THE AGRARIAN DISPUTE

THE EXPROPRIATION
OF AMERICAN-OWNED
RURAL LAND IN
POSTREVOLUTIONARY MEXICO

John J. Dwyer

DUKE UNIVERSITY PRESS   DURHAM AND LONDON   2008

Printed in the United States of America on acid-free paper ∞

Designed by Heather Hensley

Typeset in Minion Pro by Keystone Typesetting, Inc.

Library of Congress Cataloging-in-Publication Data appear

on the last printed page of this book.

Duke University Press gratefully acknowledges the

support of Duquesne University, which provided funds

toward the production of this book.

For Alice,

All the words that follow this page pale in comparison
to those written here.

I love you with all my heart and soul.

CONTENTS

ILLUSTRATIONS

TABLES

ACKNOWLEDGMENTS

U nlike some of the debts that we acquire in life, academic ones are a pleasure to acknowledge. While traveling widely over the past fifteen years for
schooling, research, writing, and employment, I have had the honor to study
under and become acquainted with many people who helped to make this book
possible. In graduate school at the University of Illinois, Nils Jacobsen and
Joseph Love introduced me to Latin American history. I benefited greatly from
Jacobsen's expertise in agrarian history and his close guidance over many years.
William Widenor's specialization in the history of U.S. foreign relations and his
experience as a foreign service officer in Mexico were equally invaluable. From
his stories, it appears that, in some respects, the manner in which foreign policy
is made on both sides of the border has changed little since the 1930s. As an
expert on Franklin D. Roosevelt, Mark Leff provided much needed insight into
his administration and the nature of his political symbolism. Finally, Friedrich
Katz's seminar on the Mexican Revolution, which I attended while studying as a
c.i.c. Visiting Scholar at the University of Chicago, provided direction to my
work on postrevolutionary Mexico. I am very grateful to Katz for warmly
welcoming me into the course, becoming a member of my dissertation committee, and lending me his support over the years.

Field research for this book lasted two years and took me to two countries,
seven cities, and sixteen archives and libraries. Hence, it would be very difficult
to thank everyone individually who provided assistance. Nevertheless, I am
extremely grateful to the many archivists and staff members at the Archivo
General de la Nación, the Archivo Histórico de la Secretaría de Relaciones

Exteriores, the Archivo Central del Registro Agrario Nacional, the Instituto Nacional de Antropología e Historia, the Hemeroteca of the Universidad Nacional Autónoma de México, the Archivo Histórico del Estado de Baja California, the Archivo del Gobierno del Estado de Sonora, the Archivo General del Estado de Veracruz, the state branches of the Registro Agrario Nacional in Mexicali and Hermosillo, the U.S. National Archives, the Library of Congress, the Franklin Delano Roosevelt Library, the Butler Library at Columbia University, the Sherman Library (which holds the records of the Colorado River Land Company), and the University of Arizona Library (which holds the records of the Richardson Construction Company). Thank you also to Cuauhtémoc Cárdenas, who granted me a lengthy interview on his father, President Lázaro Cárdenas. Finally, I am indebted to a half-dozen ejidatarios from Ejido Michoacán de Ocampo whom I interviewed, especially Pedro Pérez, who recounted with great lucidity his participation in the Mexicali Valley agrarista movement and the 1937 peasant invasion of CRLC's property. His life story is testament to the importance of grassroots mobilization and the strength of the human will to overcome the most daunting obstacles.

Through my affiliation as a Fulbright Fellow with El Colegio de México in Mexico City and as a Guest Scholar at the Center for U.S.-Mexican Studies at the University of California, San Diego, I met a number of fellow Mexicanists who provided constructive comments on different sections of this study. In particular I am very thankful to Eric Van Young, Kevin Middlebrook, Gilbert Joseph, Lorenzo Meyer, Ben Vinson, Todd Eisenstadt, Paul Eiss, Steven Bachelor, Kenneth Maffitt, and Paul Vanderwood, among others. Vanderwood not only read the dissertation but also assisted my application for a visiting professorship at UCSD. Thank you also to Alan Knight, who read and commented upon the entire dissertation and then spent a few hours discussing it in detail with me in his Oxford office. I am also grateful for the help of a number of Duquesne University graduate assistants, including Josh Britton, Sarah Zimmerman, Jason Currie, Jamie George, and Eric Sturgulewski. Thank you also to the two anonymous readers at Duke University Press, whose insightful comments made this a better book, as did the careful work of copyeditor Kathryn Litherland. Any errors or inconsistencies are solely mine. A warm thank you to Duke University Press Senior Editor Valerie Millholland, Associate Editor Miriam Angress, and Assistant Managing Editor Molly Balikov, all of whom quickly answered my questions and patiently guided me through the long publication process. Thank you to the journals *Presidential Studies Quarterly* and *Diplomatic History*, which published some parts of the book's final chapters.

The bulk of my research and writing was generously supported by a J. William Fulbright Fellowship, a W. Stull Holt Fellowship from the Society for Historians of American Foreign Relations, grants from the Tinker Foundation, the Nelle Signor Foundation, the Franklin Delano Roosevelt Library, the University of Illinois, and UCSD's Center for U.S.-Mexican Studies. Over the last few years, Duquesne University's Presidential Scholarship Award, an NEH Faculty Endowment Grant, a Wimmer Faculty Development Award, and a Russo Faculty Development Award have supported additional research and writing in Mexico City, Washington, and Pittsburgh.

I also am very appreciative of the many friends and family members who facilitated my research, especially Claudia Dwyer-Lynch, Michael Lynch, Alicia Dwyer, Demetrios Karis, Aleck Karis, Mimi and Jim Rigassio, Nadine Rochler, Angelica Palomares, Jane Madden, Ann and Jon Sachs, and Dr. Ann Hill. Two people deserve a very special thank you. My parents, Doris and John Dwyer, have always provided me with their unending love and support, for which I am extremely grateful. My mother deserves special praise for helping me when some of my research material was lost en route to Mexico City. Unfortunately, my father passed away before the manuscript was finished and remains terribly missed by everyone who knew him.

Each author knows that it is the immediate family who sacrifices the most in order for a book to make it to press. My family is no exception, and I am very thankful for their patience and encouragement. My two young daughters, Jessica and Stephanie, are adorable and fill our home with much love and laughter. Also, this book would not exist if it were not for my beautiful wife, Alice. Ever since our time together in graduate school, she has proofread all of my work, been a helpful sounding board, and provided much-needed technical support. She also weathered, in good humor, the long hours that I spent on this project over many years. Most importantly, her love and friendship greatly enrich my life. Although I can never repay what she has done to help make this book a reality, I happily dedicate it and myself to her.

Introduction

THE INTERPLAY BETWEEN DOMESTIC AFFAIRS
AND FOREIGN RELATIONS

The trend of United States–Mexican relations today is predicated principally upon the course of Mexico's internal development.

U.S. STATE DEPARTMENT REPORT OF THE DIVISION OF THE AMERICAN
REPUBLICS, DECEMBER 29, 1937

An intimate relationship exists between our foreign policy and the efforts that Mexico makes toward forwarding its social reforms.

MEXICO'S DEPUTY FOREIGN MINISTER RAMÓN BETETA, JANUARY 4, 1940

"Land and Liberty" and "Mexico for the Mexicans" were among the most popular slogans of the Mexican Revolution between 1910 and 1920. These rallying cries made agrarian reform and economic nationalism prominent features of twentieth-century Mexican politics. However, it was only through the expropriation of American-owned rural property in postrevolutionary Mexico that both of these important issues coalesced. Between January 1927 and October 1940, 319 individual and corporate American property owners lost approximately 6.2 million acres to Mexico's land redistribution program (see map 1).[1] When President Lázaro Cárdenas's administration expropriated most of this property in the mid- to late 1930s, it sparked a serious bilateral conflict that I have termed "the agrarian dispute." This crisis severely strained diplomatic relations, due to the fact that hundreds of American-owned properties below the border were seized without compensation. Although the agrarian dispute did not end until late 1941, it marked a turning point in U.S.-Mexican relations. In the course of the conflict, Franklin Roosevelt's government abandoned a

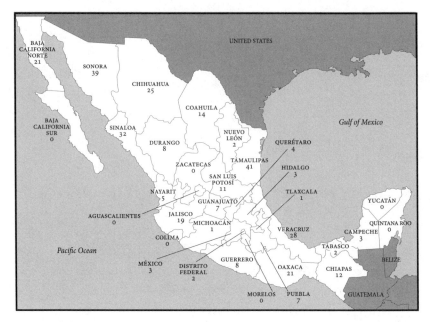

MAP 1. Breakdown, by state, of the 319 American-owned rural properties expropriated in Mexico between January 1, 1927, and October 6, 1940. SOURCE: COMMISSIONER LAWSON'S REPORT, ANNEX 2, RG 76, U.S. SECTION AGRARIAN CLAIMS COMMISSION, LAWSON CORRESPONDENCE, 1938–43, VOL. 1–3, ENTRY 203, NAW; DEPARTMENT OF STATE, *AMERICAN MEXICAN CLAIMS COMMISSION*, 475–651.

century-long tradition of heavy-handed U.S. policies against Mexico and instead accommodated its southern neighbor.

Cárdenas's attack on American holdings in the Mexican countryside can be traced back to the 1910s and the Mexican Revolution. In certain respects, the revolution increased Mexico's autonomy vis-à-vis the United States by making the country's political elite ardent nationalists. This is not to suggest that the revolution created Mexican nationalism; rather, it impelled Mexican leaders to fight for their country's national interests, even if it meant challenging more-powerful nations like the United States. Francisco "Pancho" Villa, along with Presidents Venustiano Carranza, Álvaro Obregón, Plutarco Elías Calles, Lázaro Cárdenas, and Manuel Ávila Camacho each confronted the Colossus of the North—though some with greater success than others. From the revolution until the mid-1980s, Mexico's leadership tried to protect the country against the type of foreign economic and political penetration that had marked the dictatorship of Porfirio Díaz between 1876 and 1911. And, from the 1920s onward, they were able to maintain Mexican sovereignty to a much greater degree than had been the case in the nineteenth and early twentieth centuries, when on separate occasions the country was attacked and occupied by U.S. and European military forces.

While the impact of the revolution on U.S.-Mexican relations is widely recognized, there is some disagreement as to when the new era in bilateral affairs began. Since Washington used both military intervention and non-recognition against Mexico between 1914 and 1923, most scholars see the even-handed U.S. response to Cárdenas's nationalization of American-owned oil properties in 1938 as a watershed. Linda Hall, on the other hand, argues that Cárdenas's nationalistic policies were successful only because in the early 1920s Obregón had "set the stage for a confrontation with the United States."[2] However, since the United States imposed hard-line policies against Mexico to protect American investments from expropriation—as seen with Washington's nonrecognition of Obregón's government between 1920 and 1923—it appears that a new and more respectful Mexican policy had yet to be enacted by Washington at that point.

Alan Knight also plays down the significance of the 1938 oil nationalization, arguing instead that 1927 was the "turning point" in U.S.-Mexican relations, since Washington's "renunciation of war" that year led to "a more routine form of coexistence."[3] That year the Calles administration passed new agrarian and petroleum legislation that seriously threatened American landowners and oil companies operating in Mexico. To protect U.S. economic interests below the Rio Grande, some U.S. officials called for severing diplomatic relations with Mexico City, while others advocated lifting the arms embargo or using force. Plans for a U.S. military attack against Mexico were, in fact, drawn up. Although Washington did not employ any of these high-handed policies, in part because Mexico's new nationalistic laws were never fully enforced, U.S. officials still considered such aggressive measures as part of their repertoire toward Mexico, strong evidence that little had changed bilaterally. Moreover, had the Calles government extensively expropriated U.S. economic interests, President Calvin Coolidge, Secretary of State Frank Kellogg, and U.S. Ambassador James Sheffield—all of whom believed that Washington was obligated to protect U.S. business interests abroad and use force if necessary—probably would have responded with aggression. In short, because U.S. economic interests were not widely expropriated before 1935, it is difficult to say anything definitive about Washington's renunciation of intervention and the start of a new relationship before then.[4]

In mid-1938, on the other hand, it was clear to both sides that a new era in

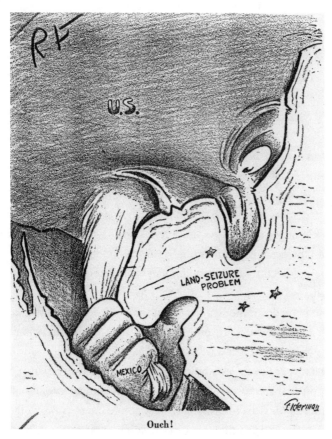

Ouch!

FIGURE 1. The agrarian dispute between the two countries stemmed from Mexico's seizure of American-owned land, which is portrayed in Elderman's cartoon by a Mexican hand pulling on Uncle Sam's beard. © 1938, *THE WASHINGTON POST*. REPRINTED WITH PERMISSION.

bilateral affairs had begun. Even though Cárdenas's administration had expropriated a number of very valuable American-owned agricultural and industrial properties, Washington did not respond to this show of Mexican economic nationalism with the sort of hard-line policies that had characterized earlier decades. President Roosevelt maintained that the United States would not forcefully intervene in the internal affairs of a foreign country to protect American citizens or their property. Below the Rio Grande, this meant that U.S. economic interests had to obey the sovereign laws of Mexico.

Unlike most scholars of U.S.-Mexican relations, I do not credit Cárdenas's nationalization of the petroleum industry, and the resultant bilateral oil crisis, for initiating this new diplomatic era. Instead, I hold that it was the agrarian dispute, which began in 1935, that was the first test of Roosevelt's Good Neighbor policy in Mexico and that marked an important watershed in U.S.-Mexican relations. By the time the foreign-owned petroleum companies were nationalized in March 1938, a precedent for Washington's accommodationist policy toward Mexican economic nationalism had already been set as a result of the prior expropriations of hundreds of American-owned estates by Cárdenas's administration. When the oil fields were seized, the response of the Roosevelt administration mirrored its evenhanded approach in the preceding conflict over land—in which the White House had simply called on Mexico City to provide adequate compensation to the affected rural property owners. Besides noting the precedents that were set during the agrarian dispute, I question the argument, put forth in much of the oil-crisis literature, that Washington yielded to Cardenista economic nationalism because of the pressures exerted by the looming wars in Europe and Asia.[5] Instead of emphasizing World War II, I will show that domestic economic and political constraints, which largely stemmed from the Great Depression, were decisive in the U.S. decision to accommodate Cárdenas's government.

I also emphasize how Mexican officials outmaneuvered their U.S. counterparts, which helps explain why the agrarian conflict ended so favorably for Mexico. Many authors who study the oil crisis fail to analyze Mexican diplomatic tactics because of their focus on the security concerns of U.S. policymakers. Due to the asymmetrical nature of bilateral relations, Mexican officials employed what could be termed the diplomatic "weapons of the weak" to resolve the land conflict in their favor.[6] In borrowing a phrase used to describe peasant agency, I do not mean to imply that James Scott's influential idea of everyday forms of resistance or Antonio Gramsci's notion of hegemony—a shared symbolic system that elites deploy and popular groups draw upon as part of the negotiation of rule—can be strictly applied to the relationship between U.S. and Mexican officials. Although policymakers in the Roosevelt and Cárdenas administrations had similar reformist agendas designed to assist the lower classes of their respective countries, U.S. and Mexican diplomats were not part of the same cultural system and therefore were not bound by a shared symbolism that Mexican policymakers could exploit to their advantage. Rather, I borrow Scott's idea to point out the similar tactics (foot-dragging, obfuscation, noncompliance) that are employed by weaker actors in a relationship marked by an unequal distribution of power (peasants versus landlords for Scott, and Mexican versus U.S. officials here). Hence, applying subaltern concepts to Mexican foreign policymaking suggests a more nuanced way to look at international affairs, forcing us to rethink how a weak state can counter an asymmetrical power structure and advance its interests against a more powerful one through well-planned and everyday forms of resistance and accommodation.

While it is vital to show how Mexican diplomatic strategies paid real dividends in their negotiations with Washington during the agrarian dispute, it is equally important to clarify the rationale behind Mexico City's foreign policy. Although scholars of U.S.–Latin American relations have demonstrated the primacy of domestic issues in shaping U.S. diplomacy, until recently few have examined fully the parallel role of domestic forces in Latin American policymaking. Ironically, although the Depression compelled FDR's government to accommodate Mexico over the expropriation of American-owned land, similar economic and political constraints led Cárdenas's administration in the opposite direction and pressed Mexico City to challenge Washington.

Since this book focuses on the fate of U.S. economic interests in Mexico's rural sector, it also addresses an ongoing debate regarding the degree to which the Mexican Revolution and the postrevolutionary era were characterized by nationalistic, antiforeign, and anti-American sentiment. Alan Knight sees little anti-Americanism during the military phase, while John Mason Hart underscores it as a major cause of the revolution and a motive for lower-class participation. Knight similarly plays down the anti-Americanism of Mexican officials during the postrevolutionary era, while Hart emphasizes it.[7] If we compare the loss of American-owned land in Sonora and Baja California—the two states analyzed in this case study—we see that both Knight and Hart make valid arguments. Consequently, what matters most to this debate is when and where researchers look.

In Sonora, American-owned agricultural properties located in the Yaqui Valley were expropriated for reasons that had little to do with the citizenship of the owners. Since a majority of Sonora's rural labor force lived in the southern Yaqui and Mayo River Valleys, these areas were targeted for land redistribution mostly for the political benefits that they would bring to the Cardenistas (supporters of President Cárdenas). Dozens of American and Mexican landowners lost their holdings because they were caught in the middle of a political conflict that pitted progressive federal officials against conservative state leaders. Had most or all of the agricultural lands in the Yaqui Valley been Mexican owned (as was the case in the Mayo Valley), Cárdenas still would have carried out the expropriations (as he did in the Mayo region). The Mayo counter case thus belies anti-Americanism and economic nationalism as root causes in the expropriation.

In Baja California's Mexicali Valley, in contrast, economic and cultural nationalism were, in fact, driving forces behind Cárdenas's expropriation of half of the 850,000 acre estate owned by the Los Angeles–based Colorado River Land Company (CRLC). Besides coveting the company's holdings for their economic potential, government officials and leading intellectuals resented the Americanization of the peninsula's border region and wanted to Mexicanize it. Likewise, many rural workers disliked CRLC and were equally antagonistic toward the thousands of Asians who worked locally. In addition to the 412,000 acres expropriated from CRLC, nearly a dozen other American property owners in the Mexicali Valley lost almost 40,000 acres of land during Cárdenas's term in office. Meanwhile, Mexican-owned holdings located in the valley were barely touched.[8] Thus, the situation in northern Baja California was the opposite of southern Sonora. Had CRLC's owners been Mexican nationals rather than Americans, and had the company's lands been worked solely by Mexicans rather than Asian immigrants, there would have been no need to Mexicanize the territory or divide the company's land outside of responding to peasant economic discontent.

As the two case studies show, some American rural holdings were expropriated due to the politics of agrarian reform, while other seizures were motivated by nationalism, xenophobia, and anti-Americanism. Just as there were "many Mexicos" during the revolution and "many Cardenismos" in the 1930s, during the postrevolutionary era there were many land reforms, and Americans were treated in correspondingly different ways.[9] Hundreds of Americans lost property throughout rural Mexico, and it would be unwise to make broad generalizations about the role of anti-Americanism in these expropriations without examining a large cross-section of the cases. Furthermore, because many American estates were among the best-developed lands in the country, we must question whether any particular example of anti-Americanism—as enunciated by peasants and presidents alike—was genuine or simply nationalistic posturing used to gain control of a valuable property.

While my arguments pertaining to U.S.-Mexican relations and anti-Americanism in the late 1930s and early 1940s will challenge much of the conventional wisdom, they are not the only scholarly contributions that this book seeks to make. In fact, most of its chapters touch on a variety of historiographical debates, some of which stretch back to the postrevolutionary era itself. For instance, as most of the book will hopefully demonstrate, the Mexican state under Cárdenas was not a capitalist "Leviathan," as revisionist historians have posited, that crushed or co-opted all that stood in its way.[10] Cárdenas was, at times, a powerful president, as illustrated by his ability to expel former president Calles from the country, easily quash Saturnino Cedillo's 1938 rebellion, and replace a handful of opposition governors. However, he also proved to be a weak chief executive who lacked full federal control over all of Mexico's regions, could not impose his lieutenants in each state, and frequently yielded to other powerful interests, both elite and subaltern, in order to maintain his authority.[11]

In line with the postrevisionist literature that questions the strength of Cárdenas's government and the efficacy of his state-building project, chapters 2 through 5 illustrate how Cardenismo both empowered and restrained subaltern groups.[12] These chapters also demonstrate that Cárdenas's agrarian policies varied from region to region. On some occasions they were shaped by political considerations (seeking to weaken the Callista opposition, for example, and strengthen his working-class base). At other times economic goals were paramount (redistributing wealth and putting more land under cultivation). Social concerns, meanwhile, almost always figured into his rural policies (such as the goal of remolding agricultural workers into modern and efficient laborers through paternalistic reforms). In addition, cultural factors were sometimes part of the equation (such as using agrarian reform to promote either indigenismo or mestizaje).[13] Lastly, nationalism at times drove Cárdenas's agrarian reform program (as seen in the redistribution of foreign-owned land to Mexican nationals). Hence, it is safe to say that no one issue alone shaped Cárdenas's rural policy; rather, a series of interrelated forces shaped it.

Chapters 2 and 4 will show that—contrary to most structuralist interpretations of the peasantry and in harmony with much of today's postrevisionist scholarship—Mexico's campesinos (peasants) were not passive victims of either the rural elite or a powerful central state.[14] Rather, as events in the Mexicali Valley will show, landless rural workers and smallholders—who often had very different agendas—resisted the Cardenista state and forced it to alter the local application of federal agrarian policy in their favor. In the Yaqui Valley, on the other hand, landless fieldworkers did not contest the federal government but instead sought its assistance in their fight against the landed elite. To achieve their goals, the Mexican peasantry in Baja California and Sonora did not rely very much on "everyday forms of resistance."[15] Instead, they were active agents who shaped their own history through overt and sometimes illegal acts. While most agraristas (activists in the agrarian reform movement) fought for land redistribution to advance their class-based interests and obtain modern material items that would improve their living and working conditions, for the majority of Yaqui Indians, their quest for land was driven primarily by cultural considerations that largely stemmed from their religious beliefs.

Although the book's various arguments concerning bilateral relations, Cárdenas's presidency, and peasant agency challenge certain scholarly interpretations and support others, none of them alone mark this study's most important theoretical or historiographical contribution. Rather, the book's main intention is to explain how they all tie together, and it is in this context that a study of the U.S.-Mexican agrarian dispute proves its scholarly worth. The bilateral conflict over land highlights the intricate relationship that exists between domestic and international affairs—one that is multidirectional and comprised of various actors of different social standings. Too often scholars separate the foreign and the domestic, as if each exists in a vacuum. In reality, though, they are closely intertwined (see figure 2). According to Enrique Ochoa, "Most studies on postrevolutionary Mexico have not fully demonstrated how complex forces, both internal and external, have coalesced to initiate, shape, and alter policies over time."[16] In Mexico, for example, landless peasants started and perpetuated the agrarian conflict between the two countries whenever they petitioned for, squatted upon, or invaded American-owned land. Unlike most of the oil-crisis literature, which provides little insight into the lives of the individual petroleum workers who instigated the international imbroglio, this book tries to be inclusive by giving a voice to those who fought for and then obtained American agricultural holdings south of the border.[17]

As such, I hope to revise our understanding of the mid- to late 1930s by illustrating how local grassroots movements in rural Mexico influenced bilateral affairs. In most studies on U.S.-Mexican relations, as Daniel Nugent rightly noted, "the peasantry and urban and rural workers figure, when they figure at all, as a *subjected* population, the passive recipients of power."[18] However, as this investigation seeks to demonstrate, peasant agency influenced the local application of Cárdenas's agrarian reform program, his regional state-building projects, and his relations with the United States. Agrarista mobilization had a ripple effect that made itself felt both domestically and internationally. Elizabeth Ferry's recent work on silver mining in Mexico similarly links worker agency within the Santa Fe Cooperative to local, national, and global develop-

FIGURE 2. Despite the fact that the cartoon stereotypes the Mexican character in a negative light (e.g., barefoot, with a very large sombrero, and oblivious of the trouble he is in), the cartoonist C. Dunning rightly notes how Mexican domestic affairs (in this case peasant and labor unrest that resulted in the expropriation of American-owned property) leads to international complications for Mexico. *Brooklyn Daily Eagle,* ca. late 1930s. REPRINTED WITH PERMISSION FROM THE BROOKLYN COLLECTION, BROOKLYN PUBLIC LIBRARY.

ments within the mining sector. The far-reaching impact of mobilized Mexican peasants and workers, as seen in this and Ferry's study, was not unique. Steve Striffler's research on Ecuador's banana industry similarly shows that peasants and rural workers, through their local struggles over land and labor relations, shaped broader economic and political processes at the regional, national, and international levels.[19]

In addition to examining the role played by *los de abajo* (those from below) in the agrarian dispute, I also focus on the parts played by the U.S. and Mexican political elite. Peasant issues gained traction in late-1930s Mexico only because

Cárdenas's domestic agenda, which was based on broad socioeconomic reforms, promoted them. Consequently, Cardenista officials at the local, state, and federal levels were equally responsible for instigating the bilateral conflict with the United States. As previously noted, domestic economic and political considerations determined how both the Cárdenas and Roosevelt administrations handled the crisis after it began in late 1935. Besides illustrating how domestic issues influenced international relations, I also demonstrate how foreign affairs impacted domestic developments both regionally and nationally, as will be seen in the delayed redistribution of land in Sonora and the denial of compensation to Mexican property owners throughout the country. By emphasizing how local forces and actors shape regional, national, and international events, and vice versa, I wish to remain sensitive to the complex web of interconnections that shape the historical past. In other words, I hope to provide a fuller understanding of postrevolutionary Mexico by analyzing the interplay between domestic and foreign affairs. By decentering the analysis and focusing on peasant mobilization in the Mexican countryside, and then recentering it on the domestic and foreign policymakers in Mexico City and Washington, we will see that distinct actors in each country not only played an important role in precipitating and later resolving the agrarian dispute, but also in recasting bilateral affairs during this volatile era. Hence, the United States did not unilaterally determine either the outcome of the crisis or the new orientation of U.S.-Mexican relations. Furthermore, by elucidating how the domestic and foreign together make the intricate whole, I hope to reconsider the standard narrative of Mexican history and contribute to a body of literature that internationalizes Mexico's domestic past.[20]

To reconceptualize both the domestic history of postrevolutionary Mexico and the international history of U.S.-Mexican relations during the interwar period, I weave together social, economic, cultural, political, and diplomatic history. The book's two parts seek to give full consideration to each side of the domestic/international equation. The first section examines the origins of the agrarian dispute and details the expropriation of American-owned agricultural property in Sonora and Baja California during Cárdenas's *sexenio* (six-year term in office). The second section of the book examines how the diplomatic crisis that resulted from the nationwide expropriation of American-owned farms, ranches, and timberlands was resolved by U.S. and Mexican officials.

I use Baja California and Sonora as case studies because of the significant amount of land taken from American property owners in both regions (see

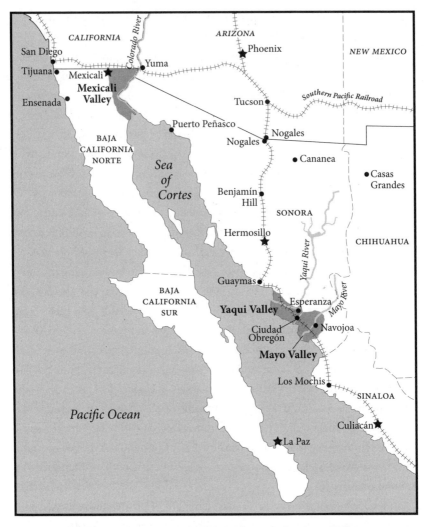

MAP 2. Baja California Norte and Sonora, highlighting the Mexicali and Yaqui Valleys.

map 2). The 412,000 acres expropriated from CRLC in the Mexicali Valley represents the single greatest loss for any one American landowner between 1927 and 1940—both in terms of its overall size and in terms of its market value and compensation award. At the opposite end of the spectrum, the twenty-nine small farms that were appropriated in the Yaqui River Valley in late 1937 represent the largest number of individual American-owned estates expropriated in any one local area of the country between 1927 and 1940. In these two valleys alone, some forty American property owners lost close to 600,000 acres—or 30 percent of the nearly 2 million acres of agricultural property expropriated from

Americans throughout the country between 1927 and 1940. All together, sixty Americans lost land in the state of Sonora and the territory of Baja California Norte.[21] Hence, few parts of Mexico were more important to either the domestic or the international side of the agrarian dispute.

However, numbers alone do not explain why I choose these two states as case studies. Because of the dramatic difference between the Mexicali and Yaqui Valleys in terms of the types of American landowners situated in each, the composition of their local populations, and the particularities of their regional politics, among other issues, studying these two states helps to illustrate important areas of commonality and difference with regard to the book's four central issues: the circumstances that spurred agrarista mobilization, the rationale behind Cárdenas's agrarian policies, Washington's reaction to the loss of American-owned land, and the diplomatic tactics employed by Mexican officials.

When we look at events in both Sonora and Baja California, we see that while economic, social, cultural, and political forces together led to the expropriation of American-owned land, the relative importance of each varied from state to state. In both locations, agrarista mobilization stemmed from the poor living and working conditions of the landless campesinos. However, in Sonora, indigenismo was also a contributing factor, while in Baja California, mestizaje was. As for Cárdenas, he used agrarian reform in both regions to improve the material conditions of the rural underclass. His redistribution of American-owned agricultural property in Baja California was also driven by economic and cultural nationalism; however, in Sonora it was precipitated mostly by political opportunism. Although U.S. policymakers tried to defend all American rural property owners in Mexico from land redistribution, some of them fought harder for the small farmers, such as those in Sonora, than they did the large agribusinesses, like CRLC in Baja California. Consequently, Cardenista officials played up their alleged concern for the small landowners and used the large property owners, especially if they were stockholders in land development companies, as a wedge issue to strengthen their hand bilaterally and further divide an already-fractious U.S. diplomatic corps. In short, comparing these two states illustrates the multifaceted nature of land redistribution in Mexico, as well as the distinct origins and erratic evolution of the bilateral agrarian dispute.

To understand both the motives of Mexico's agraristas and the policies of U.S. and Mexican officials, I draw on an eclectic mix of popular and official sources. By tapping primary sources such as the regional partisan press, peasant petitions for land, agrarista testimonials, and peasant interviews—both my own and previously published ones—this analysis stays close to the ground in explaining the agraristas' goals and actions. To clarify the domestic and international policies of the Cárdenas, Ávila Camacho, and Roosevelt administrations, I have relied on the internal and foreign correspondence, memoirs, and unpublished papers of leading officials within each government, as well as government reports and surveys, newspapers articles, photographs, and political cartoons. Such wide-ranging source material helps give shape to the multiform engagement among actors of unequal power who contributed to the agrarian dispute: namely, landless fieldworkers, colonists, indigenous groups, small landowners, multinational corporations, labor leaders, teachers, state-level officials, federal policymakers, and diplomats.

Besides including a diverse set of actors, this story focuses on events in four different locations—Sonora, Baja California, Washington, and Mexico City—and places them within the context of larger global developments, such as the Great Depression and the Second World War. Hence, the narrative's breadth requires a flexible analytical model, one that is applicable to the distinctiveness of area studies and the scope of international relations. The fact that no such model exists may, to a certain extent, help this study avoid reductionist explanations. As I hope to show, historical actors—both elite and subaltern—usually do not make important decisions based only on one factor. They, like the rest of us, are driven, knowingly or not, by a variety of underlying forces that sometimes remain constant but occasionally change, depending on, among other things, time and place.

I

Domestic Origins of an International Conflict

THE ROOTS OF THE AGRARIAN DISPUTE

The Richardson Construction Company is primarily a land and water company. Broadly stated, the purpose of the company is to place its lands under irrigation, to sell the lands but retain the water rights, and supply water at an annual rental to the lands sold; furthermore, it will enter into the general development of the entire Yaqui Valley.

DAVIS RICHARDSON, PRESIDENT OF THE RICHARDSON CONSTRUCTION CO., MAY 20, 1907

Foreigners cannot own real estate under any conditions.

MEXICAN AMBASSADOR TO THE UNITED STATES MANUEL TÉLLEZ, 1926

The person and the property of a citizen are part of the general domain of the nation, even when abroad, and there is a distinct and binding obligation on the part of self-respecting governments to afford protection to the persons and property of their citizens, wherever they may be.

PRESIDENT CALVIN COOLIDGE, 1927

Landownership has been a dominant issue in Mexico since the colonial period. From independence until today, Mexican officials have repeatedly used agrarian laws as an economic tool to alter landholding patterns and develop the national economy, as well as a political weapon to undermine opponents, support allies, and build broad-based popular coalitions. In other words, Mexican leaders have often used agrarian legislation as a state-building tool to increase their power and advance the nation's economy, as reflected by the era in which they governed, including periods as distinct as La Reforma, the Porfiriato, and the revolution.

After Porfirio Díaz overthrew Sebastian Lerdo de Tejada's government in 1876, he imposed a number of agrarian laws designed to promote capital accumulation in rural Mexico, empower regional allies, and chip away at communal Indian villages. The goal of Díaz's *Científico* advisers was to modernize the still-semifeudal countryside and promote migration to underdeveloped areas. They assumed that agricultural production and government revenue would increase with more land under cultivation—no matter the size of the holding or the nationality of its owners. By developing rural Mexico, the Porfirians hoped to transform the economy from an agriculturally based semisubsistence one to a surplus industrial one built on the nation's natural resources.

To initiate this multifaceted process and make rural Mexico attractive to both domestic and foreign investors, Díaz's administration promoted railroad construction, which would facilitate migration and trade. Also, under the agrarian law of December 1883, Díaz had all of Mexico's vacant public lands surveyed so as to begin the process of their enclosure. The survey companies, which were instrumental in privatizing and capitalizing Mexican agriculture, were entitled to keep one-third of the areas surveyed in lieu of payment. The remaining *terrenos baldíos* (vacant and untilled lands) were auctioned off in vast tracts at low prices to the survey companies themselves and Díaz's associates, as well as foreign and domestic speculators. His government also granted generous land and water concessions, along with tax incentives, to U.S. and Mexican land development companies in exchange for their agreement to improve the holdings that they usually acquired on the cheap. In 1890, Díaz reinstated some Liberal-era laws to hasten the redistribution of communal lands among residents of indigenous villages. The results were generally the same as before. Few Indians could afford to become growers, and local hacienda owners either cajoled those who could into selling their property or else took it by force. In 1894, Díaz decreed that lands without proper legal title were also considered vacant and subject to auction. This led to the further usurpation of millions of acres from indigenous communities and small property owners.[1]

By 1910, fewer than eleven thousand haciendas controlled 57 percent of Mexico's national territory. Meanwhile, small farmers and ranchers together held 20 percent of the land, and communal campesino communities controlled an additional 6 percent. The remaining lands were either national or unclaimed. The year 1911 marked the highest point of landlessness in Mexican history. As for the residents of the states analyzed here, 77 percent in Sonora and 88 percent in Baja California were landless rural workers. Land concentration and the resultant increase in peonage, tenantry, sharecropping, and migratory labor, along with the rapid industrialization of certain agricultural sectors like sugar, worsened the working and living conditions for rural laborers and impelled many to take up arms in the revolution.[2]

Mexico's revolution brought an end to the Porfiriato in 1911 and ushered in profound changes in land tenure. During both the revolutionary and post-revolutionary eras, agrarian legislation was still used as a political and socioeconomic tool by the country's ruling elite. Now, however, the agrarian laws were designed to return the land to the peasantry and ensure the political survival of competing revolutionary factions. The extensive land redistributions carried out by Emiliano Zapata in Morelos, and the more statist land reforms envisioned by Pancho Villa in Chihuahua, forced the leader of the Constitutionalist Army, Venustiano Carranza, to enact radical agrarian legislation in order to broaden his base of popular support against these rivals.[3] On January 6, 1915, Carranza decreed the restoration of village lands and the expropriation of haciendas. He also nullified all land, water, and forest concessions issued by federal authorities since Díaz entered office in 1876 and called for the distribution of land to the peasantry. The January 1915 law marked the first significant piece of national agrarian legislation that derived from the revolution and became the basis for subsequent constitutional reforms. Two years later, Carranza, who was still trying to consolidate his power nationally, accepted the radical and nationalistic provisions contained in Article 27 of the new 1917 Constitution. Article 27 reversed sixty years of federal land tenure policies by nullifying all measures passed since the Liberal's Ley Lerdo that had alienated communal lands starting in 1856. It also placed all of Mexico's natural resources under national domain, making possible the expropriation of privately owned property by the federal government.

Both the 1915 land reform and the 1917 constitution served two important purposes. First, they empowered Mexico's rural majority. Second, they weakened three important pillars of Díaz's regime, all of whom were prominent landowners: domestic hacendados, foreign investors, and to a lesser extent, the Catholic Church.[4]

At least on paper, the legislation of 1915 and 1917 simultaneously undercut the "revolutionary family's" conservative opponents and strengthened its working-class political base. But, the defeat of the Villistas and Zapatistas by the Constitutionalists dampened the enforcement of Article 27 in the first fifteen years of the postrevolutionary era. Land was given to the peasantry

FIGURE 3. On left, President Pascual Ortiz Rubio (1930–32) and former President (a.k.a. el Jefe Máximo) Plutarco Elías Calles in 1930. AGN, ARCHIVO FOTOGRÁFICO, FONDO ENRIQUE DÍAZ, 4/4.

between 1920 and 1934, but it was done not to create a more equitable socio-economic system. Rather, property was redistributed predominantly for political reasons: namely, to hasten state formation by placating campesino discontent, pacifying the countryside, and establishing federal-regional alliances. The numbers illustrate the limited nature of agrarian reform in the 1920s. From 1920 to 1924, President Álvaro Obregón redistributed only 4,142,355 acres of land, and between 1924 and 1928, President Plutarco Elías Calles parceled out just 7,891,719 acres. Rather than distribute additional government-financed *ejidos* (land granted or restored by the government, either to individuals or to communities), both leaders promoted private landownership. In 1926, for example, Calles established the National Bank of Agricultural Credit (Banco Nacional de Crédito Agrícola) to loan money to small farmers in the hope of creating a class of smallholders.[5]

The pace of land redistribution remained slow during the six-year Maximato (1928–34), when Calles, as el Jefe Máximo, dominated national politics through his control of three interim presidents (Emilio Portes Gil, Pascual Ortiz Rubio, and Abelardo Rodríguez) (see figure 3). Since the 1917 Constitution required the federal government to compensate property owners for their expropriated holdings, the fiscally conservative Callistas were wary of further increasing the government's indebtedness. Consequently, in 1930 and 1931, new conservative agrarian legislation known as the "Stop Laws" reduced land redistribution to its lowest level since the late 1910s. According to Mexican officials, the change in policy was necessitated by the nation's enormous agrarian debt, which in 1930 was estimated at $400,000,000. Also, since most affected rural property owners were not indemnified due to the lack of government revenue, Mexican leaders worried that the country's inability to meet its financial obligations was undermining its credit rating abroad and frightening away foreign capital. They also believed that a new direction in agrarian policy was needed because, according to Calles, "agrarianism was a failure." Since the ruling Callistas had lost faith in ejido farming—due, in part, to its limited output—they slowed land redistribution and instead promoted large-scale commercial agriculture.[6] In the first two decades of revolutionary agrarian legislation, approximately 26 million acres of land were expropriated. Not only did this affect just 6.2 percent of Mexico's farmland, but much of the property that was given to the peasantry between 1915 and 1935 was low quality. Worse yet, most ejidatarios were not provided adequate credit, education, or material support to facilitate their transition from landless rural workers into small independent growers or communal farmers.[7]

The limited nature of federal land reform strengthened radical agrarianism in the early 1930s, and the movement began to pose a threat to the nation's large landowners, both domestic and foreign. Spurred by the Great Depression, in the first half of the 1930s well-organized and politically active agraristas, including leaders of the National Campesino League (Liga Nacional Campesina) "Ursulo Galván" and the Confederation of Mexican Campesinos (Confederación de Campesinos Mexicanos, or CCM), pushed to liberalize Mexico's agrarian reform laws.[8]

In December 1933, delegates from the government's official party, the National Revolutionary Party (Partido Nacional Revolucionario, or PNR) met in Querétaro, nominated Lázaro Cárdenas as president, and drew up the Plan Sexenal to guide the new administration. More radical than Calles had hoped, this nationalistic Six-Year Plan (1934–40) called for accelerating the breakup of large estates and redistributing more land in the form of communal ejidos. In addition, the plan sought to modernize the countryside through increased irrigation, reforestation, rural education, and new farming practices, while promoting minimum-wage laws, collective bargaining rights, and workers' cooperatives. The Six-Year Plan also established the federal Agrarian Department, with a director who answered only to the president and whose primary objective was land redistribution. The new plan was critical of the Sonoran economic model that Presidents Obregón and Calles had imposed between 1920 and 1934, a model that had not substantially altered the Porfirian economic system, especially land tenure patterns. The economic program of Obregón and Calles was characterized by limited agrarian reform and dependent capitalist development based on foreign investment and the export of raw materials. The new Six-Year Plan reclaimed the economic nationalism of the 1917 Constitution by reinvigorating the "interventionist state" and allowing Mexicans to enjoy the fruits of their labor. This was never more apparent than when American-owned agricultural property was redistributed to landless campesinos.[9]

In addition to the Six-Year Plan, one new piece of legislation—the 1934 Agrarian Code—empowered landless rural workers. It extended the right to submit ejido petitions to not just peasants residing in free villages but also resident estate workers known as *peones acasillados,* along with seasonal workers. Also, starting in 1934, the establishment of state-level Mixed Agrarian Commissions (composed of representatives from the federal Agrarian Department, state governments, and usually six individuals from local peasant leagues) enabled community actors not only to petition for land but also to push the application along and supervise redistribution when it occurred.[10]

Just as the 1934 Agrarian Code empowered Mexico's agricultural underclass, Cárdenas's passage of the 1936 Expropriation Law strengthened the federal government's hand in the rural sector. The law made it possible for Mexico City to expropriate lands that had previously been exempt, such as properties devoted to commercial agriculture and export—as were many American-owned estates.[11] These three major pieces of legislation—the Six-Year Plan, the 1934 Agrarian Code, and the 1936 Expropriation Law—empowered Cárdenas's administration and landless rural workers alike; they also weakened the rural economic elite, promoted agricultural modernization, and enabled many more Mexicans to benefit directly from their country's natural resources. As was common throughout much of the country's history, and as we will see in chapters 2 through 5, the changes in agrarian laws that were enacted during Cárdenas's term in office reflected the president's rural socioeconomic agenda;

they also increased his power by weakening his conservative opponents and strengthening his working-class political base.

As Mexico consolidated politically in the late nineteenth century, during the thirty-five-year Díaz dictatorship, American expansion into the Mexican countryside was led by land development companies, agribusinesses, timber and ranching companies, absentee land speculators, resident colonist farmers, and individual small-scale growers and ranchers, as well as landless rural workers. American investors who obtained large estates did so by buying the concessions that Díaz's government granted to the survey companies. According to John Mason Hart, "Fraud and corruption were inherent in the process."[12] By the late 1920s, American-owned rural properties in Mexico were valued at $140 million.[13] Many of these American properties were controversial holdings that local communities believed were wrongfully taken from them either by federal and state officials or private Mexican companies and individuals. In many cases, the new American property owners, like the Mexican land-grabbers who preceded them, were resented by those whose holdings were usurped. Consequently, Hart claims the Americans sometimes became embroiled in the "intense struggle between Mexico's elites and its disenfranchised."[14] To a certain extent, this was the case on the north bank of Sonora's Yaqui River, where the Yaqui Indians violently contested the possession of their ancestral lands by Mexican and American landowners. In fact, in the first quarter of the twentieth century the largest property owner in the Yaqui Valley was a California-based company.

As Díaz had done throughout the country, in the early 1880s he ordered Sonora's public lands surveyed to foster the state's economic development. However, according to some Porfirians, Sonora's "primitive" indigenous populations stood in the way of the state's advancement.[15] After Sonora's lands were surveyed, Díaz turned the federal army on one of its most resilient indigenous groups, the Yaqui Indians who lived in the southern river valley that bore their name. After two years of brutal fighting, the Yaquis succumbed to the federal forces. Some of those who survived were deported as slaves to work on plantations in Yucatán and Cuba. Others were conscripted into the national army against their will. Some escaped the government's long arm and retreated into the Sierra del Bacatete or fled across the border to Arizona. A few, though, remained in the valley to work as field hands on the lands of their ancestors. In

1860, approximately twenty thousand Yaqui Indians lived in the valley, but by 1910 only three thousand remained.[16]

After the Yaqui were decimated by federal forces, Díaz's administration opened their homelands and the surrounding region to colonization. In 1904, the Los Angeles–based Richardson Brothers Company and its subsidiary, the Richardson Construction Company, established the Mexico-based Compañía Constructora Richardson (CCR) to purchase property in the Yaqui Valley. The owners of the Richardson companies included William and Davis Richardson, Harry Payne Whitney, Herbert Sibbet, John Hays Hammond, and the Knicker-bocker Bank and Trust Company of New York, among others.[17] As a land development firm (i.e., a colonization company), CCR bought 300,000 acres of property from the previous owners, surveyor Carlos Conant and the now-bankrupt American-owned Sinaloa and Sonora Land and Irrigation Company (SSLIC). CCR management then established the town of Esperanza ("Hope") in the Yaqui Valley, where it located the company's headquarters. By 1907, CCR had expanded its holdings to 550,000 acres, and by the end of the decade it held nearly 700,000 acres. Approximately half of this was suited for agriculture; of the remainder, more than 220,000 acres were ideal for grazing livestock, while over 81,000 acres were wooded. The company planned to use each land type commercially. In addition, because it also obtained the federal concession for regional development, CCR was obligated to build a rail line and an irrigation system throughout the entire Yaqui Valley. Both large infrastructure projects were intended to cover lands not owned by the company, including some of the Yaqui's ancestral homelands on the north bank of the river. CCR's earnings came from several sources, including the sale of land, town sites, cattle, timber; and irrigation water.[18]

CCR never undertook railroad construction and in 1905 sold those rights to the American-owned Southern Pacific Railroad Company. Within two years, Southern Pacific had laid ninety miles of track through the valley. Afterwards, the railroad giant built connecting lines northward that linked the Yaqui Valley to the nearby port city of Guaymas and the state capital of Hermosillo, as well as the border city of Nogales, Arizona. Southern Pacific then built lines southward down the west coast of Mexico to the cities of Los Mochis and Mazatlán in the state of Sinaloa, then on to Guadalajara in Jalisco state, and into Mexico City. Such an extensive rail system facilitated migration to the Yaqui Valley for U.S. colonists and Mexican workers alike and provided cheap and easy shipment of grains, fruits, and vegetables to regional, national, and international markets— thereby fostering the development of the Yaqui Valley's economy.[19]

To develop the valley agriculturally, CCR expanded its canal and irrigation systems. By 1907, the company had added twenty five miles to the main canal and fifteen miles to its lateral canals—which helped to increase the amount of irrigated land from 25,000 acres in 1911 to 100,000 by 1928. CCR paid for the construction and maintenance of the canal system and other infrastructure projects, including roads, with revenue from the sale of land and irrigation water. As stipulated by its federal concession, the company was required to sell land—commonly referred to as *campos agrícolas*—in parcels that ranged from twenty-five to one thousand acres. CCR initially sold its land at the low price of $10.50 an acre to foreign investors and U.S. colonists. In addition to the foreign property owners, by the 1920s hundreds of Mexican colonists and absentee landowners—including Presidents Obregón and Calles, along with their friends and relatives—had also purchased land from the company.[20]

To attract workers to its infrastructure projects, as well as colonists to its lands, CCR hung large billboards and distributed tantalizing posters, advertisements, and publicity pamphlets throughout Mexico and the United States (see figure 4). "Leave your troubles and double your profits!" read one series of ads. To showcase what the Yaqui Valley had to offer, CCR established a model farm next to its headquarters in Esperanza to demonstrate both the soil's fertility and the wide array of agricultural products that could be grown locally. Many of the Yaqui Valley colonists who came from north of the border were searching for a better life. Their "limited financial resources" made the valley's job opportunities and cheap land look attractive, despite the fact that the colonists, and not CCR, were responsible for clearing, fencing, and improving the land and making it suitable for irrigation. Although this meant that the colonists had significant startup costs, most remained excited by the prospect of cheap, abundant, and well-irrigated lands. Many also were drawn to the Yaqui Valley because of two nearby, relatively modern, and thriving cities—the port city of Guaymas and the city of Cajeme (today Ciudad Obregón)—that were home to mills, packing plants, warehouses, and stores. By 1910, some fifty American families had settled tracts of unimproved land along the southern bank of the Yaqui River under a colonization contract with CCR (see figure 5). Even larger numbers of Americans purchased property as resident colonist farmers after the valley's main irrigation system was completed in 1912.[21]

The landowners who arrived after Díaz left office had to weather the violence of the revolution, as well as frequent Yaqui incursions. Between 1915 and 1917, Yaqui Indians attacked both Mexican and American homesteads in the valley, and in 1918, nearly 800 Yaquis sacked a Southern Pacific train and killed

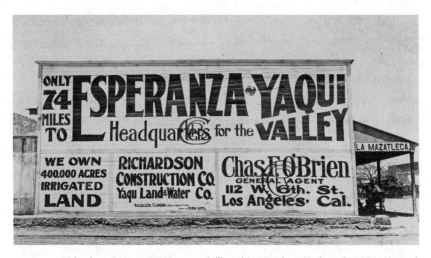

FIGURE 4. Richardson Construction Company billboard in Mazaltleca, Sinaloa, advertising irrigated land for sale in Sonora's Yaqui Valley, ca. 1910. COURTESY OF THE SPECIAL COLLECTIONS, UNIVERSITY OF ARIZONA LIBRARY, RECORDS OF THE COMPAÑIA CONSTRUCTORA RICHARDSON, MS 113, BOX 1, FOLDER 4, PHOTOGRAPHS, 1904–27.

five Americans. Yaqui raids and squatting throughout the valley—which were more examples of popular resistance than illegal acts—continued the following year and into the 1920s. Besides having their property attacked by the local indigenous population, state officials wrote legislation that threatened the holdings of the American colonists. In late 1918, Sonoran governor Plutarco Elías Calles (1917–19) passed new state laws that were designed to break up large rural properties for redistribution. Legal limits also were placed on how much land could be held: 25 acres of grazing land, 250 acres of irrigable land, and 750 acres of nonirrigated property. Any estate in excess of these amounts was to be divided among the landless peasantry. U.S. officials immediately protested Sonora's new agrarian laws on the basis that they were confiscatory, since compensation through state bonds did not ensure adequate payment for the expropriated holdings. Washington also argued that the laws denied American landowners due process, thereby violating Article 14 of the 1917 Constitution. Mexican diplomats rejected these claims, stating that Sonora's agrarian laws were in full compliance with the Constitution and were modeled on national agrarian legislation. It is noteworthy that the conflict over Sonora's land laws in 1918 foreshadowed later controversies over federal agrarian legislation as applied against American-owned estates across the country.[22]

The revolution also had a detrimental impact on CCR. The dozens of Yaqui

FIGURE 5. American settlers in the Yaqui Valley, ca. 1910. Note the automobile and the house's sturdy construction. COURTESY OF THE SPECIAL COLLECTIONS, UNIVERSITY OF ARIZONA LIBRARY, RECORDS OF THE COMPAÑIA CONSTRUCTORA RICHARDSON, MS 113, BOX 1, FOLDER 4, PHOTOGRAPHS, 1904–27.

attacks against local farmers in 1915 led CCR to suspend temporarily its operations on the north side of the Yaqui River, where most of the Indians lived. Then, in 1917, the Yaquis attacked the company town of Esperanza, killing five foreigners—including one American. Like the colonists, the company also was challenged by state officials. In 1919, the Sonoran government seized CCR's holdings and threatened to sell them because the company had not paid back taxes. CCR and U.S. officials denied the accusation and requested that the proceedings against the company be resolved legally. The tax dispute was then heard in a Mexican appellate court, where it was decided in CCR's favor. As a result, the company's holdings remained secure.[23]

Despite this victory for U.S. landed interests in southern Sonora, widespread violence in the 1910s drove many Americans to leave the Yaqui Valley. Some had their properties stolen or destroyed; others tried to sell their estates or rent them on an absentee basis. Revolutionary violence, frequent attacks by Yaqui Indians, and the expropriation provisions found in the Mexican Constitution and Sonoran agrarian legislation, however, made it difficult for the U.S. property owners to find buyers. The colonist-farmers who remained in the region, such as Edward Jesson, John Stocker, William Schutte, Malcolm Little, Benjamin Brunk, and William and James Ryan, among others, rode out these difficulties and continued to harvest wheat, rice, maize, alfalfa, chickpeas, and winter vegetables for the domestic and foreign markets. The resumption of more peaceful conditions in the 1920s led many American landowners to return to the Yaqui Valley or settle there for the first time.[24]

Due to its demographic growth and modernization, in the first four decades of the twentieth century a dynamic agrarian bourgeoisie had developed in the Yaqui River Valley. It was not long before the valley's farms began to resemble the irrigated agricultural properties found in the American Southwest. In fact, the American farms in the Yaqui Valley had little in common with either the enormous semifeudal hacienda or the subsistence-oriented peasant plot. Rather, most of the individually owned American estates were highly capitalized, relatively small, and generally employed a workforce of resident wage laborers and seasonal migrant workers. Also, unlike traditional Mexican hacendados, many of these small entrepreneurial growers personally worked their land alongside their laborers. Even CCR did not fit the usual mold of a land development company, since a couple of its directors, William Richardson and Herbert Sibbet, were not absentee owners but instead lived in the Yaqui Valley until the early 1940s. Both men also became naturalized Mexican citizens in the mid-1920s and brought their families to live with them in Mexico. In fact, they only left Mexico because Cárdenas expropriated the few thousand acres that they were granted by Calles following the 1927 sale of CCR's land to the federal government.[25]

In November 1927, Obregón arranged for the Mexican government to purchase CCR's landholdings, irrigation works, mills, warehouses, and offices for $6 million. Under federal control, CCR was renamed Irrigadora del Yaqui, S.A., and within two years the Banco Nacional de Crédito Agrícola began selling pieces of its extensive property to colonists—much like CCR had done but now with a guarantee against expropriation. The change in ownership did not set back the valley's development. In the first half of the twentieth century, the Yaqui Valley experienced rapid economic and demographic growth. At the turn of the century, only a few hundred individuals lived below the south bank of the Yaqui River, but by 1940 over 33,000 people inhabited the region. By the mid-1930s, the Yaqui Valley provided 11 percent of the country's wheat production, making it the leading producer of wheat in Mexico. Growers were not the only ones who fostered and then benefited from the region's economic expansion. Thousands of Mexican field workers had migrated to the Yaqui Valley in the early twentieth century, providing the labor to fuel its rapid growth. Prior to the Great Depression they earned better than minimum wage and had among the highest rural labor salaries in the nation. Not surprisingly, the region's growing

TABLE 1. American-owned land in the Yaqui Valley, south of the Yaqui River, December 1936

Range of Acreage	Number of Properties	Total Acres
2.5–125	64*	3,335
125–250	19*	3,417
250–370	2	642
370–620	12	5,913
620–988	11	10,561
988–2,470	7	10,339
>2,470	2	7,236
Total	117	41,454

*Small properties (*pequeñas propiedades*) not subject to expropriation
Source: Yepis to Hull, December 11, 1936, enclosure 1, RG 84, Guaymas, General Records, decimal file 350, box 3, NAW.

economy and high wages weakened the valley's agrarista movement and safe-guarded its privately held properties from redistribution.[26]

Of the 95,000 acres under cultivation in the Yaqui Valley in the mid-1930s, nearly 42,000, or 44 percent, were owned by Americans, most in the form of colonies. According to Hart, "The colony method of settlement made sense for many American small farmers. Surrounded by an alien language, culture, and customs, the majority of them were intent on retaining their language, values, and mores," and living and working among a large group of Americans facilitated this goal. In fact, many Americans in the valley kept their citizenship and called upon their congressional representatives for assistance when their properties were expropriated in the late 1930s. Most of these colonies were located in an area that had not been occupied by the Yaqui Indians; rather they were situated in what was referred to as the "Yaqui Valley proper"—a rich agricultural region located south of the river. Only a few Americans held land in the Indian-occupied "Yaqui country" on the river's north bank.[27] Some American-owned estates, such as Edward Jesson's 7,257 acre property, are not included in table 1, since they were located north of the Yaqui River.

When their lands were redistributed in October 1937, approximately 75 percent of the valley's 117 American landowners had estates of less than 250 acres.[28] Under Mexico's agrarian laws, irrigated holdings under 250 acres, and nonirrigated holdings of less than 740 acres, qualified as *pequeñas propiedades* (small properties) and were legally exempt from expropriation. While the American small landowners were spared from redistribution, as we will see in chapters 4 and 5, their compatriots who held larger estates in the valley lost most of their property to Cárdenas's agrarian reform program.

The Colorado River Land Company's development efforts in Baja California's Mexicali Valley in the early 1900s mirrored that of CCR in Sonora's Yaqui Valley. Both U.S. colonization companies promoted their regions' economic development, building infrastructure systems that delivered water, roads, or rail lines to each valley. Besides providing financial capital for some of these large-scale projects, the American firms also brought human capital to both valleys by selling or renting their lands to foreign and domestic colonists. There were, however, important differences between the two Los Angeles companies with respect to both the American colonists they brought and the local indigenous populations they encountered. Unlike the Yaquis, the Cucapá Indians of the Mexicali Valley were few in number and did not violently contest the loss of their ancestral holdings or undermine the American presence in the region. In addition, CRLC mostly rented its lands to colonists, while CCR usually sold its parcels. As a result, CRLC had more at stake in the matter of expropriation.

From the colonial period until the early twentieth century, Baja California was the backwater of the nation, sparsely populated, and mired in poverty—a situation that would change only with the advent of large-scale irrigation works.[29] As late as 1910, the territory's population numbered 9,760, with just 1,612 people living in the municipality of Mexicali and only 462 people residing in the city with the same name.[30] During the Porfiriato, the federal government offered large land concessions in northern Baja California, with the hope that capital investment would spur immigration, stimulate the territory's economy, and increase commerce. In the late 1870s, Guillermo Andrade—a wealthy Mexican living in San Francisco—and his business partner Thomas Blythe acquired extensive holdings in Baja California and Sonora. Within a few years, the two men controlled almost all the arable land in the Mexicali Valley and later gained water rights to the Imperial Valley canal just north of the border. Blythe's sudden death in 1883 allowed much of the land to pass into Andrade's hands.[31]

Andrade sought to sell his holdings in the Mexicali Valley rather than develop them. After being appointed Mexican consul in Los Angeles in 1897, Andrade met a number of prominent businessmen, including Harry Chandler and George Hunt, who were interested in purchasing his vast property. Impressed by the delta region's economic potential, in 1902, Chandler and Hunt, along with William Allen, Otto Brant, and Oliver Clark (owners of the

FIGURE 6. Left to right, Marshall Neilan, Colorado River Land Company CEO Harry Chandler, Mexican Consul to Los Angeles Lic. Garza Leal, May 1923. AGN, ARCHIVO FOTOGRÁFICO, FONDO OBREGÓN-CALLES, 11/2.

Title Insurance and Trust Company), and Harrison Gray Otis (owner and publisher of the *Los Angeles Times*) formed the Colorado River Land Company and bought most of Andrade's holdings. Because of his name recognition, his powerful contacts in Washington and Mexico City, and his ability to use his newspaper to publicize the company and its property, Otis was made CRLC's president. Chandler, who was Otis's son-in-law, would become the company's chief executive officer and its largest shareholder. These West Coast "venture capitalists" were more developers than speculators. Like the major stockholders who owned CCR in Sonora, they saw "opportunities for wealth and power" in their Mexican investments.[32]

By 1904, CRLC had acquired title to 850,000 acres of unimproved, arable land in the Mexicali Valley for $533,359. Even though the company's stockholders were all Americans, CRLC was established as a Mexican corporation, with offices in the city of Mexicali, to sidestep federal laws that prohibited foreign land-ownership near the border. The company's real headquarters, however, were in Los Angeles. Company officials were able to maintain good relations with Díaz's administration in the early 1900s, because the Mexican dictator believed that CRLC's investment would promote much needed regional development.[33] CRLC's acquisition of land led the Inter-California Railway Company to build thirty-eight miles of track through the company's holdings between 1904 and 1909. By the early 1910s, with land titles, water, transportation, and finance capital secure, the company began to undertake agricultural development. Like CCR in the Yaqui Valley, CRLC spent a great deal of investment capital build-ing and maintaining the Mexicali Valley's irrigation system. By 1922, around 134,000 of the company's 850,000 acres were irrigated. The company never engaged in farming but instead rented blocks of agricultural land, some as large as 10,000 acres. CRLC's first American lessees were modern farmers who had the financial and technical means to operate large holdings. Like CCR's colonists in Sonora, CRLC's lessees had to improve the undeveloped land and pay for their irrigation water. Although CRLC officials preferred cash, most of the early lessees paid their rents through a sharecropping agreement, in which the com-pany received 25 percent of the harvest. While the company mostly rented its land, it did sell approximately 13,000 acres in ten separate transactions between 1904 and 1932. Even though CRLC owned the lion's share of agricultural prop-erty in the Mexicali Valley, by the 1920s nearly a dozen other American com-panies and nationals together held more than 130,000 acres of land as well.[34]

With no overland route to the mainland, Baja California and CRLC's hold-ings were cut off from most of the fighting during the Mexican Revolution. Consequently, some of the territory's leaders avoided aligning with any of the various revolutionary factions until a clear winner emerged. The most powerful political figure in northern Baja California during the 1910s, Esteban Cantú Jiménez, maintained just such a neutral stance. As commander of the military garrison at Mexicali, Cantú seized the governorship by force in August 1914 and held the position until 1920, when he was pressured to resign. As gover-nor, Cantú concentrated his efforts on developing the territory. He undertook an ambitious public works program that included the construction of roads, bridges, schools, hospitals, public buildings, electric power plants, telegraph and telephone lines, and sewer and water systems. Cantú's government ob-tained some of the money for these infrastructural developments by raising property taxes 1,000 percent. Most of the territory's revenue, however, came from his taxing, licensing, and "regulating" Mexicali and Tijuana's booming vice industries, which served a predominantly American clientele. As Joseph Werne notes, in these two border cities "every kind of vice could be found: white slavery, prostitution, horse track gambling, opium dens, cocaine, morphine and heroin dealers, saloons and dives of all descriptions, open extortion, and gambling halls that offered a variety of seductions."[35]

Cantú's building projects were well timed, since the region's economy boomed after he took office due to the outbreak of World War I and the increased demand for cotton in Europe and the United States. During this period, northern Baja California, and especially the city of Mexicali and its surrounding valley, became closely tied to the U.S. economy through the vice, agricultural, and stock-breeding industries. As the economy expanded, hundreds of immigrants came to the Mexicali Valley and leased land from CRLC— mostly Americans but also Asians and, to a lesser extent, Europeans, along with a small number of Mexicans. Thousands of seasonal migrant laborers, most of whom were Chinese or Mexican, also entered the delta region looking for work. In 1915, Cantú began to promote Chinese emigration to the valley as a solution to the labor shortage that stemmed from low populations, increased demand for cotton, and the availability of better-paying jobs just north of the border. By some estimates, Mexicali's population was soon 40 percent Chinese. Cantú, CRLC, and its lessees were happy to have cheap Chinese, Japanese, and South Asian contract laborers picking cotton, since they were usually paid less than Mexican field hands. By the end of WWI, CRLC's cotton holdings were producing $18 million annually, which made the valley one of the world's largest cotton-producing regions.[36]

In the 1910s, CRLC's holdings, and those of other Mexicali Valley landowners, remained secure for a variety of reasons. First, there was little popular pressure for land redistribution, since throughout the decade Baja California's population remained low, the economy grew, wages were high, and revolutionary agrarianism never gained a foothold in the territory due to its isolation. Also, local and national leaders were sympathetic to the interests of the company. For instance, Governor Cantú was antilabor, befriended U.S. capitalists, ignored progressive federal laws, and favored the more-conservative 1857 Constitution over the one written in 1917. Likewise, since Carranza did not strongly endorse Article 27, he was not apt to redistribute CRLC's property, especially since the region remained underpopulated. Also, his government simply could not afford to purchase the company's extensive and well-developed holdings.[37]

Following Carranza, the Sonoran dynasty of Adolfo de la Huerta, Obregón, and Calles did little to threaten CRLC during the 1920s. As northern property owners who were themselves engaged in agribusiness, their interests coincided with that of the company. CRLC, Mexico City, and Mexicali—which was under the governorship of future president Abelardo Rodríguez between 1923 and 1930—sought rail lines, roads, ports, irrigation works, and other forms of infrastructure that would facilitate the transport of agricultural goods from the valley to the market. Likewise, all sides wanted to increase the region's population and agricultural production, but through private hands and not government-financed ejidos. According to Dorothy Kerig, CRLC's owners were not latifundistas (typically absentee owners of a very large private estate that is underutilized in terms of its agricultural production) but instead developers who "hoped to build a vibrant modern community of independent commercial farms that would naturally expand as allied industries grew up nearby." Nothing could have made the Callistas happier. As governor, Rodríguez tried to increase cultivation in the Mexicali Valley by promoting colonies of Mexican private landowners. To assist them with loans, he established the Peninsular Agrarian Bank (Banco Agrícola Peninsular). Likewise, as president, Rodríguez established the National Bank of Agricultural Credit in Mexicali to provide financing to the region's small growers. Before Cárdenas, Baja California's governors and Mexico's presidents had no intention of undermining successful large-scale commercial properties like CRLC's, which, according to Alan Knight, they considered essential to the "rapid development of the Mexican economy along capitalist, free enterprise lines." Finally, like Carranza before them, Obregón and Calles usually redistributed land to the peasantry to quell rural political unrest or create a basis for federal support and dependence. Social justice was not their first priority.[38]

Besides their similar agendas, company officials also were able to maintain their holdings by gaining favor with Mexican leaders—which they did in a variety of ways. For instance, CRLC frequently entertained Mexican officials, granted leases to them on favorable terms, and helped to secure large loans for presidents, governors, and other policymakers. The company also hired attorneys who had close ties to powerful political figures in Mexico City.[39] Company officials also acted as liaisons between Mexico City and Washington over important bilateral issues. CRLC's CEO, Harry Chandler, for example, met with President Warren Harding at the White House in the early 1920s to recommend that the United States recognize Obregón's government. The company also championed Mexican water rights in front of U.S. officials, especially its access to half of the water from the Imperial Valley's main canal at "moderate prices." Finally, fraud helped the company safeguard its investment. In one case, CRLC's attorney Augustín Loroña acted in collusion with Baja California's Treasurer General José Eliseo Muñoz. The two men assessed CRLC's property at a figure below market value, which lowered the company's property taxes and cheated the government of revenue.[40]

Powerful friends in Mexicali, Mexico City, and Washington meant little when the Depression struck. The global economic crisis reduced the international price of cotton and made it difficult for many of CRLC's investors to find the capital needed to keep operations running. In 1931 and 1932, the company made an average of just $30,000 annually from all its land rentals, down from a high of $1,118,000 in 1924. Soon the company was $4 million in debt, and some of its largest investors wanted to sell their holdings to the Mexican government — as CCR had done in Sonora in 1927. After Mexico City expropriated 136,000 acres from CRLC between 1932 and 1934 for restitution to the hundreds of Cucapá Indians who lived in the Mexicali Valley, company's officials became even more eager to sell. In April 1934, they proposed an $11 million instrument of transfer to President Rodríguez's office. In light of his and Calles's connections in Baja California, both men wanted to go forward with the purchase. By 1917, CRLC's holdings had a market value of approximately $40 million, a value they maintained through the 1920s. Despite the low sale price of 1934, the new Cárdenas government told the company that it could not afford to purchase its holdings. Instead, as the next chapter will show, Cárdenas had something else in mind for the company's property.[41]

THE BILATERAL CONFLICT OVER LAND

To a greater extent than Díaz had, most of Mexico's presidents between 1911 and 1940 challenged the United States. Nevertheless, Mexico's revolutionary and postrevolutionary leaders found it difficult to promote their national interests vis-à-vis their northern neighbor because of Washington's sometimes heavy-handed policies against them. Such U.S. behavior was rare during the Porfiriato because American investments in Mexico were secure. Although Washington no longer sought Mexican territory, after Díaz fell from power in 1911 one of the primary objectives of U.S. foreign policy over the next three decades was to protect American economic interests in Mexico. As early as 1913, U.S. Ambassador Henry Lane Wilson conspired with Félix Díaz, the dictator's nephew, and

General Victoriano Huerta to overthrow the democratically elected Francisco Madero, due to his supposed unwillingness to show special favors to American investors and his alleged inability to safeguard U.S. businesses.[42]

Getting rid of Madero in 1913 did little to protect American investments, since the agrarian legislation passed by Carranza in 1915 began to threaten U.S. rural interests. In the quarter century that followed passage of the 1917 Constitution, Mexico's nationalistic laws undermined U.S. economic interests and sparked the most significant bilateral conflicts of the interwar period. The severity of these international crises stemmed from the fact that Americans had approximately $1.3 billion invested in Mexico, and the security of those investments was at risk. Besides being the leading target of U.S. foreign investment in Latin America, Mexico also was the world's leading nonindustrialized importer of U.S. goods. In addition, approximately 61 percent of all Mexican imports came from the United States, and 52 percent of its exports went north of the border.[43] Hence, as has long been the case, American investments in Mexico and bilateral commerce were at the center of the U.S.-Mexican relationship throughout the revolutionary and postrevolutionary eras.

In part a reaction to foreign domination of the Mexican economy during the Díaz's dictatorship, the 1917 Constitution sought to gain domestic control of Mexico's natural and industrial resources and limit the rights of foreigners. Article 3, for instance, limited the number of foreign priests in Mexico. Article 28 cancelled tax exemptions for foreigners. Article 33 forced foreigners to give up extraterritoriality: that is, subject themselves and their properties to Mexican law. Most notably, Article 27 gave the government the power to expropriate both domestic and foreign-owned property. According to one contemporary observer, 90 percent of the disagreements between the United States and Mexico during the interwar period stemmed from Article 27 and the subsequent petroleum and agrarian laws that threatened U.S. economic interests.[44] The two issues that most frequently disrupted bilateral affairs concerned Mexico's attempts to enforce these laws retroactively and U.S. attempts to extract appropriate compensation for the American property owners who were adversely affected.

From May 1920 to September 1923, Presidents Woodrow Wilson and Warren Harding used "conditional recognition" as a diplomatic weapon to prevent Obregón's government from retroactively enforcing Article 27 against American-owned property. The U.S. Congress proved equally aggressive and, according to Benjamin Harrison, "pressured Wilson's administration ruthlessly." In June 1920, the Senate Foreign Relations Subcommittee on Mexican Affairs, headed by Senator Albert Fall, produced a lengthy report recommending that the White House withhold recognition of Obregón's government until it signed a treaty with the United States declaring Articles 3, 27, 33, and 130 of the Constitution were not applicable to American interests. And, if such an agreement could not be reached, the Senate recommended sending "naval and military forces of our government into the Republic of Mexico."[45]

Despite such belligerent threats, and even though he was not that confrontational with Washington, Obregón refused to guarantee protection for American property until the United States first recognized his government. In 1921 and 1922, Washington repeatedly protested the agrarian legislation passed by Mexican state legislatures and the national Congress, which affected American landowners. U.S. officials complained that the laws were being applied retroactively and that improvements made to the properties were not being compensated. They also argued that the agrarian bonds which state and federal governments offered to affected landowners as compensation did not constitute adequate indemnification. U.S. officials were rightly concerned that the bonds had "little market value"; should either the federal or state governments default on them, the property owners "would be remediless." In addition, U.S. policymakers were critical of the lack of legal due process afforded the Americans and the short notification that they were given prior to the division of their holdings. Washington also complained that Mexican officials were targeting large U.S. estates for redistribution and ignoring nearby unused public lands. Because of these and other problems, Secretary of State Charles Evans Hughes told U.S. embassy officials that they should urge Obregón's government to repeal its agrarian laws. Not only did Obregón's administration refuse to do so, but Mexican authorities repeatedly claimed that they and the state governments were acting within the law.[46]

Although little headway was made in the early 1920s toward resolving the bilateral differences that stemmed from Mexican agrarian reform, the standoff over U.S. recognition and the Constitution's retroactive enforcement ended when Obregón was forced to compromise due to the impending uprising led by de la Huerta—which was partly driven by the perception that Mexico City had been too conciliatory toward Washington. Since Obregón's administration rightly believed that U.S. recognition, arms, and loans would help defeat de la Huerta's forces, while a continued international standoff would work to the rebel's advantage, Mexico City conceded to Washington. The Bucareli agreements of August 1923 ensured U.S. support of Obregón's government during the rebellion; in exchange, Mexico City would meet U.S. demands concerning land and oil. Mexican officials agreed that Article 27 would not apply to either rural or industrial titles acquired before May 1917. As a result, most American properties remained secure.[47]

The Bucareli agreements quickly improved Mexican-American relations, both in the national capitals and in the Mexican countryside. The two nations soon exchanged ambassadors and had their embassies fully staffed. In addition, Obregón's government began to detach federal troops to protect American-owned rural holdings from agrarista invasions and squatting—subaltern actions that sometimes precipitated land redistributions. Also, regional officials started showing a "friendlier spirit toward and greater cooperation with the resident Americans." After Calles took office in late 1924, his government returned some rural properties to their American owners, against the interests of the local agrarians.[48]

However, the rapprochement engendered by the Bucareli agreements was short lived. In 1925, bilateral tensions again increased as Calles's administration expropriated a number of American-owned rural properties. Shortly thereafter, U.S. Secretary of State Frank Kellogg demanded that Mexico City "restore the properties that were illegally taken" (usually by squatters) "and indemnify American citizens" for those that were legally expropriated. Mexico City did neither. In his rebuff, Calles stated that he would not modify his nation's agrarian policy. Furthermore, although Mexico City agreed to provide compensation, agrarian bonds were not awarded to any of the U.S. landowners who had recently lost their holdings.[49]

Diplomatic relations worsened when the Mexican Congress debated new land and petroleum legislation in late 1925. U.S. officials tried to influence the process, which angered Mexican authorities. While they were drafting the new laws, Kellogg told the international press corps that Mexican politicians should throw out the Alien Land Act, which he considered confiscatory, and restore American properties or provide affected landowners with appropriate compensation. He also claimed, in light of the rumors of another Mexican rebellion, that Washington would not back Calles's administration until the American landowners received fair treatment. Mexico City did not take this threat lightly. Calles replied publicly to Kellogg through the American press, stating that agrarian reform was a domestic matter and that Washington had no right to interfere in it. He also claimed that Kellogg's announcement about a possible uprising only served to destabilize his government. Mexican Foreign Secretary Aarón Sáenz similarly complained to Washington that it should not try to influence the Mexican Congress and that the rights of Americans in Mexico were not being destroyed, as U.S. officials had charged, but simply changed. Seeing that the Callistas were not humbled by his tough talk, in late December, Kellogg directed Ambassador James Sheffield to submit a formal protest with the Mexican Ministry of Foreign Affairs. In the note, U.S. officials argued that Mexico had broken the Bucareli agreements and had failed to recognize the vested rights of American property owners. Washington's strong stand made Sáenz nervous. The Mexican foreign minister declared to Sheffield that the new Alien Land Act would not be retroactive; he also asked the U.S. ambassador not to use force against his country.[50]

Despite Kellogg and Sheffield's blustering, Calles's administration did not yield. Consequently, the conflict that stemmed from Mexico's proposed agrarian and petroleum legislation wore on through 1926. In fact, bilateral relations worsened as each side repeated their well-worn arguments. Although many, including Calles, expected Washington to recall its ambassador, it never happened. Instead, U.S. officials continued to argue that Mexico had violated the Bucareli agreements by expropriating rural properties whose titles predated 1917. In response to Washington, Sáenz stated that the promises made by Obregón in 1923 were not binding on Calles and merely expressed Obregón's position at that time.[51]

To make matters worse, in April 1926, Mexico's Congress passed the Law of Colonization, which called for the colonization of state and federal lands, as well as oversized privately held estates. Rather than expand Mexico's class of ejidatarios and further strain the federal treasury, colonization was seen as a more cost-effective way to give land to the peasantry. For example, colonists had to prove their solvency by depositing 30 percent of the property's value into the National Bank of Agricultural Credit. Hence, rather than the federal government footing the bill, the colonists would pay for the colonized holdings over time. According to the new law, should landowners reject a colonization proposal, then the government had the right to expropriate their property. Indemnification for the colonized land would be made in bonds, paid for by the colonists and backed by the National Bank of Agricultural Credit—again placing the cost on colonists rather than the government. The same month that the Law of Colonization was passed, Calles issued an executive decree that ordered the restitution and expropriation of irrigation waters to local villages. Washington protested both the Colonization Law and executive decree for water on the usual grounds of due process and compensation.[52]

In early 1927 the Alien Land Act became law. It required foreign landowners to surrender their diplomatic rights, sell their properties near the coast and border within ten years, and if they were corporations, to sell their majority shares to Mexican nationals. When almost 35,000 acres of land were expropriated from William Randolph Hearst's massive holdings in Chihuahua later that year, the newspaper magnate railed against Calles's government in his periodicals. Meanwhile, a new 1927 petroleum law required foreign oil companies to exchange their ownership titles for fifty-year leases. Although tensions over oil heated up in 1927, the controversy over the Alien Land Law cooled down because few American-owned estates were expropriated. In fact, the largest transfer of American-owned rural property in 1927 occurred when the Richardson Construction Company *sold* its extensive holdings in the Yaqui Valley to the Mexican government for $6 million. Although the conflict over land became less caustic, bilateral affairs continued to worsen due to the oil controversy and Calles's support of the liberal uprising in Nicaragua led by Dr. Juan Sacasa against the conservative, U.S.-backed government of Adolfo Díaz. Relations became so strained that many contemporary observers again expected Washington to recall its ambassador and break diplomatic relations.[53]

To protect American oil firms and rural property holders from seizure, Ambassador Sheffield advocated using force or lifting the arms embargo. When Calles obtained documents stolen from the U.S. embassy indicating a possible U.S. military attack against Mexico—allegedly to safeguard American lives and interests—the prospect of war between the two countries grew frighteningly real, especially since Coolidge had recently ordered the U.S. Marines back into Nicaragua. Although invasion plans existed and were in Mexico City's possession, the White House never seriously considered implementing them, due to the lack of public support. Because military intervention was off the table, U.S. officials continued to bluster and demand that Mexico stop expropriating American-owned rural properties or to pay for them in cash or gold soon after they were taken. Neither unrealistic demand was met. Rather, if American landowners were compensated by the Mexican government in the 1920s, it was usually in the form of depreciated agrarian bonds.[54]

In early 1926, Calles authorized the issuance of fifty million pesos worth of bonds to compensate domestic and foreign landowners. The chance that American or Mexican rural property owners would obtain full indemnification appeared unlikely, since Mexico City was only paying interest on the bonds (which lacked a retirement date). As the *New York Times* accurately summarized, "The crux of the agrarian question between Washington and Mexico City is the fact that the expropriated lands are to be paid for in agrarian bonds and not in cash." However, according to Chandler Anderson, Mexico's agrarian bonds were "worthless." Anderson was a former Taft administration and State Department official who had the ear of each Republican administration in the 1920s; he also was seen by many as the "perennial lobbyist" for U.S. investors in Latin America and was a friend of Ambassador Sheffield. Although Arturo Elías viewed him as an "acrimonious enemy of the Mexican government," the U.S. lawyer nevertheless showed some foresight when Mexico defaulted on the agrarian bonds in the early 1930s. Like many "dollar diplomats," Anderson did not advocate the use of force against Mexico. Moreover, because Mexico could not afford reparations, he argued against international arbitration as a way to resolve the conflict over land. Instead, Anderson called for quiet yet firm diplomacy that would lead Mexico City to revise Article 27 or not enforce it.[55] Coincidentally, this is what happened after Sheffield resigned as U.S. ambassador in mid-1927.

Bilateral tensions decreased when the hostile Sheffield—who for years had advised American businessmen not to invest in Mexico until conditions improved—was replaced by Dwight Morrow, a lawyer for J. P. Morgan. The new and more genial U.S. ambassador improved U.S.-Mexican relations by gently persuading an increasingly conservative Calles that Mexico would be better off economically if it did not enforce its nationalistic laws, because doing so would frighten away foreign capital. Since Morrow, unlike Sheffield, publicly advocated American investment below the Rio Grande, Calles was probably willing to listen to him. The fact that Calles believed Washington's new ambassador respected Mexican laws and institutions, and was sympathetic to his country rather than antagonistic, also helped to improve bilateral affairs.[56]

In November 1927, the Mexican Supreme Court ruled that Articles 14 and 15 of the new oil legislation were unconstitutional, since they were retroactive and turned a legally acquired title into a temporary concession. When Mexico City repealed these and other parts of the petroleum law in early 1928, diplomatic relations quickly improved. American-owned rural properties, though, remained at risk. However, only a handful of American estates were taken by the end of the decade, and their loss did not undermine the warming trend between the two capitals. Washington demonstrated its appreciation of Mexico

City's land and oil policies by unequivocally backing the Callista government of Emilio Portes Gil during the 1929 Escobar Rebellion—when one-third of Mexico's states rose in arms against the federal government. During the uprising, Washington imposed a strict arms embargo against the Obregonista rebels, while allowing arms, munitions, and other war materiel to be sold to Mexico City.[57]

In Mexico, 1929 was marked by a military uprising and the foundation of the country's long-standing one-party political system. It also ushered in six years of conservative rule under the Callista Maximato and an equally long period of friendly bilateral relations. Simply put, diplomatic affairs improved because of the increased security afforded to U.S. economic interests in Mexico. American oil firms were no longer at risk of being nationalized, and in mid-1929 the *New York Times* reported that "expropriations of lands owned by foreigners have been very infrequent in recent times." While Washington's heavy-handed policies can account for some of this, the relatively conservative economic orientation of Mexican leaders before Cárdenas also helped to maintain American investments south of the border. That same year, both nations, along with eighteen other countries within the hemisphere, signed the Inter-American Arbitration Treaty. The international agreement required the signatories to pursue arbitration in the event that a dispute between two or more nations could not be resolved diplomatically.[58] Should the expropriation of American-owned property in Mexico produce a bilateral crisis sometime in the future, it would be more difficult for the United States to justify the use of force against its southern neighbor, since the arbitration treaty put mechanisms in place to ensure a peaceful resolution to the conflict.

In the first half of the 1930s, bilateral affairs reached their most amicable point since 1910. In fact, according to President Rodríguez, they were "extremely cordial."[59] Contemporary observers claimed this improvement stemmed from the general belief that the Mexican Revolution, and the threat which its nationalistic laws posed to U.S. economic interests, had run its course. Although many American-owned rural properties were seized between 1915 and 1935, the majority of U.S. rural and industrial interests in Mexico were still secure when Rodríguez left office on December 1, 1934.[60] The claims of American landowners who lost their holdings between 1917 and 1927 as a result of official expropriation or peasant squatting were handled by the General Claims Commission. This commission, which was agreed to at the 1923 Bucareli Conference, was designed to resolve thousands of diverse U.S. and Mexican claims for monetary compensation that had arisen since 1868, included losses related to cross-border Indian raids, cattle rustling, and personal injury cases. To expedite a resolution of the general claims, in April 1934 both governments removed all the pre-1927 agrarian claims from the General Claims Commission and tried to negotiate a separate agrarian settlement. However, because Mexican officials undermined the bilateral proceedings by appearing to be ill prepared for them, the talks went nowhere and an agrarian claims resolution was never reached.[61] According to David Cronon, the State Department hoped that diplomatic pressure on the pre-1927 agrarian claims would dissuade the new Cárdenas administration from expropriating additional American-owned rural property.[62] U.S. officials could not have been more wrong.

In October 1935, Mexican Foreign Secretary José Ángel Cisneros proposed to halt additional expropriations of American-owned land as long as the pre-1927 agrarian claims were settled, without discussing the legality of the 1917 Constitution and Mexico's right to expropriate foreign-owned property under international law. Because U.S. officials liked hearing that the expropriations would cease, they approached the Mexican Ministry of Foreign Affairs for further talks. Cardenista officials, however, would not repeat Cisneros's offer.[63] Two months later, Mexican Ambassador to the United States Dr. Francisco Castillo Nájera told Assistant Secretary of State Sumner Welles that "no further American property of any kind would be taken over for agrarian purposes."[64] This, too, was an empty promise, one that we will return to in the final chapters of the book when we examine U.S. and Mexican diplomacy during the agrarian dispute. Suffice it to say that over the next five years, more American-owned land was officially expropriated by the Mexican government than during any time in the nation's history. The largest of all those expropriations began in early 1937, when Cárdenas's administration expropriated 412,000 acres from CRLC in Baja California's Mexicali Valley. It is to this subject that we now turn.

EL ASALTO A LAS TIERRAS Y LA HUELGA
DE LOS SENTADOS

How Local Agency Shaped Agrarian Reform in the Mexicali Valley

There is a line dividing this place between a Los Angeles company and a government [on one side] . . . and at the other end an ideal which brought rivers of blood since 1910. . . . All of the petitions made before Governor Gavira were nullified, demonstrating to the commission that there is no law nor revolutionary principles [in Mexicali], that there is nothing more than Mr. Chandler, and he is the owner of everything.

SECRETARY GENERAL OF THE UNION OF PEASANT DAY LABORERS,
JULY 24, 1936

Mr. Chandler, the government under my post, adjusting itself to the necessities of the moment and social conditions that prevail [in Mexicali], will not forgo any effort to try to improve the life of the working sector.

PRESIDENT LÁZARO CÁRDENAS TO CRLC'S CEO, HARRY CHANDLER,
FEBRUARY 4, 1937

On January 26, 1937, a large group of Mexican agraristas marched to the office of the governor of Baja California, Rafael Navarro Cortina, and demanded that he execute their petitions for land in the Mexicali Valley. Jesús Cibrián Zamudio, president of the Union of Peasant Day Laborers and one of the leaders of the demonstration, shouted, "Look, Mr. Governor, Article 27 of the Constitution says that the lands are the property of the nation; that is why we request them. If you are going to deny us our constitutional rights as

Mexicans, we will use force to take the lands, and if you do not give us water, we will break the floodgates."[1] Cibrián kept his word. At 6:00 a.m. the next morning, almost four hundred agraristas met at the Yamada Ranch, located in Colonia Michoacán de Ocampo. According to another agrarista leader, Jesús Andrade Romero, some of the participants "were armed with axes, some with machetes, and others only with the spirit of battle."[2] Later that day, groups of landless peasants seized Rancho Nagasaki, Campos Nuevos, Field no. 7 of Laguna Station, Field Miomoto, and Ranches nos. 2, 3, and 15, all part of the 850,000 acres owned by the Los Angeles–based Colorado River Land Company. The agraristas threw off the Asian tenant farmers, proudly waved Mexican flags (along with a number of red ones), and planted signs that read "Land and Freedom."[3] Within two months of the invasion, nearly 200,000 acres of CRLC's best irrigated property were redistributed by the federal government to Mexicali field workers in the form of communal ejidos. Said Pedro Pérez, a rank-and-file agrarista who took part in the invasion, "We workers finally got what we deserved, some land and water. Now we could have more things and live better." The expropriations did not stop there; by 1940 almost 412,000 acres of CRLC's property had been redistributed to landless campesinos.[4]

Like most subdisciplines, peasant studies have undergone major interpretive changes over the years. Initially, modernization and dependency theories (i.e., the traditionalists and revisionists) both portrayed peasants as passive participants who adapted to changes brought upon them from the outside. Over the last generation, these structural interpretations have been rightly challenged by postrevisionist scholars who argue that peasants are active historical agents who have vigorously and openly tried to transform their oppressive social order or have quietly manipulated it to ensure their survival. The agraristas in the Mexicali Valley fall in to the former group; they did not rely on "everyday forms of resistance" to achieve their objectives.[5] Rather, they organized into peasant leagues, aligned themselves with national labor unions, filed ejidal petitions, held marches and demonstrations, performed political plays, voted for representatives, gathered arms, and invaded an enormous private property owned by a powerful U.S. company. Many of these methods of activism, with the exception of the large-scale land invasion, were employed by the valley's agraristas in the 1920s and 1930s. However, they were only able to obtain their goals in 1937 because of the priority afforded campesino issues by Cárdenas's administration. Ironically, though, Cárdenas's government initially tried to carry out a private colonization program in the Mexicali Valley. The region's landless campesinos not only resisted this plan but forced Mexico City to reconfigure its agrarian program and the structure of land tenure in the valley in a manner that advanced their class interests as landless rural workers. This direct attack on American-owned property in rural Mexico was part of a nationwide movement by the peasantry to reclaim the land for those who worked it.

The agraristas' grassroots initiatives and the Cardenistas' statist project (which is covered more fully in the next chapter) did not go unchallenged. Much of the literature on Mexican land reform focuses mostly on agrarian legislation, the political, economic and cultural forces behind state-sponsored projects, and peasant agency. This chapter offers yet another perspective, demonstrating that disenfranchised property owners, both Mexican and American, also influenced the local application of land redistribution. Hence, agrarian reform under Cárdenas was not a linear process controlled solely by federal officials; rather, it was shaped by a variety of actors from different socio-economic classes and characterized by starts, stops, and reversals. And when agrarian reform impinged upon foreign-owned land, it became a transnational process subject to American influence.

COLONIZATION AND THE "PLAN PRO-BAJA CALIFORNIA"

In September 1934, during Cárdenas's year-long, 18,000 mile, nationwide campaign tour, he visited the territory of Baja California, including the agricultural *colonias* (communites) in the Mexicali Valley and the capital city of Mexicali. Cárdenas later recorded some ideas on how best to develop the region. He proposed "to distribute among Mexicans the enormous *latifundio* (large estate) owned by the Colorado River Land Co., which occupies the Mexicali Valley, [and] to organize agricultural colonies in the valley with Mexicans resident in the United States." During his visit he also envisioned tying the peninsula to the mainland through railroad construction. He called for building railroad lines from Mexicali to Puerto Isabel, Santa Ana, and Puerto Peñasco in order for the valley's agricultural production to reach the country's interior. After Cárdenas nationalized the railroads in 1937, such large-scale infrastructure projects became easier for the government to undertake.[6]

Cárdenas was not alone in seeing the need to focus attention on Baja California. The region's military zone commander, General Ernesto Aguirre Colorado, contrasted the easy access that the United States had to the peninsula via road and rail with Mexico's limited access. According to the general, not only did this result in American domination of the territory's economy, but many Mexican migrant workers died when crossing the desert in a vain attempt to reach the peninsula from neighboring Sonora. Aguirre warned the new president, "Either immediately deal with that part of your country's land, or it will be lost [to the Americans] within ten years." He suggested that the federal government purchase CRLC's lands, promote agricultural development, increase Mexican access to Colorado River water, and develop the territory's infrastructure in ways initially envisioned by Cárdenas himself.[7]

In April 1935, Secretary of Agriculture Tomás Garrido Canabal informed CRLC that the federal government could not afford to purchase its property as the company had proposed a year earlier. Instead, Garrido Canabal strongly recommended that CRLC sign a colonization contract with the federal government. Undersecretary of Agriculture Dr. José Parrés warned the company's well-connected Mexico City attorney, Ismael Pizarro Suárez, that unless CRLC agreed to a formal colonization agreement, "the lands would always be in danger of being affected by other means of land redistribution"—meaning expropriation. On the other hand, noted Parrés, "if such a contract is signed then the Government would be legally and morally obliged to avoid any cause of trouble that might hinder the normal course of the contract." Because of the legal restrictions on foreign landownership near the border, CRLC could not sell its property to another foreign interest. And few Mexicans had the capital to acquire such extensive and well-developed holdings. Consequently, company officials spent a year negotiating a colonization agreement with Mexico City to avoid nationalization of their property. Meanwhile, CRLC hoped (in vain) that Article 27 of the 1917 Constitution—which empowered the federal government to expropriate private property—would be repealed by the Mexican courts or legislature. As talks got under way, Cárdenas ordered a number of government agencies to study agricultural colonization in the Mexicali Valley, as well as Baja California's economic development and its integration into the larger national economy.[8]

On April 14, 1936, CRLC's owners signed a colonization agreement with the Mexican government. Over a twenty-year period, the company was obligated to survey, subdivide, and sell all of its agricultural and stock-raising property at prices that were below market value.[9] The agreement smacked of Cardenista economic nationalism, since it was specifically designed to divest CRLC of its holdings and transfer ownership to Mexican nationals. This was especially the case insofar as the contract stipulated that only Mexicans could become colonists, thereby preventing the large foreign-born population that resided in Baja California from acquiring any of CRLC's land. Also, upon the signing of each individual colonization contract, CRLC had to immediately transfer the property title to the colonist, rather than retain it until the final mortgage installment was paid to the company.[10]

In many ways, colonization was part of a larger state-building process that characterized much of postrevolutionary Mexico. As with Cárdenas's extensive public works projects, rural colonization programs were designed by the elite to develop the country's agricultural regions, give work to the underemployed, and build a loyal base of political support for Cárdenas and the government's official party, the National Revolutionary Party (Partido Nacional Revolucionario, PNR). In 1935 the president established a number of intersecretarial commissions to study colonization, both at the national level and in the territories of Baja California and Quintana Roo.[11] The Baja California commission was headed by one of Cárdenas's most trusted advisers, a former Zapatista and the sitting governor of Baja California Norte, Lieutenant Colonel Gildardo Magaña. The territory's governor suggested that to develop the region quickly, Mexican repatriates from the United States and mestizo families from the nation's interior should be settled in the Mexicali Valley.[12]

In his separate study on Baja California, Secretary of Agriculture Saturnino Cedillo referred to CRLC's extensive holdings as a "latifundio." He, too, called for colonizing the company's property immediately with repatriated Mexican families, as well as establishing agricultural experiment stations, revising the government's water agreement with CRLC, and obtaining an international water treaty with the United States.[13] In November 1935, Cedillo visited Baja California and initiated work toward colonizing CRLC's holdings with Mexican nationals. As Dorothy Kerig points out, settling migrants from the nation's heavily populated interior would act as a "safety valve" by shifting an overabundant supply of labor to a sparsely populated region. This would not only relieve pressure in areas of land scarcity but would also put more land under cultivation in the Mexicali Valley and thereby hasten the development of the territory's economy.[14] That December, Cedillo made a well-publicized trip to Los Angeles to recruit Mexican repatriates to colonize Baja California. The company's holdings were among the most developed lands in the country, and Cardenista officials believed that colonizing it with Mexican repatriates, who could employ the modern farming techniques that they likely acquired while working in the United States, would increase the valley's agricultural production.[15]

Colonization was linked to another central component of Cárdenas's state-building process: reining in Mexico's outlying territories. In September 1936, Cárdenas announced, via nationwide radio broadcast, a program designed to accelerate the economic development of northern and southern Baja California and Quintana Roo and hasten their integration into "*la patria*" (homeland).[16] Improving the nation's infrastructure was central to the government's state-building drive, since public works projects provided jobs to the underemployed and tied many local communities closer to the federal government. They also were seen as a means to modernize the nation, facilitate economic growth, and promote agricultural, mineral, and industrial development. All of Mexico's postrevolutionary governments constructed irrigation works, roads, highways, bridges, railway lines, port facilities, schools, and hospitals, with both socio-economic and political objectives in mind. Cárdenas's campaign tour not only further radicalized him but also made him into a fervent developmentalist. His diary is replete with calls for new public works in every region of the country. Although the National Treasury estimated that 892 million pesos were needed for government expenditures for the years 1935, 1936, and 1937, the Cárdenas administration spent nearly 1.2 billion pesos and ran a 258 million peso deficit—due, in part, to its large-scale public works campaign.[17]

The federal improvement programs for the territories, known collectively as the Plan Pro-Territorios Federales, as well as the one for Baja California, called the Plan Pro-Baja California, produced numerous government studies and news reports on how to develop Baja California's infrastructure, increase its agricultural output, and incorporate the region into the national economy. Some suggestions for stimulating trade included establishing a free trade zone, reforming customs and tax laws, promoting mining, fishing, and tourist development, improving communication links to the mainland via railroad, highway, and port construction, modifying irrigation works, and, most importantly, colonizing CRLC's vast holdings with Mexican nationals in order to put more land under cultivation. This latter goal was considered critical for stimulating regional economic growth.[18] In short, the Plan Pro-Baja California and colonization were nationalistic projects designed by the country's political elite to Mexicanize the region.

Nationwide, hundreds of individuals, as well as peasant, labor, government, and civic organizations, endorsed the Plan Pro-Baja California; some groups even collected money to assist the federal government in developing the territory.[19] Thousands of campesinos wrote directly to Cárdenas and volunteered as colonists; many of them were peasants who lacked ejidos in their home states and others were Mexican nationals residing north of the border. In the United States, organizations such as the National Club for the Homeland, which mostly was composed of unemployed Mexican immigrants, responded enthusiastically to the president's call to colonize Baja California.[20] In central Mexico, a group of thirty-nine families together wrote to Cárdenas and asked for financial assistance, since they could not afford a deposit for the land. Individual campesinos—including Camilo Alvarado from Guanajuato, Pedro Gálvez from Sinaloa, and César Ruíz from Veracruz, who were denied ejidos in their home states—moved to the Mexicali Valley with the hope of receiving a land grant.[21]

In November 1936, CRLC issued its first deeds to the colonists. Less than six weeks before the invasion of CRLC's property, in mid-December 1936, Mexicali's military commander, Brigadier General Juan Castelo Encinas, informed Cárdenas that the company had settled 175 colonists on twice the amount of land that was required by the colonization agreement.[22] Although CRLC was obligated to colonize only 12,000 acres in the first year of the agreement, within its first six months the company had sold or leased over 27,000 acres of land to hundreds of Mexican nationals.[23] Despite the successful start to colonization, Cárdenas seemed dissatisfied with the pace of settlement. On January 20, 1937, one week before the agrarista invasion, Cárdenas wrote to Baja California's governor, Rafael Navarro Cortina, and stressed the need to accelerate the colonization process. Cárdenas told him that he wanted to see all of CRLC's property divided among the peasantry within five to six years—as opposed to the twenty years stipulated in the colonization agreement. Although Cárdenas made no mention of redistributing the company's land as ejidos, the urgency of settling Mexicans at a faster pace and divesting CRLC of its property was abundantly clear.[24]

THE AGRARISTA MOVEMENT IN THE MEXICALI VALLEY

Although the 1936 colonization contract appeared to be proceeding according to plan, it had one very serious flaw: it was a state-sponsored project designed by domestic and foreign elites that did not take into consideration the landless rural workers in the Mexicali Valley. The field workers employed on CRLC's holdings had their own vision for the company's property that was distinct from the colonization program agreed to by the federal government and a small group of wealthy Los Angeles businessmen. The successful and rapid implementation of the colonization program was the spark that ignited the January 27, 1937, agrarista invasion of CRLC's property. In previous years the agraristas held out hope that someday they would receive ejidos. And, since Cárdenas had courted the rural vote during his presidential campaign, that dream appeared more likely once he took office. Now, however, it seemed that Cárdenas had a different plan in mind, one that depended on workers having enough money or credit to purchase the land for themselves directly from CRLC. Since field workers lacked the financial means to become colonists, many worried that they would never acquire their own property, should colonization be carried to fruition. Therefore, they felt compelled to act quickly and boldly before it was too late, before the colonization program transformed "their valley" and made them into a permanent class of landless laborers who toiled endlessly on other people's property.[25]

While it would appear that the invasion of CRLC's property by hundreds of militant agraristas was "spontaneous," its roots stretched back to the 1920s, when Baja California's population grew rapidly despite a regional economic slowdown that caused job opportunities, working conditions, and salaries to decline for most agricultural workers. Moreover, since cotton production dominated the Mexicali regional economy, even in good economic times employment levels for rural workers fluctuated greatly. In the spring cotton was planted. During the summer the land was irrigated, and in the fall—when labor demand peaked—the cotton was picked (see figure 7). Consequently, from July to November migratory laborers flooded the Mexicali Valley in search of work, but there was usually little work during the "dead season" between December and April. Not coincidently, the invasion of CRLC's land occurred in January.[26]

Most of the rank-and-file agraristas were young mestizo campesinos who came to Baja California in the 1920s and 1930s looking for employment. Some were sharecroppers who grew cotton on lands leased from CRLC. As lessees, they often complained of high rents that were paid either in cash or crops, or both. The majority of agraristas reflected the local rural labor force: overworked and underpaid day laborers and resident estate peons who worked for the Asians, Americans, and Mexicans who rented property from CRLC. Few landless workers in the valley were contracted through debt peonage. While many were from the nation's interior, part of its "increasingly large floating population of migratory workers," others arrived in the Mexicali Valley from the United States.[27]

One leader in the agrarista movement, Jesús Andrade Romero, had a per-

FIGURE 7. Mexican fieldhand picking cotton, ca. mid-1930s. Note his tattered clothes. AGN, ARCHIVO FOTOGRÁFICO, FONDO CÁRDENAS, 437/2.

sonal history similar to other rural workers in the valley, which he recalled during a mid-1980s interview. Andrade was born in Guanajuato in 1903 and at the age of twenty-one migrated to the United States, "like many others, to find a better life." After working for a year as a fieldhand on a sugar beet and potato farm in Idaho, Andrade received a plot of land from the farm owner. Over the next five years, he shared the costs and profits of farming with him. However, the onset of the Depression forced Andrade to move to California, where he worked for several agricultural companies. Since he had relatives in the Mexicali Valley, in 1934 he relocated there to "support his family and settle in a place of his own." For many Mexican immigrants like Andrade, working north of the Rio Grande was a consciousness-raising experience that exposed them to higher salaries and better working and living conditions than those encountered in Mexico. Consequently, scholars have long speculated that the experiences of migrants in the United States made them unwilling to accept Mexican labor conditions when they recrossed the border. Some, like Andrade, in turn become labor activists.[28]

Those migrant laborers such as Andrade who were lucky enough to find work in the valley still toiled under horrendous conditions. Besides engaging in stoop labor and working ten-hour days, six or seven days a week in the extreme Mexicali heat, most were underpaid. According to a recent interview that I conducted with Pedro Pérez, a rank-and-file agrarista who took part in the 1937 invasion of CRLC's land, they "worked like dogs and were given three pesos for picking one hundred kilos of cotton, despite the fact that a person needed six pesos a day to get by." Like most fieldhands in the Mexicali Valley, Pérez also suffered from underemployment and had a difficult time finding work during the slower months of the production cycle. Moreover, the fact that many *jornaleros* (day laborers) in the valley worked on estates that Asian immigrants rented from CRLC added insult to injury and for some, including Pérez, increased their nationalist ire. In other words, the agraristas in the Mexicali Valley were not only class conscious but race conscious as well.[29]

Living conditions for the valley's rural proletariat were as poor as their working conditions. Most lived in one-room thatched huts or cardboard shacks without electricity, refrigeration, running water, doors, or windows (see figure 8). Consequently, not only did they live at nature's discretion, but their bedding and furniture was minimal and uncomfortable. Finally, the landless rural workers in the Mexicali Valley occupied the lowest rung on the socioeconomic ladder and lacked access to basic healthcare and education for themselves and their families.[30]

In spite of their hard life, or maybe because of it, many field workers were not driven by strong ideological convictions; instead, bread-and-butter issues were the driving force behind their militancy. This may help explain why agrarista leaders periodically changed their labor union affiliation, probably siding with whichever local or national union would best advance their cause. Most agraristas believed that owning property, whether in the form of a communal or individual ejido, would allow them to stop migrating in search of work and pass the land down to their children so they too could avoid the difficult life of migratory labor. They expected that property ownership also would enable them to earn enough money to purchase basic necessities and a few modern conveniences—canned food, an oil stove, a watch. More important than appropriating some symbols of modernity, however, was the agraristas'

FIGURE 8. Example of poor housing conditions for Mexicali field workers, ca. early 1930s. Note the house's flimsy construction and lack of modern material items. Museo del Asalto a las Tierras, Ejido Michoacán de Ocampo, Mexicali, Baja California Norte. PHOTOGRAPH BY AUTHOR.

belief that ownership would allow them to obtain better clothing and housing, as well as access to healthcare and education for themselves and their families. The landless agricultural workers acquired some of their "modern" acquisitiveness by working on the small- and medium-sized colonies that dominated the valley, where they saw the higher living standards of the colonists (see figure 9). Ejidatario Manuel Encinos, who inherited his plot of land, recalled, "My father wanted things like the *colonos*. Before the distribution, we were so poor we had nothing." Although many rural workers were illiterate, advertisements in local newspapers also shaped their interests. Mexicali's landless proletarians simply wanted to make life at work and home easier, more comfortable, and secure and claimed that they were entitled to CRLC's land as stipulated by the 1917 Constitution.[31]

Mexicali's agrarista movement—which culminated in the 1937 invasion of CRLC's holdings—can be divided into four distinct periods: 1921–22, 1923–27, 1930, and 1934–37. Throughout these periods the movement was marked by both continuity and change. During each, the desire for land and the reasons for obtaining it—along with the inability to afford it or even rent it—remained constant for the valley's rural proletariat. Likewise, because CRLC was a foreign absentee landowner that appeared to favor Chinese, Japanese, and South Asian

FIGURE 9. Women from colonist families in the Mexicali Valley, ca. early 1930s. Note that their dress shoes, stylish clothing, and jewelry indicate that they lived above the subsistence level. AGN, ARCHIVO FOTOGRÁFICO, FONDO RODRÍGUEZ, 25/9.

tenants and workers, the company was usually unpopular with most local Mexicans. Discontinuity, on the other hand, is seen in the turnover of agrarista leaders and various union affiliations held by the local peasant leagues.

The first phase of the agrarista movement in the Mexicali Valley began during the post–World War I recession of 1921 and was precipitated by a lack of jobs in the United States—which impelled many Mexicans north of the border to return home in search of work. The slumping demand for cotton and the return of thousands of Mexican immigrants created a labor surplus in the valley that increased unemployment and class tensions.[32] Population pressure led some workers to call for the expropriation of CRLC's holdings and the creation of ejidos; it also increased the incidence of squatting, as seen by the seventy-two families who moved onto the company's property in 1921. Earlier that same year, job shortages prompted the labor union Libertarian Workers (Obreros Libertarios) to march on Governor Epigmenio Ibarra's office and demand increased employment opportunities. Ibarra, who generally sided with capital against labor, responded to the protest by arresting local labor leaders. The following year, a group of two hundred field workers, led by Marcelino Magaña Mejía, petitioned the Mexicali government to redistribute vacant and untilled lands that were part of CRLC's property. Although their request was ignored, these initial and meager steps of rural labor mobilization in 1921 and 1922 marked the beginning of the agrarian movement.[33]

Agrarista mobilization entered its second and lengthier phase in 1923, as economic conditions in the valley failed to improve. That year, two landless cotton pickers who worked on company property, José Martínez and Anastacio Reyes Uzquiano, began to organize the field workers in their agricultural communities. Both men—like many subsequent agrarista leaders in the valley, including those who would lead the 1937 invasion—identified with the field workers they represented because they, too, had worked the land and were not outsiders—unlike the urban-born schoolteachers who in some places sought to organize the rural proletariat from the top down. After working in the valley for a number of years, Martínez established the Peasant Union of Colonias Gómez and Alamo Mocho, which he then affiliated with the Syndicate of Mexicali Workers (Sindicato de Obreros de Mexicali) headed by Reyes. The latter union, which incorporated both rural and urban workers, was aligned with the Industrial Workers of the World (IWW).[34]

Because the IWW's clout weakened as the decade wore on, in 1927 the Sindicato de Obreros de Mexicali switched its affiliation to the more powerful Regional Mexican Workers' Confederation (Confederación Regional Obrera Mexicana, or CROM). The CROM, led by Luis Morones, dominated the Mexican labor movement in the late 1920s and early 1930s and was closely tied to President Plutarco Elías Calles. The CROM—and other national labor and peasant organizations that the agraristas subsequently affiliated with—gave legitimacy to the local movement and increased its leverage vis-à-vis state and federal officials.[35] Consequently, in 1927, Reyes and Martínez requested that some 35,000 acres of CRLC's property be distributed as ejidos. As with many petitions filed by agraristas during the postrevolutionary era, they cited specific agrarian laws to make a solid legal case. In addition, they used revolutionary rhetoric to illustrate the origin of their demands. Most also justified their petitions by describing the personal and economic hardships of the workers and their need to provide for their families. In their joint petition, Reyes and Martínez cited the Agrarian Law of January 6, 1915. They argued that because the field workers lacked their own plots, they were forced to work for low wages; this made it difficult for them to earn enough money to educate their children, who had to work to supplement the family income.[36]

As president of the Sindicato de Obreros de Mexicali, Reyes had enough clout to meet with both Governor Abelardo Rodríguez and CRLC officials, including CEO Harry Chandler. Rodríguez pointed out that Baja California did not have the economic means to support the peasantry on government-financed ejidos and that he and CRLC officials were not inclined to divide lands that were already under production. Chandler asked the agrarista leader to wait another five years for the company to open new, irrigated lands which the government would distribute. The situation did not look good for Reyes, since CRLC officials and Governor Rodríguez held similar views regarding the company's property and regional development. Moreover, neither side in this public-private, U.S.-Mexican partnership sought to change land tenure patterns in the Mexicali Valley in favor of the rural working class. According to Reyes's son, Rosalío, after the meeting his father became so "disillusioned by the results, after having made such a fight and effort," that he left the labor movement and moved to the other side of the Colorado River to open new lands in Sonora.[37] The outcome of Reyes and Martínez's petition was hardly unique: all requests for ejidal lands filed by the Mexicali peasantry in the 1920s and early 1930s were denied by the Secretary of Agriculture in Mexico City.[38]

Following Reyes's departure, the agrarista movement in the Mexicali Valley waned for a few years, in spite of the region's continued economic decline. The onset of the Great Depression further exacerbated the plight of the valley's landless rural workers. The price of cotton peaked in 1919 at 44 cents per pound, then dropped for the next dozen years. By 1928, cotton averaged only 19 cents per pound, and in 1931 it hit a record low of 6 cents per pound. Plummeting prices forced growers in the valley to reduce cultivation, both to cut labor costs and to drive up prices. In 1928, nearly 160,000 acres of cotton were being farmed in the valley. However, by 1932 cotton cultivation had declined to 27,000 acres. To make matters worse, the valley's population doubled between 1920 and 1930, from 15,000 to 30,000. Population pressures and economic competition among valley workers increased further during the early 1930s following the arrival of thousands of repatriated Mexicans from the United States and Chinese immigrants who were expelled from Sonora and Sinaloa. Reduction in public works projects, falling wages, growing unemployment and homelessness, widespread hunger, unpaid rents, and unfulfilled ejidal petitions led to an increase in Mexican squatters on CRLC lands. Not surprisingly, the political and socio-economic climate in the Mexicali Valley during this period was volatile. The territory's instability worsened due to the frequent turnovers in the governor's office. In the two years following Rodríguez's departure in January 1930, five different governors were appointed by Mexico City to Baja California Norte.[39]

The austerity measures enacted in 1930 by Rodriguez's successor, Governor José María Tapia, precipitated the third phase of the agrarista movement. During a mid-1980s interview, Macrina Lerma Álvarez recalled what conditions were like. In 1929, at the age of nineteen, Lerma and her husband worked as day laborers in Colonia Alamo Mocho where they barely made enough money to eat. She remembered the time as being very difficult, because "people had no money to sow the land." Recalled Lerma, "Mexicali was a desert; it was too small, and there were lots of poor people like us." In 1929, her husband joined the agrarista movement, which, according to Lerma, was encouraged by speeches made by the former "radical populist" governor of Michoacán, General Francisco Múgica. In 1930 he visited the Mexicali Valley and gave the agrarista movement a much-needed shot in the arm. According to Lerma, Múgica told rural laborers, "If we want the lands, we had to fight for them whether we had food or not . . . And sooner or later we would have to throw the company off." Although it appears that Múgica may have been suggesting a land invasion, it would be another seven years before the agraristas found the courage to seize CRLC's property. Besides telling the field workers to be more militant, Múgica suggested that they join the Mexican Socialist Party. According to Lerma, at that time many agraristas also were members of the anarcho-syndicalist General Workers' Confederation (Confederación General de Trabajadores, or CGT).[40]

Taking their lead from Múgica, some of the valley's agraristas decided to challenge elite interests in a novel way by performing a play that was written by the Mexican revolutionary Ricardo Flores Magón entitled "The Slave and the Bourgeoisie." The parody criticized the government for starving the Mexican people and denying them land. Using theater as a vehicle to raise class consciousness and promote social change was not taken lightly by regional authorities. Hence, after one of the performances in May 1930, soldiers arrested the play's organizer, Felipa Velázquez, along with her brother, some of her children, and fourteen other agrarista leaders.[41] They were described by local officials as "agitators and incendiaries" and were jailed at the nearby Islas Marías Federal Prison. However, since Múgica was the prison warden and he supported their fight against CRLC, he worked for their release and made their stay as comfortable as possible.[42] The agraristas also gained support from Baja California's congressional representative, who brought national attention to their arrest after introducing a bill in the Chamber of Deputies calling for the cancellation of CRLC's titles. In addition, the CGT pressured the federal government to release the prisoners and threatened a nationwide general strike of tens of thousands of union members. As the agraristas won widespread support, organized labor directed harsh criticism at Governor Tapia and the CRLC. Five months after their arrest, Felipa, her children, and the other agrarista leaders were released. Tapia's repression of the agrarista movement and his austerity measures made him too unpopular to retain in the office. Consequently, President Pascual Ortiz Rubio replaced him after only eight months as governor. Upon their release, the agrarista leaders went back to their colonies of Alamo Mocho, Michoacán de Ocampo, Francisco Javier Mina, Guadalupe Victoria, and Colonia Ocampo. Although these would be the same colonias that would lead the January 1937 invasion of CRLC's land, for years after the prison release the valley's rural labor movement stalled.[43]

Cárdenas's presidential campaign and visit to the region in 1934 breathed new life into the agrarista cause, which initiated the final stage of Mexicali's agrarian movement and led to the 1937 invasion of CRLC's holdings. Inspired by Cárdenas's call for greater worker and campesino rights, in May 1934, rural workers formed the Syndical Federation of Workers and Peasants of the Mexicali Valley (Federación Sindical de Jornaleros y Campesinos del Valle de Mexicali) and aligned with the CROM.[44] Clearly, they were conscious of their rights under the law, citing articles within the 1917 Constitution and the new 1934 Agrarian Code to justify their most recent petitions for land. Furthermore, not only did the agraristas know how much land CRLC owned and that Article 27 prohibited foreign land ownership within fifty miles of the border, but they reminded agrarian officials of these facts and described CRLC as "a horrible company that hoarded the land."[45]

Since no action was taken on their petition, in 1936 agraristas in the rural community of Alamo Mocho established the Union of Peasant Day Laborers and named Jesús Cibrián Zamudio as president. The union's secretaries included Leonardo Prado and Ignacio Sánchez—both of whom had been jailed in 1930 following the theatrical performance. Rather than affiliate with the conservative and discredited CROM, which was tied to the weakened Callista faction, the Alamo Mocho peasant league aligned with the CGT—which had played up its independent status and its support for Cárdenas. In the Mexicali Valley, the CGT represented the interests of estate-dwelling peons and day laborers, both of whom were sometimes overlooked by other national peasant leagues, by federal officials, and even by agrarian law—all of which usually focused on the needs of campesinos in independent villages. Consequently, the CGT found a ready rank and file that resented the fact that their status excluded them from either privately colonizing CRLC's land or obtaining government ejidos. Since the CGT's national influence had declined by the early 1930s, championing the interests of rural wage laborers rather than smallholding campesinos was a way to rehabilitate the federation. Moreover, the migratory status of many field workers in the Mexicali Valley probably increased their independent character, thus making the autonomous CGT an attractive choice. Finally, the fact that the CGT often called for land redistribution based on individually owned parcels rather than large-scale collective ejidos struck a responsive cord with those agraristas who put self-interest ahead of their collective goals.[46]

While Ben Fallaw correctly notes that during Cárdenas's sexenio many CGT unions in Yucatán opposed agrarian reform and worked on behalf of the hacendados, this was not the case in Baja California. The reasons are numerous. Unlike in Yucatán, a "cozy relationship" did not exist between Baja California's CGT leaders and wealthy landowners such as CRLC. Traditional "patron-client bonds" did not exist in the Mexicali Valley because most agraristas had a negative view of CRLC and often referred to it as an "octopus" that had tentacles which reached far into their lives. Pedro Pérez believed many field workers held this characterization and that "nobody liked the company." Moreover, not only was the company an absentee landowner, but it was controlled by a small group of wealthy Los Angeles businessmen who never soiled their hands. These factors worked against the sort of patron-client relations that existed between estate owners and laborers in Yucatán. Also, many agraristas in Baja California worked on Asian properties that were leased from CRLC, and northwestern Mexico's rampant xenophobia further hindered bonds of clientage. Finally, although Fallow rightly argues that the isolation of Yucatán's haciendas "reinforced peon attachment to the estate and hacendado," this was hardly the case with CRLC's 850,000 acres in the Mexicali Valley. Not only was the region underpopulated by contemporary standards, but it attracted migrant rural laborers from around the country who used it as a stopping place as they headed to or returned from the United States in search of work.[47]

After establishing the Union of Peasant Day Laborers and aligning with the CGT, in June 1936 Cibrián met with Governor Gabriel Gavira and asked that three Japanese ranches be redistributed. Gavira not only denied the request but also painted a bleak picture of local politics. Proclaimed the governor, "Article 27 does not apply here, nor do the principles of the revolution, just Mr. Chandler rules since he is the only landowner in the Mexicali Valley." Gavira even implied that the company's chairman had Mexico City's support, as evidenced by the fact that after he was appointed by Cárdenas as governor, federal authorities ordered him to dine with Chandler in Los Angeles. In an attempt to undermine the agrarista movement, Gavira offered to pay Cibrián's expenses should he relocate to national lands in Sonora. Cibrián declined. The governor then suspended public works projects and, according to Paul Vanderwood, "offered the discharged workers $10 to leave Baja California and find their fortunes elsewhere."[48]

Rather than leave the Mexicali Valley, Cibrián and the league organized a massive rally in Mexicali, to which they invited Cardenista officials. With more than three thousand people present at the June outdoor meeting, agrarista leader Alfonso Tovar spoke on behalf of most field workers and made their demands clear to Mexicali and Mexico City. In his speech, Tovar suggested to the keynote speaker, Interior Secretary Silvano Barba González, that "the lati-fundios which belong to the foreigners should be acquired by the government and divided into ejidos; rather than be sold under a colonization system."[49] The following month, the Union of Peasant Day Laborers complained to the federal Agrarian Department that Governor Gavira had consistently voided their petitions for land. To initiate the land redistribution process, they requested that a Mixed Agrarian Commission be sent to Baja California to resolve the many petitions that already were filed. Cibrián later wrote to federal officials and voiced similar demands.[50]

To strengthen its case, Alamo Mocho's Union of Peasant Day Laborers called on the CGT's national office for help. Jesús García, secretary of the CGT's campesino wing, asked the chief of the Agrarian Department, Gabino Vázquez, to resolve Alamo Mocho's ejidal petitions. García noted that there were "many cases like this throughout the region," and because no Mixed Agrarian Commission existed in Baja California, Gavira had too much power in deciding agrarian matters. According to García, the governor "favored the American landowners of the large latifundio" and did not enforce Article 27, which restricted foreign-owned land on the border.[51] García did not exaggerate the pro-CRLC/anti-agrarista posture of Governor Gavira, who denied the ejidal petitions of not only Alamo Mocho but also a number of other colonias, including Cucapás, Tierra y Patria, and José María Morelos.[52] In addition to the CGT, local labor unions such as the Bar and Restaurant Employees Union of Mexicali supported the agraristas. Interestingly, the latter union was more strident in their anti-CRLC, revolutionary rhetoric than were the campesinos. According to the Bar and Restaurant Employees Union, their "comrades," the peasants, constituted "the human machine of those great foreign capitalists, whose only thought is of making money, forgetting the collective welfare of their laborers," pointing the finger specifically at "the first great institution" of Baja California, "the Colorado River Land Co., owners of the great extensions of land." The union spokesperson prevailed upon the governor "to divide the company's lands" among the peasants, as had been done in the Laguna region and Yucatán, "where great holdings were subdivided." "Comrades," he continued, "we should cry out from our very soul that Mexico is for the Mexicans." "The general constitution of the Republic prohibits foreigners from acquiring property less than 50 kilometers from the boundary line," he pointed out, while in Mexicali, "the heart of the city is owned especially by Chinese, Japanese, and Jews and other nationalities, and we are ready to make them see, on behalf of our country, that the people of Mexicali cannot permit them to continue to be proprietors of large holdings and buildings." He concluded, "Comrades: our movement aims for the following: That every foreigner, who resides and dedicates themselves to commercial activities, be expelled."[53]

Popular pressure against Gavira—some of which stemmed from his appointing friends to government jobs—forced Cárdenas to replace him after six months in office. In the fall of 1936, Cárdenas named General Rafael Navarro Cortina, a native of Michoacán, as the territory's governor. The field workers rejoiced and hoped that the new government would address their needs. Again the agraristas in Colonia Alamo Mocho petitioned for CRLC's property and complained to the new governor that the company only had "a minimum of its 850,000 acres of land open to cultivation."[54] The new governor appeared unresponsive, probably due to the recent signing of the colonization contract between CRLC and the federal government in April 1936.

According to one surviving agrarista, since Alamo Mocho had little success in gaining land, field workers in the colonias of Michoacán de Ocampo and Pacífico stepped to the front of the movement and would soon lead the 1937 invasion of the company's estate. Agrarista leader Hipólito Rentería Rangel quickly took hold of the movement's reins. Rentería was from Michoacán, which he left in 1926 after trying to organize peasants there against the local latifundios. He arrived in the Mexicali Valley in 1927, worked as a day laborer for a number of years, and then began organizing the local peasantry in 1935. Rentería, like other agrarista leaders who migrated to Baja California from Michoacán in the 1920s—including Filiberto Crespo and Jerónimo and Leonardo Guillén—was not too far removed from the traditional village life and communal agriculture of southern Mexico. It may have appeared to Rentería that Alamo Mocho's Union of Peasant Day Laborers had not succeeded because it did not represent enough of the region's landless rural workforce, which thereby limited its influence. In the summer of 1936, Rentería, along with Crespo and Jesús Andrade Romero, established the Federation of Agrarian Communities of the Mexicali Valley in order to incorporate more colonias into the labor struggle. The new federation did not align with any national labor or peasant unions because, according to Pedro Pérez, they had failed to bring the field workers any results. As secretary general of the federation, in December 1936 Rentería twice wrote to Cárdenas on behalf of "all the sharecroppers, leaseholders, and laborers" who had been "victims of exploitation by the company" and asked him to resolve their numerous petitions for land.[55] To the agraristas, their situation was one of misery and "moral outrage" stemming from poor living and working conditions, as well as years of unanswered ejidal petitions.[56]

Governor Navarro Cortina, like his predecessors, not only ignored the field worker's demands but also tried to bribe Rentería, who refused to acquiesce.[57] Cárdenas's administration also gave little attention to the agraristas' demands. This probably stemmed from Mexico City's fiscal concerns; financing such a large-scale ejidal project in a highly developed region would have been very costly. In fact, just two years after the expropriation of CRLC's land in 1937, the federal government turned to the Compañía Industrial Jabonera del Pacífico, a subsidiary of the American-owned Anderson & Clayton Company, to help finance Mexicali's ejidatarios.[58] Also, since the territory was underpopulated and the president was already empowered to appoint Baja California's governor, expropriation would bring little political gain to Cárdenas regionally. Moreover, his administration had just spent a year negotiating the colonization contract with CRLC, and the recently initiated program was proving successful. In other words, Cardenista officials viewed the colonization agreement and the Plan Pro-Baja California, rather than land redistribution, as the cornerstones for the territory's economic development.

An unsympathetic local government, poor economic conditions, and the implementation of the colonization program pushed the agraristas to move against CRLC. According to the Mexicali newspaper *El Hispano Americano*, the federal government exaggerated the economic opportunities that were available in the Mexicali Valley to spark interest in the colonization program. Consequently, the newspaper opined that in 1936, the entire country became preoccupied with the territory's development, which produced a great migration of unemployed persons and families to the area. Population pressures and growing unemployment in the valley drove down salaries and forced workers to accept jobs below minimum wage.[59] The seasonal nature of cotton production only exacerbated the problem, and according to Pedro Pérez, many hardworking campesinos could not find jobs during much of the year.[60]

Without consistent employment, most rural workers lived at or below the subsistence level, making it financially infeasible for them to purchase, colonize, or rent CRLC land. The only chance they had to obtain property in the valley was by squatting or receiving ejidos from the federal government. As noted earlier, most agraristas were motivated primarily by material conditions, rather than "any structured political theory," when they decided to invade CRLC's holdings in January 1937. According to Pérez, the agraristas "did not care much about parties; they just wanted land, water, and schools." He continued, "We would have supported the governor if he gave us land, but he would not. Cárdenas did, but only after we took it first; that is why we attacked the company." The desires of Gonzalo Cárdenas Lizarraga, another field worker who participated in the movement, were simple and similar to Pérez's. According to Cárdenas Lizarraga, many field workers like himself wanted to end a life of migration and hoped for a "good cotton farm where they could raise animals and settle in one place with their family."[61]

The aim of the agraristas was to create a conflict that would force the federal government to intervene against CRLC and impel Cárdenas to visit the region. The movement's leaders believed that if Cárdenas came to the Mexicali Valley, he would see to their needs. In his many telegrams to the president in 1936 and early 1937, Rentería repeatedly asked him to visit Baja California. Since Cárdenas not only spent one-third of his time outside of Mexico City while president but at times used impromptu trips to the countryside to circumvent both federal and state bureaucracies and thereby quickly resolve outstanding local issues, Rentería's requests made perfect sense.[62]

In early 1937, rather than embark on a strike (as did rural workers in the Laguna), Mexicali's field workers began planning their invasion of CRLC's holdings. In part, the bold and illegal tactics employed by the Mexicali agraristas stemmed from the enmity that some held toward CRLC and the numerous Asian immigrants who occupied company lands. The threat posed by the colonization agreement added a sense of urgency to their actions. Unlike the drawn-out labor strike in the Laguna district on the Durango-Coahuila border, time was not on their side. On January 21 and 25, hundreds of agraristas armed with machetes, hoes, and sticks met at Emiliano Zapata Elementary School in Colonia Pacífico. During their meeting, the agraristas requested arms from the military commissioner, General Jaime Carrillo, who was sent by Cárdenas to the valley just days before. The agraristas also gave Carrillo petitions for land, which he agreed to take to Mexico City and discuss with Cárdenas.[63] After the agraristas voted to invade the camps upon which they worked, Rentería wrote to Cárdenas and asked him to arm the agraristas so that they could defend their rights under Article 27.[64]

On January 27, 1937, nearly four hundred armed and landless campesinos met in Colonia Michoacán de Ocampo and then invaded parts of CRLC's holdings, where they planted flags and banners with revolutionary slogans. When doing so, they expelled the company's tenants and precipitated another conflict in the ongoing agrarian dispute between Mexico and the United States. Events moved quickly. Two days later the agraristas briefly occupied the governor's palace, where they sang revolutionary songs honoring Pancho Villa, Emiliano Zapata, and Cárdenas. When federal forces threatened to remove them, their response was steeped in revolutionary prose: "If you kill us, then you kill us, but we are willing to die for the land." The standoff was, according to Pedro Pérez, "a little frightening, but exciting, too." The impasse ended on the third day, when Governor Navarro Cortina ordered federal troops to clear the building of protestors, remove the agraristas from CRLC's property, and arrest some of the movement's leaders—who were then sent to Islas Marías Federal Prison.[65] Navarro Cortina also wrote an open letter to the rural community, stating, "The expropriation of land must be carried out through legal channels and not by force."[66] The governor then informed Cárdenas that "in conformity with the disposition of the president" and in light of the complaints of the small farmers, he had removed the agraristas from CRLC property. Since land invasions were illegal, Navarro Cortina believed he was upholding the law and federal agrarian policy.[67] The governor had plenty of local support for his actions.

With the aid of CRLC employees, the lessees and colonists immediately protested the invasion of their property to the governor. Arnold Haskell, CRLC's general attorney, recalled:

> About four hundred of the Agrarians (Reds) moved onto our property throwing off tenants and taking possession. Fortunately, Guajardo [CRLC's Mexican counsel] organized our tenants and colonists into a farmer's organization. Guajardo acts as their attorney and leader. This organization immediately demanded protection from the governor and we as a company did not have to appear as an active participant. The governor ordered out his army and within three days the Agrarians were all off our property and the

leaders were in jail. . . . We have Guajardo at the head of the farmers, principally lessees; Fernando España [the Mexican leasing agent for CRLC] at the head of the colonists; . . . sometimes they act independently of one another, then it is necessary for me to act as co-coordinator so that we present a solid front.[68]

Clearly CRLC was working behind the scenes to strengthen the position of those with whom they held common cause, which, in turn, advanced the company's interests. Despite this favorable turn of events for CRLC, the drama was far from over, as powerful political groups came to the defense of the agraristas. Consequently, this put Cárdenas in a difficult position, especially with regard to his own policies on illegal property invasions and federal agrarian reform.

Agrarista land invasions and squatting became so frequent during Cárdenas's first year in office that in March 1936, he outlawed the seizure of vacant property without government approval. Land redistribution, Cárdenas stated, "must be carried out . . . with strict adherence to the law." Although in many ways land invasions and squatting were forms of popular resistance, in the president's mind, invasions were "treasonous." By branding land invasions as such, outlawing them, and ordering state governors and military zone commanders to halt any independent agrarista action, Cárdenas had forced landless campesinos to rely on the federal government to dole out property. This not only undermined the autonomy of many agrarista movements but also made them dependent on federal patronage and tied them more closely to the ruling party, thereby empowering the newly established political elite. Despite federal attempts to control labor militancy, agraristas and industrial laborers continued to resist and act on their own to advance their economic interests.[69]

The president was in a bind. Events in the Mexicali Valley gained nationwide attention, and dozens of peasant and labor organizations protested Governor Navarro Cortina's crackdown against the valley's rural labor movement. The CTM, the CGT, and Federation of Mexican Peasants (Confederación Campesina Mexicana or CCM) all publicly endorsed the agraristas' cause and complained to Cárdenas about the use of federal troops against Mexicali's peasantry. Jesús García of the CGT traveled to Acapulco and met with Cárdenas in order to press the agraristas' case. Such criticism impelled Cárdenas not only to recant his initial support of Navarro Cortina's actions but to cancel the colonization contract with CRLC and redistribute the company's property as communal ejidos to the valley's field workers.[70]

The above organizations were among the largest peasant and labor groups in the country and comprised an important segment of Cárdenas's base of support. It would have made little political sense for him to defend a monopolistic American company, lest he invite criticism for ignoring the interests of rural workers and dampening the spirit of revolutionary economic nationalism. To maintain his legitimacy among the peasantry, in early February Cárdenas met with an agrarista commission from the Mexicali Valley composed of Filiberto Crespo, Leonardo Guillén, and Francisco Hirales. They requested that their petitions for land be executed and that Governor Navarro Cortina be removed from office. On February 12, 1937, Cárdenas reversed course and sent the agraristas' petitions to Gabino Vázquez at the Agrarian Department. He also ordered agrarian officials to tour the rural population centers in the valley and take an agrarian census to determine the needs of the local peasantry. In addition, the president authorized the establishment of a Mixed Agrarian Commission in Baja California to begin work on the ejidal petitions; he then informed the agraristas that their demands would be met within a month and that the federal government would provide the "services necessary to improve the lives of their families."[71] Cárdenas then turned his sights on the territory's governor.

It was long customary in Mexico for presidents to remove governors when their state became unruly. According to Fallaw, "If popular forces convinced Cárdenas that a governor was unpopular and opposed to the interests of workers and peasants, then by 'right of the majority' they could demand his removal."[72] Also, because Baja California's territorial status meant the president appointed its governor, removing him from office was easy and did not carry the political backlash that sometimes came when elected officials elsewhere in the republic were replaced. Four weeks after the invasion, Cárdenas replaced Navarro Cortina and separated the civil and military gubernatorial authorities for the first time in the territory's history. The fact that Navarro Cortina not only allowed gambling in Baja California but also enriched himself in the process—despite Cárdenas's 1935 nationwide ban on casinos—was one more reason to remove the untrustworthy governor he had appointed less than a year earlier. Cárdenas then selected a close political and military ally, Lieutenant Colonel Rodolfo Sánchez Taboada, as civil governor, and Brigadier General Manuel Contreras as Baja California's military commander. The agraristas were happy to see Navarro Cortina's departure and Taboada's appointment.[73]

Besides receiving CRLC's divided lands, the ejidatarios also obtained low-interest loans and two pesos for daily expenses from the Banco Ejidal. In addition, the government established consumer cooperatives and built irrigation works and schools. The schools provided a public education not only to the field workers' children but also to the ejidatarios themselves, because, in the words of one ejidatario, they "needed to be taught how to be growers."[74] Taboada's popularity among rural workers, which continues until today, and lengthy seven-year term in office stems from his being credited with meeting agrarista demands for land and for distributing federal largesse.

Cárdenas then sent Vázquez and a number of engineers from the Agrarian Department to the Mexicali Valley. In mid-March, he ordered Vázquez, Secretary of Agriculture Saturnino Cedillo, and Taboada to carry out the execution of the agrarian petitions in Baja California.[75] After establishing the Mixed Agrarian Commission—to which the agraristas voted Filiberto Crespo as their representative—Vázquez began to solicit and receive petitions for CRLC's property from the local peasantry. In March 1937 the first expropriations were made, and the government redistributed nearly 200,000 acres of the company's farmland to thirty-six communal ejidos. By early July, four more collective ejidos were established, and a total of 4,800 ejidatarios received 237,360 acres of CRLC's best agricultural property—a large part of which was irrigated. By the end of Cárdenas's term in office, the company had lost 412,000 acres of land, of which 285,330 went to over fifty communal ejidos. The remainder was slowly sold off by the government to individual colonists. Meanwhile, the company's undeveloped and less-valuable grazing lands were barely touched by Mexican authorities.[76]

Although they were by far the most extensive, CRLC's holdings were not the only American-owned lands expropriated by the federal government in the Mexicali Valley. By mid-1937, seven other American property owners lost 33,000 acres when their small and medium-size holdings were redistributed. In a very short period of time, in comparison to most cases of land redistribution, much of the American-owned agricultural property in the Mexicali Valley was parceled out to landless campesinos.[77] By early 1938, according to the U.S. consulate in Mexicali, "practically all of the cultivated lands belonging to American owners" in this district had been redistributed. Meanwhile, few Mexican landowners were affected by redistribution. Many of them saved their estates by subdividing their holdings and registering their lands in the names of friends and relatives, since properties smaller than 250 acres were exempt from seizure.[78] Clearly this was something that CRLC could not have done, due to the overwhelming size of the company's property and the negative repercussions that it would have engendered, both locally and nationally.

Those who lost their land in the Mexicali Valley did not accept the expropriation without contest. What is interesting about the response of CRLC, its tenants
and colonists, and the small landowners in the valley was the blurring of
identities between groups representing "local" and "outside" interests. In addition, claims as to who constituted the "authentic" peasantry were contested
by the small property holders. Most colonists, and even some leaseholders—
including those of Asian origin—considered themselves independent farmers
who wanted neither to become members of ejidos nor to forfeit their individual
property rights. Dámaso Lemus Vargas spoke for many colonists when he
stated that he preferred colonization because the colonists held more than twice
as much land as the ejidatarios.[79]

Divisions between contending rural factions were common in the Mexican
countryside when Mexico City imposed its agrarian reform policies. Land
redistribution unmasked underlying hatreds and class divisions and led opposing sides to portray themselves as self-righteous and industrious and their
adversaries as crass and incompetent.[80] Many of the colonists and small landowners in the Mexicali Valley were critical of the entire land redistribution
process and correctly believed that the National Bank of Ejidal Credit (Banco
Nacional de Crédito Ejidal) would not be able to adequately finance such a large
undertaking. Consequently, they predicted (wrongly, as it would turn out)
economic catastrophe for the region.[81]

The expropriation set CRLC, the colonists, independent growers, and some
tenants in the Mexicali Valley against the ejidatarios and the state and federal
governments. Although the leaseholders and some colonists may not have
qualified as part of the middle class, it is with that set of interests that they
identified, and not those of the landless rural workers. After the January invasion, peasant smallholders formed a number of conservative organizations to
protect their interests, including the Federation of Unions of Small Farmers
(Federación de Sindicatos de Pequeñas Agricultores), the Mexicali Agricultural
Association, and the Committee for Justice. They complained to Cárdenas that
they were violently attacked by armed agraristas who forced them off their
properties, plowed under their fields, and stole their crops. They, too, asked
Cárdenas for both arms and protection and begged that the federal government

respect their property rights. These groups reflected the growing dissatisfaction that the Mexican middle class felt toward Cárdenas's reforms, which led them to establish the Civic Action Party of the Middle Class midway through his presidency.[82]

Many of the small property owners, leaseholders, and colonists who obtained plots of land during the 1920s and 1930s saw themselves differently from the field workers who recently migrated to the region. Baja California was not unique in this regard. As one scholar recently noted, the countryside in postrevolutionary Mexico was characterized by a great deal of "economic diversity" in peoples' relationship to the land.[83] Consequently, in both the Mexicali Valley and Sonora's Yaqui Valley, each side of the rural divide employed identity politics to advance or safeguard their positions. While the agraristas appropriated the identity of Mexico's revolutionary heroes to rally public support to their cause, the nonagrarista rural sector—both Mexican and non-Mexican— labeled themselves as "locals" and the recently arrived agraristas as "outsiders" in order to convince local and national policymakers of their long-term roots in the region, which made them worthy of protection. For similar reasons, this latter group referred to themselves as "traditional" campesinos and the agraristas as rural workers.

In one of the many letters sent to Gabino Vázquez and the Mixed Agrarian Commission, a group of small landowners from Mexicali's Rancho Dieguinos referred to themselves as "authentic peasants" who "personally cultivated their own parcels." In another case, Victoria Aldama de Cota wrote to Cárdenas and asked that her one hundred acre farm in Colonia Alamo Mocho—the center of the agrarista movement—be protected, because she had used it since 1924 to raise and support her family. When requesting protection of their land and crops, the small property owners told federal officials their personal history and the "great efforts and sacrifice" they made in bringing their families to the Mexicali Valley and building their homes there. The smallholders also noted the irrigation systems that they had installed and the other improvements which they had made to the land; they also claimed that they "never bothered the government." While some cited the "law of endowments" to claim the "safekeeping" of their lands, other small property holders defended their interests by appealing to articles within Mexico's Civil Code—possibly believing it represented a higher moral authority than did the agrarian legislation. Ironically, like their agrarista counterparts, they employed revolutionary rhetoric when they decried the loss of their lands and what they saw as their resultant

FIGURE 10. Well-dressed Mexicali Valley colonists, ca. early 1930s. Note the jackets and ties and lack of tattered clothing. AGN, ARCHIVO FOTOGRÁFICO, FONDO RODRÍGUEZ, 25/11.

subjugation.[84] As Christopher Boyer shows in Michoacán, in many Mexican states such as Sonora and Baja California, "revolutionary and traditional peasant identities were not incompatible." Rather, different peasant groups made revolutionary ideology applicable to their own political culture.[85] Hence, when the objections of the smallholders and tenants failed to convince the Agrarian Department to protect their lands, they—like the agraristas—took their fight to the streets.

Having received no support from either Governor Taboada or Cárdenas, on April 22, 1937, leaseholders, colonists, and independent small property owners began a large-scale, sit-down strike in front of the governor's office in Mexicali, which lasted for three weeks. They chose Taboada's office because the colonists identified the recently appointed governor as representing the "outside" interests of Mexico City, rather than the local interests of the small farmers. Thousands of peasants, including entire families, occupied the park in downtown Mexicali. The strikers were supported by moderate labor organizations such as the CROM, as well as more conservative groups such as the Union of Veteran Soldiers of the Revolution (UNVR), the Mexicali Chamber of Commerce, and local merchants—who supplied food to the strikers. Meanwhile, CRLC's local agent in charge of the colonization program, Fernando España, played a leading role in both the strike and the Federation of Unions of Small Farmers. To distance themselves from the counter-agrarista movement, Augustín Loroña, one of CRLC's attorneys, suggested to Chandler that "the Company must not be identified with any part of this movement, and if any financial aid is given Mr.

España, it should be done with the utmost secrecy." Although it is difficult to determine CRLC's exact role in the strike, clearly there was common cause between the company and the protesters, as both sought the return of their property.[86]

On April 30, 1937, Cárdenas met with officials from CRLC and representatives of the strikers. The two groups convinced the president to spare a small section of the company's land from expropriation. Following the meeting, Cárdenas again reversed himself and ordered ten colonies that fell under the April 1936 colonization contract to be exempt from seizure.[87] Since most smallholders, colonists, and tenants were still threatened by expropriation, the strike continued. Cárdenas soon yielded to the strikers too and in mid-May ordered Vázquez to make a second trip to Mexicali, where he informed them of the president's position. On May 14, 1937, after twenty-one days of protest, the strike ended, and the colonists, tenants, and small farmers vacated the park across from the gubernatorial palace. Many of the strikers' demands were met. Besides exempting the original ten colonies from expropriation, Cárdenas decreed that farms with less than 370 acres would not be seized (larger than the legal exemption of 250 acres). The extra 120 acres ensured the protection of almost all the colonists and most small landowners. In addition, the National Bank of Ejidal Credit would compensate all groups for their investments in the land, work and improvements carried out on it, loss of tools, and damages to their property. Also, parcels already planted would not be handed over to the ejidatarios until after harvest. However, CRLC tenants—many of whom were Asian—were not allowed to keep their lands. Also, the requests that the agraristas be disarmed and the head of the Mixed Agrarian Commission be dismissed were both denied.[88] To ensure that he did not lose the support of colonists and small landowners in the Mexicali Valley, in mid-August 1938 Cárdenas agreed to transfer 603 property titles to them.[89]

Company officials also worked assiduously to have their lands returned, meeting with high-ranking policymakers in both Mexico City and Washington. Knowing that expropriation was not final until Cárdenas signed the presidential resolution, CRLC first tried to delay the expropriation process by renegotiating the terms of their 1936 colonization agreement with Cárdenas and Secretary of Agriculture Saturnino Cedillo. In March 1937, Albert Vierhus, CRLC's general manager, submitted the company's formal protests to Baja California's new Mixed Agrarian Commission. Although CRLC filed a separate defense against the creation of each ejido, most of the company's objections to each land grant were the same. Vierhus argued that Cárdenas's administration had violated the company's rights under the 1936 colonization contract and that the Mixed Agrarian Commission had violated numerous statutes of the 1934 Agrarian Code. According to CRLC, these violations included the expropriation of private property when government lands were available, the expropriation of colonized holdings, the lack of agrarian petitions before the governor, and the excessive acres awarded to each ejidatario.[90] Despite the fact that Vierhus's arguments were mostly valid, in early April 1937 he nevertheless flew to Mexico City and presented Cedillo with a "formal protest." Vierhus laid out in detail, with maps and aerial photographs, how the invasion and expropriation of the company's property was illegal because the centers of rural population that were listed in the recent agrarian census, and which were to receive CRLC lands, did not exist.[91]

CRLC officials then called on the U.S. State Department to help them buy more time and then plotted their course. In his letter to Chandler, CRLC's general attorney Arnold Haskell noted that if Washington would ask Cárdenas's administration to investigate the legality of the expropriation, it would demonstrate the State Department's concern and might delay the process "and stall the signing of the agrarian petitions by President Cárdenas." Haskell added that such an approach would "also give Al Vierhus more time to work with our friends in Mexico City" and him "to study the situation here with the hope of getting the State Department to take more drastic action."[92] In mid-April Haskell flew to Washington and met with Secretary of State Cordell Hull. After he told Hull about CRLC's long and productive history in the Mexicali Valley, Haskell requested that he ask Cárdenas to "resurvey or recheck the agrarian situation on the Company's property before approving the agraristas' petitions for CRLC lands."[93] Hull willingly obliged. In its petition to the Mexican government on CRLC's behalf, the State Department wrote, "The government of the United States very earnestly hopes that the government of Mexico will accord prompt and sympathetic consideration to the request of the Colorado River Land Company and that the appropriate Mexican authorities, before reaching a final decision in the matter, cause an investigation to be made regarding the legality of the proceedings by which provisional possession of large areas of land owned by the company has been granted by the local agrarian authorities to certain groups who had filed petitions for such grants."[94] After the State Department's formal request, U.S. Ambassador Josephus Daniels met with Cárdenas to discuss the situation in the Mexicali Valley.[95] Even though the State Department was willing to assist CRLC, Roosevelt's administration would not employ any heavy-handed measures to defend the company; rather, U.S. officials relied solely on normal diplomatic procedures when it addressed the predicament of CRLC (one of the hundreds of American property owners affected by land redistribution).

Seeing that Washington's assistance and their direct appeals to the Cardenistas had made little headway, CRLC officials tried to portray themselves not as a disinterested "foreign" firm, but as a "local" company that had Baja California and Mexico's best interests at heart. In late April 1937, Chandler asked his friend, former Baja California governor and former president Abelardo Rodríguez, to intercede on the company's behalf. Chandler reminded Rodríguez how he helped to secure arms and airplanes from Washington for both the Obregón and Calles governments during the 1923 de la Huerta and 1929 Escobar rebellions. Chandler asked Rodríguez to remind Cárdenas of this and to tell him that CRLC always supported every "forward-looking Mexican enterprise" and that he was "a life-long friend of Mexico" who contributed "to the country's general welfare." Chandler was able to make a strong pitch because, during the preceding twenty years, CRLC's interests coincided with those of Mexico City. During the Carranza and Obregón administrations, Chandler pressed Washington for a water settlement favorable to Mexico. In 1918 and 1919, he had strongly and publicly opposed the construction of the All-American Canal in the Imperial Valley north of the border because it seriously threatened Mexicali's water supply from the Colorado River. He had also petitioned the Harding administration to recognize Obregón's government in 1923. Throughout the 1920s, Mexico City and CRLC each sought to develop the delta region and construct railroad lines, port facilities, roads, and other infrastructure. What Chandler failed to realize was that Cárdenas, unlike the administrations he was used to dealing with, was not part of the Sonoran dynasty, and his plans for rural development were not based on foreign-owned, large-scale commercial agriculture but instead favored the interests of Mexico's small-scale colonists and ejidatarios.[96]

In Rodríguez's letter to Cárdenas, the former Callista president described Chandler as a "great friend" of Mexico who "every time ha[d] sided [with the] constituted government." Rodríguez also stated that he hoped a "just and equitable" solution would be found to the land problem in the Mexicali Valley.[97] As one could imagine, the letter bore little fruit. Although Cárdenas agreed to meet with CRLC officials as Rodríguez had requested, he told them that his government would not return the company's land. According to Cárdenas, "the Government would insist on continuing the granting of lands which are the property of the company, but that the company would be reimbursed practically immediately for these lands . . . [with] a fair and equitable settlement."[98] This was the standard reply of most Mexican policymakers to U.S. officials and American property owners who had lost their holdings in Mexico. Although CRLC hoped to reach a settlement directly with Mexico City, the Cardenistas refused to negotiate with the company and instead threw CRLC into the pool with the other American claimants.[99]

Because CRLC officials believed that compensation would likely be made with worthless federal agrarian bonds, they sought to avoid indemnification and instead briefly considered suing the Mexican government. Article 177 of the 1934 Agrarian Code, however, denied property owners affected by land re-distribution the right to *amparo* (legal recourse in the Mexican courts to over-turn an expropriation decree). Instead, affected property owners could only seek indemnification from the federal government.[100] Nevertheless, Chandler considered a lawsuit against the Mexican government for breaching the 1936 colonization contract. The idea was dropped in late 1937 because company law-yers believed there was "no solid legal ground on which to base such action."[101]

In October 1937, having received no compensation from the Mexican gov-ernment in the first six months following the expropriation, Vierhus and his assistant, J. H. Risheberger, traveled to Mexico City. During their visit they discussed indemnification with Ambassador Daniels, the chief of the Latin American Division at the State Department, Laurence Duggan, and the U.S. consul from Mexicali, John Bowman; they also met with Cárdenas. According to the president, Mexico's ambassador to the United States, Dr. Francisco Cas-tillo Nájera, was "empowered to negotiate directly with the company regarding a settlement for their expropriated land." Since Castillo Nájera was unable to meet Vierhus and Risheberger on their initial trip to Washington in late Octo-ber, the two CRLC officials returned to the U.S. capital to see him in November and December. During their meetings, the Mexican ambassador told Vierhus and Risheberger that they should discuss compensation with the new Secretary of Agriculture, Dr. José Parrés. Risheberger and Vierhus then flew back to Mexico City in January 1938 to see Parrés. During their meeting, the secretary of agriculture told them that he "had no power to discuss indemnification" and instead suggested that they address the question of reparations with Gabino Vázquez at the Agrarian Department. However, officials at the Agrarian De-partment also refused to discuss compensation with them, and, after waiting in vain for two weeks to meet agrarian authorities, Vierhus and Risheberger left Mexico City frustrated and empty handed.[102] Since key officials in Cárdenas's administration, including Vázquez, blamed CRLC for "misleading the small owners, tenants, and settlers" in the Mexicali Valley and for "using them as an instrument" to halt the redistribution of land through the sit-down strike, it is not surprising that they gave the company a hard time.[103] CRLC officials were not the only ones subjected to such delay and obfuscation. Similar tactics characterized Mexican diplomacy vis-à-vis other American landowners and U.S. officials throughout the bilateral agrarian dispute.

Although CRLC officials took their case to the most powerful decision makers in Washington and Mexico City, not only were their holdings not returned; they also did not receive a prompt cash settlement as Cárdenas initially indicated. In a letter to a colleague, Haskell bemoaned, "We have been shunted back and forth" between the two capitals.[104] In 1938, Vierhus voiced similar complaints to Daniels, stating that Mexican officials had given him the "run around" regarding compensation.[105] After realizing that Cárdenas's government had misled them and was not going to provide the company with a cash payment, Vierhus reported in late 1938 that CRLC would not press for an independent settlement with Mexico City but instead would "apply for compensation in the routine way." In other words, like hundreds of American property owners who were adversely affected by land redistribution, CRLC would file its claims for reparations with the recently established Agrarian Claims Commission.[106]

On February 25, 1939, CRLC filed the first of its three claims with the U.S. section of the Agrarian Claims Commission requesting indemnification for the 412,000 acres that were expropriated by Cárdenas's government. Chandler also filed two additional claims: one for the expropriation of 8,000 acres from the 32,000 acre Imperial Valley Land and Irrigation Company of Lower California (also owned by CRLC's investors and located in the Mexicali Valley) and one for the seizure of 3,500 acres that he held individually in the valley. As was the case with all the American-owned rural properties expropriated in Mexico, the company's holdings were appraised on their declared tax value. CRLC officials claimed a total loss of $6,708,831 but were only awarded $2,941,209 by the commission—or 44 percent of the total amount claimed. This was the case despite the fact that an independent appraisal by Mexican officials shortly after the initial expropriation in mid-1937 valued 235,000 acres of the company's agricultural lands at $4 million. Although the first compensation check was issued to the company in 1943 for $837,244, it took until 1955 for the Mexican government to complete its indemnification payments to CRLC.[107] The reasons why Cárdenas decided to incur such costs by expropriating the company's land are numerous and will be the focus of the next chapter.

THE EXPROPRIATION OF AMERICAN-OWNED
LAND IN BAJA CALIFORNIA

Political, Economic, Social, and Cultural Factors

Ójala, now that we are given the lands to form patrimony with our children, we
will always remember the noble figure of General Cárdenas and his honorable
collaborators, who, with great valor and patriotism, resolved the problems and
needs of the village. We hope that after so many years of fighting and misery, we
will have a small place where we can make our home and raise our children.

PRESIDENT OF THE AGRARIAN COMMITTEE OF ALAMO MOCHO,
IGNACIO SÁNCHEZ, MARCH 1, 1937

The grants that you will initiate today unify the movement throughout the country in favor of the most important aspiration of the people, for which it threw itself
into the Revolution. . . . Justifiably, Ejido Islas Agrarias [formerly Colonia Alamo
Mocho] is a secure, well-deserved place established by a group of campesinos
who had suffered persecution for their ideals. . . . Send my congratulations to the
peasantry of Baja California represented by the ejidatarios of Islas Agrarias.

SECRETARY OF COMMUNICATIONS AND PUBLIC WORKS
FRANCISCO MÚGICA TO DIRECTOR OF THE AGRARIAN DEPARTMENT
GABINO VÁZQUEZ, MARCH 19, 1937

Peasant agency alone does not explain the expropriation of CRLC's land.
Rather, subaltern mobilization, along with the larger aspects of state building, precipitated the seizure of the company's holdings. The immediate underlying force that led Cárdenas's administration to reverse its policies, cancel its

colonization agreement with the company, and seize its property was political. Redistributing CRLC's land helped to solidify and expand the president's base of support, both regionally and nationally. Following the establishment of ejidos in the Mexicali Valley, dozens of peasant leagues and labor unions wrote to Cárdenas, applauded his efforts, thanked him for redistributing the land, and pledged that they would "always be ready to defend his government."[1] During the official redistribution ceremony held in a large Mexicali auditorium, a huge banner draped the width of the stage and read "con Cárdenas al triunfo, o a la muerte" (with Cárdenas to victory or to death). Such propaganda was illustrative of the support engendered for the president by the expropriation. Also on the wall above the stage were huge portrait photographs of Cárdenas, Baja California's new governor, Lieutenant Colonel Rodolfo Sánchez Taboada, former president Francisco Madero, and peasant revolutionary leader Emiliano Zapata. The portraits were designed to legitimize the expropriations by linking the federal and territorial officials who appropriated CRLC's land (Cárdenas and Taboada) to the symbolic heroes of the revolution (Madero and Zapata). As such, Cárdenas's government redeemed the deaths of these ever-popular revolutionary martyrs.[2]

The political alliance between Cárdenas and mobilized agrarian forces made the government's continued cooperation with CRLC difficult. As the agraristas received land, the president and the official party gained a loyal following among ejido recipients, who became dependent upon the federal government for most of their farming needs. Although Cárdenas was driven by a genuine desire to help the nation's landless rural workers, he also surely recognized that the expropriation of CRLC's property would enhance Mexico City's position in Baja California.[3] However, although political considerations were a major reason why Cárdenas's administration expropriated the company's land, it was by no means the only one; rather a number of social, economic, and cultural issues that advanced his state-building program also shaped the president's rural policies in the northern peninsula.

The literature on state formation in postrevolutionary Mexico spans the usual schools of thought: traditionalist, revisionist, and postrevisionist. The traditionalists' favorable account, which emphasized Mexico's socioeconomic achievements after 1920, gave way in the 1970s to a highly critical revisionist argument that characterized the Mexican state as a Leviathan which co-opted the masses, centralized political control, and maintained the capitalist political economy of the preceding Díaz regime. Today's postrevisionists generally eschew the economic reductionism that surrounds the idea of an all-powerful Leviathan and rightly focus on the role played by both elite and subaltern actors in either advancing or thwarting Mexico's state-building process after 1920. This study continues in that direction. While the previous chapter sought to demonstrate how Mexicali's landless rural workers, colonists, and smallholders shaped Cardenista agrarian policies, this chapter will try to show how Mexico City then used these same policies to impose its own agenda locally.

As governor of Michoacán from 1928 to 1932, Cárdenas implemented many of the socioeconomic and political policies that would later characterize his populist, paternalistic, and inclusive presidency and which marked some of his programs in Baja California. These included promoting agrarian and labor reforms, expanding access to public education, attacking social vices, incorporating workers and peasants into a corporatist political structure, and using various local leaders to carry out his statist project and broaden his base of support. During his term as governor and his presidential campaign in 1933 and 1934, Cárdenas recognized the need to simplify and speed up Mexico's land redistribution process.[4] While traveling the country during the campaign, he saw firsthand the plight of the rural poor and became further convinced that dividing the haciendas and redistributing them to the campesinos would improve peasants' living and working conditions. He also believed that rural wages were too low and that there was too much underutilized land throughout the country—including that of CRLC in the Mexicali Valley. In Cárdenas's mind, land redistribution would kill two birds with one stone. By ending the monopoly that unproductive landlords had over the country's agricultural property, it would aid the national economy by putting more land under cultivation; it would also boost the individual economy of landless campesinos by making them property owners.[5] With this in mind, Cárdenas made it clear during his presidential campaign that he wanted to advance the interests of Mexican peasants and workers—which, in turn, energized the country's rural and industrial labor movements.

After Cárdenas took office in late 1934, the number of strikes nationwide increased dramatically, jumping from 202 in 1934 to 642 in 1935. The number of agrarista land invasions and ejidal petitions also increased substantially during his first years in office.[6] He upheld his campaign pledges and responded eagerly to campesino discontent by making agrarian reform, and especially land redistribution, the cornerstones of his domestic policy.[7] One month after taking office, Cárdenas instructed the head of the Agrarian Department, Gabino Vázquez, to resolve immediately all pending ejidal petitions and to intensify land redistribution throughout the country in order to rid Mexico of its haciendas.[8] The president and most landless campesinos believed that agrarian reform would redistribute national wealth, reduce rural underemployment, improve the material conditions and living standards for the nation's majority, and free the peasantry from its dependence on the rural elite. Also, unlike earlier presidents, Cárdenas's agrarian reform program provided much-needed financial, educational, and technical assistance to the ejidatarios. The goal of Cárdenas's agrarian policy, Ben Fallaw astutely observes, was "economic democracy" for the rural proletariat.[9]

The Cárdenas administration also hoped that agrarian reform would provide the foundation for Mexico's economic growth. Many Cardenistas believed this would be achieved through federal food policies and by creating a market for industrial raw materials.[10] In October 1936, the president declared, "The ejidal institution has a double responsibility: as a social system that liberates the rural worker from the exploitation from which he has previously suffered . . . and as a system of agricultural production that largely provides the food supplies of the country."[11] The head of the Agrarian Department concurred: "The revolutionary program will be defeated if the farmer produces only enough for himself. He must provide for the nation as well. The government has given the land to the man who works it, but we cannot expect national prosperity to derive automatically from this. All of the land must be cultivated, modern methods used, and unproductive lands opened to farming."[12] In 1937, Cárdenas created Mexico's first State Food Agency to control the price, distribution, and marketing of wheat, beans, corn, and rice. While Cárdenas wanted rural producers to receive a fair price for their harvest, he also sought to keep the price of staples low so as to keep the cost of living in check for urban industrial workers. In response to pressure from the CTM, federal food policies that purchased basic grains and sold them at reduced prices in the cities were designed to appease urban workers and thereby offset social unrest and maintain industrial productivity.[13]

One way to keep food prices low was to increase agricultural yields by cultivating more land. Unlike previous administrations, Cardenista officials believed that communal ejidos would be able to maintain the high levels of agricultural production of the large, privately owned commercial farms that had been expropriated. Collective agriculture also would maintain the commercial value of the large expropriations and facilitate the use of collectively organized labor, marketing, and credit systems. Expanding agricultural production through communal ejidos would not only alleviate rural unemployment but would also provide both urban and rural workers with more disposable income by containing the inflation rate for basic staples. Both groups, it was hoped, would then foster the growth of light industry by consuming a larger quantity of domestic manufactured goods, especially from Mexico's growing textile industry.[14] The textile sector, in turn, needed increased agricultural output, which would also be achieved by putting more acres under cultivation, especially in cotton-producing regions like the Mexicali Valley and the Laguna.

In order to increase redistribution, expand cultivated acreage, and boost agricultural production nationwide, Cárdenas nearly doubled government expenditures targeted for agriculture compared to his predecessors. The ejidatarios were not the only ones to benefit from federal largess. Small, private producers also gained greater access to federal credit and new irrigation works.[15] However, it was the expropriation, in late 1936, of 8 million acres of land in the Laguna region that truly distinguished Cárdenas's agrarian reform program from that of earlier administrations.

Laguna marked the first time in postrevolutionary Mexico that enormous productive farms—as opposed to vacant or underproductive lands—were redistributed. Besides the Laguna region, in his first three years in office "Cárdenas supported union formation, labor agitation, and strikes among rural workers in a number of modernized latifundios, including the rice and cotton fields of Michoacán's *tierra caliente,* the sugarcane plantations of Morelos, Puebla, Tamaulipas, and Sinaloa, the wheat fields of Sonora, and the henequen estates of Yucatán."[16] Also, rather than divide all of the holdings into small, individual plots, the government sought to maintain the Laguna's economy of scale (and hence its productive capacity) by installing a system of large-scale, collective farming that used modern farming machinery and other advanced methods of agriculture.[17] The Laguna expropriation was a bold experiment in rural economic development. The Cárdenas administration not only provided credit, seeds, fertilizers, tools, mechanical equipment, irrigation works, and many other farming-related necessities; it also built schools and hospitals and provided other social services for the ejidatarios. Within a year, the federal government undertook additional large-scale expropriations against domestic and American-owned agricultural properties—much of which were then collectivized—in Baja California, Sonora, Michoacán, and Yucatán.[18]

The economic results of Cárdenas's agrarian reform program were impressive, but mixed. By the end of his presidency, Cárdenas had redistributed nearly 50 million acres of land to 811,157 individuals. After his term in office, ejidos covered 47 percent of Mexico's cultivated land, compared to less than 15 percent in 1930, and the ejidal population had more than doubled from 668,000 to 1.6 million during the same decade. By 1940, nearly one-third of the population had received land.[19] However, although the poverty index dropped 8 percent between 1930 and 1940, much of the rural population remained destitute. And agricultural production during Cárdenas's sexenio generally declined or remained flat, depending on the sector. Still, Alan Knight argues that over the long term his agrarian reform program paid off, because output and productivity both rose. While the annual growth rate in agriculture averaged 4.9 percent between 1935 and 1946, from 1946 to 1955 it increased to 7.6 percent. Higher rates of agricultural production made a significant contribution to Mexico's export earnings in the two decades after Cárdenas left office and provided some of the capital that underwrote Mexican industrialization during the post–World War II era.[20]

As the chapters on Sonora will illustrate, in addition to its economic components, agrarian reform assisted the Cardenistas with their domestic political agenda. Even though some sectors of the old landed elite survived land redistribution, nationally it eliminated many hacendados, foreign property holders, and intermediary *caciques* (rural political bosses); it also politically empowered workers and peasants and broadened support for Cárdenas and the official party. In July 1935, after Cárdenas had ousted Calles from power, he ordered the establishment, in every state, of peasant leagues that incorporated all local, state, and regional campesino organizations. Cárdenas then created a national peasant confederation to better control independent campesino organizations. In 1938, when he reorganized the official party, Cárdenas established the present-day National Peasant Confederation (Confederación Nacional Campesina, CNC) and incorporated it into the federal political structure. Thereafter, as independent peasant leagues such as the CCM were disbanded, the CNC began to dominate state and local agrarian organizations, placing the agrarian movement more fully under the direction of the federal government. Also, all agraristas with pending petitions, as well as all ejidatarios, automatically became members of the state leagues.[21]

The CNC promoted campesino interests, broadened Cárdenas's base of support, and strengthened his government against its conservative political opponents. But the corporatist agrarian structure that integrated both independent peasant groups and individual campesinos into the state bureaucracy, especially through its ties to the official party, also thwarted any serious or radical challenge to federal authority over agrarian matters by *los de abajo*. As a state-building tool, therefore, land reform empowered the federal government by eliminating rivals and incorporating the popular classes. Although the Cardenista state remained relatively weak and did not completely centralize power in Mexico City, nor politically stabilize or control the entire country by 1940, it did help to initiate a corporatist process that would enable seventy years of one-party rule.[22]

ECONOMIC DEVELOPMENT, INDUSTRIALIZATION, AND WATER

The government's rationale behind the expropriation of CRLC's property, like the colonization program that preceded it, was driven by economic nationalism. Throughout his tenure, Cárdenas sought to transfer some control of his country's natural resources from foreign to Mexican hands so the nation could profit from their development. According to Cárdenas, "the distribution of the land," both domestic- and foreign-owned, was "indispensable for developing the national economy."[23] As with other large-scale agricultural enterprises, Cárdenas expropriated CRLC's property because he believed land redistribution would reduce rural underemployment, increase agricultural productivity, stimulate domestic and international trade, and foster economic growth. Together, these domestic developments would have an international impact by making Mexico economically stronger and bolstering a far-off territory that was targeted by nineteenth-century American filibusters and twentieth-century U.S. investors. As one federal commission tied to Baja California's development concluded, "Mexicanizing the territories would strengthen the homeland."[24]

Although Cárdenas's agrarian program differed from that of his predecessors and successors, like them he sought to steer Mexico down the industrial road. Cárdenas assumed, as did many Mexican policymakers, that industrialization and commercial growth would increase employment, create investment capital, and bring material prosperity, social development, and modernity. To stimulate output and new methods of production, Cárdenas promoted state-level agricultural and industrial expositions. The expositions, along with the generation of domestic capital and a host of other domestic and international factors, led to a doubling of Mexican manufacturing production between 1933 and 1940.[25] How, then, did federal expropriation of CRLC's land figure into the agricultural/industrial equation?

By redistributing the company's extensive holdings, Cárdenas's government was able to put more land under cultivation, increase agricultural output, stimulate the regional economy, and hastened the territory's integration into the national economy via the Plan Pro-Baja California. Furthermore, because cotton production nationwide had fallen by nine thousand tons between 1936 and 1938, at a time when Mexico sought to expand textile manufacturing, federal control of CRLC's holdings took on added importance. The company owned some of the most productive cotton lands in the country, and their output could be channeled away from export to the United States, where it had gone previously, and redirected toward Mexico's growing textile industry.[26] According to the Federal Territories Development Commission, which oversaw the implementation of the Plan Pro-Baja California, the federal government sought to "prevent Baja California's riches from being carried away to foreign countries so that Mexico can take advantage of their development."[27]

It made good economic sense for the federal government to increase the supply of cotton, since output in the cotton textile industry grew by more than 60 percent between 1932 and 1937. Cárdenas and his labor secretary, Antonio Villalobos, sided with textile owners when workers sought labor contracts that would reduce the work week from six days to five, a stance that helped maintain high production levels. Villalobos also capped the minimum wage for textile workers at a figure that was acceptable to the industrialists—and far below labor's demands. Consequently, CIDOSA, Mexico's largest cotton textile producer, posted hefty profits in the mid-1930s. According to Stephen Haber, by 1935 CIDOSA, San Rafael, and a number of other large cotton textile producers began to reinvest significant sums into their manufacturing enterprises, the first time that this had occurred since the turn of the century. In 1935 and 1936 alone, CIDOSA more than doubled the value of its mills through reinvestment, from 4.2 to 9.2 million pesos. An increase in the number of active firms also fueled widespread growth after 1932. For instance, between 1933 and 1937, the number of cotton textile mills operating in Mexico increased from 153 to 224.[28]

Cárdenas sought to foster the significant growth in the cotton textile industry already underway. He probably realized this as early as 1934, when he remarked that "Mexicali should make itself into an industrial city" by building on the valley's agricultural sector.[29] During his August 1937 meeting with CRLC's colonizing agent, Fernando España, Cárdenas spoke of the economic rationale behind the expropriation. According to the president, having more people cultivate the valley's land would increase output and benefit both the national and Baja Californian economies. In order to maximize agricultural yields from the company's holdings each ejidatario in the underpopulated valley received 50 acres of land, rather than the standard 10. And as he did elsewhere, Cárdenas also allowed earlier colonists and small property owners in the valley to retain their lands.

Besides putting more land under cultivation, the federal government also invested greatly in the region. In the first year after the expropriation, the Ejidal Bank spent over $1.7 million pesos to ensure that Mexicali's ejidatarios had sufficient short- and long-term credit, animals, seed, fertilizer, and farm machinery and equipment.[30]

Had Cárdenas relied solely on the 1936 colonization contract to settle the Mexicali Valley, it might have taken twenty years for this very valuable cotton-producing region to reach its full economic potential. In fact, the initial colonization of 27,000 acres in the first six months of the colonization agreement comprised a small percentage of the company's 850,000 acre holding. Expropriation was the only way for the federal government to quickly gain control of the company's property and rapidly expand cotton cultivation during Cárdenas's term. Ironically, expropriation actually fit better with the Plan Pro-Baja California than did the colonization scheme that was first proposed under its rubric. In the colonization scenario, CRLC remained a powerful player in Baja California's rural economy. However, with expropriation, the federal government determined to a large degree the pace and direction of the territory's development, which facilitated and hastened its integration into the larger national economy as envisioned by Mexican officials.

One contemporary magazine observed that Cárdenas expropriated CRLC's holdings because he believed the method of agricultural production in the valley was bankrupt.[31] In comparison to the pace of agribusiness development in southern California's Imperial Valley, CRLC had developed its lands in Baja California much more slowly. At no point did the company have more than 122,307 acres (approximately 12 percent of its 850,000 acre total) under cultivation. Moreover, this high point was not reached until 1936 and stemmed primarily from the colonization agreement that the company was forced to sign with the federal government. In fact, each year between 1922 and 1936, on average only 90,000 acres of CRLC's land was cultivated. James Henson argues that CRLC's stockholders in Los Angeles never invested the capital necessary for extensive development of the region, because their holdings in Baja California were a peripheral part of their overall investment portfolio that also included extensive agricultural holdings in the Imperial Valley, real estate in Los Angeles, ownership of the *Los Angeles Times,* and stock in the Southern Pacific Railroad, among other economic ventures. Also, the fact that CRLC did not open up any additional lands after 1924 and shipped all its cotton to the United States illustrated the company's limited commitment to the valley's overall development and its ambivalence toward Mexico's textile industry.[32]

Cárdenas's administration wasted little time in building up northern Baja California. After a slow start, land redistribution in the Mexicali Valley helped to increase both the number of acres planted to cotton and the number of bales produced.[33] Within a year of the agrarista invasion, over 400,000 acres of land in the Mexicali Valley were developed or being prepared for farming. In 1938, the Department of Communication and Public Works began constructing new highways and improving old ones throughout northern Baja California. New railroad lines were laid that not only connected the peninsula to neighboring Sonora, but specifically the Mexicali Valley to shipping ports on the Sea of Cortes. Cárdenas's government wanted to make it easier for the valley's cotton crop to get to Mexican factories both in Mexicali (for example, the Compañia Industrial Jabonera del Pacífico, which manufactured soap and cattle feed from cotton seed oil) and elsewhere in the republic. According to one contemporary Arizona official, these infrastructure projects enabled farmers "to ship the produce of Mexicali into Mexico for use by the Mexican people."[34] Road and rail construction—long seen as symbols of modernity and tools of nation building—also brought large amounts of direct federal expenditures to Baja California, provided jobs in the vast undeveloped regions of the peninsula, and gave average Mexicans a role in carrying out the Plan Pro-Baja California.

Throughout much of the postrevolutionary era, Mexico City used road and railroad construction to bring Mexicans together in a controlled manner. Wendy Waters concludes, "Cárdenas's approach to road construction reflected his special interest in making workers and peasants prosperous, enthusiastic contributors to Mexico."[35] Hence, by building new roads and rail lines, average Mexicans could partake in a nationalist project that pulled Baja California away from the U.S. economic orbit and tied it more closely to Mexico's. Furthermore, the new highways and rail lines would Mexicanize the territory by bringing thousands of Mexican laborers to the Mexicali Valley, where they could work on agricultural lands that previously had been American owned. The only threat to this well-planned nationalistic program, federal officials believed, was the region's inhospitable heat and humidity.

Government advertisements and news reports played down the region's harsh climate and instead highlighted the economic opportunities that awaited Mexican migrants as a result of the increased demand for cotton products during World War II. This propaganda worked. Between 1940 and 1950, the valley's population increased dramatically, from 45,569 to 137,200 residents. The onset of the Korean War in 1950 again increased demand and raised prices for cotton to five times their prewar value. Baja California continued its rapid economic and demographic growth in the 1950s, more than doubling its population to 520,165. The city of Mexicali grew by 12.8 percent between 1940 and 1950, and by 10.4 percent from 1950 to 1960. The territory's development in the post-WWII era fostered its transition to statehood, which Baja California Norte achieved in 1952—nearly two decades before such rights were granted to its southern neighbor.[36]

One factor that is critical for increasing agricultural production in Mexico is water. In mid-1935, federal officials, including Foreign Secretary José Ángel Cisneros, stressed the need for an agreement with the United States that ensured enough water from the Colorado River "to meet the agricultural and industrial needs of the Mexicali region." Baja California's Secretary of Agriculture and Development Antonio Basich and Department of Public Health Minister Bernardo Batiz championed Cisneros's call and pressed Mexico City and Washington for greater access to Colorado River water to expand irrigation in the Mexicali Valley. Dorothy Kerig and Evan Ward agree that Cárdenas rushed the development of the Mexicali Valley because of his concerns regarding water. Mexico and the United States had not yet agreed on the amount of water that Mexico would receive from the Colorado River, and the completion of the Hoover Dam in 1937 along with impending completion of the Imperial Valley's All-American Canal both threatened the Mexicali Valley's water supply by diverting Colorado River water. Cárdenas was thus forced to act quickly. The more land that Mexico could cultivate in the valley before the All-American Canal was completed (which occurred in 1942), the more water Mexico City could claim was already being used by Mexico when negotiating a water treaty with Washington.[37] Cárdenas pressed this point to Baja California's governor. In his letter to Navarro Cortina, Cárdenas declared, "It is important to remember that the more land we put under cultivation, the better our chances for a larger volume of water from the U.S. reserves of the Colorado River." Consequently, before a bilateral water treaty was signed, between 1938 and 1941 the Mexican government increased the amount of irrigated land in the Mexicali Valley from 172,164 acres to 301,600.[38]

For many Mexican officials, water was an important component of economic nationalism. While the acquisition of CRLC's property significantly increased the economic power of the Mexican federal government in Baja California and simultaneously decreased that of an entrenched, foreign-owned enterprise, the lands had little value in such an extremely hot and arid climate without access to a sustainable water supply. Because Washington desired good relations with Mexico following the U.S. entrance into World War II, the Roosevelt administration began negotiating a water treaty with Cárdenas's successor, Ávila Camacho, after the All-American Canal was completed in 1942. In February 1944 the two governments signed a bilateral water treaty that ensured Mexico an adequate water supply for irrigation (1.5 million acre-feet of water per year). Mexico immediately began to construct a number of dams to control the delivery of the Colorado River water into the municipality of Mexicali. According to Ward, the aptly named Morelos Dam "broke Mexico free from the capricious control that Americans exercised over Mexico's share of water" from the Colorado River and "symbolized Mexican independence from asking the United States for water in times of drought."[39]

The resultant influx of people, water, and profits sparked the irrigation and mechanization (i.e., modernization) of Mexicali Valley farms and ushered in its "golden age" of cotton production. When Cárdenas took office in the mid-1930s, only 134,000 acres of land in the valley were irrigated by the Colorado River. In the late 1950s, over 475,000 acres were under irrigation. Not surprisingly, the greater distribution of water led to a dramatic rise in agricultural productivity and made the valley's ejidatarios and independent farmers more prosperous.[40] Consequently, former cotton pickers took their children out of the fields and sent them to school, and primary school enrollment in Baja California shot up from 14,207 to 76,001 between 1940 and 1960. Ejidatarios were now able to purchase items that they identified as modern and that they expected would improve their quality of life. Some bought tractors for their farms, as well as cars, trucks, electric fans, refrigerators, radios, watches, and dress clothes for themselves and their families. In addition, between 1940 and 1950 the number of housing units in the territory nearly tripled, to 48,472, of which 55 percent had piped water and sewers.[41]

Even though living standards of Mexicali's rural workers improved greatly when they became ejidatarios, this does not mean that agrarian reform was a resounding success throughout the republic. While conditions improved in both the Mexicali and Yaqui valleys, in regions outside of northern Mexico most ejidatarios continued to live and work in misery—leading many to migrate, during the last seven decades, to Mexico City and the United States in search of work and a better future for themselves and their families. In fact, the economic position of many Mexican peasants and workers declined in the 1940s. While some of this stemmed from the rising cost of living associated with wwii, along with the slowing of land reform and the reallocation of federal resources away from the working classes by the Ávila Camacho and Miguel Alemán administrations, it also resulted from Cárdenas's agrarian reform program. Although the northern ejidos—including those studied here, as well as the Laguna region—were relatively well off, many that were located in the central Bajío region and southern Mexico were mired in poverty because they were poorly planned by Cárdenas's government and lacked sufficient subsidies. Besides curtailing agrarian reform in their last years in office, too often Cardenista officials simply divided the land, declared victory, and went home, leaving thousands of new ejidatarios in dire economic straits.

SOCIAL ENGINEERING, MESTIZAJE, RACISM, AND MEXICANIZATION

Cultural factors, including social engineering and racism, also figured into the expropriation of crlc's land. In the eyes of many Cardenistas, agrarian reform was, at minimum, a two-stage process. Land redistribution was followed by the dispatch of a plethora of government agencies and programs that sought to transform the countryside by building a more modern republic. The Agrarian Department's Gabino Vázquez noted, "Social and educational action is given special attention, since land and credit alone are not sufficient to transform the rural agricultural economy."[42] Hence, federal intervention in rural Mexico via the ejidal system was part of an elite nation-building project designed to remold rural workers into healthier, modern, and more productive citizens. For Cárdenas, economic reforms such as landownership, higher salaries, and better working and living conditions were not an end in themselves; they had to be accompanied by cultural changes that would improve moral values and make peasants and workers more efficient.

Just as Cárdenas believed that breaking up the haciendas, putting more land under cultivation, and modernizing agricultural production would promote economic growth, he also thought that attacking social vices and promoting education would stimulate rural development. For many Cardenistas, economic, social, and cultural reforms had to be mutually reinforcing, just as were many of Mexico's social ills. To combat ignorance and illiteracy and promote the types of socioeconomic changes that he envisioned, Cárdenas established cultural missions throughout the country comprised of teachers, doctors, engineers, and agricultural and industrial experts. He relied on public schools not only to create an educated and skilled workforce but also, in his words, to "transform the spirit of the Mexican people" by liberating them from their "misery and ignorance."[43] In addition to the Ministry of Public Education, Cárdenas also called on the office of the Secretary of Agriculture to propagate scientific agricultural methods—such as pest control and storage—to fight the "metaphysical explanations," "superstitions," and "local legends" that were often professed by priests and which made rural workers "docile" and inefficient.[44]

Many observers felt it would be easier to change the peasants' worldview and modernize their methods of farming once their position in society improved. According to Cárdenas's friend and confidant, Columbia University Professor Frank Tannenbaum, the first step in "converting the peon into a citizen" was to "give him some land."[45] Thereafter, the Cardenistas believed it was necessary to provide ejidatarios with a socialist education that stressed the benefits of good health, nutrition and hygiene, athleticism, self-improvement, sobriety, and other positive social habits. Besides remolding rural citizens in the classroom, federal policymakers also used their increased power at the local level to undermine religious fervor and crack down on social vices such as alcoholism, gambling, and prostitution. Both before and during his presidency, Cárdenas often commented on the detrimental socioeconomic impact of these and other vices. To promote a wholesome, productive, and politically correct lifestyle, Cardenista officials in the Department of Public Health closed bars, casinos, cabarets, brothels, and "zones of tolerance" around the country. And, in mid-1935, Cárdenas issued a presidential decree that closed all casinos nationwide.[46]

Like some of their revolutionary predecessors and successors, puritanical Cardenistas replaced popular religious festivals and scurrilous activities with state-sponsored sporting events, parades, and other civic celebrations—most notably Revolution Day on November 20. Public spectacles fostered a "hegemonic discourse" that redefined Mexican manhood, developed a national campesino and worker identity, built community solidarity, institutionalized the revolution, and created a new class of modern, healthy, disciplined, and politically loyal *gente decente* (decent people) from "those from below." For many, such social reforms reflected Mexico's new, more enlightened "revolutionary morality" and enhanced the country's international reputation.[47] For most Cardenistas, land redistribution without social reform would place in jeopardy their goals of improving material conditions for the rural population, modernizing the countryside, and fostering greater agricultural productivity.

To Cárdenas and Vicente Lombardo Toledano, leader of the CTM, social vices, especially gambling and alcohol consumption, along with the public and private individuals who profited from them, were enemies of the revolution, since they undermined workers' health and efficiency and abetted political corruption. Consequently, Mexicali's saloon culture, red light and casino districts, and drug trade—all of which had been thriving since the early 1900s—drew the attention of the moralizing president. The fact that many of Mexicali's cantinas, casinos, brothels, and opium dens were owned by Chinese and used by Americans gave Cárdenas's paternalistic social reforms a nationalistic edge. Politics figured into the equation, as well, since the corrupt Callista governorship of Abelardo Rodríguez (1923–30) was closely tied to Mexicali and Tijuana's vice tourism industries. Callista political control was directly maintained when Arturo Elías governed the territory in 1933. Even former president Plutarco Elías Calles himself—who had a large estate outside Ensenada—gained financially from his relationship with Baja California's foreign casino owners. Hence, Cárdenas probably thought that clamping down on them would weaken his political rivals.[48]

The stage for social reform in Baja California Norte was set as early as 1934. During his presidential campaign visit that year to the Mexicali Valley, Cárdenas visited some of the territory's most famous casinos. He also noted that gambling and alcohol consumption in the region inhibited Baja California's economic development. Because Governor Navarro Cortina ignored Cárdenas's federal ban on casinos and lined his pockets with proceeds (as had many previous governors), the president was forced to act directly. In 1936 Cárdenas closed Mexicali's popular ABW Club (formerly the Owl) and the following year expropriated Tijuana's "sumptuous" Agua Caliente Spa and Resort. Then, after the expropriation of CRLC's land in the spring of 1937, he revoked the liquor licenses from the cantinas that operated within centers of agricultural production and suppressed liquor sales and border vice tourism throughout the region. Casinos that operated illegally in Tijuana, Ensenada, and elsewhere also were closed by the president.[49] Moralizing Cardenistas called upon Mexican women to assist them in the campaign against vice. According to Gabino Vázquez, following CRLC's expropriation, government officials in Baja California organized Feminine Leagues for Social Action to help "reduce vicious customs, better manage the domestic economy, improve the schools, and collaborate with the ejidatarios."[50]

By cracking down on social vices, the federal government took away with one hand. But, it also gave with the other by constructing hundreds of sanitation works, introducing drinkable water, and establishing model ejidos within the Mexicali Valley ejidal system. Since administration officials believed that the peasants needed their own public space, the Casa del Agrarista was built in the valley to temporarily house campesinos and function as a meeting place for the peasantry. Such buildings were used for group activities, which empowered rural workers and raised their class consciousness.[51] Cardenista officials also hoped that Casa activities would broaden their base of support. In this regard, rural schools were even more important. Following the expropriation of CRLC's holdings, Cárdenas significantly increased Baja California's overall education budget, established thirty-six new schools, and assigned eighty new teachers to the ejidos and agricultural colonies in the Mexicali Valley. In fact, the number of schools throughout the territory increased dramatically by the end of Cárdenas's term in office, from just 21 in 1930 to 140 by 1940 (see figure 11). As a result, primary school enrollment nearly tripled over the same period.[52] Both educational and social advancement were not ends in themselves. Coupled with the belief that land redistribution gave rural laborers a stake in society and increased their morale, most Cardenistas believed that social and economic reforms together would create a more modern and industrious rural workforce.

Besides molding a new peasantry through progressive reforms, the expropriation of CRLC's land allowed the government to supplant American values with Mexican ones. As Alan Knight has shown, some of Mexico's leading postrevolutionary thinkers were critical of American mores. Manuel Gamio, a leading anthropologist, archaeologist, and public administrator, "deplored the Americanization of Baja California," which stemmed from a variety of sources, including the vice tourism industry in which Americans were both providers and consumers, CRLC's domination of Mexicali's rural economy, and the colonization of land by American farmers. According to John Mason Hart, because

FIGURE 11. Ejidal school in the Mexicali Valley built by Cárdenas's administration in 1938 in Ejido Islas Agrarias. PHOTOGRAPH BY AUTHOR.

many American colonies were concentrated as enclaves in specific areas, they were "partially closed and culturally isolated" communities that barely assimilated. As a result, many American colonists did not speak Spanish or understand Mexican culture.[53]

In addition to Gamio, José Vasconcelos, philosopher, political activist, and public official, denounced "*pochismo* (the hybrid U.S./Mexican culture of Northern Mexico)" and the region's "pro-Americanism."[54] Rather than look to the United States or Europe for theoretical and spiritual inspiration, intellectuals like Gamio and Vasconcelos championed a new nationalism that was based on the cult of the mestizo. Throughout the postrevolutionary era, "mestizophilia" became a prominent part of Mexican artistic culture, especially in murals, theater, and film. According to Alexandra Minna Stern, in the late 1920s and early 1930s Mexico's eugenics movement was formalized, and "eugenicists, like Gamio and Vasconcelos, loudly carried the banner of mestizophilia and saw homogenization as fundamental to the health of the nation."[55]

The political rhetoric of mestizaje allowed the postrevolutionary elite, including Cárdenas's administration, to distinguish itself from the Porfiriato's "cosmopolitan, Europhile ethos" and rebuild the state based on Mexican norms, values, and ethnicity. Porfirian Eurocentric racism—which was anti-mestizo and anti-Indian—was replaced by a positive, yet often paternalistic, view of mestizos and indigenous groups. Although the revolutionary nationalism fostered by the country's political and economic elite celebrated Indian and mestizo culture in very different ways—the former as an abstract cultural value from the past, the latter as a model for Mexico's future—both were part of a new way of thinking that appealed to the mestizo and Indian masses and sought to hasten the state-building process. This new philosophical orientation, however, was not fully inclusive; rather, it tended to be exclusionary and smacked of reverse racism, because it sometimes denigrated non-Mexican racial groups, including Asians, Africans, and Jews.[56] Like their predecessors, Cardenistas theorized national history around the myths of the Indian and mestizo for a variety of socioeconomic and political ends.

The political elite's view of Americans, Europeans, mestizos, and indigenous peoples influenced national policies on population density and economic development. Some Cardenistas, including the president, believed that Mexico's low population contributed to the underutilization of the nation's agricultural lands and hampered productivity. According to Stern, while the Científicos promoted European migration to offset this problem, many postrevolutionary leaders preferred to stimulate natural population growth. In 1936, Cárdenas passed the General Population Law, which tried to increase Mexico's population through campaigns for public health and against infant mortality, the modernization of Indian and mestizo communities, the promotion of internal migration, and the repatriation of Mexicans from the United States. For many eugenicists, including Gilberto Loyo, rapid population growth would significantly improve the quality of life for most Mexicans and allow the country "to fulfill its historical destiny."[57]

Population levels in Baja California depended on one's perspective. According to many landless field workers, the Mexicali Valley was overpopulated in the 1930s due to the recent influx of Chinese migrants from Sonora and Mexican repatriates from the United States. Increased population pressures in the valley during periods of economic decline, especially during the Great Depression, increased job competition and unemployment, while driving down wages. Thus, local rural workers were very present-minded when they reflected on population levels. Cárdenas's government, on the other hand, held a long purview and rightly believed that Baja California was one of the most underpopulated regions of the country, which in turn reduced the region's economic capacity. Moreover, since the territory had the largest per capita foreign-born population in the nation, as well as the lowest per capita mestizo population—both of which stemmed from its large Asian presence—no place was in greater need of "Mexicanization." In fact, not only was the population more than 10 percent non-Mexican, but the ratio of Chinese to mestizos was more than sixty times the national average. Furthermore, 75 percent of the Chinese immigrants in Baja California arrived via Mexicali and lived in that region.[58] Addressing the population imbalance was central to the territory's Mexicanization program and had roots that stretched back to the mid-1920s. At that time, Governor Abelardo Rodríguez had bemoaned the large number of Chinese residents in the territory and had tried in vain to promote Mexican colonization by smallholders who would farm their own private parcels. Now, however, for leaders such as Vázquez, land redistribution would be "the first step toward obtaining a more numerous Mexican population in the peninsula."[59]

Thus, the Plan Pro-Baja California was designed not only to boost the economy but also to maintain cultural and racial unity. According to Cárdenas, populating the Mexicali Valley with Mexican nationals would enable the residents of the territory to live within "the economic and social rhythm of our nation" and "maintain the racial characteristics of *la cultura patria* [the native culture]." After CRLC's lands were expropriated, Vázquez similarly argued that the redistribution of land in Baja California was part of a "great recovery program that strengthened the racial community, cultural solidarity, and economic intercourse between the distant territory and the rest of the republic, so as to make it an integral part of the Mexican nation."[60] Hence, expropriating CRLC's property presented the Cardenistas with a unique opportunity to meld economic and cultural nationalism under the rubric of mestizaje.[61] The revolutionary cult of mestizaje, which was based on the racist assumption of the innate superiority of the Indian and mestizo over other racial groups, provided an additional rationale for the expropriation of the CRLC's holdings. Although the government's April 1936 colonization agreement permitted only Mexican nationals to colonize CRLC land, Mexicanization through colonization was hampered in Baja California by the fact that foreigners, primarily Asian immigrants, continued to rent plots of land from the company. However, the expropriation of all rented parcels and their redistribution only to Mexicans, plus the exemption of the Mexican-owned colonies from seizure, diluted the foreign presence in the Mexicali Valley and added to the climate of popular sinophobia.[62]

In the 1920s, anti-Chinese sentiment was rampant in those areas of Mexico that had a sizable Asian population. As was the case in other parts of northern Mexico, attacks against Chinese immigrants in Baja California Norte had both economic and sociocultural roots, and often stretched backed decades. In the early 1920s, anti-Chinese sentiment in the territory expressed itself in both official and popular rhetoric. For instance, Baja California's federal congressional representative, José María Dávila, wanted the Chinese out of Mexico since, he said, "They do not represent a step forward in the ideal mestizaje . . . but rather signify a step backwards in the anthropological search for the prototypical man."[63] As Alan Knight points out, sinophobia "embodied a range of powerful 'irrational' prejudices which served to legitimatize persecution and lend it 'theoretical' justification." The Chinese "were stereotyped as filthy, disease-ridden, money grubbing, parasitic, and sexually threatening. They spread sickness, gambling and drug-addiction" and were seen as " 'corrupting the organism of [the Mexican] race.' " The city of Mexicali was well known for its Chinese bars and opium dens. When the Mexican Nationalist League of Baja California (Liga Nacionalista Mexicana en Baja California) was established in 1935, it wanted to clean up the territory's cities. To do so, the organization championed prohibition and called for closing the Chinese cantinas and cabarets that fomented social vice. In their place, athletic activities and cooperative organizations would be organized. In short, as Gerardo Rénique notes, Mexico's "preoccupation with the 'Chinese problem' expressed a deep concern with the future of the nation, its racial makeup, and its progress."[64]

Throughout most of the postrevolutionary era, Chinese immigrants in Baja California were physically attacked, verbally insulted, and exhorted for money by their Mexican neighbors. In 1924, fifty Chinese were expelled from the northern territory. The situation for Asian immigrants in Baja California worsened in the early 1930s, when thousands of Chinese arrived from neighboring Sonora after being fined, arrested, exhorted, attacked, and then finally deported. Although examples of Chinese discrimination and persecution could be found throughout Mexico during the postrevolutionary era, it was most prevalent during the Depression, and it was strongest in the northern and western parts of the country, where Asian populations were highest.[65]

In response to the growing Chinese presence in and around the Mexicali Valley, in May 1933 the Nationalist Party in Support of the Race (Partido Nacionalista Pro-Raza) was founded in Mexicali. This racist party, which was largely comprised of Mexican merchants, demanded that the territory's government segregate the Chinese population of Mexicali into a separate barrio. The logic behind this, one could assume, was to reduce commercial competition for Mexican merchants. Shortly thereafter, some Chinese-owned businesses in Mexicali and Ensenada were forced to close. Anti-Asian sentiment was entrenched in business groups, as well as local and national labor unions, including the Confederation of National Chambers of Commerce and Industry (Confederación de Cámaras Nacionales de Comercio y Industria), the CROM, and the Syndicate for Proletarian Control of Mexicali (Sindicato Control Proletario de Oficios Varios de Mexicali). These and other organizations called for limiting Chinese immigration to Baja California, expelling Chinese from the territory who were there illegally, denying citizenship to both Chinese and Japanese residents, and limiting Asian commercial activities; they also demanded that 80 percent of the employees of any business be Mexican.[66] Both local actors and national organizations found a sympathetic ear in Mexico City. The same year that the Partido Nacionalista Pro-Raza was established in Baja California, President Abelardo Rodríguez gave a warm endorsement to Chinese deportation. According to Rodríguez, they were "not asking that the deportation of the Orientals be discontinued" but instead "that the deportation of Chinese be handled by people who will respect the laws of the land."[67]

Anti-Asian sentiment often stemmed from economic competition between Asian immigrants and Mexican nationals, as was the case on CRLC's property. Prior to the 1937 invasion, hundreds of Chinese and Japanese nationals had rented land from CRLC. Some organized cooperative societies that only employed Asians workers. A few of the wealthier Chinese lessees imported workers from China. In the mid-1930s, Governor Agustín Olachea estimated that 25,000 acres of land were farmed by six thousand Chinese and four thousand Japanese.[68] Because of the large Asian presence, in 1934 a number of Mexican labor confederations in Baja California wrote to President Rodríguez and complained that agricultural cooperatives and other commercial establishments run by Chinese and Japanese in the Mexicali Valley had hired mostly members of their own race, without employing the proper percentage of Mexican workers as required by Article 90 of the Federal Labor Law. According to union officials, this not only increased Mexican unemployment but also was "injuring the economic interests of the country."[69] Pedro Pérez had a similar impression of the Asian population in the city and valley of Mexicali. According to the agrarista, "There were a lot of Chinese everywhere, and they always took care of their own people first."[70] When referring to Asian immigrants, the racist Bar and Restaurant Employees Union of Mexicali argued, "In order to accomplish our improvement, [we must] get rid once and for all from our small Country, those foreign races which annoy us." According to the same union, Mexicans in and around Mexicali were "controlled by foreign capitalists, especially the Japanese and Chinese," who forced Mexicans, through "their ruinous competitions," to live in miserable conditions, "always to be their slaves for a small salary" that was not enough to survive on. "Comrades," implored the union speaker, "The Chinese and Japanese compete with us with bars, grocery stores, meat markets, laundries, 'tortilla' factories . . . All the commercial life in the Territory of Lower California is in the hands of the everlasting yellow octopus, who continues sucking the Mexican workers' blood." The workers' movement, he continued, brought about the improvement of the working class and freed them "from the domain of the exploiters," making "Mexico for the Mexicans." He concluded, "Comrades: Every nation has looked to nationalism to protect its citizens. We have for example in the U.S., that every time their labor situation is aggravated they expel all the foreigners to secure the improvement of their own people."[71]

Asians were not just seen as commercial competitors. Many Mexicans felt "cheap and servile Chinese workers" worsened labor conditions for everyone by flooding the labor pool, driving down wages, and increasing unemployment.[72] According to Cardiel Marín, nearly 30 percent of Baja California's workforce was Chinese. Economic jealousy also probably fomented anti-Asian sentiment, since hundreds of Chinese and Japanese could afford to own or rent farms in the Mexicali Valley—something that was beyond most mestizo field workers.[73] Since the Chinese were seen as both a "parasitic" racial group and as economic competitors, they made easy targets "against whom the populist nationalism of the Revolution could be safely vented."[74] Not surprisingly, when armed agraristas invaded CRLC's holdings in January 1937, Asian plots of land were among the first to be seized by them and subsequently expropriated by the federal government. By driving Chinese and Japanese tenants off their land, the agraristas targeted individuals who lacked any substantial political or diplomatic strength. And, due to popular sinophobia, Asian tenants received no sympathy or support at the local and national levels.[75]

Just as mestizaje was intended to "forge the nation" by integrating the mestizo, it also sought to cleanse it by expelling the Chinese, Japanese, and other foreigners from regions like the Mexicali Valley.[76] As indicated in table 2—whose numbers are conservative in light of the comments by Governors Cantú and Olachea that indicated a much larger Chinese presence in the Mexicali

TABLE 2. Population of Baja California Norte, 1930 and 1940

	1930	1940
Total population	48,327	78,907
Immigrant population	5,372	1,306
Chinese	3,089*	618
Japanese	958	346
Americans	576	172
Russians	473	76
Italians	169	37
Spaniards	159	54
Germans	54	3

* The Chinese population had risen to 4,434 in 1933.
Sources: Secretaría de la Economía Nacional, Dirección General de Estadística, *Quinto Censo de Población, Mayo 1930, Baja California (Distrito Norte)*; Secretaría de la Economía Nacional, Dirección General de Estadística, *Sexto Censo de Población, 1940, Resumen General*; Consejo Nacional de Población de México, *Baja California demográfico*, 17, 39; Peritus, "La población en Baja California," *La Voz de la Frontera*, October 1969; Rénique, "Race, Region, and Nation," 230; Cardiel Marín, "La migración china," 212; Lorey, *United States–Mexico Border Statistics*, 7.

region—dispossessing foreigners of their land was one way to hasten the Mexicanization of Baja California and promote both racial and cultural homogeneity. Between 1930 and 1940 the territory's foreign-born population dropped from roughly 12 percent to less than 2 percent.

The flight of foreigners from Baja California, especially those of Asian origin, reflected national trends. Between 1927 and 1940, the number of Chinese-born immigrants in Mexico declined from 24,218 to 6,661. From 1930 to 1940, the number of Japanese immigrants dropped from 4,310 to 2,181.[77] Finally, in January 1942, Manuel Ávila Camacho's government relocated all of Baja California's remaining Japanese to Guadalajara and Mexico City, due to U.S. security concerns.[78]

In hard economic times, it is common for popular and elite groups to target minorities as scapegoats and use racism to secure broad support for diverse goals. The fact that 84 percent of the Chinese population in Baja California was between the ages of fifteen and thirty-nine increased job competition for Mexican workers. Consequently, the battle over land and jobs in the Mexicali Valley was cast by organized labor in ethnonationalist terms that appealed to the local Mexican population and received a sympathetic ear in Mexico City.[79] Not only was CRLC seen as a powerful and intrusive foreign-owned entity; many Mexicans also viewed Asian groups as a threatening foreign presence. In short, both groups of foreigners were seen as an economic and cultural threat to the region and the nation. Hence, during the 1937 invasion agraristas planted Mexican flags on land owned by Americans and farmed by Asians to symbolize their reclaiming Mexico's territorial integrity.

Despite the events in the Mexicali Valley, we should not conclude that all the seizures of and petitions for American-owned rural property in Mexico during Cárdenas's administration were motivated solely by either anti-Americanism or xenophobia. In fact, the agrarista invasion of CRLC's property in 1937 would most likely have occurred had the company been Mexican owned—as seen by similar types of land invasions of Mexican properties around the country. Furthermore, since the parcels of Mexican colonists and tenants also were invaded by the agraristas, one can conclude that the popular movement was not solely motivated by a bias against foreigners; instead the field workers' desperate working and living conditions, their anger at having earlier ejidal petitions rejected, and especially the threat posed by colonization were the main roots underlying their bold invasion of CRLC's property. Anti-Americanism and xenophobia, while very critical, were probably of secondary importance to the agraristas' class-based needs. On the other hand, if CRLC was owned and worked only by Mexicans, then there would be little need for the federal government to Mexicanize Baja California, making it less likely that Cárdenas's administration would have endorsed the agraristas' actions by expropriating the company's holdings.

EPILOGUE

In 1937, Mexico expropriated 237,000 acres of CRLC's land to create forty collective ejidos. Mexican policymakers, though, did not rely solely on collective agriculture when they divided CRLC's property. In addition to all of the colonies that were saved by the sit-down strike, by December 1937 federal officials established eleven new colonies, totaling 72,500 acres, from CRLC's appropriated holdings. More colonies were similarly sold by the Mexican government in coming years. Also, the individualist priorities of most ejidatarios worked against the long-term success of communal farming. After a few years of working together, between 1940 and 1942 the ejidatarios were given a choice between individual ejido plots or communal forms of land tenure. Most opted for individual plots that they or their descendants still possess today. Meanwhile, Pedro Pérez, when I interviewed him in 2001 at the age of ninety-one, lived quietly in his three-room cement house, which had electricity and plumbing and was located in Ejido Michoacán de Ocampo. As one of the original agraristas, he is proud of his participation in the labor movement and the January 1937 land invasion—especially since his words are memorialized on the wall of the nearby museum that celebrates these events. Like most of the other ejidatarios interviewed, Pérez claims that his life improved after 1937, as shown by the federal pension that supports him, the car in his driveway, and the modern appliances and electronics that fill his home, including a refrigerator, television, radio, and electric fan.[80]

In March 1944, CRLC swapped the stock that covered its remaining property for valuable Los Angeles real estate owned by businessman and former U.S. consul William Jenkins. In 1945 Jenkins sold the stock that he acquired from the company to the Mexican government at the request of President Ávila Camacho.[81] On May 12, 1945, a Mexico radio bulletin proudly announced the end of CRLC. The broadcast announced, "The territorial government is pleased to inform all of the inhabitants of Baja California, and especially the farmers of the Mexicali Valley, that Governor Juan Felipe Rico Islas has signed historic documents that restore forever, and in the favor of the country, the lands of the Mexicali Valley that until yesterday had been the property of the Colorado River Land Company. . . . Today's restitution to [our] nationals restores for future generations a legitimate patrimony of Mexicans that inhabit this region of the homeland."[82]

Each year on January 27, Baja California celebrates as a state holiday the 1937 invasion of CRLC's property, commonly referred to as "el asalto a las tierras." In 1987, fifteen thousand people gathered in Ejido Michoacán de Ocampo to see President Miguel de la Madrid, Governor Xicotencatl Leyva Mortera, and many other Mexican dignitaries celebrate the golden anniversary of the seizure. Leyva's scathing speech illustrates the historical significance of the invasion. According to the governor, "Fifty years ago, in the territory usurped by the insolence, exploitation, and abuse of the foreign owners, a handful of patriots, who shouldered the past glory of their ancestors, planted here the flags of national dignity, sovereignty, and independence."[83]

Laden with nationalistic, revolutionary rhetoric, Leyva's speech was designed for domestic political consumption. Nonetheless, this does not negate two facts. First, Mexico's economic autonomy vis-à-vis U.S. business interests, as represented by CRLC, increased substantially in Baja California following the expropriation of the company's land. Second, the Mexicali peasantry played an integral role in reshaping the territory's political economy and the valley's land tenure system by precipitating a conflict with CRLC that impelled the Cárdenas administration to intervene on the agraristas' behalf and redistribute the company's holdings to local field workers. Agrarista mobilization by itself, however, was not powerful enough to bring about the expropriation of CRLC's land. Had it not been for the multifaceted Cardenista state-building project, the aspirations of Mexicali's rural workers probably would have been thwarted, as they had been throughout the 1920s and early 1930s.

DOMESTIC POLITICS AND THE
EXPROPRIATION OF AMERICAN-OWNED LAND
IN THE YAQUI VALLEY

It would be really pitiful if hundreds of foreign residents in the [Yaqui] Valley can cultivate thousands of hectares, and we, the children of Mexico, in full possession of our rights are not able, unfortunately, to be owners of one piece of land.

SECRETARY GENERAL JESÚS ALATORRE, UNION OF WORKERS AND
PEASANTS, PUEBLO EL YAQUI, NOVEMBER 8, 1935

The expropriation of American-owned land in Sonora in October 1937 was linked to the development of Sonoran politics since the late 1920s. From 1929 to 1935, Sonora was controlled by three relatively conservative governorships that used revolutionary rhetoric to promote developmental capitalism. Each was closely tied to the former president and political strongman Plutarco Elías Calles, including his uncle Francisco Elías (1929–31) and son Rodolfo Elías Calles (1931–34). In late 1935, growing opposition to Callista continuity in office sparked an armed uprising against the third Callista governor, Ramón Ramos (1934–35) by conservative Sonorans who included opposition politicians, large landowners, Catholics, and Mayo Indians. After this group, led by Román Yocupicio, gained control of the state in 1936, Cárdenas used land redistribution to weaken their political power while simultaneously broadening his own base of support among rural workers. It was within this context of a domestic political conflict that American-owned farms in the Yaqui Valley were seized.

The opposition politicians who led the 1935 revolt against Governor Ramos were comprised primarily of Obregonistas (supporters of Álvaro Obregón) who expected to reclaim power at the state and national level after Calles left office in 1928 and Obregón reassumed the presidency in 1929. However, when Obregón was assassinated after his presidential reelection in mid-1928, his supporters saw their prospects for regaining control dissipate. Rather than fade into the dustbin of history, many Obregonistas—including one-third of the army, under General José Gonzalo Escobar—took up arms in the spring of 1929, in an unsuccessful attempt to overthrow the Callista-imposed presidency of Emilio Portes Gil. After federal forces crushed the rebellion, Calles purged the remaining Obregonistas from power at the federal, state, and municipal levels and filled the new vacancies with his supporters. These events had a significant impact in Obregón's and Calles's home state of Sonora. Although some of the leaders of the Escobar rebellion fled to the United States, many remained in Sonora and formed a conservative anti-Callista opposition that eventually would topple Governor Ramos in 1935.[1]

In Sonora, the anti-Callista faction contained not only these Obregonista politicians who sought to regain control of the state government but also Catholic lay persons and priests who resented the Callista anticlerical campaign, large property owners and Mayo Indians who opposed the Callista agrarian reform program, and Sonoran businessmen who were outside the Callista political machine and thus excluded from its lucrative business contracts. The goal of this diverse faction was to prevent the imposition of another Callista governor following the end of Rodolfo Calles's term. Despite organizing statewide political organizations and opposition rallies, these groups failed to prevent the 1934 gubernatorial election of Rodolfo's close associate, Ramón Ramos. As a former secretary of the interior (*gobernación*)—a powerful post in Mexican politics—Ramos won the election because he was endorsed by both the official party (the PNR) and by Cárdenas, and was backed by well-organized groups of teachers, agraristas, and urban workers in Hermosillo, Ciudad Obregón, Nogales, and Agua Prieta. Ramos was inaugurated governor in September 1935. To solidify his position, he installed his supporters in municipal governments, toppled conservative factions linked to the rural and urban elites, arrested opposition leaders, and established *defensas sociales* (social organizations that were often armed) to combat "reactionaries" and "enemies of the government." Faced with rumors of a conservative Obregonista uprising against his administration, Ramos purchased arms in the United States and smuggled them into Sonora.[2]

Ramos had every reason to expect trouble. One month after his inauguration, the anti-Callista groups rebelled against his government. Mayo Indians in southern Sonora took up arms against the municipal governments that they perceived as radical and which were controlled by anticlerical Callistas, federal schoolteachers from the Ministry of Education (Secretaría de Educación Pública, SEP), and powerful agraristas. In the eastern Sierra Madre, widespread discontent similarly led Catholic villagers, priests, and ranchers to fight a "mini-Cristiada." In the northern Altar district of Sonora, cattlemen, growers, and merchants rebelled in order to gain political power and prevent land redistribution. The elite and popular grievances that sparked these uprisings, according to Adrian Bantjes, stemmed from agrarian reform, "socialist education, control of the press, electoral fraud, the closed shop system, agrarista manipulation of the peasantry, and the economic hegemony of revolutionary elites." The opposition's limited resources made them too weak to overthrow Ramos, whose control of the defensas sociales and Sonora's political apparatus enabled him to mobilize well-organized urban and rural workers, teachers, and sectors of the economic elite tied to the official party. In other words, without federal assistance, the state's conservative anti-Callista movement had little chance to depose Ramos.[3]

Unable to overthrow the governor, the Sonoran opposition used the conflict between former president Calles and current president Cárdenas during the latter half of 1935 to oust Ramos and the state's Callistas. In June 1935, Calles undermined Cárdenas's authority as president and publicly blamed him for the tumultuous rural and urban labor unrest that engulfed the nation during his first six months in office. Hundreds of industrial strikes had erupted throughout the country soon after Cárdenas took office, due to his strong support for labor.[4] The battle between the two national leaders represented a fight between Calles's dominant, conservative coalition and Cárdenas's rising progressive block. Realizing the importance of military support to the presidency, Cárdenas already had begun to reform the institution and promote promising junior officers. Following Calles's public attacks, Cárdenas swiftly transferred or retired many army generals who did not express their loyalty to his government. Likewise, he removed some Callista officials from important government posts and the cabinet. With the support of a number of state governors, key sectors of the military, and most national peasant and labor federations, Cárdenas was determined not to follow the path of former president Ortiz Rubio—whom Calles had forced from power due to policy disagreements and Ortiz Rubio's attempts to break out of his shadow. Instead, Cárdenas would be the one who would send Calles out of the country. After el Jefe Máximo was sent into a brief political exile, Cárdenas dismissed his pro-Calles cabinet and immediately formed a new, more radical one. He then again purged most remaining Callistas from the official party, the federal Congress, the military, and state governments.[5]

Although Cárdenas had prevailed over Calles in June 1935, he was by no means in complete control of Mexico. For the remainder of the year, and during the first half of 1936, his administration was besieged by Callista threats from around the country. Former head of the military General Joaquín Amaro mentioned on several occasions his plans to overthrow the new president.[6] To strengthen his hand in northern Mexico, Cárdenas backed the conservative Obregonista anti-Ramos rebels in order to purge Sonora's political system of Callistas. Cárdenas's decision to back Sonora's conservatives was made after Calles returned from exile in December 1935. Many domestic and foreign observers believed that Calles was planning to seize power when he returned from the United States. Clearly, the situation did not bode well for Cárdenas when, on December 15, 1935, Sinaloa governor Manuel Paez met with Rodolfo Calles to discuss arms shipments that the Sinaloa state government had received in preparation for an armed uprising. The following day, there were rumors of a Callista rebellion in Xalapa, Veracruz, headed by Humberto Escobar. In the state of Mexico, Callistas carried out acts of terrorism; in Puebla, peasants were attacked by armed men shouting, "Viva Calles." Arms were reported to have been smuggled from the United States and Honduras into the states of Sonora, Chihuahua, Veracruz, Tabasco, and Durango in preparation for a January 1, 1936, coup to be led by Generals Pablo González and Jacinto Treviño. In early January, fifty armed Callistas terrorized villagers in Oaxaca. In Yucatán there were reports of a Callista uprising against local Cardenista authorities.[7] Despite the numerous threats, it is unlikely that the Callistas posed a serious military challenge to Cárdenas's government. Nevertheless, because the Cardenistas needed to firm up their support at the state level, they used legitimate threats and false alarms alike to consolidate or expand their regional hold on power. With Sonora under Callista rule, and lacking a loyal base to back him against el Jefe Máximo, Cárdenas removed Ramos from office and aligned with the conservative Obregonista faction.

In December 1935, Cárdenas replaced Ramos with the head of the Yaqui Military Zone, General Jesús Gutiérrez Cázares; he then deposed most of Sonora's executive, legislative, and judicial authorities, replaced all of the local police chiefs, and purged the defensas sociales, as well as many Callista-controlled municipal-level peasant and labor councils, assigned new military zone commanders, and granted amnesty to all anti-Ramos rebels. Sonora's anti-Callista/anti-Ramos conservative opposition laid down their arms in order to gain control of important positions in the new state and municipal governments. Political expediency and factional alliance, rather than ideological convictions, pushed Cárdenas into backing Sonora's anti-Callista opposition. Domestic politics surely made for strange bedfellows in Sonora.[8]

SONORAN POLITICS AFTER RAMOS

Although Cárdenas purged the Callistas from the Sonoran political establishment, he had difficulty putting together a loyal political base, because the interim Gutiérrez government lacked legitimacy and had alienated many segments of the population. In addition, Sonora's branch of the PNR was in shambles. Gutiérrez also was unable to lift Sonora out of the economic slump of the Depression, and in 1936 unemployment hit a ten-year state high. Economic conditions were so poor during Gutiérrez's year in office that rural workers complained of "a horrific crisis" in the Yaqui Valley. Lacking work, agraristas in the Peasant Union of Quechehueca petitioned the Gutiérrez government for 12 acres of land for each union member. Although the state government refused the request, it suggested that the agraristas should rent unused land from the valley's large property owners. When the growers—who had recently established the Confederation of Agricultural Associationes of the State of Sonora (Confederación de Asociaciones Agrícolas del Estado de Sonora, CAAES) to protect their properties—objected to the proposal, the Gutiérrez government sided with them and left the agraristas without assistance.[9] During his brief governorship, Gutiérrez also alienated the Yaqui Indians, a relationship that was already damaged during his tenure as military zone commander in the Yaqui Valley from 1931 to 1935. The interim governor viewed the Indians as backward, lazy, barbarous alcoholics who were jaded by their "ancestral hatred of white people."[10] When it became clear that the favored candidate in the upcoming gubernatorial elections was the conservative, anti-Cardenista Román Yocupicio (see figure 12), Cárdenas postponed it.

Yocupicio was a Mayo Indian and mayor of Navojoa, Sonora, from 1920 to 1923. As a brigadier general and a diehard Obregonista, Yocupicio rebelled against Calles in the failed 1929 Escobar rebellion. He was also infamous for leading a brutal military campaign against the Yaqui Indians in 1926 and 1927.

FIGURE 12. Sonoran Governor Román Yocupicio (1937–39). LORENZO GARIBALDI,
MEMORIA DE LA GESTIÓN GUBERNAMENTAL DEL C. GRAL. ROMÁN YOCUPICIO, 377, © 1939.

By 1936, however, in order to gain Yaqui support, he portrayed himself as an
Indian leader who championed the repatriation of the Yaquis that lived in
Arizona. Initially, Yocupicio was a member of the Sonoran Democratic Party
(Partido Democrático Sonorense), and his campaign for governor was financed
by Obregón's widow, María Tapia, landowners in the Mayo and Yaqui Valleys
who feared Cardenista agrarian reform, and merchants who opposed Cárdenas's pro-labor policies. At the national level, Yocupicio was tied to one of
Cárdenas's principal rivals, the conservative Secretary of Agriculture Saturnino
Cedillo—who would lead an armed uprising against Cárdenas in 1938. Yocupicio employed a regionalist discourse to establish his own power base and
promised to stem anticlericalism, keep national labor leaders at bay, and thwart
federal agrarian reform. By also positioning himself as a defender of Sonoran
autonomy, Yocupicio gained the endorsement of the disparate anti-Callista
factions, both elite and popular, who had rebelled against Ramos and now

wanted to prevent the imposition of an outside Cardenista carpetbagger on Sonora.[11]

Cárdenas's "semiofficial candidate," General Ignacio Otero Pablos, was unable to gain widespread support for a number of reasons. First, Gutiérrez's difficulties as interim governor undermined Otero Pablos's candidacy. Also, despite the fact that Otero Pablos was from Sonora and widely distributed his "substantial campaign funds" among the press and supporters, many Sonorans disliked having officials imposed on their state by the federal government. In fact, Otero Pablos was an odd pick on Cárdenas's part, since, as recently as early 1936, the general often sided with the landed elite against the interests of workers when he was the federal military commander in Yucatán. As Ben Fallaw shows, Otero Pablos ordered his Yucatecan troops to harass communists and urban and rural labor unions. Besides forming close ties with the local elite through marriage and political appointments, Otero Pablos also accepted money from Yucatecan hacendados for his Sonoran gubernatorial campaign. In light of their political differences, one could assume that Cárdenas encouraged Otero Pablos's candidacy in order to appease the military.[12]

In any event, Otero Pablos faced a formidable opponent, since Yocupicio remained popular throughout Sonora. Yocupicio's decision to run as a PNR candidate put the state's political bureaucracy behind him and facilitated his victory over Otero Pablos in the official party primary, which, in turn, assured his victory in the subsequent general election. His acceptance of the PNR candidacy was seen by Mexico City as an "olive branch" and an indication that he would work within the political system when challenging the Cardenista project. Yocupicio won the gubernatorial general election in November 1936 by a large majority and threatened to take up arms should electoral shenanigans by the federal government deny him victory. Such ultimatums were taken seriously. In fact, many contemporary observers believed that even a small, state-based revolt could spark a nationwide, "fascistlike" uprising like Spain's. Cárdenas's administration let Otero Pablos's defeat go uncontested because it preferred to confront Yocupicio in office, through political infighting and compromise, rather than on the battlefield. This does not mean that Cárdenas did not use force against his opponents. On the contrary, if the negotiations that surrounded state formation (in this case, relations between Sonora and the federal government) had not produced the desired result (in this case, reducing the military threat posed by Yocupicio and keeping him tied to the officials party), then Cárdenas probably would have used force to remove Yocupicio from office and install Otero Pablos. Cárdenas used force against Cedillo because, unlike Yocupicio, he very publicly broke from the revolutionary family and took up arms against the federal government. Yocupicio was smart enough not to follow such an ill-fated path.[13]

After 1935, Cárdenas's attempt to alter the Sonoran political landscape met with mixed success. Although he removed the immediate Callista threat by deposing Ramos, he was unable to build a powerful progressive political alliance and peacefully impose Otero Pablos as governor. The president now had three years before the next gubernatorial election to build a formidable anti-Yocupicio political coalition based on worker and campesino support. Not surprisingly, Yocupicio made it very difficult for him to do so. After he took office in January 1937, Yocupicio created an administration based on an informal network of patron-client relationships with local, regional, and national factions that were channeled through state and municipal governments, the state legislature and judiciary, and the Sonoran branch of the PNR. Yocupicio's tight control of the state's official party allowed him to purge municipal governments and use electoral fraud to ensure statewide victories for his supporters in the 1937 mayoral elections. Soon after entering office, Yocupicio also forced the State Supreme Court to resign and made the Sonoran legislature into a "mere rubber stamp body."[14]

As governor, Yocupicio pursued a conservative economic policy that thwarted agrarian reform, protected small landholdings, and promoted the development of Sonora's infrastructure through the construction of roads, dams, and irrigation canals. He did not want to see the American landowners leave the Yaqui Valley, since he rightly believed they ran industrious and progressive yet moderately sized agricultural enterprises that were evenly distributed throughout the valley. Yocupicio opposed Cárdenas's agrarian reform program for a number of reasons. First, he argued, the federal government did not have the resources to properly finance the ejidatarios. Second, he believed most ejidatarios were unprepared to farm using modern agricultural methods. Third, it would destroy productive farms, such as those operated by the Americans, even though the Mexican government held large amounts of idle lands throughout the state—including in the Yaqui Valley. Fourth, Yocupicio argued, Sonora's agrarian problem was not one of land scarcity but rather insufficient water.[15] Fifth, he was "disgusted politically" by agrarismo, as he declared on a number of occasions. In other words, he was upset that Cárdenas used agrarian reform to garner political support from the rural working class.[16] In short, because Yocupicio endorsed the Sonoran model that had characterized the political economy of his state and the federal government since 1920, he opposed the structural economic changes that the Cardenistas sought to bring to his region and much of the nation.

To combat the formation of a Cardenista power bloc in Sonora, Yocupicio assembled a conservative coalition of state government and PNR bureaucrats, municipal officials, the state police, veterans, state teachers, landowners, and cattle ranchers. He also established a number of state-sponsored unions that organized urban and rural day laborers and state bureaucrats. One of them, the Workers' Confederation of Sonora (Confederación de Trabajadores de Sonora, CTS), was created by Yocupicio, according to the U.S. vice consul in Guaymas (Sonora's main port city), "for the special purpose of fighting the CTM." The CTS also channeled labor demands against capital and backed Yocupicista candidates in official party primaries and state elections.[17] It would be wrong to assume that the formation of the Yocupicio coalition was solely from the top down (just as it would be wrong to view the formation of the Cardenista bloc in those terms) or that working-class solidarity is the historical norm. There are many examples of political splits among rural and industrial workers in postrevolutionary Mexico. As Jonathan Brown demonstrates in his study of the petroleum labor movement, not only did workers pressure their leaders, but divisions and competition existed within both the rank and file and among union leadership.[18]

Yocupicio also employed the "weapons of the strong" and violently repressed the Left. During his second month in office, Yocupicio deposed agraristas from the Huatabampo and Ciudad Obregón (Yaqui Valley) town councils; he also arrested Maximiliano "Machi" López, leader of the Worker and Peasant Federation of Southern Sonora (Federación Obrera y Campesina del Sur de Sonora, FOCSS)—which stood in opposition to Yocupicio's more conservative CTS—when López called a peasant unification congress.[19] Said Vicente Padilla, former secretary general of the Central Syndicate of the Valley (Sindicato Central del Valle)—which also stood in opposition to the CTS—"Yocupicio tried to stop us with threats and pressure, using leaders of the CTS and the judicial police, who would turn violent at any moment." During the summer of 1937, pro-Cárdenas CTM delegates, agraristas, and federal schoolteachers and inspectors were harassed, arrested, kidnapped and murdered by Yocupicio's henchmen. Thousands of campesinos and CTM unionists demonstrated against Yocupicio in June, as Cárdenas's office was flooded with complaints from Sonora and around the country regarding Yocupicio's brutality.[20]

The Cárdenas administration's primary concern stemmed from the belief that it could not rely on Yocupicio's support during a political or military crisis, since the conflict between the Yocupicista and Cardenista power blocs in Sonora was, according to Steven Sanderson, "a political expression of opposing class interests."[21] Consequently, Cárdenas set out to build a loyal political base that would counterbalance Sonora's conservative coalition and endorse a Cardenista candidate for governor in 1939, who, once elected, could implement far-reaching socioeconomic reforms and further solidify the progressive Cardenista political bloc. Land redistribution, irrigation works, technical support, and agricultural credit for the Yaqui and Mayo Valleys were federal political weapons designed to undermine Yocupicio's municipal dominance in Huatabampo, Ciudad Obregón, and Navojoa (Mayo Valley) and weaken the governor's conservative supporters.

Immediately after Yocupicio was inaugurated on January 4, 1937, the political climate in Sonora became stormier. As the CTM and those on the Left attacked Yocupicio, American landowners realized that their holdings would become political rewards given to the agraristas for their support of Cárdenas. One month after Yocupicio entered office, Gabino Vázquez, head of the federal Agrarian Department, met with the agraristas in the Yaqui Valley and promised them ejidos. Since Vázquez's office was empowered to redistribute land, and because it took another nine months for his offer to materialize, it is safe to conclude that he was probably acting without Cárdenas's consent. Whether Vázquez realized it or not, the invasion of CRLC's property in the Mexicali Valley had complicated matters for the president in terms of the impact that expropriating more American-owned property would have on U.S.-Mexican relations. Nevertheless, the administration had shown its hand. According to the U.S. vice consul, Alfonso Yepis, Vázquez "aimed at depicting President Cárdenas as the benefactor of the peasants" in order to broaden his base of support against Yocupicio. "There is no doubt in my mind," wrote Vice Consul Yepis, "that Cárdenas is now taking steps to weaken the conservative element in this country (of which Cedillo apparently is a principal leader), and that in Sonora the president's action might materialize in the form of granting all the demands of the Yaqui Valley agrarians. It is obvious that a strong political factor has entered into the purely agrarian problem in the Yaqui Valley."[22]

Contemporary observers believed that the president had used land reform in Sonora as a political weapon to undermine his opponents in the state and broaden the Cardenistas's political base of support.[23] However, to conclude that Cárdenas was motivated only by domestic politics when he chose to expropriate American-owned agricultural land in the Yaqui Valley would misread his presidency. Although Cárdenas used agrarian reform for political ends, he also was driven by a desire, as he was in the Mexicali Valley, to improve the living and working conditions of the region's rural proletariat. Prior to any political conflict with either Calles or Yocupicio, Cárdenas and future CTM leader Vicente Lombardo Toledano visited the Yaqui Valley in 1934 and discussed land reform with labor and peasant leaders Pascual Ayón, Maximiliano and Jacinto López, Vicente Padilla, and Saturnino Saldívar. Also, four months after assuming the presidency, in March 1935, Cárdenas ordered the federal Agrarian Department to establish a Mixed Agrarian Commission in the Sonoran capital of Hermosillo. Establishing commissions in each state, a process begun by the previous president, Abelardo Rodríguez, after the passage of the 1934 Agrarian Code, was part of a nationwide bureaucratic restructuring by the newly formed Agrarian Department intended to speed up agrarian reform. In any case, it appeared that from early on that Cárdenas intended to redistribute land in Sonora.[24]

THE AGRARISTA MOVEMENT IN THE YAQUI VALLEY AND CÁRDENAS'S ANTI-YOCUPICIO BLOC

Despite agrarista mobilization in the 1920s and early 1930s, as in Baja California, there was no meaningful land reform in Sonora before 1937, when Cárdenas redistributed more than 2.5 million acres of land statewide in the form of ejido grants and Indian restitutions. Although Obregón's government did redistribute 184,000 acres of land in Sonora between 1920 and 1924, most were for grazing. In fact, just 16,000 acres were suitable for cultivation, and only 6,200 acres were irrigated. Also, the one restitution made to the Yaqui Indians covered nonirrigated lands and was "more a symbol of reform than a precursor" of further indigenous restitutions. During Calles's administration from 1924 to 1928, some 67,000 acres were redistributed, which included a paltry 5,300 acres of cultivable land and 3,700 acres of irrigated land. During his term, no restitutions were made to the Yaqui Indians. Land redistribution increased some between 1928 and 1934, during the three administrations of Portes Gil, Ortiz Rubio, and Abelardo Rodríguez. By the early 1930s, however, only 3.6 percent of the five thousand square kilometers under cultivation in Sonora belonged to ejidos. In all, thirty-eight ejidos consisting of low-quality lands were granted to 4,071 ejidatarios. Because of the limited nature of agrarian reform prior to 1937, 90 percent of the Sonoran population was without land, while 919 latifundios—

each possessing more than 2,500 acres—controlled 89 percent of the state's agricultural holdings. Despite the radical nature of the revolution's agrarian laws, little substantive progress was made toward changing Sonora's land tenure system between 1920 and 1935, a period in which the rural economic policy of Mexico City and Hermosillo politicians mirrored that of Díaz. In other words, Mexico's postrevolutionary leaders before Cárdenas favored capital-intensive, privately owned, commercial agricultural production—as seen in the Yaqui and Mexicali Valleys. Moreover, since the Obregonistas and Callistas often redistributed national lands to quell agrarista unrest, their policies had little impact on the structure of private landownership.[25]

During the revolutionary and postrevolutionary eras, the Yaqui Valley's rich land and well-developed agricultural estates, like those in the Mexicali Valley, drew migrant laborers looking for work and a better life: an escape from violence, higher wages, and improved working and living conditions. Most migrants sought work as fieldhands, packers, loaders, and mill workers. Some rented plots of land from larger U.S. and Mexican property owners, and a few migrants even acquired their own small farms. The prosperous and productive Yaqui Valley employed some five thousand day laborers, several thousand migrant workers, and about six hundred Mayo Indians. As in the Mexicali Valley, debt peonage does not appear to have been used as a labor system.

Although most came from Sonora, a large percentage of migratory workers traveled from Chihuahua, Sinaloa, and the other western states of Jalisco, Nayarit, and Zacatecas. Before arriving in the Yaqui Valley, many migrant workers took jobs wherever they could find them, such as in mining and railroads. One example was the Saldívar family. Eulalia and Domingo Saldívar, along with their son and daughter, left Nayarit in the early 1920s for the border town of Nogales, Sonora, where Domingo worked on the railroads. The family then headed south with the hope of finding work in the Yaqui Valley's agricultural camps. "We walked like nomads," stated daughter Marcelina, until they settled in the pueblo El Yaqui. Domingo found work as a fieldhand elsewhere in the valley and returned every eight days to be with his family.[26] Another example was Vicente Hernández Padilla, who would later become a leader in the Yaqui Valley labor movement. Inviting ads in his local newspaper in Culiacán, Sinaloa, boasted about the opportunities in southern Sonora and raised his interest in the prospect of acquiring land and living near a modern city like Cajeme. Hoping to improve his life, in 1929 the twenty-year-old Padilla headed to the Yaqui Valley, intent on becoming a small landowner.[27]

Unaware that the Depression impelled many Mexican repatriates and miners in northern Mexico to flood the Yaqui Valley, thereby limiting land availability and job opportunities, Padilla found conditions more difficult than he was led to expect. Although he was unable to afford to purchase land, he still desired his own plot. After working in the fields for a number of years, Padilla realized that the only way he or the other field hands could gain land was by receiving an ejido. According to one agrarista descendant, the workers wanted to see and taste for themselves, as had the foreigners, what it meant to be an owner. Not only was that "their passion," but it was also their "revenge" for years of exploitation as rural laborers.[28]

Not all agraristas, however, were vengeful. For some, the passion to own land was inspired not by exploitation but by their admiration of the property owners and the amiable relationship that they had with them. Unlike the large and more traditional haciendas found elsewhere in Mexico, many owners of small- and medium-sized estates in the Yaqui Valley worked side by side with their employees. This was especially the case with the American farmers. The Americans not only got their hands dirty but also employed advanced farming techniques, showed their workers how to use modern machinery, and paid their staff comparatively well. Said one field worker, Alfonso Encinas García, "The farmers taught me to think." Some showed their employees how to grow crops. Such relationships contradict conventional wisdom regarding plantations and rural labor relations that depicts owners as maintaining brutal control through a cycle of debt and submissive agricultural workers as ready to explode against the repressive system under which they toil.[29] Moreover, as Christopher Boyer illustrates in postrevolutionary Michoacán, the lack of a dominant political ideology in many states, including Sonora and Baja California, meant that rural workers viewed their particular situations differently and had a variety of political discourses to choose from. Some were simply apolitical, while others held multiple, and at times contradictory, positions concomitantly.[30] The lack of a unifying campesino ideology and the distinct views of social reality held by Sonora's rural workers were exploited by conservative leaders like Yocupicio— which in turn weakened the Yaqui Valley agrarista movement.

As in the Mexicali Valley, the agrarista movement in the Yaqui Valley was influenced by ideas of modernity. Southern Sonoran landowners, both American and Mexican, modernized the region by bringing packing plants, processing mills, irrigation works, reapers, tractors, cars, trucks, motorcycles, and machines to the Yaqui Valley. According to Mary Kay Vaughn, agraristas also sought these tools of modernity, as well as their own land on which to use them, in order to make their work easier and their lives richer. As in Baja California, many agraristas associated a higher standard of living with the ability to purchase modern conveniences such as sewing machines, oil stoves, corn-grinding mills, canned food, medicines, beds, shoes, perfume, and more fashionable clothing. In other words, while some agraristas fought for land redistribution in the Yaqui Valley due to a radical ideological conviction that was based on a utopian vision of communal agriculture, most of Sonora's rural workers simply sought a "more modern and convenient lifestyle," which they believed would stem from landownership, whether individual or communal.[31]

Not surprisingly, when increasing unemployment and falling wages during the Depression pushed greater numbers of Yaqui Valley field workers to mobilize, they often sought to gain possession of the American-owned estates because they usually were the most valuable holdings in the valley. Most American properties were in close proximity to Ciudad Obregón, employed modern technology, had access to irrigation, and boasted substantial improvements—including fences, canals, drainage works, pumping plants, storage facilities, and other buildings. In fact, both U.S. and Mexican claims commissioners later estimated that in the Yaqui Valley, American-owned lands were four times more valuable than Mexican-owned properties.[32]

Notions of modernity were propagated by federal teachers who started organizing peasants around the country, including the Yaqui Valley, during the Maximato. Since the rural labor movement in the valley needed and actively sought influential allies in Mexico City, when Cárdenas entered office, his administration had little difficulty mobilizing Sonora's landless campesinos. Cárdenas simply used the CTM, as well as federal teachers from the Ministry of Public Education who already were working in Sonora, to align the Yaqui Valley's agrarian movement more closely to the interests of his government. There was a clear commonality of economic and political interests, as both sides realized that they could not obtain their complementary goals without each other's support. Although federal teachers and the CTM were important nonagrarian actors shaping the movement of rural proletarians in the Yaqui Valley, to see either the agrarian movement or the October 1937 *reparto* (land grants) as solely the work of secondary mobilization (i.e., subordinate groups organized from the top down) would misrepresent the grassroots initiative and perseverance of the valley's agraristas.[33]

If we consider the important role played by both local and outside actors in

Sonora's land reform program, and note the factionalism among Sonora's rural workers, as well as the different views of the Yaqui and Mayo Indians toward their respective ancestral homelands, the categorization of the agrarian reform process as either "primary" or "secondary" does not account for its inherent complexity.[34] The agrarista movements in both the Yaqui and Mexicali Valleys challenge the revisionist interpretation that sees subordinate groups merely as pawns manipulated by a Machiavellian federal power structure that was controlled by Cárdenas. As Alan Knight rightly argues, the top-down model of agrarian reform "should be replaced by a dialectical model which sees 'manipulation' (or reciprocal political bargaining) as proceeding both ways, top-down and bottom-up."[35]

Sonora did not experience the same agrarian revolution from below that took place in central Mexico in the 1910s. In fact, agrarista pressure did not manifest itself until the end of the decade, and it was distinct from the more militant movement of rural proletarians that coalesced during the 1920s and 1930s. Most of Sonora's land petitions during the late 1910s were presented by peasant villages seeking to regain communal grazing lands lost during the mid–nineteenth century Reforma. However, the rapid expansion of commercial agriculture in the Yaqui and Mayo Valleys during the 1920s, plus the region's high rural wages, attracted impoverished migrant workers from other parts of the state and country. This fundamentally altered the character of rural labor relations.[36] According to one contemporary observer, the majority of the agraristas involved in the Yaqui Valley movement were "not old-time residents of this section" but instead had arrived "within the past few years from Sinaloa and other parts [of Mexico]." It would not take long for the valley's newly arrived rural proletariat to mobilize.[37]

One of the most important leaders of the agrarista movement in the Yaqui Valley during the 1920s and 1930s was Pascual Ayón. A blacksmith from Durango, many of Ayón's supporters saw him as a "responsible and morally reputable man" who was "the moving spirit of the agraristas." Many American landowners, on the other hand, referred to him as "a bad hombre." According to one biased American source, Ayón claimed that he would "not be satisfied until he [brought] about the ruin" of leading American landowners in the Yaqui Valley. Prior to Cárdenas's 1937 reparto, the U.S. consulate in Guaymas reported that of all the *pueblos* (villages) in the Yaqui Valley, Ayón's was "the most vehement in its demand for lands under the Agrarian Code."[38] Ayón, like many agraristas in the valley, did not align with political movements for ideological reasons; rather, he sided with the faction that best addressed the needs of his pueblo, fittingly named El Yaqui. In the 1920s, for instance, Ayón was an Obregonista. In 1929, after Obregón's assassination, he became a Callista and received a political post and land for his *poblado* (settlement). Following Ramos's overthrow in 1935, Ayón sided with Cardenas, who promised to redistribute land in the valley. By the early 1940s, Ayón rejected the Cardenistas and their communal ejidos and again sided with the Obregonistas/Yocupicistas, who called for parcelization of the communal ejidos.

With little more than his typewriter and inspired by the "ideal of land, water, work and justice," from 1921 to 1937 Ayón fought for land redistribution in the valley. According to one of his descendants, Aurora Ayala de Ayón, it would have been a betrayal of both the working people of Sonora and the revolution if land was not redistributed in the valley. As head of the valley's branch of the Obregonista National Agrarista Party (Partido Nacional Agrarista), Ayón denounced the massive concession held by the Los Angeles/Sonora-based Richardson Construction Company (Compañia Constructora Richardson, CCR). When he requested land for his settlement in 1921, Ayón argued that the Constitution's Article 27 prohibited foreign-owned companies such as CCR from possessing property within fifty miles of the coast. In 1936, Ayón would make the same argument against individual American-owned farms located within the prohibited zone.[39]

Two years after Ayón's complaint against CCR, he submitted a formal petition in April 1923 for ejidal land on behalf of his pueblo. In the early 1920s, approximately 30 families lived in the center of El Yaqui, with another 150 on the outskirts of the settlement. The grant, according to Aurora, would allow the pueblo "to cover its needs and establish its economic independence." A few weeks later, on the symbolic Cinco de Mayo, a group of radical day laborers invaded part of the Richardson holdings, planted a number of red and black flags, menaced some American growers, and paralyzed their works. Worried that the invasion would lead to expropriation, company officials argued that their property was exempt from appropriation, since federal law prohibited the expropriation of land that was held under a colonization contract. To allay the company's concerns and, more importantly, quell agrarista discontent, in October 1923 Obregón's government bought 800 acres from CCR and the following spring made the first land grant in the Yaqui Valley to a group of mestizos near the city of Cajeme. No grant was made to Ayón's poblado. In fact, Ayón's 1923 petition was rejected by President Calles in 1926 on the grounds argued earlier by CCR officials. Such excuses led one valley worker, Alfonso Encinas García, to refer to the Richardson brothers as the "untouchables."[40]

Obregón gained a great deal of support in the Yaqui Valley following the 1923 grant, and his popularity increased further when he negotiated the federal government's 1926 purchase of CCR's holdings. According to Aurora Ayala de Ayón, "the farm workers were jubilant over the Richardson sale to the federal government," and the "handing over of the [company's] lands to the people inspired their fight." Not surprisingly, pueblo El Yaqui endorsed Obregón's reelection in 1928. However, the negative economic impact of the Great Depression and President Calles's declaration that the Richardson tract would be nationalized through colonization and not ejidal redistribution led many agraristas to "lose hope" and become "demoralized," recalled Ayala de Ayón. Like their counterparts in the Mexicali Valley, rural workers in the Yaqui Valley were too poor to purchase tracts and become colonists. After Calles's announcement, some became convinced they were "destined to remain day laborers and slaves for the rest of their lives."[41]

Although Calles virtually ignored the demands of the Yaqui Valley agraristas during his administration, Ayón's grassroots leadership helped the rural labor movement to grow. Besides writing prolifically and filing repeated petitions on behalf of his fellow agraristas, Ayón organized nighttime meetings in which rural workers could discuss politics, the 1928 presidential succession, and agrarian issues. Following Obregón's assassination and Calles's subsequent formation of the PNR in 1929, Calles either purged the Obregonistas from positions of power in Sonora or co-opted them to broaden his support. As such, in 1929 Calles appointed Ayón—a noted Obregonista—as PNR secretary for the Yaqui Valley. To keep Ayón's loyalty, later that year the Callistas who controlled the Sonoran state government made a small provisional ejidal grant to Ayón's poblado. Unfortunately, in 1933 President Rodríguez refused to sign the definitive resolution granting the ejido, and so pueblo El Yaqui never received the land. Surely this must have increased the moral outrage of Ayón and the other workers in his village and explained why he again petitioned for lands.[42]

The Depression had a significant impact on the Yaqui Valley and the agrarista movement. Unemployed mineworkers from northern Sonora and repatriated Mexicans from Arizona filled the valley's agricultural camps. By the mid-1930s, nearly 90 percent of Sonora's rural labor force was concentrated in the southern Yaqui and Mayo Valleys. The flood of migrants depressed rural wages, fomented labor militancy, and stimulated new petitions for land from repatriados who wanted their own plot to sow. Labor leaders such as Ramón Olivarría and Vicente Padilla organized flour mill workers at Campo 65. In 1932, they formed the Sindicato Central del Valle and pressured the growers to regulate work hours and adhere to federal labor and agrarian laws. Olivarría also had rural workers study the new labor codes and read magazines, newspapers, and illustrated accounts on the labor movement and abusive bosses. Like the agraristas in the Mexicali Valley, the mill workers from Campo 65 also used theater as an educational vehicle to promote social change. Outside one of the Yaqui Valley mills, workers, artists, and a schoolteacher performed political plays that targeted the owners. The Sindicato Central del Valle became the kernel of the Union of Workers and Peasants (Unión de Obreros y Campesinos), which later became part of the Federación Obrera y Campesina del Sur de Sonora (FOCSS). During the early 1930s, labor leaders like Padilla and Olivarría traveled throughout the Yaqui Valley and held assemblies, established unions, and negotiated work contracts; they sought higher wages, better living and working conditions, direct worker control over certain aspects of agricultural production, agrarian reform, and political power at the regional and national level. The fact that Cárdenas would later use Sonora's unified worker and peasant federations to promote his own political interests and facilitate land redistribution throughout the state runs counter to the revisionist argument that posits he purposefully separated these two subordinate groups to weaken each, in order to control them more easily.[43]

Despite their activism, the Yaqui Valley agraristas were unable to win ejidal grants. Consequently, some of them tried to obtain land through colonization. In 1932, the Union of Workers and Peasants of Pueblo El Yaqui petitioned local officials for land in the name of hundreds of "poor workers . . . who have lived and are still living a ridiculous life of misery and slavery, . . . who want to dedicate themselves to agriculture" and improve their "well-being." The campesinos requested ten colonies from the former CCR holdings now under federal control, citing the federal colonization law of April 1926 to justify their claim.[44] Two years later, the union still had no answer to their request. After the passage of the 1934 Agrarian Code, the campesinos again petitioned for land. This time, however, besides requesting colonies from the CCR holdings, the union cited Article 27 of the 1917 Constitution and asked for ejidal grants from the nearby American-owned estates. Mary Kay Vaughan argues that these petitions, based "on collective rights as expressed in the Mexican Constitution and in subsequent labor and agrarian law," represent the adoption of a "language of modern legality" based on "a modern notion of class." Since Governor Rodolfo

Calles had little interest in undermining the Yaqui Valley's privately owned productive enterprises, he rejected the petition without explanation.[45]

During the early 1930s, field workers in Sonora's southern agricultural valleys remained landless, but not for lack of trying. Before Cárdenas took office, Mexico's paternalistic political elite had little interest in empowering subaltern groups and disrupting the socioeconomic and political status quo. After a decade of mobilization that had achieved very little, in the early 1930s Sonora's agraristas sought to increase their strength by unifying with nonpeasant worker organizations. Driven by a desire to obtain land, and impelled by high unemployment, falling wages, and economic insecurity resulting from the Depression, peasant leagues and worker unions throughout the state conglomerated into larger, regional Federations of Workers and Campesinos (Federaciónes de Obreros y Campesinos, FOCs) headquartered in Hermosillo, Hautabampo, Guaymas, Ures, Nogales, Alamos, Navojoa (Mayo Valley), and Ciudad Obregón (Yaqui Valley). The different regional FOCs varied in their militancy and political muscle, with the most radical ones located in the southern agricultural valleys and the most conservative ones aligned with Yocupicio in the state capital of Hermosillo.[46]

A critical event in the Yaqui Valley agrarista movement was the formation, in May 1934, of a regional FOC in Ciudad Obregón. The new FOCSS unified the militant rural workers in Campos 60, 74, and 80 under the leadership of Jacinto and Maximiliano "Machi" López, Matías Méndez, and Rafael "Buqui" Contreras. The López brothers had previously worked with organized railroad workers in Empalme, Sonora, and brought "mature" union experience to the agrarista movement. Boyer refers to these types of labor leaders as "village revolutionaries," whose personal experience—including travel, employment, and work with "well-organized labor unions" in Mexico or the United States—influenced how they organized rural workers. As an umbrella organization for rural proletarians, the FOCSS incorporated the most militant unions in the Yaqui Valley, such as the Industrial Syndicate of the Bácum Valley (Sindicato Industrial del Valle Bácum), led by Saturnino Saldívar and Vicente Padilla, the Progressivist Industrial Syndicate (Sindicato Industrial Progresista), led by Pedro Retamoza, and the Syndicate of the Eastern Yaqui Valley (Sindicato Oriental del Valle del Yaqui).[47] Thus, when Cárdenas assumed the presidency seven months later, the agraristas in the Yaqui Valley were already mobilized, and during the 1935 anti-Ramos revolt, Mexico's new president began to address their needs and seek their endorsement.

As in the Mexicali Valley, in the Yaqui Valley agraristas invited Cárdenas's government to play an important role in state socioeconomic and political affairs by petitioning the federal government for land and demanding improvements in infrastructure, along with the fruits of modernity. And, as it did with Baja California, Mexico City welcomed the opportunity to increase its political and socioeconomic presence in Sonora. The agraristas' demands for things associated with social progress and economic development aligned well with the interests of federal officials, who eagerly sought to deliver to these far off regions. Neither location, however, was unique. Similar quid pro quo arrangements existed throughout the country, as Cárdenas's administration literally delivered the goods in exchange for local support.

The Yaqui Valley's status as a colonization concession that was exempt from expropriation ended in November 1935, when Cárdenas opened the valley to ejidal grants.[48] Cárdenas's move, which came shortly after he forced Calles from power, indicates his early decision to increase the federal government's economic and political presence in Sonora and to use land redistribution as a political weapon within the state. Not surprisingly, agrarista activity in the Yaqui Valley increased substantially after Cárdenas's decree in late 1935. Now with the tools of the state at their disposal, when the agraristas in pueblo El Yaqui petitioned again for ejidos, they wrote directly to the president.[49] Ayón, who still headed the agrarista movement in his pueblo, was now president of its Special Committee of the Agrarian Executive Council (Comité Particular del Ejecutivo Agrario)—a small and seemingly independent organization with local concerns that later would affiliate with FOCSS and be tied to the CTM. In his petition, Ayón decried the difficult conditions that existed in the Yaqui Valley and argued that the high unemployment rate forced many campesinos to steal in order to eat.[50] The income of farm workers in the Yaqui Valley had dropped precipitously during the Depression, from $2.33 pesos a day in 1929 to $1.56 pesos by 1935.[51]

To improve El Yaqui's chances of receiving land, Ayón undertook an impressive writing campaign, typing seven letters a day with the hope of gaining the support of any agency that was connected to agrarian reform. As seen with the Mexicali agraristas, and as will be shown with the Yaqui Indians, Sonora's agraristas appropriated the elite's revolutionary ideology and political rhetoric when making demands on federal officials and their respective agencies. Subaltern groups were cognizant of their constitutional rights; they frequently cited specific agrarian reform legislation (for example, the 1915 Agrarian Law, Article 27 of the Constitution, and the 1934 Agrarian Code), and invoked revolutionary slogans ("land for those who work it" and "Mexico for Mexicans") in their correspondence. It is difficult to tell whether the agraristas and indigenous groups employed such rhetoric in a Machiavellian attempt to reach their particular goals and obtain federal largess or if they were sincere in their convictions. Most likely it was a little of both and varied in degree from community to community and even from person to person. In any case, Cárdenas's administration responded favorably to such petitions, since they fit well with the federal government's socioeconomic and political agenda for rural Mexico. While most government ministries, peasant leagues, and political parties endorsed Ayón's call for ejidos, the Confederación Campesina Mexicana was the most supportive. The CCM, which would later be replaced by the Confederación Nacional Campesina, was the centralized peasant organization employed by the Cardenistas to facilitate ejido distribution. León García, secretary general of the CCM, repeatedly wrote to numerous government agencies on behalf of their "*compañeros*" (comrades) in pueblo El Yaqui, asking for help in resolving the campesinos' agrarian problems.[52]

The Yaqui Valley agrarista movement was assisted by federal schoolteachers. To hasten the construction of a national coalition based on worker and peasant support, Cárdenas called on Mexico's federal teachers to suspend their antireligious campaign and focus on redistributive reforms. Most federal teachers, like Cárdenas, believed that the state could emancipate and redeem the peasantry through public education. Many teachers in the Yaqui Valley, including Cornelio Ramírez Vásquez of Campo 6, Eusebio Morales of Campo 7, and Jesús Madrigal of Campo 27, helped agraristas to organize, file ejidal petitions, and fight for minimum-wage labor contracts, a six-day work week, vacation pay, medical care, union recognition, and cooperatives, as well as better working and living conditions. Federal teachers throughout the 1930s remained at the forefront of the revolution and sought to infuse a leftist ideology into the countryside that, according to Vaughan, was "populist" and "nationalist" as well. In the Centers for Pedagogical Cooperation (Centros de Cooperación Pedagógica), for instance, they taught rural workers about agrarian and labor laws, cooperativism, and the subordination of Mexico's economy to foreign imperialism.[53]

After the passage of the Expropriation Law in 1936 and the government's expropriation of millions of acres in the Laguna later that year, expectations rose among radical groups and tensions increased in the Yaqui Valley. Agraristas went to Mexico City and personally asked Cárdenas to break up the estates in the valley. Meanwhile, the Mixed Agrarian Commission in Hermosillo was flooded with petitions for ejidos, and "marches, conventions, and demonstrations proliferated in the Valley." The landowners grew concerned over the turn of events and tried to frighten the agraristas by throwing some of them out of their homes and using white guards as hired guns to intimidate field workers against petitioning for land. Ayón feared for his life and avoided leaving his house because of the death threats made against him by some of the growers. In October 1936, Ayón and his supporters stole all of the rifles from the El Yaqui police station; a week later he wrote to Cárdenas asking for more arms to form the *defensas rurales* (organized groups of armed peasants).[54]

Initially, Cárdenas did not hesitate to arm the agraristas in the Yaqui Valley or other regions of the country. To strengthen his position, as well as those of his most ardent supporters, in October 1936 Cárdenas created a seventy thousand member national peasant militia known as the Agrarian Reserve, which was often trained and armed by the military.[55] By late 1936, over three thousand Sonoran agraristas were armed, and in the Mayo and Yaqui Valleys the defensas rurales were considered a powerful force. Moreover, in a state like Sonora—which was a great distance from Mexico City and controlled by an antagonistic government—arming the campesinos provided the Cárdenas administration with political and military leverage against unruly local officials who opposed federal reforms. It also kept the national military and state forces in check. According to U.S. observers, the Yaqui Valley police had been disarmed by armed agraristas, who were now "in complete control of the Valley."[56] According to one American landowner, since the Yaqui Valley agraristas were armed, they "pretty much do as they please."[57] The president also provided weapons to individual campesinos, agrarista leaders, agrarian committees, teachers, and local officials when they requested arms to protect themselves or organize rural defense units.[58]

In organizing his rural base, Cárdenas relied heavily on the CTM, which was led by one of his strongest allies, Vicente Lombardo Toledano (see figure 13). Formed in February 1936, the CTM was a national labor organization comprised of three thousand independent labor unions, with more than one million members. With Lombardo Toledano as its strident secretary general and enjoying broad federal support, the CTM soon became the most powerful labor organization in the country. The CTM did not just organize urban and industrial workers but also successfully targeted rural agricultural workers and repeatedly called for hastened land redistribution. In fact, not only did the CTM

FIGURE 13. CTM leader Vicente Lombardo Toledano addressing a rally in Mexico City ca. 1938.
AGN, ARCHIVO FOTOGRÁFICO, FONDO ENRIQUE DÍAZ, 59/27.

play a critical role in organizing rural workers in Laguna's cotton district, but—
from as early as June 1935—Lombardo Toledano called for dividing the Laguna
haciendas into ejidos. In Sonora, the CTM similarly mobilized the rural proletariat in the state's southern valleys. This does not mean, however, that the
Yaqui Valley labor movement was only a product of outside forces. Quite the
contrary, from the outset, the already-organized agraristas in the Yaqui Valley's
FOCSS provided the CTM with both its Sonoran leadership and rank and file
after the national union arrived in the valley in early 1936. This, in turn, facilitated the CTM's work in the state and allowed it to play an important role in
Sonoran municipal politics.[59]

Besides organizing workers and campesinos, the CTM attacked the administration's conservative opponents. Once Yocupicio took office, Lombardo Toledano launched a state- and nationwide campaign against the new governor.
Because Cárdenas allowed some important decisions to be made by his key
collaborators and at times had them intervene on his behalf vis-à-vis the states,
and in light of the shrill exchange between the CTM chief and the Sonoran
governor, Lombardo Toledano was likely acting to some degree on his own.

Lombardo Toledano portrayed Yocupicio as a conservative who suppressed Sonora's workers and peasants, frequently referred to the governor as a "reactionary" and "fascist," and accused him of smuggling arms into Sonora for an anti-Cardenista rebellion. Throughout Yocupicio's two years in office, the CTM leader repeatedly called for his resignation.[60] By the spring of 1937, Yocupicio's position as governor had weakened to such an extent that many predicted "his administration would not last unless he completely abandoned his conservative stand," and acted, or at least appeared, more radical. To save his governorship, Yocupicio spoke rhetorically on behalf of workers and peasants while simultaneously defending the state's conservative interests and attacking its radical groups.[61]

As the year progressed, federal support and the success of the worker and peasant movements around the country helped strengthen Sonora's peasant and labor organizations. In Cárdenas's opinion, divisions among workers were an "obstacle" to their "economic liberation."[62] In June 1937, the CTM sponsored a unification congress in Ciudad Obregón and formed the Workers' Federation of Sonora (Federación de Trabajadores de Sonora, FTS)—an umbrella organization designed to unite the regional FOC organizations from around the state. Many rural laborers now joined previously organized mineworkers, railway workers, and urban artisans under a single federation. With the exception of the military zone commanders, by 1938 the FTS/CTM represented most of the Cardenista coalition in Sonora: workers, agraristas, federal employees, and SEP teachers. One of the leaders of the Yaqui Valley FOCSS, Jacinto López, was elected the first secretary general of the FTS when it was established, indicating the importance of the Yaqui Valley rural labor movement to the overall state. The FOCSS and the agraristas of the Yaqui Valley were now officially a CTM affiliate and closely tied to the federal government. Reflecting back on the significance of the unification congress, Padilla stated, "We were adding to the national labor current of which agricultural workers constituted its main strength."[63]

No CTM labor congress in Sonora would have been complete without public attacks on Yocupicio. Labor and agrarista leaders called the Sonoran governor a "blind instrument of the landowners" and criticized his "tolerance of religious fanaticism" and repression of workers. Yocupicio responded to the verbal attacks by arresting CTM leaders Fidel Velázquez, Rodolfo Piña Soria, and eight other delegates at the June 1937 unification congress. The governor's aggressive reaction impelled thousands of agraristas and urban workers to

FIGURE 14. Cárdenas (right) meets a Mexican peasant (left), ca. late 1930s. AGN, ARCHIVO FOTOGRÁFICO, FONDO CÁRDENAS, 63/24.

march in Ciudad Obregón, which was the center of Sonoran radicalism, and demand the release of their comrades. The CTM held a one-hour sympathy strike in Mexico City, and Lombardo Toledano intensified his anti-Yocupicio campaign. Shortly thereafter, the Sonoran governor released the labor leaders. By mid-1937, the conflict between Lombardo Toledano and Yocupicio had turned into a violent feud. According to the CTM leader, when he arrived in Hermosillo in September 1937, Yocupicio's supporters greeted him with shouts of "death to Lombardo Toledano" and tried to assassinate him. Yocupicio denied the charges and claimed that Lombardo Toledano had been secretly traveling throughout the state, creating disturbances and avoiding authorities by disguising himself in women's clothes.[64]

Even though Yocupicio continued to attack radical groups throughout the first half of 1937, the FOCSS, the FTS, the CTM, and Lombardo Toledano continued to press Cárdenas to break up the lands in the Yaqui and Mayo Valleys. In July 1937, agraristas from both regions sent a delegation, including Ayón, to meet with Cárdenas in Mexico City and pressure him to resolve their agrarian problems. The same month, Cárdenas sent a group of engineers from the Agrarian Department to the southern valleys to survey the land and conduct an agrarian census. Meanwhile, the head of the Agrarian Department, Gabino Vázquez, promised Ayón that the land would be divided in three months' time—which it was.[65] By September it was clear that the lands were to be parceled out, and agrarista leaders Maximiliano López, Rafael Contreras, and Aurelio García went to Mexico City to receive instructions from federal authorities. When they returned to the Yaqui Valley, they organized commissions throughout the camps to receive land.[66] Seven weeks later, on October 27, 1937, Cárdenas issued the long-awaited presidential *acuerdo*, the resolution that decreed the redistribution of approximately 1.3 million acres of land in the Yaqui Valley to both the agraristas and the Yaqui Indians. Ayón and the campesinos in El Yaqui immediately thanked Cárdenas for their ejidal grant and pledged to serve him and the republic. Although the Yaquis received most of the land, more than 2,160 nonindigenous ejidatarios obtained 108,000 acres on the south bank of the Yaqui River, of which half was American-owned. Meanwhile, Ayón's settlement, El Yaqui, became Ejido El Yaqui and received 19,200 acres of land, of which half were irrigated and half were grazing lands. Plots of 20 acres were distributed to 470 campesinos from El Yaqui, twice the size of standard ejido grants. And only 750 acres of Mexican-owned land, as opposed to 18,450 acres of American property, were distributed to the new ejido.[67]

RESTITUTION OF THE YAQUI ANCESTRAL HOMELANDS

For over four hundred years, the *Yoeme* (the name the Yaquis call themselves in their native language) fervently defended their homelands from Spanish and later Mexican incursion. After Mexican independence in the early 1820s, the Yaquis had fought the federal army to maintain tribal and territorial autonomy against the encroaching Mexican state. They also sought to halt the advance of the *Yori* (Mexicans, Europeans, Americans, or other foreigners) and their "capitalist" forms of land tenure and labor relations, into the valley.[68] Despite this resistance, the Yaquis were attacked and either massacred, pacified, or deported to other parts of Mexico by Díaz's regime in the late nineteenth century. The Porfirians' heavy-handed policies were designed to transfer control of Yaqui lands to private interests and hasten their assimilation into mainstream mestizo culture. Despite deportation, many Yaquis outside Sonora "maintained their identity through a strong awareness of their homeland and by continuing to practice their socioreligious institutions in the new locations," claims anthropologist Thomas Sheridan.[69] Such ethnic consciousness, ritual behavior, and tenacity facilitated their return to the Yaqui Valley after Díaz left office in 1911.

During the Mexican Revolution and continuing throughout the 1920s, thousands of surviving Yaqui exiles and their descendants returned to their ancestral homelands in southwestern Sonora. Although they were kept out of the valley's most fertile lands, located south of the Yaqui River, they nevertheless tried to re-establish their autonomous indigenous communities. Most resettled on the north bank of the river and became landless agricultural workers. In the mid-1910s, the Yaquis began to attack or squat on local homesteads throughout the valley. Although they had fought initially alongside the Constitutionalist Army during the revolution—mostly to regain their lands—Venustiano Carranza's government responded to their sometimes violent incursions with military force in May 1917. Federal troops rounded up the Yaquis and placed them in concentration camps, an action that resulted in more than thirty Yaqui deaths. Shortly thereafter, the Yaquis who were sequestered in the concentration camps fled, and violent raids against the valley's landowners resumed. Over the next few years, little improved with respect to the Yaquis' living condition or their relations with federal authorities.[70]

Since force had only worsened the Yaquis' plight in the mid-1920s they shifted tactics and—like many indigenous groups throughout Mexico—tried to take advantage of the new constitutional laws that restored lands to Indian villages. In 1925, Yaqui Indian chief Francisco Pluma Blanca (see figure 15) petitioned the federal government for land under the constitutional provision that provided for the restitution of usurped property to indigenous communities. Pluma Blanca specifically asked that the lands surrounding the village of Bácum, Sonora, be returned to them, since it was one of the eight original Yaqui mission communities established by the Jesuits in the early 1600s.[71] For their part, the Yaquis sought to turn back the clock to an earlier period, when they held extensive areas of land and were relatively independent of both the Mexican and Sonoran states.

Probably for these and other reasons, Calles's administration denied Pluma Blanca's request. Meanwhile, as the valley's nonindigenous population increased in the mid-1920s, the situation worsened for the Yaquis. Greater amounts of water were diverted away from the north bank (the Yaqui side) and toward the agriculturally rich south bank, where American growers had most of their lands. Peaceful petitions to the federal government brought them no dividends, so in late 1926 and early 1927 the Yaquis again took up arms. In September 1926, at the Yaqui Valley train station of Vícam, one thousand armed Yaqui Indians pinned down former president Obregón and 150 federal troops prisoner and held them for two days. After he was allowed to leave without incident, with the

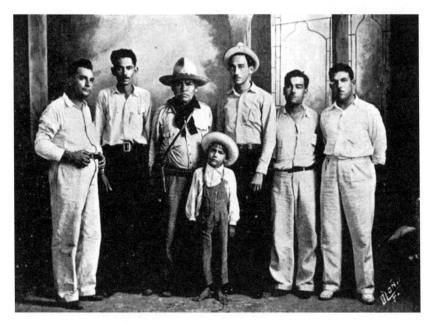

FIGURE 15. Yaqui Indian chief Francisco Pluma Blanca (center, with gun holster) meets with Secretary General of the CGT Julio Ramírez (center, with hat) and CTS leader Porfirio Valencia (far left), along with other CTS officials, ca. mid-1930s. LORENZO GARIBALDI, *MEMORIA DE LA GESTIÓN GUBERNAMENTAL DEL C. GRAL. ROMÁN YOCUPICIO*, 125, © 1939.

aid of additional federal troops, Obregón vowed to annihilate the Yaquis. A few months later, twenty thousand federal troops under generals Yocupicio and Antonio Ríos Zertuche attacked the Yaquis living in the valley and "inflicted severe losses" on them. Hundreds of Yaquis were killed, and more were chased into the nearby Bacatete Mountains, where they were bombed by military aircraft. Many of the Yaquis who fled from the mountains during the bombardment were either captured and conscripted into the army or else deported. Yocupicio then took command of the so-called Yaqui country on the river's north bank, and in March 1927 some one thousand Yaqui men, women, and children were forcefully resettled into small towns in Mexico's interior. From that point until the mid-1930s, repression pervaded the Yaqui country, which resembled a military camp with thousands of federal troops stationed in Yaqui villages.[72] Indian leaders' requests for land and water were repeatedly denied by either state or federal authorities. Despite (or maybe because of) official repression and intransigence, the Yaquis continued to resist the entrenched powers by invading or squatting upon privately held valley lands.[73]

When Cárdenas became president, Yaqui leaders, including Chief Pluma

Blanca, again requested the return of their homelands from the federal government. Asserted one governor of the eight Yaqui pueblos, "The lands expropriated and occupied by the whites . . . , in addition to the towns of Bácum and Cocorit . . . , belong to this Yaqui tribe. . . . And, Ciudad Obregón, where the lands are cultivated and occupied by the whites, is also the property of the Yaqui tribe. For this reason the governors of the eight towns request that the property that was taken from us in past epochs by ambitious men be returned in some definite way for the progress of the Yaqui tribe."[74] In light of decades of Yaqui oppression and resistance, Cárdenas recognized the mutual distrust between the Yaquis, their nonindigenous neighbors, and state and federal officials. He also realized it would take a great deal of time and federal effort to overcome these divisions, bring prosperity to the region, and, as he put it, "incorporate the Yaquis into the social life of the Mexican nation."[75] To reach these goals, Cárdenas believed that he needed to respond to Yaqui demands and initiate a federal interventionist project in the Yaqui Valley. According to one Mexican newspaper, Cárdenas sought to "right the wrongs inflicted upon the Yaquis over the past half-century, especially the seizure of tribal property and the sale of their most fertile lands to foreigners."[76] Cárdenas sincerely desired to improve the living and working conditions of the Yaqui Indians, just as he did for agraristas in the southern half of the valley.[77] During his campaign tour through Yaqui country in 1934, Cárdenas called for land restitution, along with the establishment of agricultural zones and irrigation canals, "to resolve definitively the eternal Yaqui problem." In Cárdenas's mind, the Yaquis were "a strong and pure race that should fully expect vindication for the despoliation of their lands by past governments."[78]

During his nationwide presidential campaign in 1933 and 1934, Cárdenas witnessed the abject poverty of Mexico's Indians, including the Yaquis, and promised many of them that he would restore their ancestral lands and develop their economic and educational infrastructures. The indigenous peoples usually responded warmly to such pledges.[79] Cárdenas believed that the country's indigenous populations were "not conservative" in the sense that they "opposed improvements"; rather he claimed that the Indians' "misery and ignorance impeded their evolution." Cárdenas held a similar view of the country's poor mestizo population. Cardenistas saw each group primarily in terms of class; both groups were oppressed rural workers who remained backwards due to the mutually reinforcing social woes of illiteracy, religious fervor, alcoholism, and isolation.[80] This stance shaped Cárdenas's egalitarian, statist project throughout the countryside. He thought, as did many contemporary teachers and social scientists, that the "Indian problem" was a material one that could be rectified through federal intervention. According to one of Mexico's leading anthropologists, Manuel Gamio, addressing the Indians' material needs would foster their acculturation and help to homogenize the nation. In other words, Cárdenas wanted to incorporate the country's indigenous populations into mestizo Mexico rather than have them preserve their unique ethnic and cultural identities.[81]

Federal officials also believed that addressing indigenous needs would politically benefit the ruling elite. In return for gaining land and material assistance, indigenous groups were expected to become a "grateful constituency" that supported the federal government against domestic or foreign opponents. For many groups, including the Yaquis, this was indeed the case. Such policies not only helped build long-term alliances between the country's indigenous communities and the federal government but also extended state authority into the rural sector and strengthened the official party's hand locally. In fact, the restitution of Indian homelands, like the distribution of ejidos to landless rural workers, facilitated the formation of Cardenas's corporatist state. In this state, workers, peasants, and Indians were given the space and official channels to communicate their demands to the federal government. To reach these ends, in January 1936 Cárdenas created the Department of Indigenous Affairs (Departamento de Asuntos Indígenas, DAI) and ordered the new agency to organize Indian congresses where federal bureaucrats would meet directly with Indian representatives and listen to their complaints and demands.[82]

Despite Cárdenas's seemingly pro-Indian policy, he still adhered to an incorporationist ethos and assimilationist model that sought to Mexicanize indigenous peoples. The Yaquis, however, were an exception to his homogenizing agenda. Due to their resilience, militancy, and tendency to side with any political faction that endorsed the return of their homelands—and in light of his political weakness in Sonora—Cárdenas gave the Yaquis more material largess and political autonomy than he did most other indigenous groups. Also, unlike many other Indian peoples in Mexico, the Yaquis had a written literary tradition and preserved their institutions outside of the religious cargo system, which made their cultural restoration more acceptable to Cárdenas and other revolutionary political leaders.[83] Administration officials believed that land redistribution, economic support, and education would modernize the Yaquis, orient them toward the marketplace, and facilitate their incorporation into the

Mexican nation. Such reforms also would preserve their artistic and religious heritage—which was often defined by outdoor ceremonial dances—and help maintain Yaqui culture.[84] Besides returning 1.2 million acres of land to the Yaquis, the October 1937 presidential acuerdo also recognized the civil authority of the Yaqui governors and their control over land use. According to Sheridan, "Yaqui public rituals are the single most important expression of Yaqui ethnic identity in the modern world," and the reparto allowed them to revive, after decades of exile, their "elaborate political and religious systems that had bound them together for centuries."[85] While such indigenous empowerment reflected a shift in thinking about Mexico's "Indian problem" among indigenista officials at the DAI and the SEP in the mid-1930s, including its undersecretary Moisés Sáenz, Cárdenas's Yaqui policy was nevertheless an exception—largely influenced by state and federal power relations—rather than the rule.

For their part, the Yaquis wanted to reclaim the land in the valley not for the sake of profit but, according to one U.S. landowner, because "they consider it tribal property."[86] According to Yaqui myth, God gave them the lands in 1414, and they held an unquantifiable spiritual value. The Yaquis' homelands were central to the maintenance of their ethnic identity and culture, as most commonly seen through the Yaqui Deer Dance (see figure 16). For these reasons, the highly productive agricultural properties on the left bank of the Yaqui River were less important to the Indians than the sacred lands that surrounded the eight original Yaqui pueblos.[87] Specifically, they wanted restitution of their ancestral lands so that these eight pueblos, which from 1740 to 1887 had enjoyed a state of relative autonomy and exclusive control over their communal lands, could be restored and governed by Yaqui institutions.[88]

Cárdenas realized that returning 1.2 million acres of ancestral lands to the Yaquis would not by itself end their poverty or promote a peaceful, agriculturally based lifestyle for them. After the reparto, he frequently met with a council of Yaqui governors, and together they designed a broad-based development project to empower the Yaqui peoples, both politically and socioeconomically. Cárdenas also promised to visit the Yaqui towns and did so in 1939 when he held open public meetings in Potam and Vícam. According to the Mexico City daily Excelsior, the Yaqui project was a "vast agricultural development program designed to raise the indigenous race."[89] The goal of the program was to help the Yaquis pursue a modern lifestyle based on farming, ranching, and permanent settlement in established villages, and to support the federal government. Hence, altruism and political expediency dovetailed within Cárdenas's Yaqui

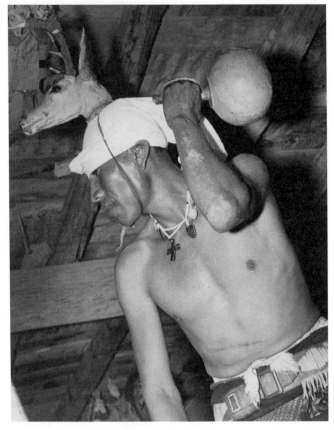

FIGURE 16. Yaqui Indian Deer Dancer, ca. mid-1950s. COURTESY OF THE
ARIZONA HISTORICAL SOCIETY, PHOTOGRAPH NO. 22611.

policy. As seen earlier with the agrarista invasion of and petitions for American-
owned agricultural property in the Mexicali and Yaqui Valleys, the Cardenista
government viewed indigenous demands for land and the tools of modernity
as welcome invitations and opportunities to establish itself in local community life.

After the Yaquis received their lands, the development program that Cárdenas's administration and the Yaqui chiefs had negotiated was announced. In
short order, the Department of Agriculture completed a number of irrigation
projects and furnished the Yaquis with the trappings of modern rural life:
cattle, goats, mules, tractors, reapers, trucks, plows, shovels, machetes, hatchets,
barbed wire, seeds, and fertilizers. Cárdenas, through the National Irrigation
Commission and the Yaqui Regional Commission on Irrigation, guaranteed

the Yaquis half of the water from the new Angostura Dam, located 250 miles upstream on the Yaqui River, after its construction was completed. The Department of Agriculture and the Bank of Agricultural Credit financed loans for the Yaquis. The Commission for Yaqui Agricultural Development and the Subsistence Regulatory Committee also provided credit and guaranteed wheat purchases from them at inflated prices. The Department of Public Health financed the construction of drinking water and sanitary systems and expanded their access to public health services. The Department of Public Assistance established maternity homes and parks for Yaqui women and children. Finally, the SEP and DAI constructed new schools and resupplied the Yaquis' *internados indígenas* (Indian boarding schools). Some boarding schools hired Yaqui teachers and trained others in the Yaqui language, enabling instruction in the indigenous tongue—something that did not occur for most indigenous groups until the 1970s. Yaqui students learned about the history and myths of their ancestors, as well as the sacredness of their territory. Murals were painted on school buildings to celebrate Yaqui culture. Schools also were used to conduct tribal affairs and hosted activities of the newly established Mothers' Society. The schools, which promoted Yaqui ethnic identity and empowerment and were sometimes used for nonacademic functions, became "an important center for community life."[90]

Land restitution and the federal development programs were designed to rehabilitate the Yaqui Indians by making their material life more modern. These policies were, in the words of the local U.S. vice consul, "a strategic necessity." Even though the Yaquis had begun to lead a more sedentary life, contemporary observers were still wary of their military potential. During this period, the U.S. consulate in Guaymas filed frequent reports of an impending Indian uprising and believed that the "Yaqui would go on the warpath" if kept away from their traditional homelands.[91] According to Enrique Guzmán, chief of military operations for Sonora, the object of returning the lands "was to create a Yaqui Indian Reservation as in the United States in an attempt to keep the tribe at peace."[92] Cárdenas realized that forcing the Yaquis to assimilate fully into Mexico's mestizo nation also might cause them to rebel, which would add to Sonora's political instability and weaken the federal government's position in the state. Moreover, as Bantjes points out, since the Yaquis were the "wild card in Sonoran politics," should Yocupicio take up arms against the federal government or join a Cedillo-led rebellion, Cárdenas did not want the Yaquis aligning with the governor.[93] To achieve such ends, Cárdenas astutely combined two rather contradictory federal Indian programs—special protection and partial incorporation. The Yaquis would gain special territorial autonomy over their eight sacred pueblos, while at the same time they would be tied to the state and the national economy through land reform, federally sponsored rural development projects, and the expansion of agricultural production and commerce.

It would be misleading to think that Cárdenas folded in the face of Yaqui pressure and met all of their demands for land and government aid. In spite of Yaqui requests, the president did not return the rich agricultural properties south of the Yaqui River to the Yaquis, which instead were earmarked for the valley's agraristas. Consequently, the 1.2 million acre restitution covered only one-third of the Yaquis' original homelands. Also, in spite of repeated requests, Cárdenas would not restore Yaqui governing authority to the towns of Bácum and Cocorit, which were heavily populated by Mexican mestizos. He also refused Yaqui demands for federal funds to restore or reconstruct church buildings.[94]

One also should not overstate the initial success of the Yaqui project. Many Yaqui leaders complained about the "woeful inadequacy of land reform" and contested over which among them would be chosen to speak on the Yaquis' behalf to Mexico City. Also, according to both Stephen Lewis and Alexander Dawson, many SEP teachers and inspectors in the valley were monolingual racists who denigrated Yaqui culture. Soon after the presidential acuerdo, ongoing conflicts in the Yaqui country prompted the DAI to limit Yaqui autonomy, taking control of all the local indigenous schools in 1939. Many federal SEP schools refrained from teaching Yaqui history and using their native language in the classrooms, and thus it took another two decades before the Yaquis began to use SEP schools in large numbers.[95]

Although Marjorie Becker argues that campesinos forfeited "their cultural knowledge to outsiders" when engaging the state, this was not the case with the Yaquis.[96] From their perspective, Cárdenas not only delivered the lands and territorial autonomy that they had long fought for but also provided both the material and financial support that would allow them to prosper and maintain their cultural heritage. With restitution and federal assistance, the Yaquis regained, in perpetuity, exclusive possession of their ancestral homeland and full political autonomy. This allowed them to revive their nineteenth-century religious and secular arts, as well as their "intensive ceremonial life."[97] After the Yaquis gained possession of their ancestral lands, they expressed their "gratitude, admiration, and respect" to Cárdenas for his assistance. When he announced the development programs, the eight Yaqui governors and many rank-and-file Indians wrote to Cárdenas and thanked him, declaring their "unconditional support" for his government.[98] In June 1939, Cárdenas spent a week in the Yaqui country, where he toured Yaqui towns and agricultural camps, met with Yaqui representatives, and celebrated the land restitution with the indigenous people.[99]

The Yaqui River Valley was not the only agricultural region in southern Sonora that was targeted by Cárdenas's agrarian reform program. Agraristas in the Mayo River Valley, located just south of the Yaqui Valley, also benefited greatly from the October 1937 reparto. Nearly four thousand ejidatarios received 114,662 acres of land, of which 61,500 were irrigated. Few Americans owned property in the Mayo Valley, and only one lost land as a result.[100] Consequently, events there had little impact on the U.S.-Mexican agrarian dispute and therefore are outside the scope of this study. Nevertheless, since most of the landowners in the Mayo Valley were Mexican, the expropriations there demonstrate that the nationality of Sonora's rural property owners was of little concern to the Cardenistas. In other words, since Mexican estate owners lost approximately 160,000 acres of land in the Mayo and Yaqui Valleys—as opposed to the 65,000 acres seized from the Americans—it is safe to conclude that the Yaqui Valley expropriations were not driven by economic nationalism or anti-Americanism. Instead, what mattered most to the Cardenistas were the political benefits of the statewide reparto—which the president used as a political tool to weaken his conservative opponents throughout Sonora.

Did land redistribution in Sonora pay political dividends to Cárdenas? Also, how did the American landowners and Washington contest the expropriation of American-owned rural property in the Yaqui Valley? Finally, how did the latter question affect the former? These are some of the subjects to which we now turn.

THE SONORAN REPARTO

Where Domestic and International Forces Meet

Most of us have invested all of our savings [in the land], the product of years and years of intense labor in the region and even of placing our lives in danger during the sad periods of the Revolution, Yaqui Indian incursions, financial and agricultural crises, and other similar calamities. Many of us introduced agriculture to the Yaqui Valley; others of us were called to establish ourselves here under the colonization and subdivision contracts . . . and all of us consider ourselves factors in the prosperity and progress of the Valley.

JOHN STOCKER, REPRESENTATIVE OF THE YAQUI VALLEY AMERICAN LANDOWNERS, DECEMBER 11, 1936

Edward Jesson was one of dozens of American landowners who lost their property in Sonora under President Lázaro Cárdenas's agrarian reform program. Although Jesson's estate was three times larger than the average American-owned property in the Yaqui River Valley, it was by no means a large agribusiness like the Colorado River Land Company in Baja California. Rather, Jesson's property typified that of many small American landowners who worked alongside their employees in Sonora's southern agricultural valleys. Born in Kansas in 1869, Jesson and his brother Levi left for Sonora's Yaqui Valley in 1910 and bought 7,250 acres of unimproved land on the north and south bank of the Yaqui River, with the intention of starting a commercial farm. The property was formerly part of the ancestral homelands of the Yaqui Indians but was taken from them by Díaz's government around the turn of the century. After years of arduous work, the Jessons and their laborers had cleared the mesquite brush covering the estate, developed 2,000 acres of land, constructed twenty-six kilometers of canals, and built sixty-five houses for tenants. Although Jesson's holdings were periodically overrun by the Yaqui Indians during the 1910s and 1920s, it was not until the arrival of militant agraristas during the mid-1930s that his real problems began.[1]

In late 1934, when Jesson was sixty-five years old, over fifty agraristas began squatting on his property on the north bank of the Yaqui River. As the number of squatters increased to more than one hundred, they seized 625 acres of land and formed their own agricultural colony, Colonia Esperanza. In January 1935, the municipal president in Guaymas granted the squatters legal possession of the 625 acres for three years, under Mexico's Idle Lands Law. Jesson was unable to collect any rent from the squatters, even though they cut timber for sale, cultivated small agricultural plots, and built an irrigation canal on his property. In February 1936, members of the colonia filed an ejidal petition to obtain 2,200 acres from Jesson's estate.[2] A year later, frustrated by the government's silence regarding their petition, the squatters illegally expanded their possession from 625 to 1,850 acres. When their three-year "contract" expired in January 1938, the squatters not only refused to leave but grew more militant.[3] Said Jesson, "The squatters have taken control of most of my ranch to suit themselves, occupying three or four times as much land as the government was to give them. They cut, burned, and destroyed thousands of dollars worth of my best timber, . . . [and] cut my fences, running horses, mules, burros and cattle in my fields. . . . They have threatened to kill me many times and the American consul has advised me to keep away from my ranch."[4] The situation grew even more complicated for Jesson in the spring of 1938—following Cárdenas's October 1937 presidential decree that returned the Yaqui homelands to the Indians—when truckloads of armed Yaquis arrived and ordered Jesson, his tenants, and the illegal peasant squatters off the property, claiming that the land was theirs.[5]

Jesson was emotionally distraught. According to the U.S. vice consul in Guaymas, Jesson had become "so desperate over losing his life's savings with the loss of his property that he seem[ed] to be on the verge of losing his mind." Jesson pleaded his case to anyone who would listen. Local officials in the Yaqui Valley, such as the municipal president at Empalme and the police commissioner at Pótam, claimed that they were unable to assist him because many of the agrarista and Indian occupants were armed.[6] Indeed, remarked Jesson, "Squatters on my land have thirty rifles and plenty of ammunition with which they intend to run or shoot me and my friends and tenants off my ranch."[7] The governor's office agreed that the squatters had occupied Jesson's estate illegally, but it refused to interfere since the federal government planned to return his land to the Yaqui Indians.[8] To protect his property, Jesson hired an attorney and wrote to his congressional representatives in California; he also wrote frequently to the U.S. consulate in Guaymas, the U.S. embassy in Mexico City, and the State Department in Washington. U.S. Ambassador Josephus Daniels was directed by the State Department to keep Jesson's case active before the Mexican Ministry of Foreign Affairs and press for a resolution. In July 1938, Jesson finally abandoned his property—not to the agraristas, but to the Yaqui Indians.[9]

Like Jesson, dozens of American landowners in southern Sonora found themselves caught in the middle of a political dispute between state and federal officials that included opposing class interests. According to the U.S. consulate, the distribution of rural property in the Yaqui Valley was "due more to political conditions than the government's agrarian policy."[10] While the observation made by Vice Consul Alfonso Yepis was accurate, the politics of land reform in Sonora differed somewhat from Baja California. Since Cárdenas was empowered as president to replace Baja California's territorial governor at will, his decision to do so following the expropriation of American-owned land was a political move that, like the redistribution of CRLC's land, was designed to appease national peasant organizations and labor unions. Since the target of the Sonoran reparto was Governor Román Yocupicio and the regional conservative faction that he represented, the politics behind agrarian reform in Sonora were driven mostly by state-specific issues rather than national ones—although the two were never entirely separate.

There is widespread consensus within the literature that Cárdenas used agrarian reform as a political weapon both to undermine Sonora's conservatives and to broaden his local base of support among landless rural workers and the Yaqui Indians. The literature, however, fails to explain why Cárdenas waited two and a half years after establishing Sonora's Mixed Agrarian Commission in March 1935, almost two years after deposing Ramos in December 1935, and one year after Yocupicio's November 1936 election victory, to announce the reparto in October 1937. The rapid and extensive redistribution of land in the Laguna region, Yucatán, the Mexicali Valley, and elsewhere illustrates that Cárdenas had the power and confidence to move quickly and decisively when expropriating large areas of land—especially when it was politically expedient. Had Cárdenas carried out the reparto by mid-1936, it would have strengthened Ignacio Otero Pablos's gubernatorial campaign against Yocupicio. Likewise, although

Cárdenas visited states such as Puebla, Nuevo León, Yucatán, Durango, Coahuila, Morelos, Oaxaca, and Guerrero to resolve labor disputes, redistribute land, consolidate his popular support, and strengthen his fellow Cardenistas, he failed to do the same in Sonora prior to the 1936 election for governor. In fact, Cárdenas did not travel to Sonora until May 1939, well after both the November 1936 and the January 1939 gubernatorial elections.[11]

Scholars have not explained these paradoxes because they have failed to analyze the international dimensions of the reparto. In other words, they have not examined the influence that the American landowners in the Yaqui Valley and the U.S. government had on Cárdenas's agrarian reform program in Sonora. Demonstrating the role played by foreign actors in land redistribution not only illustrates the complexity of the overall agrarian reform process but also shows how non-Mexicans influenced federal-regional power relations and state building in postrevolutionary Mexico. On one hand, we could interpret Cárdenas's absence from Sonora as an indication that his key collaborators, such as the CTM's Vicente Lombardo Toledano and the Agrarian Department's Gabino Vázquez, had a role in shaping policy and intervened on his behalf vis-à-vis the state. On the other hand, because of the international delicacy of land redistribution in Sonora, Cárdenas may have wanted other officials to take center stage there in order to mitigate the diplomatic complications that stemmed from the redistribution of tens of thousands of acres of American-owned property. By physically distancing himself from events in Sonora, Cárdenas could rightly emphasize the popular roots of the reparto, rather than have it appear primarily as a federal initiative that was designed to strengthen his government. In a similar fashion, Cárdenas claimed that the 1938 oil expropriation was precipitated first and foremost by the demands of the petroleum workers and not federal energy policy.

Since the American landowners in the Yaqui Valley received more attention from Washington than did any other group of U.S. property owners who lost land in Mexico, Cárdenas's administration needed to consider the impact of the reparto on U.S.-Mexican relations. In order to keep bilateral relations from unraveling, Cárdenas had to appear as a "Good Neighbor." This meant discussing plans other than expropriation with both U.S. officials and the affected landowners prior to the reparto. Ignoring U.S. concerns and seizing the American-owned estates in 1936 or early 1937 would have stirred up much more criticism against the Cárdenas administration north of the border. By opening a dialogue with U.S. officials and property owners and delaying the reparto,

Cárdenas was able to mitigate its bilateral repercussions. This, in turn, impeded efforts by Sonora's conservatives to find a powerful and disgruntled foreign ally. Had Washington strongly opposed the reparto and lifted its arms embargo against Mexico, especially in a border state like Sonora, it would have empowered Cárdenas's opponents, undermined his progressive coalition, increased the threat of rebellion in Sonora, and thwarted the president's political objectives throughout the state. As in Baja California, the expropriation and redistribution of American-owned agricultural property in Sonora required Cárdenas's administration to walk a diplomatic tightrope.

In December 1936, eleven months before the reparto, Cárdenas met with the U.S. ambassador to Mexico, Josephus Daniels, and informed him of his plans to redistribute dozens of American-owned estates in the Yaqui Valley. To reduce bilateral tensions that were sure to erupt, Cárdenas told Daniels, "If President Roosevelt insisted on it, the Mexican government would wish to make any settlement that he desired with regard to the Yaqui Valley in order to save him from embarrassment and difficulty in the United States." The State Department replied that it would agree to any proposal for the Yaqui Valley that was "acceptable to the American landowners in that area."[12] Cárdenas's offer probably did not surprise Roosevelt's administration, since they were well aware that the Mexican president had been discussing alternative plans to expropriation with the American landowners and the U.S. consulate in Guaymas as early as March 1936.

As the agrarian movement gained momentum in early 1936, Yaqui Valley landowners organized into the Confederation of Agricultural Associations of the State of Sonora (Confederación de Asociaciones Agrícolas del Estado de Sonora, CAAES) to protect their interests. CAAES was comprised of Mexican and foreign growers (although Edward Jesson does not appear to have been one of them) who owned parcels of varying sizes and sought to safeguard their holdings by presenting federal authorities with alternative plans to land redistribution. For example, in March 1936 a group of U.S. and Mexican landowners from CAAES met with Cárdenas and offered to form an ejidal district for the agraristas by purchasing government-owned property at the mouth of the Yaqui River, as well as clearing and fencing the land and constructing canals, roads, houses, and schools for the campesinos out of their own pockets. Cárdenas accepted the offer and assured the growers that their estates would not be expropriated for at least ten years. Surprisingly, the Mexican president even suggested that they "parcel out their land to relatives, friends, and companies" to reduce the size of their holdings on paper and minimize the number of acres that the government could legally expropriate when the time came. The Mexican Agrarian Department also endorsed the proposal. The agraristas, however, rejected the offer because the proposed lands were farther from the railway station and Ciudad Obregón than were the lands for which they had petitioned, thereby increasing their transportation costs. According to the U.S. vice consul, Cárdenas "did not wish to force the agrarians to take the lands offered," since it might have cost him their support. The Mexican president then reversed his position and rejected the landowners' offer.[13]

Cárdenas initially favored the landowners' proposal for many reasons. First, productive growers would have retained their properties in the valley, bringing much-needed tax revenue to the federal and state treasuries. Second, the number of acres under production, and hence agricultural yields, would have increased by settling agraristas on vacant federal land elsewhere in the valley. Third, these thousands of acres of land would have been cleared and improved by the property owners at no cost to the federal government. Fourth, Cárdenas would have been credited with providing land to the agraristas—thereby gaining their support—without generating tensions with the United States over the expropriation of American-owned property. Yet, Cárdenas rejected the growers' proposal because he needed the support of the local agraristas who opposed it. In other words, Cárdenas was willing to disappoint the Americans because Yocupicio, Cedillo, and Mexico's conservatives posed a greater and more immediate threat to his regional and national interests than did the U.S. landowners or Washington. As in Baja California, political expediency shaped his decisions in Sonora.

To prevent the seizure of their holdings, the American growers in the Yaqui Valley independently devised a second proposal—similar to the first one suggested by CAAES—offering to purchase, clear, improve, and cede to the campesinos some 20,000 acres of idle land previously owned by the Richardson Construction Company.[14] While Interim Governor General Gutiérrez endorsed the proposal, Cárdenas "merely reiterated his previous stand: i.e., that any plan acceptable to the agrarians would be acceptable to him." Passing the buck was a convenient way for Cárdenas to avoid being held accountable for his failure to reach an agreement with the U.S. landowners. All the communities that petitioned for land in the valley agreed to the new offer, except pueblo El Yaqui. Pascual Ayón demanded the agraristas be given the lands for which they had petitioned—the irrigated properties located in the "Yaqui Valley proper," south of the Yaqui River. Ayón probably worried that it would take a number of years before the unimproved Richardson lands would be ready to plant and that Cárdenas would be out of office by then. Ayón bemoaned that the growers had been pressuring the agraristas to accept each of their proposals in turn; he also claimed that CAAES was planning to have him murdered because he stood in the way of a solution that would have safeguarded their estates.[15]

After Mexico City rejected both of the growers' proposals, the American landowners contacted their congressional representatives in Washington and asked them to intervene on their behalf. Although many congressmen and senators wrote to the State Department in 1936 and 1937, they could not convince the Roosevelt administration to take the hard line against Mexico that many property owners urged.[16]

At the request of the American landowners, and with the State Department's blessing, Vice Consul Yepis negotiated a third proposal—this one too was rebuffed by the agraristas.[17] Although each proposal was rejected, the landowners succeeded in buying more time. In October 1936, the American growers formed their own committee, headed by one of the valley's principal U.S. property owners, John Stocker, who held nearly 5,000 acres. Even if Stocker could not convince Cárdenas's administration to accept one of the growers' plans, he hoped at least to delay government action for several months, until the governor elect Yocupicio took office in January 1937.[18] The landowners expected that Yocupicio would defend their interests' against the federal government. It was clear that Cárdenas was still hoping for a compromise that was agreeable to all sides, since in November 1936 he ordered the Agrarian Department "to stop all action on the Yaqui Valley agrarian petitions."[19]

The following month, the American landowners alone presented their final offer to Cárdenas's administration and suggested a colonization agreement similar to the one that the Mexican government and the Colorado River Land Company signed in April for the Mexicali Valley and that was still enforced. Under the contract, the growers would sell their holdings in 10 acre plots to Mexican nationals over a twenty-year period; they also would help finance the campesinos by paying a 3 percent tax on their crops over a four-year period. According to the head of the Agrarian Department, Gabino Vázquez, "The President was considerably interested in the proposal."[20]

To reach a solution that was acceptable to both sides, Cárdenas ordered Vázquez to meet with the agraristas, landowners, and U.S. and Mexican officials in the Yaqui Valley. In February 1937, Vázquez met with the radical municipal president of Ciudad Obregón, Matías Méndez, and visited the agrarian communities in the valley. In his meeting with the agraristas, Vázquez raised their hopes by promising them that "the entire Yaqui Valley would be divided in the same manner as the Laguna district." After Vice Consul Yepis met with Vázquez, he reported that the Agrarian Department "was ready to offer [the agraristas] land or anything else in order to have them on Cárdenas's side."[21] Mexico City needed the campesinos' support, according to Yepis, because "Cárdenas was expecting an uprising soon in which Cedillo would be one of the principal leaders, and they [Cárdenas's administration] thought that even Governor Yocupicio would fight against the central government."[22] Although Cedillo did not take up arms against the federal government for another year, the Cardenistas were clearly worried and intended to use land reform to solidify campesino support for the impending conflict. If land redistribution would thwart a possible uprising in Mexico, or hasten its defeat, sympathetic leaders in Roosevelt's administration, as the next chapter will show, would endorse it.

A few days after meeting with the campesinos, Vázquez informed Yepis and Stocker that Cárdenas was "still studying the [colonization] proposal" made by the American landowners in December 1936.[23] Vázquez's trip to the Yaqui Valley was not intended to find a solution that was acceptable to the opposing sides; rather, by telling both sides what they each wanted to hear, it appears that Vázquez hoped to avoid any new diplomatic problems for the administration. Cárdenas probably put the Yaqui Valley agrarian issue on hold due to the unexpected strain on U.S.-Mexican relations caused by the invasion of CRLC's holdings in Baja California by hundreds of armed agraristas in January 1937. The rapid expropriation of 237,360 acres of CRLC's land, along with the seizure of nearly 33,000 acres from seven other American landowners in the Mexicali Valley between March and July 1937, increased the bilateral tensions that already existed as a result of the widespread expropriation of American-owned rural property by Cárdenas's government. By delaying the expropriation of American-owned estates in southern Sonora until after expropriations in northern Baja California had subsided, Cárdenas avoided the appearance of being a tool of the workers and peasants or a fervent communist bent on seizing all forms of private property—charges that many of his domestic and foreign critics had leveled at him. Rather, Cárdenas placated Washington by informing U.S. officials that he was studying the landowners' colonization proposal and by appearing interested in a compromise, which was central to the idea of reciprocity as defined by Roosevelt's Good Neighbor policy. Cárdenas was astute enough to realize that rapid and excessive seizures of American-owned land would further destabilize relations with Washington and possibly precipitate a hard-line U.S. policy. Telling the agraristas and American growers in the Yaqui Valley what they each wanted to hear illustrates how his administration adeptly balanced domestic politics and international affairs.[24]

It took Cárdenas nine months to give a formal reply to the American land-owners' colonization proposal. With the Baja California expropriations behind him, and unable to work out an agreement that was acceptable to both the U.S. property owners and the agraristas, in October 1937 Cárdenas met with Daniels, one week before he announced the reparto. To reduce the repercussions that would stem from the expropriation of American-owned land, the Mexican president offered to indemnify U.S. property owners for their losses with unimproved lands elsewhere in the Yaqui Valley.[25] However, unbeknownst to both U.S. officials and growers, the region that was to be set aside for the American landowners was located north of the Yaqui River and was already slated as restitution to the Yaqui Indians.[26] The growers "emphatically rejected" the offer because they believed the unimproved lands offered in compensation would not be ready for planting for several years, and in the meantime they would lose most of their assets almost immediately to expropriation.[27] Instead, many U.S. property owners applied for an *amparo* (injunction) to legally overturn the seizures. The Mexican courts refused, however, to hear any suits filed against the government.[28]

Cárdenas was clearly concerned about the ramifications of the Yaqui Valley reparto on U.S.-Mexican relations. On October 29, 1937, two days after he announced the presidential resolution, he wrote to the Mexican ambassador to the United States, Dr. Francisco Castillo Nájera, that his "government wanted to demonstrate in this case, that it tried to the utmost to decrease frictions and avoid . . . having the affected parties look to the American government and make political problems."[29] While Cárdenas offered to indemnify all American landowners nationwide who were affected by expropriation with almost worthless federal agrarian bonds, he offered compensation lands to the Yaqui Valley property owners in hopes that it would appeal to Roosevelt's desire to protect the "little man" and thereby temper U.S. policy toward Mexico.[30] Favorable treatment for the Yaqui Valley landowners stemmed from the State Department's request that the Americans who owned small and medium-sized parcels in the valley be given special treatment, in comparison to large U.S. property owners who had lost their estates elsewhere in Mexico, due to their "limited means."[31] It appears, however, that Cárdenas's land-swap proposal was merely a ploy designed to show Roosevelt's administration that he took Washington's concerns seriously. Just as the American growers and the State Department finally accepted the compensation lands offer in the spring of 1938, the Cárdenas administration rescinded it and instead proposed to indemnify them with cash—an offer that Mexico City never carried through.[32]

Cárdenas initially used the agraristas' intransigence as an excuse for why his government failed to reach a compromise that was acceptable to all sides and which would have spared the American properties from redistribution prior to October 1937. After the reparto, though, the issue was no longer one of avoiding expropriation but simply of compensation. Again, Cárdenas would not assist the American landowners. Why not? Perhaps Cárdenas's nationalist leanings made it difficult for him to give twenty-nine Americans valuable Mexican property located in a rich agricultural region. More importantly, though, domestic politics made it almost impossible for Cárdenas to meet the Americans halfway. Over the previous two years, the American landowners had been supported by Sonora's conservative faction, including Yocupicio. Since Yocupicio and his henchmen had brutally oppressed the labor and agrarian movements, divided the lower classes, and were against the redistribution of land to the agraristas and the Yaquis, it would have been too great a political risk for Cárdenas to bail out the American landowners, who endorsed Yocupicio's candidacy and governorship. Had Cárdenas provided the Americans in the Yaqui Valley with a special compensation plan, he may have lost some much-needed political support among Sonora's working class and further angered the Mexican landowners who also lost their holdings but received no compensation whatsoever. Hence, international considerations influenced domestic issues in Mexico at the same time that domestic concerns also shaped Cárdenas's foreign relations.

U.S. property owners argued that the seizure of their holdings was illegal, since the 1934 Agrarian Code prohibited the expropriation of land held under a colonization contract. Although some American landowners talked of launching an armed rebellion against the Mexican government, most seemed content to allow John Stocker and Vice Consul Yepis—both of whom had represented their interests before the reparto—to work on their behalf regarding indemnification.[33] After the reparto, however, Stocker played less of a role in negotiations, because the Yaqui Valley case became an important part of the bilateral talks regarding Mexico's compensation of hundreds of the American-owned rural properties that had been expropriated nationwide. In fact, as the last chapters of this book will show, Cárdenas's government shrewdly used the U.S. landowners in the Yaqui Valley as part of its diplomatic strategy of delay and subterfuge against Washington.

Most of the thirty-nine American rural properties that were expropriated in Sonora between 1927 and 1940 were located in the southern part of the state: twenty-nine in the Yaqui Valley alone. In fact, of the approximately 90,000 acres that were expropriated from the Americans statewide, nearly 65,000 were located in the Yaqui Valley and were seized during Cárdenas's term in office. As instructed by Mexican agrarian authorities, the landowners in the valley turned over their holdings to the ejidatarios in the middle of 1938, immediately after harvesting their crops. Most affected American property owners subsequently sold their remaining land and equipment, abandoned farming, and left the Yaqui Valley entirely. After the United States and Mexico signed the 1941 Global Settlement that ended the agrarian dispute, in 1943 the Yaqui Valley growers, like American landowners who had lost property elsewhere in Mexico, began to receive their first reparation checks. And like most other U.S. property owners, they received between fifteen and twenty cents on the dollar from their compensation claim and even that amount they did not receive in full until 1955. Edward Jesson, meanwhile, returned to California in late 1938. Sadly, he died before receiving any of the $30,368 that was awarded to him for the land which he had poured his life into and that now belonged in perpetuity to the Yaqui Indians.[34]

THE REPARTO'S POLITICAL BENEFITS FOR CÁRDENAS

The president's decree affected nearly 65,000 acres of American-owned agricultural property. The reparto was intended not only to extend socioeconomic justice for the agraristas and right the wrongs of the past for the Yaqui Indians but also to weaken Sonora's conservative bloc and strengthen that of the Cardenistas. Did this move, which jeopardized relations with the United States, pay off for Cárdenas? To a certain extent, the trade-off was worth it. According to Yepis, Yocupicio was "impotent as regards to agrarianism." Indeed, Cárdenas did array a powerful contingent of actors to ensure the Sonoran governor did not prevent the implementation of land reform.[35] For many of the agraristas, including Marcelina Saldívar, Cárdenas became "a great god."[36]

The October 1937 reparto established thirteen ejidos in the Yaqui Valley from 108,000 acres of redistributed land. A total of 2,159 agraristas received land grants. On average, each ejidatario received 20 acres of land, double the usual amount. By 1941, additional expropriations had increased the number of ejidal acres in the valley to 132,240 and ejidatarios to 3,969. Few lands south of the Yaqui River were awarded to the Yaquis; instead they received 1.2 million acres, now referred to as an "indigenous community," that were located primarily on the north bank of the Yaqui River and adjacent to the Bacatete Mountains.[37]

The reparto largely succeeded in addressing the demands of Yaqui Indians. Under Cárdenas, the Indians were incorporated into the economic and political life of the nation while maintaining their cultural heritage; this finally eliminated the Yaqui military threat. The reparto also succeeded economically by expanding agricultural production, thanks to two factors: first, the American farms that were converted into ejidos were modern and efficient agricultural enterprises; and second, unlike other rural parts of the country, the Yaqui Valley received a large amount of federal support. By 1940, the amount of land under cultivation, and the output of cash crops such as wheat and rice, exceeded pre-1938 levels. In fact, between 1938 and 1943, the collective ejidos averaged higher yields than did privately held farms in the region. Consequently, most Yaqui Valley ejidos quickly turned a profit, and by 1943, only three of the fourteen collective ejidos in the valley were in debt to the Ejidal Bank.[38]

The construction of three dams in the Yaqui Valley watershed starting in 1938 also helped increase agricultural production. While only 123,500 acres were irrigated in 1937, by 1955 that number was nearly 520,000. Today, the irrigation system includes more than 2,700 kilometers of main, lateral, and secondary irrigation canals that deliver over two billion meters of water each year to the valley's farmers. In addition to expanding irrigation, the federal government also used its enhanced position regionally to promote agricultural experimentation—making the Yaqui Valley the home of the Green Revolution for wheat. In the early 1960s, an international team of scientists worked at the the Yaqui Valley research station of the International Maize and Wheat Improvement Center to produce a more productive wheat germ plasma. Since 1965, the center's wheat varieties have remained universal among Yaqui Valley growers, and some have even been exported to other developing countries.[39]

In comparison to the reparto's success in the realm of economics and indigenous politics, it was less successful in the area of campesino and institutional politics. Even though Cárdenas gained the support of thousands of agraristas and future ejidatarios, his candidate, Ignacio Otero Pablos—who lost the 1936 gubernatorial election to Yocupicio—was again defeated at the polls in January 1939 by Yocupicio's handpicked successor, General Anselmo Macías Valenzuela. Despite the reparto and the worker-peasant Cardenista alliance, the president and his followers were too weak to defeat Sonora's entrenched conservative machine.[40] Otero Pablos did carry the Yaqui Valley by a two-to-one margin over Macías, but he lost the rest of the state. It would be misguided to assume that voter sentiment alone determined the outcome of the election or that the final vote count accurately reflected the popular mood within the state. Electoral fraud was rampant throughout much of the country in the 1930s and Sonora was no exception. Not surprisingly, after the state's 1939 official party primary, Lombardo Toledano complained to Cárdenas that Yocupicio and his supporters stole the election through their usual dirty tricks. However, electoral fraud cut both ways, a fact that the CTM leader appeared to ignore.[41]

Besides the all-too-common electoral shenanigans, the vote count also reflected the strength of each candidate's political machine. Otero Pablos failed to win Sonora's 1939 PRM (Partido de la Revolución Mexicana, which succeeded the PNR as the official party in 1938) primaries due to regional and national political developments that occurred after the October 1937 reparto that empowered the Yocupicistas and made it easier for them to win the election. The March 1938 nationalization of the foreign-owned oil industry and the subsequent military uprising by Saturnino Cedillo marked a turning point in Cárdenas's agrarian program, as the president shifted authority over ejidal petitions back to the state level. In 1938 land redistribution also slowed and labor militancy waned as Cárdenas appeased conservative governors in exchange for their support during the two crises.[42] Yocupicio, like many other anti-Cardenista governors, backed the president during the oil conflict and Cedillo rebellion, since he correctly believed that the federal government's need for support would force it to relinquish some authority at the state level, which, in turn, would strengthen his position in Sonora. Even after these two tumultuous events were behind him, from mid-1939 until his term ended in December 1940, Cárdenas yielded to the conservative regional machines not only in Sonora but also in Yucatán, Campeche, Puebla, and Zacatecas. According to Fallaw, "Cárdenas compromised" the interests of the populist groups and "much of his own corporate political apparatus" within these states to "maintain political control of Mexico for the remainder of his term and impose Manuel Ávila Camacho as president."[43]

Prior to the fall 1939 PRM primaries, Yocupicio took advantage of the power that Cárdenas ceded to the governors in 1938 by manipulating national institutions for his own advantage and keeping the PRM committees and electoral delegations under his control. More specifically, he filled political vacancies with his supporters and attacked his progressive opponents throughout Sonora. One of Yocupicio's first important moves was to appoint a close friend and former state prosecutor, Adolfo Ibarra Seldner, as president of the Sonoran branch of the PRM. Yocupicio then dismissed the Ejidal Bank director who supported the agraristas in the southern valleys. He also used conservative municipal presidents to alter the composition of some agrarian committees while separating them from their teacher advisers. The recomposed agrarian committees were then pressured to join Yocupicio's conservative National Peasant Confederation (CNC affiliate, the League of Agrarian Communities and Peasant Unions [Liga de Comunidades Agrarias y Sindicatos Campesinos]). Yocupicio also fired the Cardenista SEP director Elpidio López and appointed a conservative education secretary who, in turn, replaced the radical federal teachers and school inspectors with conservative state instructors. According to Bantjes, by filling posts with his supporters, Yocupicio ensured that "state officials spread Maciista propaganda and pressured the electorate." Government employees also were "threatened with dismissal if they did not vote for the correct candidate" (i.e., Macías).[44]

The governor also called upon state agencies, such as the Labor Department and the Office of Conciliation and Arbitration Junta de Conciliación y Arbitraje, to break up federally sponsored CTM-affiliated unions. And, if this failed, bribes of money, gifts, and labor contracts were employed to woo workers to his straw union, the CTS. In July 1938, Yocupicio cracked down on the radical labor movement in the Mayo Valley by arresting both leaders and rank-and-file members of the CTM. It was clear Yocupicio had made a significant political comeback when, in October 1938, he convinced Cárdenas to replace the pro-labor military zone commander with Sonora's former conservative interim governor General Jesús Gutiérrez. By January 1939, army officers had joined in the repression of the Sonoran Left, which increased the number of arrests, beatings, and murders of radical labor leaders, ejidatarios, agraristas, and federal teachers. Not surprisingly, agraristas and CTM-istas protested vociferously, and CTM leader Lombardo Toledano sought federal intervention.[45] Threats and violence from Yocupicio supporters probably kept many of Otero Pablos's backers away from the polling centers during the 1939 PRM primaries, while cronyism and bribery won Macías additional votes and the governorship.

Otero Pablos's loss also reflected the conflict between those Sonora rural workers who received ejidos and those who did not. Even the ejidatarios were themselves divided between those who preferred communal farming (collectivists) and those who sought individual exploitation of ejidal lands (individualists). As in other areas of Mexico, these divisions stemmed from a variety of issues, most notably campesinos' differing views of the land and the tendency of many to put individual familial interests before those of their social class. In January 1939, more than eighty individualists and two hundred collectivists clashed in the Mayo Valley, resulting in four deaths and dozens of injuries. Throughout Sonora, Yocupicio exploited the division between the two groups by arresting collectivists, who supported Cárdenas and Otero Pablos, and convincing many individualists to join his conservative League of Agrarian Communities and Peasant Unions. While campaigning for governor, Macías advocated the parcelization of the collective ejidos, which attracted a significant percentage of disgruntled individualist ejidatarios. In addition, the Yaqui Valley was split between voters (such as day laborers) who "followed the official line" and supported Otero Pablos, and the many ejidatarios who resisted it, including those in Pascual Ayón's Ejido El Yaqui. Democratically minded ejidatarios who were against the federal imposition of an outside candidate voted for the third choice, General Francisco Bórquez, rather than Otero Pablos or Macías.[46]

Unable to impose Otero Pablos as governor or make the state's conservative opposition fully compliant to his populist agenda, Cárdenas did not fully achieve his political goals in Sonora. However, the political picture is much muddier than that simple observation. For instance, to Yocupicio's dismay, Macías did not continue his conservative, anti-Cardenista policies. Instead, this handpicked successor turned out to be a moderate governor who reached a rapprochement with the CTM and pursued conciliatory policies that kept the labor and agrarian movements at bay. And, although regional actors in Sonora refused to acquiesce to Cárdenas's administration, the president did advance the postrevolutionary state-building process. To have an immediate, short-term view of nation building that analyzes it as a state-by-state zero-sum game misreads the ways it evolved over time. According to Gerardo Otero, Cárdenas's policies in Sonora were politically successful in the long run, as they built popular democratic institutions within the state that the rural working class would employ to its advantage in later decades. Likewise, the president carried out a massive land redistribution program that dramatically redirected Sonora's land tenure system away from the large landholders and toward the ejidatarios and Yaqui Indians. As Christopher Boyer rightly concludes, both agrarismo and the "system of regimented empowerment" that characterized Cárdenas's national peasant and labor organizations gave popular groups a permanent, albeit limited, "political voice" that allowed them "to advance their collective interests from within the Mexican state over the long term."[47] Empowerment via corporatism, however, does not mean that workers and peasants did not suffer setbacks in the coming decades or were always able to advance their agenda. To get a sense of the limited nature of popular empowerment, one need only look at the 1940s and 1950s to see how rising prices and flat wages reversed many of the gains won by labor in the latter half of the 1930s.

Like subaltern politics, elite politics also presents a mixed picture. Although Cárdenas could not stop Yocupicio and Macías from winning Sonora's governorship, he was able to count on Yocupicio's support during the Cedillo uprising, the agrarian dispute, and the oil crisis. By making both men confront Mexico City within the constraints of the official party and the electoral system, rather than on the battlefield, Cárdenas and the nation won an important political victory. As one scholar of the Latin American countryside astutely notes, nation building is a long and complicated process that is based on a network of relationships that cut across heterogeneous groups, classes, and social categories, and that is characterized by a process of contention and negotiation. According to Guillermo de la Peña, the "populist pact" which characterizes modern Mexico is based on a "combination of grass-roots demands and community organization, personalized leadership-cum-brokerage, selective repression and ubiquitous factionalism [all of] which laid the foundations of the successful policies of stability."[48] In other words, Otero Pablos may have twice lost Sonora's gubernatorial election, but neither he, Cárdenas, Yocupicio, nor Macías ever resorted to arms to establish control in Hermosillo. Since the most powerful actors worked within the accepted parameters of the political system, they minimized Mexican instability and augmented the postrevolutionary state-building process. And, for the Cardenistas, like each of Mexico's postrevolutionary administrations, this was a central part of their overall political agenda.

EPILOGUE

The reparto had a significant impact on the lives of the agraristas in the Yaqui Valley. "Before the reparto," remembered Lina Saldívar, "Valley people were nomads, wandering from camp to camp." Receiving 20 acres of land enabled rural workers to settle permanently in one place and build homes and communities. Also, living standards improved for most of the valley's rural population under the ejido system, as the annual income for ejidatarios increased from 1,559 pesos in 1943 to 4,500 by 1950. With some disposable income, many of them were able to buy a few modern conveniences and take their children out of the fields and enroll them in school. "As the teacher Manuel del Cid recalled: 'It was no longer a question of battling to meet basic needs. Now they harvested and reaped. The children could finally get proper clothes, purchase supplies, and come to school with full stomachs.'"[49] Equally significant to the improved material conditions were the "psychological rewards" that accompanied the reparto. Arturo Saldívar recalled what land redistribution meant to a former field-worker: "Before he had been a peón; now he was a farmer. As a peon, if he had not been abused, he had been indifferently treated by the owner. When he became an ejidatario, he was an individual who had to be noticed and taken into account. He got his first share of the profits, and his dreams were fulfilled. He worked harder, with more *sabor*. He was off and running."[50]

The impact of the reparto on the Yaqui Indians was equally positive. The Mexican state, after a century of fighting the Yaqui, finally recognized their territorial and political autonomy. The restoration of 1.2 million acres of ancestral land and the large-scale development project for the Yaquis enabled them to preserve their ethnic identity and revive a ceremonial culture that was dedicated to ritual and social cohesion, putting it into practice in both religion and collective land use. The trust that Cárdenas instilled between himself, as Mexico's chief executive, and the Yaqui governors—which had never before existed—produced new linkages between the Yaqui and the Mexican state. These new ties facilitated their inclusion into the nation's economic and political life and, like the land restitution, counteracted any reason for them to rebel. The Yaquis' demands for their homeland, as well as the agrarista petitions for ejidos, could only be met through increased federal power at the regional level. As was the case in Baja California, many local actors did not resist the intervention of Mexico's postrevolutionary state; quite to the contrary, they invited the federal government into their respective regions because they viewed it as a powerful and necessary ally that would help them achieve their particular goals—whether they were socioeconomic, political, or cultural.[51]

Had Cárdenas redistributed land in Sonora shortly after deposing Governor Ramos and by the fall of 1936 (that is, prior to the state's PNR gubernatorial primary in late 1936), it would have assisted Otero Pablo's 1936 campaign against Yocupicio, due to the state of flux that characterized Sonoran politics throughout that year. Moreover, at that time, Yocupicio was not yet governor and therefore had not yet established the repressive state government and corporatist political machine that together would blunt the federal weapon of land reform when it was belatedly wielded by the Cardenistas in October 1937. Had there also been no American farmers in the Yaqui Valley, Cárdenas probably would have issued the reparto sooner. To decrease bilateral tensions, starting in March 1936, Mexican policymakers began to discuss options besides expropriation with U.S. officials and landowners alike in order to come across as a "Good Neighbor" who was willing to negotiate. Even after the Americans in Sonora lost their property, they remained important because Mexican diplomats used them as a wedge to divide officials within the Roosevelt administration over the issue of compensation. Before addressing Mexico's diplomatic strategies during the agrarian dispute we will first examine why Washington decided to accommodate Mexico City in the bilateral conflict over land.

II

Diplomatic Resolution of an International Conflict

THE END OF U.S. INTERVENTION IN MEXICO

The Roosevelt Administration Accommodates Mexico City

The situation created by the recent decree affecting the oil companies raises no new question of policy, and we have already informed the Mexican government that our position with respect to the agrarian expropriations applies with equal validity with respect to the Mexican government's action in taking over the American petroleum interests.

PRESIDENT FRANKLIN ROOSEVELT, APRIL 11, 1938

I fully recognize the right of every sovereign government such as Mexico to expropriate property under its jurisdiction.

PRESIDENT FRANKLIN ROOSEVELT, FEBRUARY 15, 1939

From January 1, 1927, through October 6, 1940, at least 319 American rural property owners had approximately 6.2 million acres of land legally expropriated by the Mexican federal government. Of this total, approximately 1.8 million acres were agricultural lands, 3.6 million acres were pasture, range, grazing, and scrub lands, 450,000 acres were timberlands, and more than 300,000 acres were unclassified. As table 3 shows, since 65 percent of the compensation claims filed by American landowners were for less than $50,000, and 85 percent for less than $100,000, it is safe to assume that most of the expropriations affected either small and medium-sized estates or else limited parts of a larger property. Some Americans lost all of their land, while others lost just a fraction of it. All told, more than two hundred Americans had their holdings seized during Cárdenas's presidency—which is not surprising, since his

TABLE 3. Dollar amount and number of claims filed with the Agrarian Claims Commission (ACC) and the American Mexican Claims Commission (AMCC) for American-owned land expropriated between January 1, 1927, and October 6, 1940

Value	ACC[a]	AMCC[b]	Total
$8,000,000 to $9,000,000	0	1	1
$7,000,000 to $8,000,000	0	0	0
$6,000,000 to $7,000,000	1[c]	1	2
$5,000,000 to $6,000,000	1	0	1
$4,000,000 to $5,000,000	0	1	1
$3,000,000 to $4,000,000	1	3	4
$2,000,000 to $3,000,000	2	2	4
$1,000,000 to $2,000,000	7	5	12
$900,000 to $1,000,000	1	2	3
$800,000 to $900,000	1	0	1
$700,000 to $800,000	1	2	3
$600,000 to $700,000	3	0	3
$500,000 to $600,000	2	1	3
$400,000 to $500,000	5	0	5
$300,000 to $400,000	11	0	11
$200,000 to $300,000	20	2	22
$100,000 to $200,000	36	10	46
$50,000 to $100,000	52	12	64
$25,000 to $50,000	38	12	50
$10,000 to $25,000	63	14	77
Less than $10,000	54	26	80
Value not indicated in claim	25	0	25
Total claims filed:	324	94	418
Total claims disallowed:	67	32	99
Total claims awarded:	257	62	319

Notes:
[a] The bilateral Agrarian Claims Commission was established in January 1939 to settle the agrarian dispute by determining the amount of compensation that the Mexican government would pay American landowners whose properties were expropriated between 1927 and 1940.
[b] The American Mexican Claims Commission was established in December 1942 to distribute reparations from Mexico City to the American landowners and also evaluate ninety-four new claims (known as the Series E Claims) filed by Americans who missed the ACC application deadline of October 6, 1940, or failed to submit sufficient documentation in their initial claim with the ACC.
[c] CRLC's property.
Sources: RG 76, Office of the Commissioner of the U.S. Section, Agrarian Claims Commission, Lawson Correspondence, 1938–43, vols. 1–3, entry 203, NAW; Department of State, *American Mexican Claims Commission*, 475–651.

agrarian reform program was massive. Nationwide, Cárdenas's government redistributed nearly 50 million acres of land, more than double the total for the previous two decades. In the process, close to 5 million acres were expropriated from a variety of American landholders, including individual small farmers and ranchers, as well as large land development, agricultural, timber, ranching, and even mining companies. The individual losses suffered by American rural property owners during Cárdenas's term in office ranged from as few as 6 acres to as many as 412,000.[1]

The number 319, however, represents only those American landowners who were compensated by the Mexican government in the 1940s for the loss of their holdings to federal expropriation and does not include all the rural properties that were taken from Americans in postrevolutionary Mexico. For instance, while 324 agrarian claims were initially filed by American landowners with the Agrarian Claims Commission, 67 of them were denied compensation by U.S. claims officials. Although there were legitimate reasons for rejecting many of these latter claims, the fact remains that in some cases land was seized and never paid for.[2] In addition, both governments agreed that only lands which were officially expropriated by Mexican agrarian authorities would be indemnified. This meant that an untold number of estates which were illegally occupied by squatters did not qualify for compensation.[3] Also, according to U.S. officials, many Americans affected by land redistribution, both official and otherwise, did not file claims because they were afraid of the violent repercussions that might befall them at the hands of local agraristas.[4] Furthermore, some absentee landowners did not know that their properties were taken, and therefore did not file indemnification claims in time. Finally, according to Lawrence Lawson, head of the U.S. section of the Agrarian Claims Commission, for reasons left unsaid, "Many Americans known to have suffered agrarian losses between 1927 and 1940 did not file claims with the Commission."[5]

Since there are few definitive records in either the U.S. or Mexican depositories that clearly indicate the total number of acres lost by Americans in rural Mexico between 1920 and 1940, legal or otherwise, it is hard to know exactly how much American-owned property was seized and squatted upon. John Mason Hart believes that not just hundreds, but "thousands" of American landowners were adversely affected, and "by 1940, American residents and absentee investors had lost most of their material assets in Mexico."[6] Without accurate records of the amount of land taken from Americans, it is impossible to determine its total value. Nevertheless, it is safe to say that Mexico did not pay for all the land seizures, since reparations covered only those American properties that both sides recognized as being legitimately expropriated by federal agrarian authorities.[7] Hart mistakenly claims that U.S. and Mexican negotiators "agreed upon $200,000,000 as the total sum to be dedicated to the payment of damages caused to American property as a result of the agrarian reform program."[8] In reality, although the 319 American landowners who received compensation claimed a total loss of nearly $136 million, Mexico City paid only $22 million for all the American-owned rural holdings that were officially expropriated between 1927 and 1940.[9] While this figure may seem paltry, it is worth noting that Mexico similarly paid just $24 million for all the American-owned petroleum properties it nationalized in 1938.[10]

Comparing these two figures, it would appear that the American-owned oil properties were only slightly more valuable than the rural American-owned lands. This, however, was not the case. First of all, Americans who lost land before 1927 submitted their requests for compensation to the General Claims Commission. There were more than three thousand such general claims, some stretching as far back as 1868, and it is likely that dozens, if not hundreds, of rural land seizures between 1917 and 1927 were part of the general claims settlement rather than the separate and subsequent agrarian claims settlement.[11] Also, each affected U.S. petroleum company filed a reparation claim and was fully indemnified. Many rural landowners, in contrast, were afraid to seek indemnification out of fear of physical retaliation by rural workers, and numerous others missed filing deadlines.[12] In addition, no petroleum holdings were seized by extralegal means that stymied rightful compensation, unlike the hundreds of estate owners whose lands were occupied by squatters. In other words, had every American rural property owner been properly indemnified for the loss of their land, no matter who seized it (squatters or federal officials), the total amount of compensation for the rural properties would have easily exceeded that of the American petroleum firms. In spite of the greater monetary value of the rural properties, the historical scholarship has focused overwhelmingly on the oil nationalization and paid little attention to the land expropriations. This may stem from the fact that the rural land seizures were carried out over the course of two decades and affected hundreds of property owners across Mexico, parcel by parcel. Hence, they lacked the nationalistic drama of the March 18, 1938 oil nationalization that, through its abruptness, boldness, and simplicity, gained the attention of politicians, the press, the general public, and academics on both sides of the border.

Despite the centrality of agrarian issues to the Mexican Revolution, Cárdenas's sexenio, and U.S.-Mexican relations, scholars are just now beginning to investigate the loss of American-owned rural holdings south of the border. According to Stephen Niblo, "During the late 1930s petroleum was not viewed, either by U.S. diplomats or Mexican political figures, as the central issue of the period. Agrarian claims against Mexico exceeded the value of petroleum expropriation. Not only expropriation but also more generally the rules governing foreign landowners were in question."[13] Although it is important to put the expropriation of American-owned land in its proper context vis-à-vis the oil nationalization, simply correcting the historical record with more accurate figures is not the end of the story. Because historians value new research that challenges commonly held views about what occurred in the past and why events evolved as they did, in the following three chapters I seek to revise our understanding of U.S.-Mexican diplomatic relations from the mid-1930s to the early 1940s through an in-depth examination of the agrarian dispute.

Historians have not only failed to recognize the importance of the bilateral conflict over land, but they have also ignored the policy precedents that were set by each side during the dispute. The reaction of both hard-liners and accommodators within the Roosevelt administration to Cárdenas's nationalization of the petroleum industry mirrored their earlier responses to the expropriation of American-owned rural property. As FDR's quote at the beginning of this chapter demonstrates, not only did the agrarian dispute shape the U.S. position during the subsequent oil crisis, but U.S. officials saw no need for a new policy toward Mexico following oils nationalization. In fact, the U.S. ambassador to Mexico, Josephus Daniels, showed a good deal of foresight when he stated that the November 1938 bilateral agrarian agreement "would have a good effect" on resolving the oil conflict.[14] The 1941 Global Settlement signed by Mexico and the United States proved Daniels to be correct, since the procedures that were designed to resolve the oil controversy (the bilateral claims commission) were based on those established in late 1938 to settle the agrarian dispute. Moreover, it is safe to assume that had the United States employed heavy-handed policies against Mexico after 1935 to protect American landowners from redistribution, Cárdenas would likely not have risked further U.S. aggression by nationalizing the petroleum industry.

It would be wrong to conclude that because the land and oil conflicts ended peacefully, Mexico's attack on American-owned property did not strain bilateral relations. It did. With the exception of the Soviet Union during the 1920s, Mexico in the late 1930s mounted the most significant challenge to U.S. economic interests by a foreign government anywhere in the world. Although the USSR's extensive nationalization program predated much of Mexico's, U.S. investments there were small in comparison to those it held south of the border, where the United States was the largest foreign investor. This explains why the State Department believed that Mexico under Cárdenas, more than the USSR under Joseph Stalin, was setting a dangerous precedent for other developing nations—especially in Latin America, where the United States was also the largest foreign investor.[15]

In light of the overt and forceful role played by the United States in Mexico's internal affairs throughout its history, it is surprising that Washington did not respond forcefully when a wide range of American economic sectors—including land, oil, and railroads—were appropriated by the Mexican government in the mid- to late 1930s. As recently as the 1910s and 1920s, the United States had intervened in Mexico's internal affairs in a very vigorous manner, twice invading the country and repeatedly using nonrecognition as a diplomatic tool. Since many of the hard-line U.S. policies during this period were intended to safeguard U.S. investments or shape Mexico's political future, why did Roosevelt's administration not intervene militarily, display a show of force, break diplomatic ties, levy a trade embargo, or lift its arms embargo against Mexico to protect American landowners when Cárdenas's government began to expropriate their properties in late 1935?

In explaining why Washington accommodated Mexican economic nationalism during this period, the scholarly literature has focused overwhelmingly on Cárdenas's nationalization of the foreign-owned petroleum industry. The oil crisis dominates the historiography because most scholars view it as a watershed, when the United States abandoned a century of belligerent policies against its southern neighbor.[16] Unfortunately, most researchers who study the oil controversy lean toward reductionism and argue that one issue—World War II—enabled Mexico to resolve the conflict favorably. The general consensus is that Washington did not pursue a hard-line policy against Cárdenas's administration because the United States needed Mexican military bases and raw materials in the lead-up to war and sought its diplomatic support for collective hemispheric security against the growing Axis threat. Yet, according to María Paz, Washington did not see the Axis as a threat to U.S. security that necessitated hemispheric defense until November 1938.[17] Thus, while national security and World War II partly explain the U.S. accommodation of Mexico after 1938, they do not adequately explain why Roosevelt's administration did not respond aggressively to the expropriation of millions of acres of American-owned land between late 1935 and early 1938. In this earlier period, U.S. officials were not constrained by events in Europe and Asia, nor were they in need of Mexican strategic materials and military bases. If global politics did not determine U.S. policy during the early stages of the agrarian dispute, what did temper the Roosevelt administration's response to the loss of American-owned rural property? Looking beyond the security issues that most scholars have invoked to explain the U.S. response to the oil expropriation, in this chapter I examine the domestic political, economic, and ideological forces behind U.S. policy and argue that the Great Depression was the primary event which shaped it.

THE ACCOMMODATORS

Because a number of key U.S. officials were willing to accommodate Mexico over the expropriation of American-owned land, the United States responded evenhandedly during most of the agrarian dispute. The two most important leaders, President Roosevelt and Ambassador Daniels, sympathized with the plight of Mexico's peasantry and saw land redistribution as a legitimate way to address their deplorable working and living conditions. Their empathy derived from idealized Jeffersonian values, which they hoped Cárdenas was applying to Mexico. Both U.S. policymakers believed that the strength of the American republic derived from the yeoman farmer, whose love for the soil and desire to own a parcel of land helped to diffuse wealth and promote democratic principles. Subscribers to what Frederick Pike refers to as the "agrarian myth" (a belief in the "redeeming, uplifting effect of proximity to, and intimacy with, the land"), Roosevelt and Daniels thought that happiness and human virtue lay in the countryside. These ideals colored a number of New Deal projects, including the Farm Security Administration, the Rural Resettlement Administration, the Rural Electrification Administration, and the Tennessee Valley Authority, and led FDR and Daniels to support Cárdenas's agrarian reform program.[18] In some ways, Roosevelt's romanticized notion of transforming rural America was similar to the self-sufficiency goals that drove the distribution of individually owned ejidos in Mexico. According to Frank Freidel, "Roosevelt was keenly interested in rural planning and conservation, and in romantic Jeffersonian terms talked of the necessity to move millions of permanently unemployed city dwellers back onto the land, where they could produce their own food on small plots."[19] A 1937 article in *Harper's Magazine* illustrated Daniels's like-minded philosophy toward Mexican land redistribution. "Mexico now likes Daniels and Daniels likes Mexico," the magazine declared. "His Jeffersonian nerve centers tingle with pleasure as he sees the land cut up into little squares and parceled out to the people."[20]

Just as New Deal legislation was designed to bring much-needed change to the U.S. countryside, FDR believed that the bold transformations underway in rural Mexico were integral to Mexico's future. In a letter to Texas governor James Allred, FDR wrote, "The settlement of Mexican farmers on arable lands of the Republic is a very urgent need and . . . has been long delayed. . . . Unless the people can have their own fields to till and gain a growing sense of responsibility which comes from individual and family application to the daily problems of the farm, I am convinced that [Mexico's] progress will be postponed. As a sincere friend of Mexico I have a profound sympathy with the basic objectives of the agrarian program."[21]

Roosevelt's empathetic position, which to some degree may have stemmed from his battle with polio and the time that he spent with the other disabled patients at Warm Springs, Georgia, was mirrored by Daniels. The ambassador —a North Carolina native who as a journalist had cut his teeth in that state's politics—saw in Mexico's rural reality a reminder of the discrimination, poverty, unemployment, and land exploitation that characterized the tenant farming and sharecropping system of the American South. After eight years of firsthand experience as U.S. ambassador, Daniels concluded that Mexico was "cursed with over-grown haciendas" and "absentee ownership." Like the president, he saw Mexico's future intimately tied to land reform. "The future of Mexico," Daniels wrote to FDR, "rests upon giving the Indians, who constitute three fourths of the population, a better chance than they have ever enjoyed."[22]

Roosevelt and Daniels were not alone in the endorsement of land redistribution in Mexico. Secretary of Agriculture Henry Wallace was supportive of it, while Laurence Duggan, chief of the State Department's Division of American Republics, also saw its potential. To Duggan—an astute young career diplomat and protégé of Undersecretary of State Sumner Welles—agrarian reform was the lynchpin to Mexican prosperity and democracy. As a supporter of land redistribution throughout Latin America, Duggan argued, "Agrarian reform and industrialization are indispensable pre-requisites for a democratic and prosperous [Mexico]. Without these, the most favorable financial and trade position can only palliate a fundamentally unhealthy situation. . . . Politically, *latifundismo* negates democracy by giving the small class of landowners excessive power over the mass of peons. Economically, it favors backwardness and poverty by permitting the landowner to make a profit from cheap labor while using the most antiquated agricultural methods."[23]

The formula that Roosevelt, Daniels, and Duggan prescribed for their southern neighbor coincided with the views held by many contemporary, left-leaning observers of Mexico, including the anthropologist Robert Redfield; the historian Frank Tannenbaum; the economist Stuart Chase; the journalists Carleton Beals and Betty Kirk; the fiction writers Waldo Frank, Katherine Anne Porter, John Dos Passos, and Anita Brenner; the missionary William Cameron

Townsend; Secretary of Agriculture Henry Wallace; Director of the Resettlement Administration Rexford Tugwell; and Commissioner of Indian Affairs John Collier. For them, Mexico in the 1930s was a "laboratory of socioeconomic innovation." Disappointed by the tenancy bill that passed Congress in mid-1937, Tugwell wrote to Roosevelt, "I shall have to go to Mexico if I am ever to see the aims of the Resettlement Administration carried out. . . . It is really too bad that the tenant bill as it passed allowed nothing for communal and cooperative activities."[24]

Many of these "political" and "cultural pilgrims," as Helen Delpar describes them, did not endorse Mexican industrialization. Instead, they believed that Mexico's future lay in the rural sector and should be based on the communal village, whose cooperative nature was "spiritually fulfilling." Even scholars who championed Mexican industrialization, such as the sociologist Eyler Simpson and the economists Nathaniel and Sylvia Weyl, saw land redistribution as a prerequisite. Not only did these prolific American writers help to convince some members of Roosevelt's administration, the general public, and popular magazines like *Time* and *Life* that land redistribution and Cárdenas's nationalistic policies were appropriate for Mexico, but they also stimulated a general interest in Latin American music, dance, art, fashion, film, and tourism. Due to an outpouring of books, paintings, and news stories, along with the popular appeal of the Good Neighbor policy, in the 1930s Mexico was in "vogue" north of the Rio Grande.[25] Not only did Roosevelt and Daniels embrace "things Mexican" (see figure 17), but many members of FDR's government, including Wallace, Tugwell, Collier, Duggan, and Secretary of the Interior Harold Ickes, also respected Mexican art and society. On one occasion Roosevelt wrote to Tugwell, "What a pity that the Yankees cannot improve the processes of their civilization by emulating Mexican culture."[26]

In the nineteenth and early twentieth centuries, numerous U.S. officials and a significant percentage of the American public had held a racist contempt for Latin America. But by the 1920s negative stereotypes began to fade as Americans acquired a more complex and politically sensitive view of the region. This stemmed from greater U.S. interest in Latin America following the Spanish-American War in 1898; it also was built on the longstanding Western Hemisphere idea—long held by intellectuals in the New World and reinforced by the horrors of World War I—that Europe was "spiritually and intellectually bankrupt" and that the United States and Latin America had a common history and culture superior to that of "old Europe." Most importantly, argue James Park

FIGURE 17. Daniels (sitting far right) listens to Mexican mariachis, ca. 1930s. AGN, ARCHIVO FOTOGRÁFICO, FONDO ENRIQUE DÍAZ, 60/7.

and John Britton, greater tolerance and understanding of Latin America were precipitated by the Great Depression. The crisis produced a sense of failure among Americans and made them humble in light of the economic hard times they now shared with the Latin Americans.[27] According to Britton, "The continuing severity of the business collapse, the eclectic experimentation of the Roosevelt administration, and the ascent of leftist cultural values in the United States gave discussions of Mexican communal agriculture, socialist education, and government management of large sectors of the economy a familiar and receptive context. In a general sense, Roosevelt and Cárdenas seemed bound in the same direction. . . . Media commentators soon discovered that the Mexico of Cárdenas made 'good copy' in harmony with the New Deal ethos."[28]

Not only did this pro-Mexican sentiment likely moderate U.S. policy during the agrarian dispute, but it also worked to Mexico's advantage in their negotiations with Washington. Because Daniels and FDR's romanticized view of Mexico was also naive and patronizing, when bilateral relations became strained over Mexico City's failure to indemnify American landowners, Daniels rarely acknowledged the evasive diplomatic tactics employed by Cárdenas's administration. Instead, he wrongly interpreted Mexico's failure to make reparations as the product of Mexico's political immaturity. On one of many occasions when Cardenista officials derailed the agrarian claims negotiations, Daniels excused it, telling Roosevelt, "Be patient with these children of our younger sister Republic. Let them grow up."[29] In a speech celebrating Pan American Day in April 1938, FDR used similar paternalistic language when he addressed the tension that resulted from the agrarian dispute and Cárdenas's recent oil nationalization. In front of dozens of Latin American officials assembled together in Washington, Roosevelt declared in a fatherly manner that the Good Neighbor policy would "not be endangered by controversies within our family."[30] By using familial metaphors, Daniels and Roosevelt (keeping in mind FDR's haughty ego) may have seen themselves as paternal benefactors of an immature people or as civilized exemplars who took up the "White Man's Burden."[31] Whichever was the case, since few members of the Roosevelt administration saw Mexican policymakers as their equals, when problems arose for Washington during the agrarian dispute they blamed their colleagues' ineptitude rather than admit that they were outmaneuvered by skillful Mexican diplomats. As we will see in subsequent chapters, such misperceptions within the U.S. diplomatic corps facilitated Mexican policymaking.

THE NEW DEAL AND THE PLAN SEXENAL

Washington's endorsement of Mexican land reform also reflected the common political and economic agendas pursued by the two administrations. The Great Depression fostered a change in prevailing attitudes worldwide regarding the relationship between the state and the economy. Not only in the United States and Mexico but also in much of Latin America, Europe, and Asia, greater state intervention in the economy was considered the most expeditious way to redress the domestic ills brought on by the global depression. Throughout the 1930s world leaders pursued policies that smacked of economic nationalism and that redefined the government's relationship with the private sector and the general public. Cárdenas, for instance, used the federal government to create a mixed economy that benefited Mexican workers and peasants.[32]

In his 1934 inaugural address, Cárdenas spoke of societal interdependence and called for increased state intervention in the economy because he believed only the federal government had the will and ability to carry out much-needed structural reforms. Said the president, "It is necessary to see the economic problem in its entirety and to observe the connections that link each of its parts with the whole. Only the state has the general interest, and, because of this, only it has the unified vision. State intervention has to be greater, more frequent, and deeper."[33] Mexico's 1934–40 Plan Sexenal (Six-Year Plan) was considered by politicians and social commentators on both sides of the border as their equivalent of Roosevelt's New Deal. In fact, the most radical period of FDR's thirteen years in office—when his administration took its most pro-labor and antibusiness stance during the so called "Second New Deal" of 1935 to 1938—coincided with the most radical years of Cárdenas's sexenio, when most American-owned rural property was expropriated. Not coincidently, in 1935 Cárdenas told Daniels that he had "great interest in the broadminded policies of the American government, especially in the direction of curing abuses and promoting measures that would benefit workers, as well as in the large-scale reforms that in their general pattern were similar to those which he had in mind for Mexico."[34]

With comments like these, and in light of his pro-Mexican posture, it should not be surprising that throughout his ambassadorship Daniels repeatedly compared Mexico's Six-Year Plan, and Cárdenas's desire to assist Mexican laborers, peasants, and indigenous peoples, to the New Deal and Roosevelt's goal of helping American workers, farmers, and Native Americans. The shared ideological convictions of U.S. and Mexican reformers, especially their tendency to side with labor in its disputes against capital, enabled Cárdenas's government to intervene in the Mexican economy and against U.S. economic interests in ways that would have brought sustained criticism from Washington less than a decade before.

Although the major rural programs of the Roosevelt and Cárdenas administrations were very different, especially with regard to land redistribution in Mexico (intended to increase agricultural production) versus crop reduction in United Sates (intended to decrease production), there were some similarities. Both governments endorsed conservationism and sought to modernize the rural sector. Each used agricultural experiment stations to teach farmers and peasants new ways to grow crops, as well as how to improve soil quality and increase agricultural productivity. Both governments saw the need to provide farmers with credit, in Mexico via the Ejidal Bank and in the United States through the Rural Rehabilitation Program and the Crop Loan Act, which loaned poor farmers millions of dollars to purchase equipment, fertilizer, livestock, and land. In the United States, between 1938 and 1945, the Bankhead-Jones Farm Tenancy Act provided $300 million in low-interest loans to tenants, farm laborers, and small property owners to purchase land. In a general sense, like land redistribution in Mexico, some New Deal programs were designed to give land to those who lacked it. Both the Resettlement and Farm Security Administrations (FSA), which assisted poor, often landless tenant farmers and sharecroppers, in some ways mirrored Cárdenas's agrarian reform program. The Resettlement Administration attacked rural poverty through a program of landownership, rehabilitation, and cooperatives. It relocated fifteen thousand rural families into 164 resettlement projects that were subdivided and leased from federal landholdings. Meanwhile, the FSA operated ninety-five camps for migrant rural workers that housed seventy-five thousand people, and its Rehabilitation Division sponsored medical and dental cooperatives for the rural poor.[35]

FDR and Cárdenas's rural programs mobilized millions of farmers and peasants and organized them into regional and national associations. Like Mexico's Plan Sexenal, Roosevelt's New Deal developed a domestic recovery program in agriculture that was based on increased state intervention in the rural economy through centralized national planning, regulation, and management. For both men, the Depression exposed the shortcomings of a U.S. corporate culture that Americans had proudly extolled at home and abroad. Each president rejected traditional laissez faire economic policies and, to varying degrees, embraced Keynesian economic principles that combined liberal capitalism with liberal statism. Also, even though Cárdenas was not a member of the Mexican upper class, his populist desire to help the nation's poor must have appealed to Roosevelt's sense of noblesse oblige. Despite their different upbringings, FDR probably saw Cárdenas as his Mexican counterpart, who, like himself, listened to the working class and implemented bold new programs that provided for their immediate relief, while seeking long-term solutions to his nation's socioeconomic problems.[36]

In addition to helping rural workers, both governments altered decades-long federal policies toward indigenous groups. Members of each administration rejected earlier assimilationist policies and instead promoted indigenismo, along with greater political autonomy and economic opportunity for Indians. The Department of Indigenous Affairs, the Regional Indigenous Congresses and Indian boarding schools were important components of Cárdenas's rural program, just as indigenismo was a guiding philosophy for many Cardenistas. Likewise, the New Deal's Indian Reorganization Act authorized the creation of indigenous governments, promoted Indian arts, crafts, religion, and culture, and discontinued the allotment of land to individual Indians in favor of communal landholdings. As commissioner of Indian Affairs, Collier made sure Native Americans were included in New Deal relief programs such as the Civilian Conservation Corps, the Works Progress Administration, and the Resettlement Administration. In the early to mid-1930s, Collier made several trips to Mexico, where he traveled to remote Indian villages and met with Mexico's leading indigenistas—including Moisés Sáenz and Manuel Gamio. He was clearly influenced by Mexican attitudes and policies toward its indigenous peoples. Collier organized Indian congresses in the United States that, like Mexico's Department of Indigenous Affairs, provided a forum for federal officials to meet with Indian representatives and hear their concerns. According to Collier, "Mexico has lessons to teach the United States in the matter of schools and Indian administration, lessons which are revolutionary and which may be epoch-making."[37]

For Collier and some Mexican indigenistas like Sáenz, U.S. and Mexican Indians should not be forced to conform to their nation's majority culture but instead allowed to maintain their rich and unique ethnic heritage. Since the restitution of ancestral homelands to Mexico's indigenous population helped to maintain Indian culture and was an important component of Cárdenas's agrarian reform program, it is not surprising that Collier enthusiastically supported it. In fact, Collier often cited Mexico as an example of the type of land tenure reforms that were needed to restore communal Indian culture in the United States. According to Collier, Mexico recognized "its moral obligation to restore to all Indians enough land for a healthy living"and was carrying out this restoration "as a matter of duty"; while the U.S. sought to restore land to "perhaps only 200,000 Indians," its poorer neighbor to the south "assumed as a moral obligation the restoration of land to more than 2,000,000 Indians."[38]

Whether it was indigenous peoples or the rural and urban working classes, Roosevelt's New Deal and Cárdenas's Plan Sexenal gave a political voice to those who often lacked one. In addition, both administrations redefined the role of government by directly addressing the needs of the poor and disenfranchised. The two governments' common ideological convictions made the White House more sympathetic and accommodating toward Mexico over the expropriation of American-owned rural property than were the Republican administrations of the 1920s. As bilateral relations strained in the late 1930s over the lack of compensation for American landowners whose properties were expropriated, Daniels not only eased tensions by frequently referring to Cárdenas as a Mexican-style New Dealer worthy of U.S. support but often reminded FDR that Cárdenas had a great deal of respect for him and his New Deal programs.[39]

In addition to its ideological component, U.S. policy during the agrarian dispute was moderated by domestic economic and political considerations that stemmed from the Depression. Many officials within Roosevelt's administration believed that greater international trade would reduce unemployment, stimulate the economy, and help to lift the United States out of its economic crisis. Consequently, Latin America received increased commercial attention from Washington and U.S. manufacturers alike. According to Duggan, one of the central goals of the Good Neighbor policy was to extend commercial relations with Latin America through the medium of bilateral trade agreements. To reach this end, the 1934 Reciprocal Trade Agreements Act granted most-favored-nation privileges to any country that signed a bilateral commercial treaty with Washington.[40] In fact, reciprocal trade agreements and the Export-Import Bank were Washington's primary tools for restoring trade levels with Latin America, which had declined as a result of the Depression and Smoot-Hawley protectionism.[41] The government's foremost proponent of lower tariffs, market liberalization, and increased international commerce as a panacea for the global economy was Cordell Hull. During his twelve years as Secretary of State, Hull made reciprocal trade agreements a priority and signed eleven of them with Latin America.[42]

In Mexico, as elsewhere in the hemisphere, Washington sought to broaden the export market for U.S. manufacturers. The logic was simple: additional exports to Mexico meant more jobs and lower unemployment in the United States. In Mexico's agricultural sector, three groups sought access to U.S. exports: the federal government, private growers, and the ejidatarios. Mexico also wanted to increase its export of raw materials to the United States to finance the importation of capital equipment and advanced technology. These types of imports were needed to build up Mexico's infrastructure, especially roads, ports, dams, canals, schools, and hospitals. Throughout Cárdenas's term in office, the largest purchaser of U.S. capital equipment in Mexico was the federal government (figure 18). In 1937 Cárdenas stated that he welcomed Hull's policy of expanding international commerce through market liberalization, despite the fact that lower tariffs would reduce Mexican government revenue. Both sides believed that the lost revenue would be offset by the increased volume of trade.[43]

Cárdenas's administration also bought mechanized farming equipment from the United States, such as tractors, reapers, combines, and trucks, to modernize

FIGURE 18. U.S. Secretary of Agriculture and Vice President Elect Henry Wallace (atop a U.S.-made Caterpillar tractor), with Cárdenas (fifth from left) and incoming Secretary of Agriculture Marte Gómez (third from left), November 1940. AGN, ARCHIVO FOTOGRÁFICO, FONDO ENRIQUE DÍAZ, 74/24.

Mexico's antiquated agricultural methods and increase productivity. He had the full support of Mexican agronomists in this undertaking. Between 1935 and 1937 Cárdenas's government imported $100 million worth of advanced farm machinery and irrigation works from U.S. manufacturers.[44] Cárdenas and the Department of Agriculture also sought to increase agricultural output through greater use of chemical fertilizers, pesticides, and high-yield seeds that were produced in the United States. To promote their use, in March 1936, the Cardenistas lowered Mexico's tariffs on imported fertilizers. Soon, wheat and rice growers in Sonora, potato farmers in the Bajío, tobacco growers in Nayarit, cotton growers in the Laguna, and wheat and cotton farmers throughout northern Mexico, along with tens of thousands of ejidatarios, were using seeds and fertilizers imported from the United States.[45]

Although scholars do not often address the role of consumerism in Cárdenas's policies, it was nevertheless an important element in his programs. To "build up" the Mexican economy, Cárdenas argued, it was necessary to provide workers with "higher wages and a higher standard of living" so as to make the "masses into constant consumers."[46] The esteemed Mexican anthropologist Manuel Gamio also believed that a higher standard of living for the majority of Mexicans would foster individual consumption, help domestic industries recover, and make the country more modern. According to Gamio, Mexicans needed to be taught to "live better" and "increase and diversify their needs, satisfying them with goods and services they currently lacked."[47] For Cárdenas's administration, the surest way to bring about this transformation was through agrarian reform—the cornerstone of the government's domestic program. According to the Cardenistas, the country's future relied on the government's ability to transform the rural economy from its backward, semifeudal system of production to a more modern one. The breakup of the haciendas and the creation of cooperative ejidos, they believed, was "Mexico's way out" of underdevelopment.[48]

U.S. officials, including Roosevelt, Daniels, Duggan, and Treasury Undersecretary Harry White, also thought that Cárdenas's agrarian reform program would help produce a stronger and more prosperous Mexico.[49] Many U.S. commentators concurred. University of Oklahoma Professor Maurice Halperin argued in the mid-1930s that progressive U.S. and Mexican businessmen understood the economic benefits of land reform. "Only when Mexican agriculture becomes modernized, when the large plantations are broken up into small holdings, when agricultural laborers become free purchasing agents and able to buy the products of modern industry," wrote Halperin in the *New York Times*, "will Mexican capitalism truly flourish." Princeton University's Eyler Simpson concurred. The young sociologist believed that peasants' demand for manufactured goods would increase as Mexico modernized, expanded its highway system, and broadened access to education.[50] This may explain why Mexican manufacturers did not see Cárdenas's government as a threat. According to Stephan Haber, because Cárdenas built up Mexico's infrastructure, integrated the national market, stabilized the political system, brought peace to the countryside, kept labor under state control, and pursued agrarian reform, but did "not eliminate the concept of private property," Mexican manufacturers saw his government and these changes positively, leading many of them to reinvest their profits in new plants and equipment.[51]

There also was a consensus within both administrations regarding how Mexican agrarian reform would benefit U.S. manufacturers who were outside of the agricultural sector. During the agrarian dispute, Mexican officials frequently told their U.S. counterparts that land reform would lead to the socioeconomic betterment of the nation's popular classes and enhance their acquisitive capacity, which, in turn, would increase exports of U.S. consumer goods to Mexico. Welles concurred and stated that he agreed with Ramón Beteta's 1937 speech, in which the Mexican deputy foreign minister claimed that a "higher standard of living for the great majority of Mexicans was not only desirable in itself, but also meant a greater market for American goods in Mexico."[52] Welles was not alone in his thinking. According to a lengthy 1938 State Department study entitled "Economic Effects of the Mexican Agrarian Program," U.S. policymakers believed agrarian reform would provide a long-term boost for U.S. exports to Mexico. The report concluded, "In the event that the [agrarian] program is maintained with its present education, health and other social objectives, it should serve to increase the standard of living of a large proportion of the country's agricultural population. Viewed from the economic interests of the United States, this might in the future prove of considerable significance in the development of this country's export trade with Mexico."[53] Thus, the idea of Jeffersonian yeoman farmers, idealized by FDR, Daniels, and Duggan, had an international component that was seen to have benefits for a depressed U.S. economy. Agrarian reform helped to modernize Mexican agricultural production by providing ejidatarios with U.S. machinery; it also redistributed wealth by breaking up the haciendas and created acquisitive landowning peasants who could now afford U.S.-made products. For U.S. officials, these developments created a more prosperous Mexico that could become America's junior partner in a post-Depression capitalist world economy.

The numbers supported the claims made on both sides of the border (see table 4). When Mexico was still under the tutelage of the conservative president Plutarco Elías Calles, U.S. exports to Mexico in the first quarter of 1935 stood at $48 million pesos. After mid-1935, when Cárdenas forced Calles from power, accelerated land redistribution, and implemented far-reaching socioeconomic reforms, bilateral trade grew. By the last quarter of 1939, U.S. exports to Mexico reached $140 million pesos. Hence, in less than five years they jumped by nearly 150 percent. In 1940, 79 percent of all Mexico's imports came from the United States, compared to 65 percent in 1935, thereby enabling the United States to gain an even larger share of the Mexican market.[54] Mexican exports to the United States also increased during Cárdenas's term in office, but at a slower rate. Moreover, the United States practically became Mexico's sole export market. In 1937 the United States bought 56 percent of Mexico's total exports, and by 1940, 92 percent of Mexico's exports went north of the border.[55]

Not surprisingly, during the agrarian dispute Mexican officials stressed that the long-term benefits of land reform outweighed the immediate economic losses suffered by a few hundred American property owners. In a November 1937 meeting, Mexican Ambassador to the United States Dr. Francisco Castillo Nájera told Welles that if the United States wanted to demonstrate the goodwill

TABLE 4. Geographic distribution of Mexican imports, 1935 and 1940 (in millions of pesos)

Year	Total	U.S.	U.S. as % of total	Europe	Europe as % of total
1935	406.1	265.3	65	127.1	31
1940	669.0	527.3	79	91.4	14

Source: Hamilton, *The Limits of State Autonomy*, 201.

it so often boasted of, it should not create obstacles by defending the American landowners, who were of little economic significance in comparison to the many benefits that the U.S. industrial and commercial sectors had gained from the Cardenista reforms.[56] In the mid-1930s, public editorializing on both sides of the border in favor of land reform led some U.S. interest groups to advise the State Department against a hard-line policy during the agrarian dispute. When the conflict reached crisis proportions in the summer of 1938, the U.S. National Foreign Trade Council reported to Hull that it preferred to see an "early settlement of the present controversy between the two governments because of the unsettling effects present differences have upon trade with [the United States'] leading Latin American market."[57] In light of the importance that Hull placed on international commerce, he surely would have given such opinions serious consideration.

Since Cárdenas's agrarian reform program benefited U.S. manufacturers of capital goods, farm products and machinery, and a variety of consumer goods, Roosevelt's administration had to balance competing interests. Undoubtedly, FDR would have liked to protect American landowners in Mexico from expropriation. However, it is safe to assume that many American farmers who relocated to Mexico did not vote in each U.S. presidential election and that the largest U.S. absentee landowners (like William Randolph Hearst) and agribusinesses operating in Mexico (like Harry Chandler's CRLC) were aligned with the Republican Party. On the other hand, the U.S. export sector—which clearly benefited from increased trade with Mexico—employed millions of workers who were part of Roosevelt's New Deal coalition. Hence, besides economic factors, domestic political considerations also would have dissuaded the White House from being too critical of Mexican agrarian reform.

MEXICAN IMMIGRATION AND REPATRIATION

In addition to bilateral trade, domestic politics over Mexican immigration and repatriation—both shaped by the Depression—also tempered Washington's policy toward Mexico City during the agrarian dispute. In the 1930s, high rates of unemployment produced a great deal of frustration and disenchantment among American workers. Many used the Mexican American and Mexican immigrant communities as scapegoats for their plight, and anti-Mexican sentiments soared. Many Americans—especially those who competed directly with Mexican immigrants for low-skill agricultural and industrial jobs—believed that limiting the number of Mexicans in the United States would decrease competition for both jobs and government handouts. Roosevelt, therefore, foresaw political gains from reducing their numbers.

From Washington's point of view, there were at least two ways to restrict Mexican migration to the United States. First was the strict enforcement of immigration laws, which aggressively blocked both legal and illegal immigrants from entering the country.[58] The clampdown worked. For the six-year period from 1935 to 1940, only 13,000 legal Mexican immigrants crossed the Rio Grande, or approximately 2,180 per year.[59] The second way to limit the number of new immigrants was to encourage land redistribution in Mexico as a way to reduce rural under- and unemployment across the border. Property ownership not only provided landless peasants in the Mexican countryside with consistent employment but also gave them a stake in the community and reduced the likelihood of their crossing the border in search of work.

While Washington actively tried to limit Mexican immigration, this policy did little about those Mexicans who were already in the country; nor did it remedy the erroneous belief, held by many Americans, that ridding the country of immigrants would create jobs for "real Americans" and save taxpayers money by reducing federal welfare rolls.[60] To reduce the Mexican presence Washington again had two options. The first was to make the United States a less attractive place to stay by limiting Mexican access to New Deal programs. The Federal Emergency Relief Administration, Civil Works Administration, and Works Projects Administration excluded thousands of Mexicans because of residency and documentation requirements. The AAA's crop reduction program caused many Mexican farmhands to lose work, as large landowners reduced the number of acres under cultivation and dismissed immigrant field workers; it also provided no assistance to migratory rural laborers. In addition, Mexican migrant workers were precluded from filing discrimination charges against their employers with the federally sponsored Committee on Fair Employment Practices.[61]

The second way to reduce the number of Mexicans north of the border was through the enactment of federal deportation laws. While recent studies show that Mexican repatriation did not significantly benefit the U.S. economy, at the time the impression was quite different.[62] During the 1930s, approximately 1.5 million Mexicans were either forcefully deported or returned voluntarily to Mexico. The repatriation of Mexican nationals and Mexican Americans was supported by opportunistic politicians, labor unions, civic and patriotic groups, and a majority of the American public.[63] Congress also jumped on the repatriation bandwagon. As late as April 1940, a joint resolution was introduced in the Senate stating that the number of Mexicans residing in the United States should be equivalent to the number of Americans residing in Mexico and that "all Mexican aliens in excess of Americans in Mexico shall be deported within one year after the enactment of this joint resolution."[64]

Cognizant of the deplorable living and working conditions of Mexican nationals north of the border, Cárdenas's government gave a good deal of attention to repatriation.[65] During his presidential campaign in 1934, Cárdenas often spoke of the need to assist Mexicans "outside of Mexico" in their return to "*la madre patria*" (the mother country). In fact, Mexico City's commitment to repatriation became official in the PNR's 1934–40 Six-Year Plan.[66] Although repatriation numbers had peaked earlier in the decade, Cárdenas's position in favor of repatriation pleased U.S. officials.

Cárdenas's repatriation program was not solely based on altruism. Besides the president, Mexican agronomists and the anthropologist Manuel Gamio—a contemporary expert on migration issues—believed that repatriates would help modernize Mexican agricultural production, boost farm yields, and stimulate the rural economy. A study by Gabino Vázquez's Agrarian Department in January 1936 noted that while in the United States, many Mexican rural workers acquired skills in advanced agricultural methods that were lacking in the Mexican countryside. According to the report, Mexican field workers in the United States learned how to use fertilizers, pesticides, and modern farm machinery; they also understood soil and irrigation management and economic planning. To persuade the more-progressive Mexican agricultural workers in the United States to return to home, Cárdenas's administration's offered them land. Once south of the border, many of these repatriates were placed in agricultural colonies where their new skills could be maintained. In addition, they could teach other Mexican peasants how to be more productive and farm like the Americans. The 1936 Agrarian Department study argued that if the more-advanced agriculturalists were isolated in rural communities in Mexico's interior, within a few years they would forget everything they learned.[67]

Vázquez's 1936 report also recommended establishing agricultural cooperatives in northern Mexico in areas with high-quality soil and irrigation works. The north was preferred because its close proximity to the U.S. border reduced transportation costs; it was also assumed that the *repatriados* were accustomed to the frontier lifestyle. Sonora's Yaqui Valley and Baja California's Mexicali Valley, as well as Chihuahua and Coahuila, were some of the regions singled out. The Agrarian Department's repatriation report even recommended colonizing the "large latifundios appropriated by foreigners during the Díaz administration" that were located on the border in Baja California.[68] As shown earlier, following the promulgation of the April 1936 colonization agreement between the Colorado River Land Company and the Mexican government, Cárdenas's administration sought to colonize some of the company's 850,000 acres with Mexican rural workers residing in the United States.[69]

The Roosevelt administration knew of Cárdenas's repatriation and colonization program, since Mexican Foreign Secretary Eduardo Hay announced it via radio broadcasts and press releases in the United States. Mexico City also established a repatriation office at the Matamoros-Brownsville border crossing. Deputy Foreign Secretary Beteta, meanwhile, suggested bringing the message directly to the Mexicans living in the United States. In 1937, he toured Mexican *colonias* (barrios) in California, Texas, New Mexico, Arizona, Louisiana, Illinois, Pennsylvania, New York, Massachusetts, Rhode Island, and Virginia. Not surprisingly, the State Department "rolled out the red-carpet" and instructed state and local officials to extend him every "diplomatic courtesy." Clearly winning Washington's support, throughout his lengthy tour Beteta announced to thousands of Mexican nationals that the Mexican government would pay transportation costs for entire families, as well as their farm animals, automobiles, and personal belongings, provide each family with 20 acres of irrigated land and 50 acres of seasonal land, and finally offer cash assistance in their first year back, as well as bank loans and private credit, if they returned to Mexico. During his visit to Houston, Beteta wrote to the Ministry of Foreign Affairs and stated that, due to the poor conditions there, Mexico City should immediately repatriate forty-three people back to their home states and pay all of the transportation costs.[70]

Many Mexicans found living and working conditions in the United States so deplorable, and attitudes toward them so hostile, that returning home was seen as the first step toward starting a better life. In March 1936, Cárdenas began making radio addresses inviting all Mexicans in *el norte* back to Mexico. The response was overwhelming. Cárdenas's presidential papers are filled with hundreds of telegrams from Mexican nationals residing in the United States asking him for money and/or transportation to facilitate their return. Many of these telegrams are filled with heart-wrenching tales of woe, along with nationalistic, revolutionary zeal and requests for a plot of land.[71] Cárdenas even appealed to the nation as a whole to assist its fellow countrymen north of the border. On November 20, 1938, in an address celebrating the twenty-ninth anniversary of the Mexican Revolution, the president stated, "Local economic depressions occur, creating a hostile atmosphere for aliens who retained the nationality of their homelands and who find themselves unwelcome competitors of the citizens of the country whose guests they have become. . . . This unfavorable circumstance does not relieve us of the unmistakable duty to respond . . . to the necessity of repatriating our fellow citizens. . . . We must lend our aid to those who left their motherland."[72]

Out of the numerous colonies of repatriates that were established in northern Mexico in 1939, Mexico City used the aptly named "Colonia 18 de Marzo" to showcase its effort. The symbolism of the colony's name stems from the fact that on March 18, 1938, Cárdenas nationalized the entire foreign-owned oil industry. Located in Tamaulipas, near the border city of Matamoros, Colonia 18 de Marzo held more than four hundred repatriated Mexican families and totaled nearly fifteen hundred people. Each family was given their own 25 acre ejido to farm. Because of the political attention given to it, Colonia 18 de Marzo was visited by high-ranking federal officials, including Beteta, who strongly endorsed the program. It also initially received a decent amount of financial and material support.[73]

Because U.S. Democrats lost eighty-one seats in the House of Representatives and eight in the Senate in the 1938 midterm elections, and because much of Roosevelt's New Deal coalition endorsed limiting the Mexican presence in the United States, electoral politics probably encouraged FDR to support Mexican land reform insofar as it facilitated repatriation.[74] In fact, it was in the White House's self-interest, both politically and economically, to endorse Cárdenas's agrarian reform program, in hopes that it would stem immigration, assist repatriation, and promote the export of capital equipment, farm machinery, irrigation works, agricultural products, and consumer goods made by U.S. manufacturers. U.S. workers, who comprised the largest percentage of Roosevelt's political base, stood to benefit from Mexico's agrarian reform, and thus FDR was not apt to challenge the program solely to protect a few hundred American property owners from redistribution.

The Roosevelt administration also accommodated Mexico during the bilateral conflict over land because there appeared to be no attractive alternative to President Cárdenas. Washington believed that Cárdenas stood between two undesirable options: the communists and the fascists, both of whom appeared eager to take over the Mexican government. To prevent this, Roosevelt's administration backed Cárdenas and hoped that economic and political conditions in Mexico would not deteriorate to the point where civil war could erupt. The American public and U.S. officials were terrified by the possibility of having a "Spanish-like" civil war on the U.S. border. If revolution came to Mexico, many contemporary observers believed, it would increase Mexican migration to the United States, disrupt bilateral trade, and hurt the U.S. economy. Also, many feared that a fascist victory would increase Germany's penetration of Mexico, while a communist takeover would result in the widespread nationalization of foreign-owned enterprises. Taking a hard line over the land expropriations and hence destabilizing Cárdenas's administration made little sense to most U.S. policymakers, especially as both sides recognized the importance of land redistribution as a tool to maintain Mexican political stability.

For many U.S. officials, including the embassy's chargé d'affaires, Pierre L. de Boal, a politically stable Mexico required a robust Mexican economy. According to a 1937 State Department memorandum, "from a long range point of view, no policy could have the same stabilizing influence" as Cárdenas's agrarian policy. "It is already evident," the memo continued, "that those Indians who have received land have lost interest in revolutions and banditry. They now have the opportunity to make a living out of the land and are satisfied. As property owners their interest is principally in protecting what they have at last secured."[75]

Both Daniels's and FDR's views on the political components of land reform were influenced by Frank Tannenbaum. The Columbia University history professor's 1934 book *Whither Latin America* argued that foreign domination of Latin American agriculture and transportation systems were not just local defects but rather the primary cause for the region's underdevelopment.[76] This landmark book was soon followed by similar arguments from journalists and economists. In addition to shaping a school of thought that was critical of U.S. foreign investment in Latin America, Tannenbaum spent a great deal of time in Mexico and often took lengthy trips with Cárdenas in the countryside. Afterwards he would meet or correspond with Daniels or Roosevelt about Mexico. So impressed was the U.S. ambassador with Tannenbaum's keen observations that on one occasion he told FDR, "Frank Tannenbaum knows Mexico better than any man except Ernest Gruening."[77] After one of his trips with the Mexican president, Tannenbaum summarized for Daniels the politics of land reform in Mexico:

> The agrarian movement is stronger than the government. . . . The present Mexican government could not stop the process of land distribution if it wanted to without precipitating either a revolution against itself . . . or universal and unorganized violence all over the country. . . . The thousands of villages which have had no land given to them will not . . . stand by and see themselves denied what other villages have been given. It would amount to political suicide if any administration in Mexico should bring the agrarian movement to an end now, without completing the process of land distribution. This process must be seen as a fundamental historical change taking place in Mexico, which, like a flood, is stronger than any obstacle which stands in its way. . . . The present administration considers it its duty to Mexico to satisfy the demands of the people—partly because of humane feelings on the part of the present administration, but largely because of a kind of political insight which makes them feel that the only way to peace and stability and democracy in Mexico is through land distribution, and that until that process is completed nothing else can be achieved in Mexico.[78]

Besides the instability produced by agrarista militancy, the political situation in Mexico grew even more precarious following the establishment of a conservative and sometimes violent opposition to Cárdenas. General Saturnino Cedillo led a brief and unsuccessful military uprising against the federal government in mid-1938. In addition to Cedillo's insurrection, during Cárdenas's tenure Mexico witnessed the growth of a rightist political movement that opposed his progressive socioeconomic policies. Among the largest conservative organizations were the Mexican Revolutionary Action (Acción Revolucionaria Mexicana, ARM) founded in 1934, the National Union of Veterans of the Revolution (Unión Nacional de Veteranos de la Revolución, UNVR) established in 1935,

FIGURE 19. Cartoonist Lute Pease depicts President Cárdenas as blinded by his political obligations, presumably to workers and peasants, which results in his being led by an expropriatory domestic policy that in turn leads him into the cactus of international complications. THE NEWARK EVENING NEWS, CA. LATE 1930S. COURTESY OF THE NEWARK PUBLIC LIBRARY.

and the Confederation of the Middle Class (Confederación de la Clase Media), formed in 1936. The UNVR had its strength in the army, while the ARM— popularly known as the Gold Shirts—was modeled upon Benito Mussolini's Black Shirts. Although it is difficult to measure the size and influence of these quasi-fascist movements, Cárdenas either saw them as a threat or, more likely, played up the threat that they allegedly posed to justify clamping down on them. In late 1936, for instance, he expelled the ARM's leader General Nicolas Rodríguez from Mexico and officially banned the organization.[79] This did not prevent the ARM from conducting propaganda campaigns against Cárdenas and launching a small-scale armed insurrection in Tamaulipas in January 1938 that resulted in the death of sixteen Gold Shirt rebels and the capture of twenty-five more.[80]

In 1937 two additional opposition groups also were established: the Mexican Social Democratic Party (Partido Social Demócrata Mexicano), founded by respected journalist Diego Arenas Guzmán, and the National Sinarquista Union (Unión Nacional Sinarquista), established by a group of young Catholic laymen. The Sinarquistas, according to Alan Knight, "rejected the Mexican Revolution, liberalism, socialism, class struggle, and gringo materialism, offering instead, the value of religion, family, private property, hierarchy, and social solidarity." By 1938, this conservative religious group had gained hundreds of thousands of members and significantly increased its organizational muscle. In light of the government crackdown against the Catholic Church during the postrevolutionary era—which in 1926 precipitated the three-year-long Cristero Rebellion—some observers in the late 1930s expected the Sinarquistas to take up arms against Cárdenas's government, especially since they were strongest in many of the same states that had earlier fought the Cristiada.[81]

Besides conservative and potentially violent Catholic laypeople, there also were a number of smaller political groups—some centrist, some center-right, and a few far right—that stood in opposition to Cárdenas's government, including the Confederation of Independent Parties, the National Civic Action Group, the Civic Action Party of the Middle Class, the Spanish Anti-Communist and Anti-Jewish Association, the Anti-Reelectionist Party, the Mexican Nationalist Youth, the National Committee in Defense of the Race, and the National Action Party (PAN).[82] Cárdenas's unpopularity, according to John Sherman, stemmed from the conservative nature of Mexican society and the radical spirit of his reforms. The conservative opposition to Cárdenas included reactionaries in the church and army, remaining hacendados, industrialists, fascists, and anti-Semites, upper- and middle-class Mexicans who abhorred socialist education, small business owners upset over rising inflation, political, worker, and peasant leaders who resented the PNR's monopoly on power, suffragists angry over women's continued disenfranchisement, and religious peasants who opposed agrarian reform.[83]

Most of the conservative nationalist movements saw parallels in the Spanish Civil War and supported General Francisco Franco's rebellion against the Popular Front government. Many Mexican industrialists and hacendados who backed the Mexican Social Democratic Party and the Sinarquistas also supported German intervention in Spain on Franco's behalf. In fact, two of Mexico's leading anti-Cárdenas organizations were under the tutelage of the Spanish Falange. As the head of a relatively weak federal government, Cárdenas must have recognized his own vulnerability, especially should any of the far-right opposition parties receive support from Germany, Italy, or Spain. Again, whether Cárdenas felt threatened or was simply using the political situation to strengthen his government is unclear. Nevertheless, he armed workers.[84]

Conspiracy rumors helped to shore up support for Cárdenas both in Mexico and in the United States, where Roosevelt's administration feared a civil war like Spain's below the border. According to Daniels, "The old 'Científicos' and wealthy people" in Mexico were "warmly sympathetic to the forces trying to drive out [Spain's Popular Front] government" and saw "a common bond between themselves and their cousins in Spain."[85] The fact that FDR, Daniels, and most State Department officials were Protestants may have had a negative affect on how they viewed right-wing Catholic opposition groups in Mexico. Also, in light of the 1917 Zimmermann telegram—in which Germany offered to support a Mexican attack against the United States to keep the latter country from entering World War I—many U.S. diplomats worried that a rightist takeover in Mexico would lead to greater German economic, political, and military presence in their southern neighbor. By linking events in Spain to Mexico, Roosevelt hypothesized a worst-case scenario during an April 1938 press conference: "Suppose . . . the European governments were to do in Mexico what they did in Spain. Suppose they would organize . . . a Fascist revolution in Mexico. Mexico is awfully close to us. Suppose they were to send planes and officers and guns and were to equip the revolutionists and get control of the whole of Mexico and thereupon run the Mexican government. . . . You could not stand for it."[86]

Roosevelt was not alone in exaggerating German involvement in Mexico. The assessments of Nazi penetration of Latin America by both U.S. policy-makers and the press were alarmist, despite the absence of proof.[87] Whether the German threat was real or imagined, one of Washington's primary concerns during the agrarian dispute was to avoid creating conditions in Mexico that would lead to civil unrest. A member of the U.S. embassy staff summed up the situation well in a conversation with his British colleague: "Roosevelt is . . . alarmed at the consequences which might ensue if anything like a pitched battle between capital and labor on the Spanish model were to break out in Mexico. Official American opinion regards this as the worst of all the disagreeable results which might follow a coup d'état or widespread revolution in Mexico, and it has never thought of any other way of preventing either than that of affording full support to Cárdenas and his present advisers."[88]

If the United States stopped backing Cárdenas and a "rightist soldier" gained control of the federal government, then, according to Daniels, the new conservative regime would either lead to a "great deal of bloodshed and another Spain," or the rightists would be forced from power and replaced by a "radical leftist who would go further to the left than Cárdenas."[89] The popular social commentator Walter Lippmann argued that what was at stake in the agrarian dispute, the oil crisis, and Mexican political stability was an issue "far greater than that of the legal claims of foreign investors." Rather, "the paramount interest of the U.S. was to prevent a Mexican civil war."[90] As bilateral tensions grew due to the continued seizure of American-owned land and the national-ization of the petroleum industry, Hull discussed the Mexican situation with the State Department's economic adviser Herbert Feis, Assistant Secretary of State Adolf Berle, and Welles. Backing away from a hard-line policy, Hull ad-mitted that he was persuaded by Roosevelt's argument that too much pressure on Mexico over the expropriations would provoke "widespread anti-American feeling . . . and . . . a revolutionary movement." [91]

Although Washington worried about civil war and a fascist takeover in Mexico, policymakers also were concerned about the growing influence of the radical Left in Mexican politics and civic organizations. The communist move-ment had gained so much support in Mexico that Washington was convinced its influence stretched beyond Mexico's borders. A 1937 State Department re-port noted that communist movements in Latin America were inspired and directed from Mexico and not the Soviet Union.[92] According to the State De-partment, three prominent leftist leaders in Mexico posed a serious threat to U.S. interests: Vicente Lombardo Toledano, who was both the general secretary of the nation's largest labor union, the CTM, and president of the Latin Ameri-can Confederation of Workers; Dr. Alejandro Carrillo, who was secretary of the Workers' University in Mexico City and Lombardo Toledano's assistant at the CTM; and Hernán Laborde, who was general secretary of the Mexican Commu-nist Party. Lombardo Toledano and Carrillo were both members of the Com-munist International operating in Mexico, and all three men stated publicly on repeated occasions that a "Soviet-style form of government would be best for Latin America." After spending much of 1935 in the Soviet Union, upon his return to Mexico, Lombardo Toledano advocated "Stalinist Communism" for his country. All three men were clearly more antagonistic toward the United States than was Cárdenas. During the July 1937 meeting of the International Federation of Trade Union Congresses, Carrillo charged that over the past twenty-five years the United States had "supported internal turmoil in Mexico to further its own selfish and imperialistic aims"; he then characterized the United States as the "Germany of the American continent."[93]

As bilateral tensions increased over the land and oil seizures, in June 1938 Daniels received a copy of a confidential report supposedly written by Lombardo Toledano to other CTM leaders. According to the radical labor leader, conditions were ripe for revolution in Mexico. First, the lack of cohesion of the Mexican people, wrote Lombardo Toledano, would allow the Left to dominate the country. Second, Cárdenas was still close to the CTM and willing to follow its lead. Third, it was necessary to take advantage of the Good Neighbor policy's noninterventionism. Fourth, Cárdenas's strong alliance with John Lewis and the Congress of Industrial Organizations (CIO) would facilitate the uprising. Fifth, the CTM's radical propaganda in Central and South America had made considerable progress. Sixth, because the CTM was among the most important labor organizations in the hemisphere, it had to take the lead in promoting revolution. At the end of the communiqué, Lombardo Toledano called for the immediate division of all lands in Mexico and the nationalization of the electric, mining, textile, and railroad industries.[94] Since the letter painted the Mexican Left as being both extremely radical and militant, it reinforced Washington's policy of backing Cárdenas so as to prevent more antagonistic groups from coming to power.

As the *Nation* surmised in mid-1938, Washington would have difficulties finding a replacement for Cárdenas among other Mexican leaders. If Roosevelt's administration discredited the Mexican president over the land and oil conflicts and helped to unseat him, the magazine editorialized, not only did Lombardo Toledano stand as his likely successor, but "American interests would have little chance of survival."[95] Mexico's lack of a centrist political opposition impelled Washington to back Cárdenas's government and take a conciliatory approach over the expropriation of American-owned rural property. This remained the case even after the March 1938 oil nationalization. At this point in his presidency, Cárdenas had demonstrated his nationalist credentials and significantly increased his popular support with the oil seizure. Consequently, he was able to thwart attempts by workers to take control of the mining industry—which American companies dominated—and keep the radical labor movement in check. Also, because Cárdenas's labor policies usually promoted traditional workweek and wage concessions for workers, some U.S. officials rightly saw him as both a populist and centrist who stood between Mexico's political extremes, thus making him worthy of accommodation.[96]

THE SPECIAL AND GENERAL CLAIMS COMMISSIONS

As increasing numbers of American landowners lost their property to expropriation during the mid- to late 1930s, many of them called for the U.S. to intervene militarily or sever diplomatic ties. Leading U.S. officials ignored such requests, not only for the economic and political reasons already discussed, but also because they recognized that previous bilateral claims agreements had put in place a set of procedures that could be used to indemnify U.S. landowners. Officials on both sides of the border saw the Special and General Claims Commissions as models for resolving the agrarian dispute through peaceful and more routine diplomatic channels.

Although the idea of a Special Claims Commission was initially proposed by Mexican officials in late 1918, it was not until the 1923 Bucareli Conference that both countries established it in order to settle all of the claims filed by U.S. nationals against the Mexican government for the damages that they or their property incurred during the Mexican Revolution (officially dated as lasting from November 20, 1910, to May 31, 1920). For losses suffered during this period, the Americans filed 2,810 "special" or "revolutionary" claims totaling $207 million.[97] Although negotiations got underway in late 1924, little headway was made in resolving the claims because the U.S. and Mexican commissioners could not agree on the amount of compensation that should be awarded to each individual claimant. Consequently, in 1927 and again in 1929 both countries extended the life of the Special Claims Commission. Since officials continued to make little progress throughout 1930, in 1931 Mexican Foreign Minister Genaro Estrada suggested limiting the number of cases to be heard; he also recommended an *en bloc* (lump sum) settlement for all of the American claims against his government. U.S. diplomats were initially skeptical of the Mexican proposal. Soon, however, the State Department realized the futility of evaluating thousands of individual claims and accepted Mexico's idea of a lump sum agreement.[98]

In late 1932, Mexico's new foreign minister, Manuel Téllez, began to discuss with U.S. Ambassador James Rueben Clark an en bloc settlement that would cover all the U.S. special claims, rather than have the commissioners discuss one case at a time. Washington demanded that Mexico pay 10 percent of the total amount applied for by the American claimants. Mexican officials argued that their country was too poor to pay such a high percentage and noted that most European governments had accepted 2.65 percent on behalf of their citizens for similar claims. Not surprisingly, talks broke down. After Roosevelt appointed Daniels ambassador in 1933, the State Department directed him to settle all of the revolutionary claims. In an August 1933 meeting between Daniels and Plutarco Elías Calles, el Jefe Máximo, endorsed the idea of a lump sum settlement, as long as it was an amount that Mexico could afford. Like his predecessors, Daniels discovered that his Mexican counterparts were difficult to pin down on details and avoided making "concrete proposals" with regard to a final settlement.[99]

Without the threat of hard-line tactics, Roosevelt's administration had little leverage against Mexico. After a year of arduous negotiations over the special claims, in April 1934 the two governments agreed to a lump sum settlement of $5.5 million. Mexican officials clearly out-negotiated their U.S. counterparts, as Mexico paid only 2.65 percent of the total amount that was initially claimed. Mexico City was granted ten years to pay off the claims, with annual installments of $500,000 to begin in January 1935, just two months after Cárdenas took office. Afterwards the U.S. government established the Special Mexican Claims Commission—comprised solely of U.S. officials—which then appraised each claim and disbursed the funds to the American claimants.[100]

A number of key officials in both the Roosevelt and Cárdenas administrations believed that the 1934 special claims agreement established a set of procedures that could resolve the subsequent agrarian dispute. As bilateral tensions increased in 1938 over Mexico's repeated failure to compensate U.S. landowners, Daniels suggested to Hull that Washington should consider a "lump sum" agreement and "settle with [U.S.] nationals" as they did "in the Special Claims on which Mexico is now paying $500,000 a year."[101] When skeptics questioned whether Mexico would compensate the American landowners or the oil companies, both Roosevelt and Daniels reminded them that the special claims filed by U.S. nationals had been resolved satisfactorily.[102] The fact that Mexico also had compensated European claimants for the losses that they suffered during the revolution indicated Mexico's willingness to pay and encouraged U.S. officials who sought a peaceful settlement of the agrarian conflict. Meanwhile, Cardenista officials pushed for a lump sum agreement of the agrarian claims and suggested following the formula used with the special claims. In April 1938, Beteta told Daniels that instead of negotiating each individual agrarian claim, "Mexico [could] pay a lump sum to the United States . . . [of] $500,000 a year in monthly installments—and [U.S.] officials could pay out to [the American] claimants in the same way as they allocated funds derived from the Special Claims payments."[103]

Like the Special Claims Commission, the General Claims Commission also provided a model for a negotiated resolution to the agrarian dispute. This commission, also agreed to at the 1923 Bucareli Conference, was designed to settle those outstanding claims filed by both U.S. and Mexican nationals since 1868 that were not related to the Mexican Revolution. More than three thousand

American claimants demanded nearly $600 million. Like the special claims, most of the general claims were greatly inflated by Americans seeking exorbitant compensation. The General Claims Commission also covered the agrarian claims that stemmed from Mexico's expropriation of American-owned rural property between 1917 and 1927. Although the commission examined thousands of nonagrarian cases between 1924 and 1930, it ruled on only two hundred of them. Since the U.S. and Mexican representatives could not agree on the value of each general claim, the commission suspended its work in 1930; it was revived in 1932 and again in 1934, each time for a period of two years.[104]

After the General Claims Commission was re-established in 1934, the two governments adopted a new approach to facilitate a settlement. Each government designated one representative whose sole function was to appraise all of the general claims, both U.S. and Mexican, within a three-year period. When Commissioners Oscar Underwood and Dr. Fernandez MacGregor met in 1937 to reconcile the claims, they eliminated 1,500 for their lack of merit. Of the remaining half, the two officials only agreed on a few. As was the case initially with the special claims, the impasse resulted from their inability to appraise each general claim equally and then agree on the amount of compensation due the individual claimant. Because of the deadlock, U.S. and Mexican officials decided to follow the special claims model. Thereafter, they no longer discussed the individual claims but instead simply negotiated the total amount of Mexico's lump sum payment to the United States.[105]

For some in Roosevelt's administration, there was little reason to take aggressive action against Cárdenas's government over his land seizures, because the expropriation of American-owned rural property already had been the subject of bilateral talks via the General Claims Commission.[106] In other words, because FDR's administration had discussed the pre-1927 agrarian claims with Mexico, it was difficult for the White House to justify taking a hard line over Cárdenas's expropriations simply because they were more numerous than those of his predecessors. Hence, the establishment of the Special and General Claims Commissions in the mid-1920s, and their revival in 1933 and 1934, put in place a set of procedures that were later used to compensate both American landowners and the U.S. petroleum companies. Likewise, the Special Claims Commission demonstrated the advantage of settling such disputes through a lump sum agreement—a model that later was applied to the general, agrarian, and oil claims and detailed in the Global Settlement that the two nations signed in late 1941.

The expropriation of American-owned rural property in Mexico during Cárdenas's administration severely strained U.S.-Mexican relations. Rather than
respond in a heavy-handed manner, Washington accommodated its southern
neighbor. As other scholars have shown for other parts of Latin America during
the Good Neighbor era, a variety of forces and actors shaped U.S. policy toward
Mexico.[107] The initial U.S. response to Mexican economic nationalism, as seen
in the bilateral conflict over land, had little to do with the onset of wwii in 1939.
Rather, the Roosevelt administration's reaction to the Cardenista assault on
U.S. economic interests in the Mexican countryside began earlier in the decade
and was determined mostly by the economic and political impact of the Great
Depression.

When the oil properties were subsequently taken over by the Mexican government in 1938, the issues were strikingly similar to those surrounding the
agrarian dispute: oil worker militancy (versus peasant agency), PEMEX (versus
communal ejidos), American-built oil wells (versus American-developed farm
and ranch lands), subsoil rights (versus future agricultural yields), $24 million
settlement for the oil properties (versus $22.5 million settlement for the rural
properties). Likewise, many of the concerns that were raised by both sides
during the agrarian dispute simply resurfaced, including national sovereignty,
economic nationalism, domestic politics, international law, property rights,
foreign investment, indemnification, Mexican political stability, bilateral trade,
the Good Neighbor policy, and nonintervention, to name a few. For Hull, like
Roosevelt and Daniels, the oil expropriation was little different from that of
American-owned land. In a State Department press release, Hull claimed that
the oil seizure was "one incident in a long series of incidents of this character
and accordingly *raises no new question. The subject under consideration*" was
"the matter of compensation for *various properties of American citizens expropriated in the past few years.*"[108] Hence, the role played by the Second World
War in determining the outcome of the oil crisis warrants reexamination. In
fact, had it not been for the agrarian dispute, U.S. officials might not have even
assisted the oil companies in gaining compensation from Mexico. In mid-1938,
Assistant Secretary of State Adolf Berle claimed that if the oil companies were
the only ones involved in the expropriation controversy, then the United States
would have considered not asking Mexico for payment, "but as there were
several hundred small landowners whose property has also been taken and
more coming," wrote Berle, Washington had to insist on indemnification.[109]

The agrarian dispute not only promoted a negotiated settlement of the oil crisis but also improved U.S.-Latin American relations. As one U.S. newspaper commented, since the Good Neighbor policy passed its first test in Mexico with the amicable resolution of the agrarian conflict, the South American republics were "really beginning to trust the United States."[110] Clearly, the bilateral clash over land played an important role in shaping both U.S.-Mexican and U.S.–Latin American relations during this period. While this chapter has examined the domestic factors that tempered U.S. policy during the agrarian dispute, the next two chapters will analyze the manner in which the conflict was negotiated by officials on both sides of the border.

DIPLOMATIC WEAPONS OF THE WEAK

The Cárdenas Administration Outmaneuvers Washington

Do not let social reforms frighten you! Without them the transformation of my country is impossible.

MEXICAN AMBASSADOR DR. FRANCISCO CASTILLO NÁJERA, ADDRESSING
THE ACADEMY OF WORLD ECONOMICS, WASHINGTON, MAY 21, 1936

From the inception of the agrarian program the question of compensation of American owners of expropriated lands was a constant source of friction between the two governments.

U.S. AGRARIAN CLAIMS COMMISSION EXECUTIVE OFFICER GEORGE
WINTERS, FEBRUARY 18, 1939

In 1936 Cárdenas's government sought to hasten the redistribution of national wealth by passing a new expropriation law that enabled the federal government to seize any type of property through eminent domain. Cárdenas assured Ambassador Daniels that Washington should not worry about the law's application against U.S. economic interests, since it was designed to gain control of industries that had suspended their operations.[1] Despite the president's assurances, the law did facilitate the expropriation of hundreds of American-owned rural estates and the nationalization of nearly a dozen U.S. petroleum companies. The expropriation law required the Mexican government to compensate affected property owners, both domestic and foreign, within ten years. It did not, however, specify either the form or terms of indemnification. Because Washington recognized Mexico's sovereign right to expropriate private property and since, as Lorenzo Meyer points out, U.S. officials capitulated on the issue of prompt payment, the main point of bilateral contention during the agrarian dispute and the subsequent oil crisis became "the amount and form of payment" that Mexico would make to the affected property owners.[2]

For Washington, the compensation agreement concerning American landowners would serve as a precedent for the petroleum companies and any other American properties expropriated in Mexico or other parts of the developing world.[3] For Mexico City, the cost of indemnifying hundreds of American landowners, and later the foreign-owned oil companies, would hurt the nation's weak economy. Consequently, Mexico City sought to avoid, or at least minimize, these additional debts. As seen by the tremendous strain put on bilateral relations, the issue of compensation was critical not only to the property owners but also to both governments. Because of the importance of indemnification, each administration used its own set of diplomatic tools to obtain their version of a favorable agrarian settlement. For Washington, this meant applying economic pressure against Cárdenas's government to reach a narrow agreement that only addressed Mexican compensation for the American landowners. For Mexico City, it meant employing what could be described as the "diplomatic weapons of the weak" to expand the agreement so as to include U.S. financial and commercial assistance to Mexico to ease the cost of indemnifying hundreds of American rural property owners.[4]

Unlike great powers, middle powers and weak nations generally are not interested in changing the structure of the interstate system; rather, they usually try to "work the system to their advantage or their minimum disadvantage."[5] To safeguard their national interests against more powerful nations, middle powers such as Mexico sometimes use diplomatic tactics that one could describe as "everyday forms of resistance." Foot-dragging, obfuscation, noncompliance, and other forms of defiant diplomacy are utilized by middle and weak states because they lack the military, economic, and political resources that great powers commonly use to gain leverage in an international conflict. Such methods of diplomacy are not often overt, nor do they usually require much planning, since they stem from an implicit understanding among policymakers of their weak position internationally—which may stretch back decades or even centuries. Mexico, having been a victim of U.S. military aggression and economic penetration in the nineteenth and twentieth centuries, developed a "culture of resistance" toward the United States that reinforced such diplomatic methods.[6] This was especially true for those Mexican officials who were a prod-

FIGURE 20. Pulitzer Prize winning syndicated cartoonist Reg Manning accurately denotes Mexican foreign policy tactics of delay and obfuscation in the face of U.S. pressure. The cartoon does not employ negative Mexican stereotypes. Instead, it depicts the Mexican character as not being afraid of Uncle Sam, as he goes about his business and uses subaltern diplomatic tactics (e.g., "No savvy señor") to thwart his northern neighbor. REPRINTED WITH THE PERMISSION OF DAVID C. MANNING.

uct of the revolution and who governed their country from 1915 to 1946. In fact, Cárdenas's mulish strategy toward the United States during the agrarian dispute was not unique, and examples of obstinacy toward Washington can be found in a number of Mexican administrations both before and after the 1930s (see figure 20).

While most scholars of bilateral relations see Mexico as weak and vulnerable and the United States as an all-powerful, self-serving hegemon, the next two chapters will explore the limitations of U.S. power and add to the growing body of literature that recognizes the sophistication of Latin American officials in negotiations with their U.S. counterparts. Unlike many traditional and revisionist accounts, which sometimes depict Latin American policymakers as inert, recent postrevisionist studies of U.S. relations with Nicaragua, Venezuela, Costa Rica, the Dominican Republic, and Mexico have, according to Max Friedman, "rightly portrayed Latin American leaders as genuine partners in the relationship, acting with autonomy and pursuing their own interests to the best of their ability within an asymmetrical framework."[7] As for Mexico, Friedrich Schuler correctly notes that in the mid- to late 1930s, the "Mexicans were better skilled in international negotiations, more realistic in the evaluation of historical contexts, and more creative in situations of crisis than their European and U.S. counterparts. With few exceptions, Mexican skills easily countered the alleged, intrinsic power advantages that are supposed to come with open hegemony and indirect imperialism."[8]

During the agrarian dispute, Mexican officials expropriated millions of acres of American-owned land over a period of five years, avoided paying immediate reparations, and negotiated an advantageous compensation agreement by manipulating the diplomatic process. This raises an important question: How did Mexico City get the better of Washington? This chapter will examine, among other factors, problems within the U.S. foreign policy establishment that afforded Mexican diplomats space in which to maneuver. Mexico's U.S. policy also successfully mixed resistance with cooperation. By dragging its feet in some places and conceding in others, Mexico City was able to secure international loans, as well as a trade and monetary stabilization agreement from the United States, among other economic incentives, in exchange for indemnifying American landowners.

Showing how Cárdenas's administration outfoxed Roosevelt's is vital to gaining a fuller understanding of how bilateral relations were actually conducted. To complete the picture, it is necessary to clarify the forces that drove Mexico's foreign policy. Just as domestic political and economic constraints brought on by the Depression led the White House to accommodate Mexico during the land crisis, similar issues had the opposite effect in Mexico and forced Cárdenas's government to challenge the United States. In short, a troubled Mexican economy and Cárdenas's political weakness at home led his administration to defy the Colossus of the North.

THE GOOD NEIGHBOR POLICY AND
U.S. AND MEXICAN DIPLOMACY

In President Roosevelt's mind, the Good Neighbor policy was designed to bring the sort of profound changes to American diplomacy that the New Deal brought to the U.S. economy. This "new deal" for Latin America meant that the United

States would abandon its imperialistic behavior and withdraw its remaining troops from the region—thereby finishing a process begun by FDR's predecessor, Herbert Hoover. Since the economic and political costs of keeping troops stationed in Latin America outweighed its benefits—a lesson learned in part from U.S. intervention in Nicaragua—from the late 1920s onward, Washington resolved its differences with its hemispheric neighbors without resorting to force. Roosevelt's Good Neighbor policy also implied that Washington would not interfere in Latin America's internal affairs and would allow its counterparts to shape hemispheric relations, or as FDR put it, "give them a share."[9] Since Roosevelt's administration never considered using force against Mexico, it is this last aspect of the Good Neighbor policy, Latin American empowerment, which proved crucial to Mexico during the agrarian dispute. For Roosevelt, the Good Neighbor was "not a solitary policy" but a two-way agreement.[10] In his address to the Governing Board of the Pan-American Union in April 1933, FDR stated that the United States and Latin America were equally obliged to improve hemispheric relations. According to Roosevelt, "Friendship among nations . . . involves mutual obligations and responsibilities, for it is only by sympathetic respect for the rights of others and a scrupulous fulfillment of the corresponding obligations by each member of the community that a true fraternity can be maintained."[11] Laurence Duggan, chief of the State Department's Division of American Republics, echoed the president's multilateralism. According to Duggan, "fair play, equity, mutual accommodation and mutual trust" were central to the Good Neighbor's success, and "any departure at any time by any country from these principles" would jeopardize inter-American affairs.[12]

Although many early studies of the Good Neighbor policy wrongly ignored the role of Latin American officials in shaping it, they rightly saw that the Roosevelt administration applied the policy in an ad lib manner that differed from one Latin American republic to another. In fact, as the experience of a number of hemispheric countries show, including the Dominican Republic, Costa Rica, Cuba, Argentina, Brazil, and Mexico, FDR's policy lacked consistency even when directed at a single nation. These inconsistencies arose from Roosevelt's tendency to abandon policies that did not produce results, as well as the varying internal dynamics of each Latin American country across space and time and the ability of regional leaders to manipulate U.S. policy for their own ends.[13]

Unlike Roosevelt, Ambassador Josephus Daniels's views of Mexico and U.S. policy toward it were more consistent, in part because he did not have to devise a larger hemisphere-wide or global foreign policy as did the White House. Daniels was a Wilsonian who strongly endorsed the principle of nonintervention and believed that the Good Neighbor policy should be guided by empathy and patience. Or, as Daniels simplistically put it, U.S. relations with Latin America should be based on "the policy of Put Yourself in His Place." On a number of occasions during the agrarian dispute, the U.S. ambassador suggested to Roosevelt that to resolve the "present delicate situation," he should put himself in Cárdenas's shoes so he could see that land reform sprang not only from Cárdenas's desire for social justice but from political necessity as well.[14] According to Daniels, because "Cárdenas was elected on the [agrarian] platform and took it seriously, Washington would be unable to get Mexico to halt land redistribution, especially since anyone who would advocate the repudiation of the agrarian policy would be doomed to defeat."[15] When Mexico repeatedly failed to provide an adequate payment plan for remunerating American landowners, Daniels told both the State Department and Roosevelt to be patient with their southern neighbor.[16]

More than any other diplomat, Daniels shaped Washington's Mexico policy. In his opinion, prior to FDR's term in office, U.S. foreign policy was based upon the "archaic doctrine" that the government was obligated to protect "its citizens and his investments wherever he goes, [and] to exert pressure on weaker . . . 'backwards' peoples" whenever those interests were threatened.[17] Despite the fact that the United States made formal declarations of nonintervention at the 1933 and 1936 Pan-American conferences, Daniels realized that old habits die hard.[18] Aware of the growing U.S. criticism of Cárdenas in both official and private circles during the mid- to late 1930s, Daniels repeatedly told Roosevelt that if the United States intervened in Mexico in order to collect compensation for the American landowners, it would "imperil the Good Neighbor dream" that they shared and return the United States to the "old days of Big Stick and dollar diplomacy."[19] Both men wanted to avoid a heavy-handed Mexican policy and not have the Good Neighbor considered empty rhetoric by Latin America's leaders. For Cárdenas's government, the policy's noninterventionism proved beneficial.

Some contemporary commentators criticized the hands-off approach of the Good Neighbor policy. Opponents of FDR's policy viewed the expropriation of American-owned land in Mexico as a "happy interlude" for the Cárdenas administration that afforded Mexico City the opportunity to "get away with things" it could not do in previous decades.[20] Roosevelt's critics were upset by his failure to protect U.S. economic interests below the Rio Grande, which, in their opinion, allowed Cárdenas's government to seize U.S. investments. Even Secretary of State Cordell Hull was wary of Daniels's and Roosevelt's sympathetic attitude toward Mexico and believed that they undermined the U.S. position vis-à-vis its southern neighbor. In Hull's mind, not only was Daniels "a little radical at times," but both he and the president were responsible for causing many of Washington's problems by giving "the Mexicans the impression that they [could] go right ahead and flaunt everything in Washington's face."[21]

The relationship between Washington's like-minded accommodators, FDR and Daniels, had deep roots. The president frequently called Daniels "Chief" because when Daniels was Secretary of the Navy during the Wilson administration, Roosevelt had served under him as Assistant Secretary of the Navy. The fact that the two men were friends for more than twenty-five years and had a "father and son relationship" (Daniels was thirty years older than FDR) boded well for Mexico.[22] Roosevelt respected Daniels's views on Mexico, and because of their close relationship, he allowed him to report directly to the White House and bypass Hull and the State Department. FDR also had Undersecretary of State Sumner Welles go over Hull and work closely with him at the White House. Roosevelt encouraged this insubordinate behavior because it allowed him to circumvent conservative State Department staffers left over from twelve years of Republican rule, who sometimes ignored directives from above.[23]

Roosevelt's diplomatic style had both positive and negative consequences for the United States. On one hand, it fit well with FDR's informal methods of policymaking and his unconventional management style. On the other hand, it produced bitter quarrels within the president's diplomatic corps and made it difficult to chart a coherent foreign policy. According to Irwin Gellman, "FDR's self-confidence, bordering on arrogance, led him to dismiss normal organizational procedures," which "resulted in confusion among his own foreign policy experts."[24] To make matters worse, according to Frederick Pike, "Roosevelt chose underlings with irreconcilably different approaches to hemispheric issues." This is not surprising, since FDR often appointed cabinet members with opposing views. While this created friction, confusion, and competition among his staff, it also ensured Roosevelt would be the final arbiter in any dispute— which is exactly what the president wanted. Unfortunately for the larger U.S. diplomatic staff, neither Roosevelt nor Hull nor Welles outlined a foreign policy agenda; nor did they give their subordinates much guidance.[25]

FIGURE 21. Secretary of State Cordell Hull (left) with Undersecretary of State Sumner Welles at the U.S. Capital to testify before the House Foreign Affairs Committee in June 1939. © BETTMANN/ CORBIS. COURTESY OF THE FRANKLIN DELANO ROOSEVELT LIBRARY.

Problems at the State Department and the U.S. embassy in Mexico City also shed light on U.S. diplomatic shortcomings. According to Assistant Secretary of State Dean Acheson, State was "a department without direction, composed of a lot of busy people working hard and usefully but as a whole not functioning as a foreign policy office. It did not chart a course . . . rather it seems to have been adrift, carried hither and yon."[26] Disorganization also existed at the U.S. embassy. According to one embassy official, because of Daniels's diplomatic inexperience, the place needed a "shake-up" and a new ambassador who was "hard boiled and a 1st class administrator." The same embassy staff member complained, "Top officials get to work about 10:30 or 11:00 and quit early. . . . There is no head to [the embassy] . . . and everybody goes his own way."[27] Roosevelt's nontraditional methods of diplomacy, as well as mismanagement at both the State Department and the U.S. embassy, gave Mexican policymakers greater room to maneuver during the agrarian dispute and allowed them to skirt the more antagonistic U.S. officials.

It is natural that the Mexicans focused their attention on Daniels during the six-year conflict over land, since he championed most Cardenista reforms and had direct access to the White House.[28] Mexican leaders also looked for allies in Washington. Mexico's ambassador to the United States, Dr. Francisco Castillo Nájera, sent Cárdenas an in-depth report profiling U.S. officials and clarifying the viewpoints of leading members of Roosevelt's administration. FDR was painted as a humanitarian who improved living conditions for workers and sought to solve social problems without changing the capitalist system. Castillo Nájera's report also noted that FDR feared fascism more than communism and was sympathetic to Mexico's revolutionary policies, which pursued some of the same objectives as his New Deal program. Hull was labeled a liberal who took a cordial attitude toward Mexico because Roosevelt did. Welles was seen as a conservative, but not a reactionary. Duggan was described as a radical leftist who was sympathetic to Mexico and its problems. Secretary of the Interior Harold Ickes also was labeled a leftist and the champion of radicalism in Roosevelt's administration. Secretary of Agriculture Henry Wallace was considered a liberal with leftist tendencies, and Treasury Secretary Henry Morgenthau was considered to be apolitical.[29] By identifying like-minded U.S. policymakers, Castillo Nájera's report was intended to fine-tune Mexican diplomacy and show the Cardenistas "which buttons to push."[30]

Cárdenas's views on foreign affairs and his overall policy toward the United States were also shaped by a 1934 memorandum that was prepared for him, as president-elect, by the office of the Secretary of Foreign Affairs. The memo stated that Mexico's relationship with the United States was impeded by larger structural forces, namely the country's "weak condition." Internal prosperity, the memo claimed, would allow Mexico to close the economic gap with the United States and enable Mexico City to conduct bilateral relations on a more equal basis.[31] Clearly, Mexican officials recognized the structural limitations that were placed on Mexican diplomacy and understood the relationship between Mexico's domestic and foreign affairs, especially how economic weakness put Mexico at a disadvantage when confronting powerful nations like the United States. For the Cardenistas, the surest way to foster development and reduce the asymmetry of bilateral affairs was by enacting socioeconomic reforms that were progressive in nature and that redistributed wealth. The synergy between Cardenista domestic and foreign policies was expounded by Deputy Foreign Minister Ramón Beteta in his 1940 article in *Mexico Today.* According to Beteta, who was the president's chief adviser on international affairs, for Cárdenas's administration "there existed an intimate relationship between foreign policy and Mexico's social reforms." In a 1940 article in *Foreign Affairs*, Mexicanist scholar Maurice Halperin reached the same conclusion. According to Halperin, "Cárdenas's foreign policy was the logical extension of his domestic policy."[32]

Cárdenas's socioeconomic reforms were designed not only to improve the living and working conditions of Mexico's urban and rural masses but also to enhance the nation's position on the world stage. Mexico's global position, though, had long been defined by its relationship with the United States. According to Sidney Weintraub, Mexico's relations with the United States fostered a national inferiority complex that stemmed from the military defeat of 1848, as well as a defensive nationalism. The latter tendency was enunciated in 1918 via the Carranza Doctrine—which repudiated the Monroe Doctrine, championed nonintervention, and warned more-powerful nations to stay out of Mexico's internal affairs. To keep Washington from influencing Mexican domestic policy, the Ministry of Foreign Affairs memo recommended against submitting bilateral disputes to a court of international arbitration. Despite U.S. pressure, Cárdenas did refuse to submit the land expropriations and the oil nationalization to arbitration.[33]

The 1934 memo also suggested that Cárdenas choose a foreign secretary who would be completely subordinate to him, a suggestion that he also heeded.[34] To ensure that he made the most of the important foreign policy decisions, Cárdenas appointed the partially deaf Eduardo Hay, "largely because of the fact," said Castillo Nájera, "that he was not identified with any political faction." In other words, Hay's political neutrality and corresponding lack of powerful allies decreased his influence and made it difficult for him to challenge the president.[35] Likewise, Cárdenas appointed the politically loyal Castillo Nájera as ambassador to the United States. While on some occasions during the agrarian dispute it appeared that Castillo Nájera contradicted Cárdenas, it would be a mistake to assume that he was advancing his own policy or being insubordinate. Rather, such behavior was a product of the ambassador's location at the diplomatic frontline. Because of the contentious nature of the bilateral conflict over land, Castillo Nájera often had to save face, backpedal, stall, accommodate, or simply tell U.S. officials what they wanted to hear in order to reduce international tensions and or postpone the agrarian settlement.

Although centralized political authority facilitated a cohesive Mexican foreign policy and strengthened Cárdenas's hand, *presidencialismo* (a domineering executive branch and president) hardly originated with his administration. And while Cárdenas was the driving force in Mexican policy toward the United States, he did not make all of his nation's foreign policy decisions alone. Cárdenas did not rely heavily on his foreign secretary, Hay, when making policy and instead gave greater voice and autonomy to Hay's subordinate, Deputy Foreign Secretary Beteta, as well as Treasury Secretary Eduardo Suárez, just as Roosevelt often sidestepped Cordell Hull in favor of Sumner Welles and Henry Morgenthau. Friedrich Schuler rightly plays down Cárdenas's role in foreign affairs, stating that during the 1930s, "the majority of Mexican exchanges with foreign countries were conceived of and executed by Mexican bureaucratic professionals." However, this was not the case when the country in question was the United States and the matter at hand concerned a bilateral conflict that—like the agrarian dispute—had domestic ramifications for Mexico and Cárdenas alike, nearly severed relations with Washington, would cost Mexico City tens of millions of dollars in reparations, and, after March 1938, could set important precedents for the oil question. Most diplomatic scholars agree the severity of an international conflict can be measured by how far it reaches up the chain of command. Suffice it to say that during the agrarian dispute Cárdenas was, to an even greater degree than Roosevelt, very much involved in policymaking.[36]

Despite the asymmetrical nature of U.S.-Mexican relations, Mexico had some diplomatic advantages during the dispute that helped to level the international playing field. These benefits stemmed from the Good Neighborly policy of noninterventionism, the accommodating attitude of leading U.S. officials, divisions within the U.S. foreign policy establishment, and greater unity among Mexican officials.[37] The fact that the United States did not have a Mexican equivalent to Josephus Daniels—that is, that there was no high-ranking Mexican policymaker who would fight on Washington's behalf—made it difficult for U.S. leaders to find wedge issues that would divide Mexico's diplomatic corps and give them the upper hand. In this, the Cardenistas enjoyed an advantage. Finally, the policymaking procedures employed by officials on both sides of the border, especially the centralized manner in which both nations formulated their respective foreign policies, also proved critical.

1935 AND THE START OF THE AGRARIAN DISPUTE: PATTERNS ESTABLISHED

Although the expropriation of American-owned rural property was a contentious bilateral issue in the early to mid-1920s, by the late 1920s and early 1930s it cooled down because few American-owned estates were seized during this time. The oil controversy also receded during this period for similar reasons and reflected the growing conservatism of Mexico's political elite. However, following Cárdenas's triumph over Plutarco Elías Calles in mid-1935 and the subsequent rapid acceleration of land redistribution, American rural holdings began to be expropriated in much greater numbers; this put the issue at the forefront of U.S.-Mexican relations. Consequently, in August and September 1935, U.S. officials laid out three objectives that would shape their policy over the next three years. The Roosevelt administration first wanted to settle the outstanding pre-1927 agrarian claims. Then it sought to obtain "prompt and adequate compensation" for all American-owned rural property seized since 1927, especially during Cárdenas's term in office. Finally, Washington wanted to receive assurances from Mexico City "that no more lands would be taken from American citizens until adequate provisions were made to pay for them."[38]

Between September 1935 and January 1936, no progress was made in obtaining compensation for American landowners who had lost their estates before 1927. Little discussion of the pre-1927 claims took place after February 1936 because of the greater number of new expropriations carried out by Cárdenas's government. As one would expect, Roosevelt's administration shifted its focus to present-day matters: minimizing additional seizures of American-owned land and obtaining payment for those taken by the Cardenistas. The increase in *afectaciones* (expropriations) stemmed from official government grants and from what U.S. officials termed "illegal acts." In growing numbers, landless peasants squatted on American-owned property and remained there until they qualified for ejidos. In March 1936, armed agraristas invaded the property of the Turno Land Company in Sinaloa. Despite repeated protests from U.S. Chargé d'Affaires Pierre L. de Boal regarding the illegal seizure, the agraristas remained on the company's property for the next eight months, until it was officially expropriated by the federal government. Similarly, in April 1936 agraristas confiscated the property of Harold Reeder in the state of Tamaulipas.[39] Some State Department officials believed that American-owned properties were targeted because they had irrigation works and better soil management. According to Assistant Secretary of State Robert Walton Moore, land redistribution in Mexico was prejudicial against American owners, since "in most cases well-developed [American-owned] property had been taken, whereas the vast undeveloped public lands, which could be readily given to landless peons were left untouched."[40] By the end of 1936, the number of invasions and expropriations of American-owned land had increased to such an extent that one U.S. newspaper noted it was the "most delicate point of conflict between Mexico and the United States since Cárdenas came to power."[41]

In 1935 and 1936, domestic politics prevented Cárdenas from reaching an agreement with Washington over agrarian issues. Few things in Mexico garner more popular support than confronting the United States, and during this period Cárdenas needed all of the backing he could find. Cárdenas split with Calles in mid-1935, and the threat—real or exaggerated—posed by the remaining Callistas made his first year in office shaky. The president's political weakness at the national and regional levels pushed him to address peasant calls for land redistribution and worker appeals for better pay; it also made any capitulation to U.S. demands over agrarian matters difficult, since his opponents would have attacked him for backing down to Washington.

Budgetary constraints also limited his policy options. It made better economic and political sense for Cárdenas to spend government revenue on public works projects, social welfare programs, and agrarian reform, all of which reduced unemployment and broadened his base of political support, than to indemnify American landowners. And, that is exactly what Cárdenas did. Instead of balancing the budget, stabilizing the peso, paying down Mexico's foreign debt, and avoiding new debts (i.e., pursuing an orthodox monetary and fiscal policy), Cárdenas's administration emphasized full employment and deficit spending. Social and economic expenditures increased from 36 percent of the federal budget in 1933 to 60 percent in 1936. As table 5 shows, 1936 marked the first of five consecutive years of federal deficits. In that year alone, Mexico City undertook extensive construction projects by building new roads, railroad lines, dams, irrigation and electric systems, schools, and libraries, among other things. In addition, land reform greatly accelerated, as seen with the massive redistribution of eight million acres in the Laguna region and federal financing of hundreds of thousands of new ejidatarios nationwide.[42]

As ever greater amounts of American-owned land were seized in 1936, Cárdenas kept relations cordial by telling U.S. officials what they wanted to hear: that American landowners would be indemnified for their losses. In his meeting with Daniels in October 1936, Cárdenas agreed to make provisions in the next budget for compensating American property owners; he added that Mexico would "pay as much on the agrarian claims as possible," and that payments would be continued after they started.[43] In a subsequent meeting, Cárdenas took advantage of Daniels's access to the White House to gain Roosevelt's

TABLE 5. Mexican federal income and expenses, 1934–1940 (in millions of pesos)

Year	Income	Expenditures	Surplus/Deficit
1934	295	265	30
1935	313	301	12
1936	385	406	−21
1937	451	479	−28
1938	438	504	−66
1939	566	571	−5
1940	577	610	−33

Source: Villarreal, *El desequilibrio externo en la industrialización de México*, 39.

assistance in dealing with the American property owners, who had become increasingly critical of his government. According to the Mexican president, because the "people had existed for many years in a state of appalling misery and poverty it was the ambition of the great mass of poor agrarian workers to own the land upon which they worked." Because the Mexican government "had sought faithfully to carry out this purpose," he asked if it would "be possible for the Ambassador to enlist the assistance of President Roosevelt and the American Government to get the American landowners in Mexico to co-operate with the Mexican Government so that this end might be achieved."[44] Daniels assured Cárdenas that since "Roosevelt had an interest in the forgotten man [he] would give sympathetic consideration to his request." Cárdenas told Daniels that he appreciated Roosevelt's understanding of Mexico's problems, and as a goodwill gesture he would accept any settlement that FDR desired for the American landowners in Sonora's Yaqui Valley.[45]

The U.S. farmers in the Yaqui Valley received special consideration on both sides of the border for a number of different reasons. The Yaqui Valley expropriations—twenty-nine individual American-owned estates in October 1937—marked the largest number of American land seizures anywhere in Mexico. And, by presenting themselves as a unified block, the valley's landowners received Washington's attention and a good deal of press. As medium-sized estate owners who usually improved and farmed the land themselves, they stood apart from the absentee domestic and foreign landed elite who dominated much of the Mexican countryside. And on at least one occasion Undersecretary of State Welles told Ambassador Castillo Nájera that the Americans in the Yaqui Valley "deserved special attention from the Mexican government" because many had put their entire life savings into their properties. In the same vein, Secretary of State Hull told Mexico's Treasury Secretary Eduardo Suárez that the Yaqui Valley landowners deserved the same lifestyle after the expropriation as they had before it. Meanwhile, throughout the agrarian dispute, Daniels was repeatedly instructed by the State Department to press the Yaqui Valley case.[46] Because of the attention U.S. officials gave the valley's growers, Cárdenas's administration was impelled to respond in kind.

When Daniels returned to the United States after his meeting with Cárdenas in late 1936, on three occasions he met Roosevelt alone at the White House and then separately with State Department officials. Hard-liners at the State Department did not want to limit Cárdenas's settlement offer to the Yaqui Valley; rather, they hoped to extend the terms of indemnification to American landowners throughout Mexico. Assistant Secretary of State Moore drafted a memorandum declaring that the United States could not acquiesce in the expropriation of lands belonging to American citizens unless immediate cash compensation was made based on the property's market value.[47] Roosevelt became incensed by Moore's memo because it implied special privileges for Americans citizens: i.e., that they should be compensated in cash while Mexican landowners receive agrarian bonds. FDR told Moore that his memo represented a "policy of many years ago [and] certainly [was] not the policy of today." Roosevelt then enunciated Washington's position toward its southern neighbor: "In the matter of the expropriation of American-owned property of any kind in any foreign country, the United States expects prompt and effective compensation to be paid to the owners on not less than the same basis that payments are made to the nationals of the country making the expropriation."[48]

Hull saw Roosevelt's policy as "extremely dangerous" and told him that he was leaving U.S. nationals at the mercy of the Mexican government, since no reparations were being made to any landowners in Mexico, regardless of nationality. The secretary of state saw Mexico as a test case and argued that FDR's policy would "produce world-wide repercussions." Hull argued that other countries would "change their domestic private property laws overnight and encroach upon the rights of aliens and confiscate American-owned property" if they thought Washington would not defend its citizens beyond the treatment provided to the nationals of those countries.[49] Despite Hull's plea, Roosevelt stuck to his decision. He and Daniels each had little sympathy for the large American property owners in Mexico, many of whom they believed had gained their extensive holdings through bribes made to Porfirian officials in the late nineteenth and early twentieth centuries.[50] FDR then ordered all State Department divisions, especially the Division of Mexican Affairs, to be informed of his decision. Daniels returned to Mexico in early 1937 and informed the Cárdenas administration of Roosevelt's position. The division among U.S. policymakers was now clearly drawn between the hard-liners and the accommodators. According to David Cronon, this incident illustrated the influence that Daniels had with FDR and his independence from the State Department.[51]

TRYING TO SETTLE THE CÁRDENAS-ERA EXPROPRIATIONS

Although Cárdenas had stated in October 1936 that American landowners would be compensated in 1937, the weakness of the Mexican economy precluded his administration from reaching a definitive settlement with Washington. While Mexico's economy was relatively robust from 1934 to 1937, in the latter year a number of important economic indicators began to decline. According to a 1937 U.S. Commerce report, "after several years of unusual prosperity [Mexican] business had slowed down."[52] Throughout the year Mexico's inflation rate increased steadily and the value of the peso dropped—in part because the government was printing pesos without sufficient backing. Prices for some staples rose by 50 percent over 1936 levels. Meanwhile, agricultural production was flat or declined because of pests, diseases, and radical changes in land tenure. Such problems sunk real wages in the agricultural sector to their lowest level of Cárdenas's sexenio. To make matters worse, from 1937 to 1940 problems with food production and distribution forced Cárdenas to spend the country's limited foreign exchange on food imports—including large-scale wheat purchases from the United States. Not surprisingly, this brought a great deal of criticism of Cárdenas and his agrarian reform program from Calles, the National Chamber of Commerce, the Unión Nacional Sinarquista, large landowners, and the newspapers *Excelsior* and *El Universal.* As the cost of living increased for both rural and urban workers in 1937, so too did social and political unrest, as strikes and the threat of them spread nationwide.[53]

In addition to rising prices and falling wages, deficit spending also increased in 1937. According to Castillo Nájera, there was little likelihood of a balanced budget or economic recovery in the immediate future, since no one within the administration could persuade Cárdenas to cut back on public works projects or stay within the budget. One of the biggest drains on government revenue stemmed from land redistribution. Federal loans to the ejidatarios through the Banco Nacional de Crédito Ejidal were enormous, peaking in 1937 at 565,241 million pesos and dropping only modestly, to 352,641, by 1941. [54]

This significantly reduced government reserves and worried both Mexico's industrial sector and the nation's treasury secretary. According to Suárez, in 1937 many Mexican industrialists refused to reinvest their capital domestically and instead sent it overseas on account of Cárdenas's deficit spending program, the drain in foreign exchange at the Banco de México (the country's federal reserve institution), unsatisfactory agricultural output, and labor unrest. Worker militancy in the oil sector led the foreign-owned oil companies to transfer capital abroad and periodically suspend sales. In short, Cárdenas's nationalistic, pro-labor stance made it hard for Mexican leaders to halt capital flight and attract much-needed foreign investment.[55]

Although Cárdenas promised U.S. officials he would set aside $2 million pesos in the 1937 budget for compensating American landowners, the Mexican government was so strapped for cash it could not afford to do so.[56] Rather, in October 1937 Deputy Foreign Secretary Beteta announced that American landowners would be paid in agrarian bonds, because the federal government needed to increase, rather than decrease, its revenue—which is what would have occurred had cash compensation been made. Recalling that in 1934 the Mexican government defaulted on the agrarian bonds previously issued to American landowners, most U.S. officials did not see this as acceptable compensation. If history was a guide, they felt, any new agrarian bonds would soon be worthless.[57]

A few days after Beteta's announcement, a livid Sumner Welles told Castillo Nájera that the State Department was losing patience because "since 1935 the notes that Ambassador Daniels presented [regarding compensation] have not received any answers or were answered evasively." Welles complained that the expropriation of American-owned rural property had not stopped and that there was no indication from Cárdenas's administration regarding how it intended to indemnify American landowners. Welles expressed deep concern that Beteta's announcement exposed Mexico's true position—a concern that was well founded. Castillo Nájera concurred with Welles's assessment but added that his government was still studying ways of making effective payment. The problem, the Mexican ambassador claimed, was that Mexican officials were concerned about the political fallout should they pay American claimants before deciding how to indemnify Mexican landowners. They were also rightly worried about the astronomical costs of compensating all rural property owners, both foreign and domestic. In a telephone conversation between Hay and Daniels in early 1938, the Mexican foreign secretary described Cárdenas's dilemma. According to Hay, if Mexico "paid the Americans, the Mexicans would demand that they also be paid and that the amount for the large quantities of Mexican land would be so great that it would be impossible to raise enough money."[58]

To placate Washington, two days after Castillo Nájera's meeting with Welles, Cárdenas made a new offer. Realizing that it was financially impossible for Mexico to indemnify all the American property owners, and recalling Washington's concern for the Yaqui Valley growers, Cárdenas told Daniels that since "bonds would be of no material benefit to the Americans," Mexico would provide compensation lands to the American farmers in the Yaqui Valley. The Mexican president offered to give the Americans land north of the Yaqui River, which, like their present property, would be irrigated once the Angostura Dam was completed in 1940.[59] The State Department seriously considered Cárdenas's new offer and spent many months discussing it with the American landowners in Sonora.

Unbeknownst to Washington, however, the lands on the north bank of the Yaqui River were already slated for the Yaqui Indians as restitution of their ancestral homelands. Thus, the land swap deal was never a viable alternative. Moreover, just one week after making the offer, Cárdenas privately reconsidered it due to the cost. He realized that Mexico could not afford either cash or compensation lands to indemnify both foreign and domestic landowners; instead, Mexico had to use agrarian bonds. "Mexico will not be able to pay the agrarian debt in any other form," the president declared. "It will go up to more than a thousand million pesos and it is unfair to burden the present and future generations for the accumulation and plundering of the land by past generations."[60] Because the offer of compensation lands in the Yaqui Valley was never a real possibility, Mexican officials rarely elaborated on it. Instead, they let U.S. officials study the proposal. By repeatedly offering different forms of indemnification, Mexican officials were able to drag out the bilateral conflict over land—a tactic that proved so successful they employed a similar version of it during the subsequent oil crisis.[61]

Some in Washington blamed Daniels for the difficulties in resolving the agrarian dispute. After their December 1937 meeting with Suárez, Treasury Department officials bemoaned the fact that Daniels's "benevolent outlook" and his tendency to approve everything the Mexicans did gave Cárdenas's administration the wrong impression of U.S. policy. Treasury Secretary Henry Morgenthau stated that Daniels's sympathetic attitude "developed the anticipation" among Mexican officials that Washington "would not speak up in behalf of any American difficulties" and "would not refuse them anything they asked."[62] Assistant Secretary of State Adolf Berle was even more critical of Daniels and referred to his work at the embassy as a "total loss." According to Berle, Daniels was a "bad ambassador."[63]

Although Daniels may have been too conciliatory in the eyes of some State and Treasury Department officials, proper credit should be given to Mexico's diplomatic corps. Elitism prevented some U.S. policymakers from seeing that Mexican officials were sophisticated diplomats. If Mexico was able to side-step U.S. demands, such U.S. officials chalked it up to the shortcomings of someone within FDR's government, rather than credit skillful Mexican policymaking. Undoubtedly, it behooved the Mexicans to work closely with U.S. officials who were sympathetic to their interests. And Cárdenas's government realized that keeping on good terms with Daniels meant good relations with the White House. In December 1937, Berle noted the obvious when he wrote that Roosevelt and the State Department were at odds over U.S. policy toward Mexico, since most State Department officials pushed for compensation for the American landowners more vigorously than did the president, a position that reflected the "traditional U.S. policy of protecting American interests abroad."[64]

THE CEDILLO REBELLION AND COMPENSATION LANDS

As we have seen, Cárdenas's foreign policy during the agrarian dispute was influenced by domestic issues such as opposition from the Callistas and Obregonistas, as well as the growing popularity of the far Left and Right, and Mexico's economic weakness. Similarly, Cárdenas's year-long rift with Secretary of Agriculture Saturnino Cedillo also motivated the Mexican president to avoid compromise with Washington. Cedillo, one of the most conservative members of the administration, possessed a private army of fifteen thousand soldiers in his home state of San Luis Potosí that made him a genuine military threat to Cárdenas's government. Tensions between the two men increased in 1936 and 1937 when Cedillo objected to the breakup of large estates and the accelerated pace of land redistribution.[65] It is noteworthy that Cedillo's position was supported by most domestic and foreign landowners in Mexico, as well as some U.S. officials in Washington.

In August 1937 Cedillo resigned his post in the Department of Agriculture, hoping to capitalize on the growing domestic and international opposition to Cárdenas. Although Cárdenas purged the Department of Agriculture of

Cedillo's supporters, the president still worried that a right-wing movement would coalesce around him. He therefore warned the country's conservative elements that he would not allow Mexico to become another Spain.[66] In the fall of 1937, Cedillo garnered political support among right-wing groups for a 1940 presidential bid while simultaneously preparing for military insurrection. He contacted other conservative leaders who also opposed Cárdenas— generals Juan Andreu Almazán and Antonio Ríos Zertuche, Michoacán governor Gildardo Magaña, Zacatecas governor Félix Bañuelos, and Sonoran governor Román Yocupicio. After Cedillo's resignation and return to San Luis Potosí, Cárdenas offered him an ambassadorship, hoping that he would take the traditional road to political exile. Cedillo rejected it. In the spring of 1938 Cárdenas tried to transfer Cedillo away from his personal army by assigning him to a military post in Cárdenas's home state of Michoacán. Rather than separate himself from his well-armed base of power, Cedillo retired from the army and declared—along with the San Luis Potosí state legislature—that he no longer recognized Cárdenas as president.[67] The stage was set for an uprising.

With the backing of some conservative groups, the clergy in San Luis Potosí, and to a small degree, foreign capital, Cedillo's forces rose up against the federal government in May 1938. More than ten thousand federal troops were used to contain Cedillo's rebellion to San Luis Potosí. The movement was crushed in a matter of days, with little bloodshed. The fact that Cedillo's uprising had been anticipated for almost a year enabled Cárdenas to use land redistribution as a political weapon to win over Cedillo's rank-and-file supporters. Months before the rebellion began, many of Cedillo's soldiers received land from the Agrarian Department, which quenched their enthusiasm for armed rebellion against Cárdenas's government. Also, after the uprising started federal aircraft dropped leaflets containing extracts from a recent speech by the president on social reform. Cardenista propaganda claimed that an insurrection against a government that was dedicated to helping the rural poor was absurd.[68] It seems many agreed.

Since the rebellion lacked Washington's support and did not spark a wider revolt—in part because it was never fully coordinated with other opposition groups—it was clear that it would fail.[69] Although the larger rebellion was quickly crushed, the uprising still upset Mexico's political landscape. Army officers remained divided toward Cárdenas, and, both during and after the revolt, rumors spread that other generals also intended to overthrow the president. Meanwhile, leftist leaders used the uprising to attack conservative politicians by suggesting their opponent's involvement in Cedillo's treason. With cries of conspiracy, the left wing of the new official party, the Party of the Mexican Revolution (Partido de la Revolución Mexicana, or PRM), expelled two conservative members, General Ramón Iturbe and Colonel Bolívar Sierra. The political situation deteriorated to such an extent that in July 1938, members of Congress drew their guns during a session, and Cárdenas temporarily suspended the national legislature.[70]

In such tumultuous times, Cárdenas needed to put forth an image of both domestic and international strength. He claimed that if there was to be peace in Mexico, and if he was to remain in office, then rural demands had to be met. After spending one month with Cárdenas in the Mexican countryside in mid-1938, Frank Tannenbaum wrote to Daniels and summarized how land redistribution was critical to Mexican political stability and democratization. In his letter to Daniels, it was clear that Tannenbaum was preaching to the converted, since years earlier the U.S. ambassador reported to Roosevelt that no Mexican government could "long endure if it did not give the lands to the people who have long tilled them."[71] Since it was common knowledge that Tannenbaum was closely tied to the political Left in the United States and had met or corresponded with Daniels, Roosevelt, and Duggan about developments in Mexico, Cárdenas used him to translate his vision of socioeconomic reform to U.S. officials. Better than most contemporary observers, Tannenbaum expressed an ideological premise of what was wrong with old Mexico: that *latifundismo*—the domination of the countryside by large often inefficient estates —blocked Mexico's development, and that the progressive Cardenista project, especially agrarian reform, was required to move the country forward. Cárdenas employed Tannenbaum to reaffirm Daniels's and Roosevelt's conviction of the inevitability and righteousness of land redistribution. This strategy was a smart move, according to John Mason Hart, because when Tannenbaum corresponded with U.S. officials he "understated the size of American interests, the number of American colonists affected by agrarian reform, and the violence directed toward them."[72]

By March 1938, some U.S. policymakers realized that Cárdenas's administration was not likely to provide cash compensation to American landowners. Said Chargé d'Affaires de Boal, "The possibilities of immediate cash compensation are so remote as to be negligible" and "insistence upon such immediate cash compensation might result in the elimination of other proposals now under consideration. . . . The proposal for a settlement through 'compensation' lands . . . is the best [plan] yet advanced for the relief of affected landowners and would seem to be more promising than starting all over again from scratch."[73] Unable to agree to a payment plan for all U.S. landowners in Mexico, Washington was forced to accept Mexico's offer of compensation lands for the Yaqui Valley farmers, which appeared to be Mexico's most attractive offer to date. Obtaining indemnification for the dozens of small individually owned American estates in the Yaqui Valley allowed the White House to demonstrate its commitment to protecting the interests of the "little man"—which fit well with FDR's domestic political rhetoric.[74] In fact, a year before the Roosevelt administration accepted Mexico's offer of compensation lands, in April 1937 Hull told Castillo Nájera and Suárez that Washington had little sympathy for Americans who had purchased land for a trifle and later tried to "fleece" the Mexican government by demanding exorbitant amounts in compensation. On the other hand, stated Hull, Americans who had purchased their holdings "in good faith" with "no plan to make undue or unreasonable profits" were entitled to just compensation.[75]

After notifying Mexico City that it would accept the Yaqui Valley compensation lands, Roosevelt's administration played up the agreement. When questioned about developments in Mexico during an April 1938 press conference, FDR stated,

Two things have happened over . . . a good many years, which do affect American citizens. The first is the small fellow, the small American, who has gone down there to ranch and farm, etc., and has put everything he has into his ranch or farm. Under the Mexican policy of distribution of land ownership, quite a number of those poor Americans have been stripped, and their property has been taken, or a part of their property has been taken, and so far, they have not been able to realize on a settlement. Those people, the Mexican government assures us, are going to be taken care of. They are the real hardship cases. Then you come to the Americans who went to Mexico, like William Randolph Hearst, and bought a state legislature, bribed officials and acquired title . . . to hundreds of thousands of acres of land for practically nothing except the cost of the bribe, or they paid three cents on the acre for it . . . and then claimed all kinds of damages in a sum far in excess of the amount of money that he had actually put in. We have not got much sympathy with trying to collect that excessive sum for him. The same thing in the case of the oil companies.[76]

A few days later Roosevelt met with Castillo Nájera, reiterating many of the points that he made during the press conference and suggesting some payment options that would help Mexico avoid compensating landowners who gained their large estates through bribes or on the cheap.[77]

Just as Cárdenas's diplomatic hands were tied by political developments at home, so were Roosevelt's. To garner popular political support in the United States, FDR clearly implied that his administration would not assist the large landowners in their claims against Mexico. To improve his chance for reelection in 1936, Roosevelt began to cultivate the idea that big business was an opponent of the American people. According to Mark Leff, both during and after the campaign, Roosevelt "established a politics of ostracism, uniting Americans against their common—if diabolized—economic royalist enemies."[78] Bashing big business at home and abroad gained votes for Roosevelt in a depressed economy and played an integral part in his use of political symbolism. Defending the interests of the small farmers, and not those of American hacendados like Hearst, projected the image of FDR's concern for the "forgotten man" onto an international backdrop. Roosevelt must have believed that using this type of diplomatic rhetoric would be agreeable to the American electorate.

Understanding American public opinion during the Depression and Roosevelt's diplomatic symbolism also helps to explain why FDR did not take a hard line during either the agrarian dispute or the oil crisis. The Depression caused many Americans to lose their nerve and confidence both domestically and overseas; it also made them unwilling to assume the economic burdens of intervention, as well as averse to protecting the foreign interests of the same U.S. capitalists who had failed them at home. And, because Roosevelt did not aggressively protect American property owners from land redistribution in Mexico, it was politically impossible for him to reverse course and impose heavy-handed measures against Mexico in order to protect a handful of rich and powerful U.S. oil companies from nationalization. Doing so would have contradicted FDR's platform of defending the "common man" against big business. It also may have shaken the endorsement of his New Deal coalition, since a large segment of organized labor—for example, CIO president John Lewis—both publicly and privately endorsed Mexico's appropriation policies, while pacifist organizations also petitioned the White House for a negotiated resolution to the land and oil conflicts.[79]

From November 1937 to April 1938, U.S. officials and American landowners in the Yaqui Valley discussed Mexico's offer of compensation lands. In April, just as both groups finally accepted the proposal, Foreign Secretary Eduardo Hay retracted it. As mentioned earlier, the offer appears to have been a ploy to gain time, since the lands in question were already earmarked for restitution to the Yaqui Indians as decreed by Cárdenas's October 1937 reparto. With no lands to offer, Mexican officials instead proposed cash compensation. Hay told Daniels that, starting in June 1938, Mexico would set aside $120,000 pesos in the national budget every month for compensating the American farmers in the Yaqui Valley. As for the large landowners in other parts of Mexico, the Mexican government offered agrarian bonds, arguing that these large property owners and businesses had greater economic resources than the valley's small and medium owners and could therefore wait to be indemnified. No mention was made of compensating the hundreds of other small farmers outside of Sonora. Castillo Nájera justified Mexico's limited offer on the basis of his country's financial problems; he also stated that his government differentiated between the two groups because it appeared that the large landowners "were not an immediate preoccupation of the U.S. Government."[80] Clearly, Mexican officials employed Roosevelt's political rhetoric to their own advantage and manipulated a U.S. policy that distinguished the American landowners.

Unable to see that Cárdenas's administration had used the Yaqui Valley case as a stalling maneuver, Daniels supported Mexico's new offer because it addressed Washington's preference for "payment first for the small properties." Welles, however, rejected it.[81] A number of State Department officials—not only Welles but also Hull, Moore, and Berle—now believed that Mexico's promises to indemnify American landowners were a "mere formality" and not intended to resolve the agrarian dispute.[82] To their credit, Mexican officials had sharpened the divisions within Roosevelt's diplomatic corps, which, in the long run, would pay them dividends.

Cárdenas's nationalization of the foreign-owned oil industry in March 1938 heightened bilateral tensions. Critics of the Mexican president felt vindicated that the lack of U.S. action over land had led to further attacks against American economic interests. Now on the ascendancy, the State Department's hardliners convinced FDR to cancel temporarily the U.S. silver purchase agreement with Mexico—although the U.S. Treasury Department and Federal Reserve continued to buy Mexican silver at lower prices on the "open spot market." Fearing more U.S. reprisals, Castillo Nájera told Hull in April that he would urge Cárdenas to settle the agrarian dispute "without any more delay."[83] Two weeks later, Hull complained that he had not received a compensation plan as Castillo Nájera had promised. It was clear that Hull's patience was running thin when he stated to Daniels that Cárdenas's agrarian reform program was proceeding too quickly and that Washington had waited more than three years for Mexico to present an indemnification plan for U.S. landowners.[84] Angered by the years of delay and subterfuge by Mexican officials, feeling pressure from the U.S. Congress to do something about Mexico, and disturbed by the oil expropriation, Hull and Welles were convinced that a tougher policy was needed.[85]

THE STATE DEPARTMENT TURNS UP THE HEAT

Hard-liners within the State Department saw Daniels's three-week hiatus from Mexico in June 1938 as an opportunity to press Cárdenas's administration more forcefully for agrarian compensation without interference from the U.S. embassy.[86] Welles informed Castillo Nájera that U.S.-Mexican relations were at risk on account of Mexico's failure to provide a "definite, practical, and complete proposal for making compensation representing fair, assured, and effective value to the American citizens whose agrarian properties have been expropriated." To make some headway toward indemnification, Welles gave Castillo Nájera a list of all the American-owned lands expropriated since 1927, and their respective values; he suggested that Mexico immediately assess the value of the holdings and inform Washington of its ability to pay. Welles also stated that the United States would no longer differentiate between large and small property owners, and he insisted that the expropriation of American-owned rural property be stopped immediately.[87] The Mexican ambassador was dismayed by the harshness of Welles's tone and the abrupt nature of his demands. Welles gave the Mexican ambassador a payment plan that recommended Mexico put $10 million in escrow over the next two-and-a-half years to begin the process of paying American landowners.[88] Aware of Mexico's weak economy, Welles then applied economic pressure. If the Mexican government were to begin payments for the expropriated lands, Welles stated, it would mark the "first step toward economic and financial recovery in Mexico; but if this new policy were not adhered to," he continued, he "could see no way by which Mexico could rehabilitate her national economy and much less any way in which this government could continue to cooperate in an effective manner."[89]

The State Department's more assertive policy worried Mexican officials. Nevertheless, after consulting with Cárdenas, Castillo Nájera informed Welles that his figures "were excessive" in light of the payments Mexico was already making on the special (revolutionary) claims, coupled with the payments it would have to make on the general claims and the oil properties. The Mexican ambassador affirmed that Mexico was financially unable to pay according to

Welles's plan.[90] When he returned to Mexico City in July 1938, Daniels made it very clear to Washington that he disapproved of Welles's forceful approach and agreed with Castillo Nájera that it was impossible for the Mexican government to pay $10 million so quickly.[91] Since Daniels sided with Mexico against the State Department, there was little reason for Mexico City to yield. Consequently, Cárdenas then reiterated that his country was too poor to pay cash for the expropriated American-owned estates and that Mexico would pay with agrarian bonds and compensation lands.[92] Exasperated by Mexico's rejection of Welles's proposal, Hull asked Morgenthau to place economic pressure on Mexico by lowering the world price of silver, but the treasury secretary refused.[93] Bilateral affairs had become so tense in the wake of the oil nationalization, and the mood in Washington so unfavorable to Mexico, that Castillo Nájera predicted a break in relations.[94]

Because the Treasury Department refused to apply economic pressure against Mexico, the State Department resorted to additional diplomatic pressure. On July 21, 1938, a frustrated Hull delivered a strongly worded note to Castillo Nájera and sent copies to the U.S. press. According to Hull, since Mexico had not indemnified the American landowners, its policy of taking property without compensation was not expropriation but illegal confiscation. Hull also demanded that the amount of reparations and the terms of payment be adjudicated in an international court of arbitration, which he believed would bind Mexico and force it to define the terms of payment.[95] Hull stated that Mexico had no right to take privately owned property without first having the means to pay for it. If Cárdenas abided by Hull's note, argues Lorenzo Meyer, "Mexico would have to subordinate its domestic needs to international capital and would even have to write off the agrarian reform."[96]

Surprised by Hull's note, Mexico City offered no reply at first. Cárdenas then met with his cabinet, which was split into two groups. The more radical wing, led by Deputy Foreign Minister Beteta and Secretary of Communications Francisco Múgica, advocated an equally provocative reply that appealed to the nationalistic climate pervasive in the country in the summer of 1938 following the oil nationalization. The second group, led by Secretary of War and future president Manuel Ávila Camacho, favored a more moderate response.[97] The fact that Hull had his note published in a number of major U.S. dailies forced Cárdenas's administration to respond publicly and therefore take into consideration a Mexican public that was increasingly anti-American. If the president publicly backed down, he would be attacked for being weak. Likewise, Mexico

City had to publish its response, lest the Mexican people think a secret and unfavorable agreement had been reached with Washington.[98]

Cárdenas's cabinet saw that it had three options. The first possibility was to accept Hull's demands for international arbitration. This idea was widely dismissed because they feared that if Mexico lost in an international court, immediate and extensive compensation would be required. The economic consequences of such a judicial defeat would force Mexico to halt its agrarian reform program, which would hurt the government politically. They also did not want to set a precedent that would force Mexico to arbitrate over the oil properties. The second possibility was to simply reject arbitration without suggesting any alternatives. This idea also garnered little support. The third possibility was to reject arbitration and propose to study each of the agrarian claims and thereafter submit a payment plan. The last idea was the most popular among the cabinet members.[99]

On August 3, 1938, Mexico City responded to the first of Hull's three notes, arguing that international law did not, as Hull claimed, obligate payment of immediate or deferred compensation for expropriated foreign-owned properties. Mexican officials stated firmly, "The political, social, and economic stability, and peace of Mexico, depends on the land being placed anew in the hands of the people who work it; a transformation of the country, that is to say, the future of the nation, could not be halted by the impossibility of immediately paying the value of the properties belonging to a small group of foreigners who seek only a profit."[100] Besides prioritizing the government's domestic responsibilities over its international obligations, the Mexican note also compared Cárdenas's economic reforms to FDR's New Deal and stated that had the United States not been a wealthy country, it too would have expropriated properties without paying for them. It also rejected international arbitration, since there were not any irreconcilable differences between the two countries; instead, Cardenista officials claimed that the only real problem was the failure of both sides to reach a final compensation agreement. Also, if an international court imposed economic restrictions on Mexico, the note added, it would undermine Mexican sovereignty by limiting the government's right to organize the national economy as it saw fit. Despite the note's confrontational tone, it reiterated Mexico's intention to compensate American landowners in a time and manner that was economically feasible (see figure 22). The Mexican note concluded by suggesting that both countries appoint representatives to determine the value of the expropriated American-owned lands and the manner of Mexican payment.[101]

FIGURE 22. The cartoon lacks negative Mexican stereotypes and instead rightly illustrates Mexican diplomatic stalling. It depicts a stubborn President Cárdenas, who not only refuses to address Uncle Sam's demands for payment but has his own ideas for compensating American property owners. *Brooklyn Daily Eagle,* ca. late 1930s. REPRINTED WITH PERMISSION FROM THE BROOKLYN COLLECTION, BROOKLYN PUBLIC LIBRARY.

To demonstrate that they had no intention of altering their agrarian reform program, one day after Hay delivered Mexico's reply to Daniels, Cardenista officials expropriated 1,800 acres of American-owned land belonging to Dora and Oscar Newton, located in the state of Jalisco.[102] Cárdenas's August note was published in the Mexican press, approved by the Mexican Congress, and supported by the nation's media and a large segment of its public.[103] Peasant leagues and labor unions throughout the country endorsed Cárdenas's position. His presidential papers are filled with hundreds of letters and telegrams from national and local peasant leagues in support of his stand. Likewise, numerous labor organizations backed the president, and many of Mexico's governors wrote to him pledging their support. His position was endorsed by the government's official party, as well as the right-wing Partido Social Demócrata Mexicano and the left-wing Partido Comunista Mexicana. Civic groups and professional organizations also showed their support, and hundreds of individual Mexicans sent in letters that praised Cárdenas for his stand against Washington.[104]

Daniels, who objected to international arbitration, argued in favor of Mexico's proposal.[105] However, the conservative members of the State Department were unimpressed with the reply, which they saw as another example of Mexican foot-dragging. Welles claimed that Mexico's offer of payment was typically "vague and imprecise," while Hull voiced his displeasure at Mexico's continued defiance. In late August, Hull asked Castillo Nájera to withdraw his government's note in order to nullify it. The Mexican ambassador refused without hesitation, arguing that doing so would "ruin [his] government's reputation." To assuage Hull, he stated that Mexico City "might proceed" with compensating the Yaqui Valley farmers and make "provisions to pay for other lands seized since 1927."[106] Once again, Mexico did neither.

Unsatisfied with Mexico's response, on August 22, 1938, Hull sent Mexico another long-winded and sternly worded note that repeated much of his first dispatch. The secretary of state rejected Mexico's offer to discuss the value of expropriated holdings on account of "the unfruitful negotiations held with the Mexican Government in recent years on these subjects." He added that additional talks would continue for "many years" and would not lead to an "equitable and satisfactory solution." As the next chapter will show, Hull was right. Hull also reiterated the standard State Department position: that until a final settlement was reached, Mexico should not expropriate any additional American-owned land.[107]

The reaction in Mexico to Hull's second note was similar to the first. The newspapers *Gráfico* and *Novedades* viewed Hull's demands "as a violation of Mexican sovereignty." *Últimas Noticias* described Hull's note as a "terrible, acrid document in which the strong attempt to exercise control over the weak." The Mexico City daily *Excelsior* insisted that U.S. officials had misled Cárdenas and that Washington's diplomatic "bungling" was responsible for much of the bilateral tension. This anti-American assault must have pressured Cárdenas into rebuffing Hull once more. The *New York Times* described, rather arrogantly, Cárdenas's dilemma. According to the newspaper, Cárdenas was forced either "to lose national prestige by backtracking upon all of his public declarations and policies through accepting arbitration or else defy the United States, which no Mexican president has ever done successfully."[108] Many U.S. officials probably saw the situation similarly.

The Cardenistas' initial reaction spoke louder than words. Less than twenty-four hours after Hull's second note was published, Mexico expropriated 22,692 acres of land from an American-owned hacienda in the state of Hidalgo. The property, called "La Reforma," belonged to the estate of William Mourse and was redistributed as a communal ejido to 581 peasant families.[109] The Mexican people once again rallied behind their president. According to Daniels, Cárdenas was becoming "stronger than ever with the masses of the people." The CTM-sponsored daily El Popular, the official organ of the nation's largest labor union, attacked Hull.[110] Novedades filled its pages with anti-U.S. rhetoric, stating, "The Yankees were never our friends. . . . [and] the government of the United States is principally responsible for the Mexican tragedy, for our military revolutions, our economic poverty, and our social anarchy."[111] Cárdenas's refusal to back down, in light of a century of U.S. dominance over Mexico, swelled his popular support (see figure 23). In addition, as Stephen Niblo notes, many Mexicans, like their president, were economic nationalists who saw the expropriation of foreign-owned land, oil companies, and railroads as prerequisites for developing their nation's economy to the point where it could compete with the United States.[112] Because of the link between Mexico's domestic and foreign policies, Mexicans who endorsed Cárdenas's domestic populism had to support his bold U.S. policy, since any other course of action would have jeopardized his program for national reform.

Mexico's second note, issued September 1, 1938, again rebuffed the State Department. Cárdenas's administration refused to halt land redistribution or submit the agrarian dispute to international arbitration. The Mexican note declared that its annual payments on the special claims cases involving damages incurred during the revolution illustrated Mexico's willingness to compensate Americans for their losses. Finally, Cárdenas's government again called for the creation of a bilateral commission to determine the value of the expropriated lands and the terms of payment.[113] This second note, along with a number of inflammatory anti-American speeches made by Cárdenas before the Mexican Congress and the CTM's Latin American Labor Congress—including a call to the rest of Latin America to follow his nation's lead and unite against the "common foreign enemy"—increased the breach between the two countries and made bilateral relations quite chaotic. The general reaction of the American press was equally grim. Many U.S. dailies predicted that diplomatic relations would break over the land seizures and painted the agrarian dispute as one of the most serious crises between the two countries since 1923.[114]

While Hull was "greatly disappointed" and "flabbergasted" by Mexico's sec-

FIGURE 23. Pro-Cárdenas rally in Mexico City in mid-1938. AGN, ARCHIVO FOTOGRÁFICO, FONDO ENRIQUE DÍAZ, 63/24.

ond response, Daniels endorsed it. He believed that for political reasons Cárdenas could not publicly declare that Mexico would halt the expropriation of American-owned property. After the second note was issued, Beteta told Daniels (in a move obviously intended to appease Washington) that "little additional land would be taken from American landowners." It was an empty promise. Nevertheless, upon receiving this news, the U.S. ambassador urged his superiors to accept Mexico's second reply. Worried that Washington would apply economic pressure against Mexico, as discussed in official circles and reported in U.S. newspapers, Daniels objected to canceling all U.S. purchases of Mexican silver. The U.S. ambassador argued that such a policy would hurt the Mexican mining industry, which was 90 percent American owned, and that it would also increase Mexican unemployment, since taxes on silver helped to finance Cárdenas's development projects. This higher unemployment would boost Mexican migration to the U.S.—something the White House wanted to avoid. A boycott of Mexican products, Daniels claimed, would produce similar results, and lifting the arms embargo would encourage revolution and end the Good Neighbor policy. Rather than resort to any of these heavy-handed measures, Daniels recommended that Washington pursue Mexico's proposal of a bilateral agrarian commission.[115]

In 1938, federal budget deficits, inflation, commercial bankruptcies, and capital flight increased in Mexico, while factory production, exports, federal tax revenue, the peso's value, and the world price of silver all declined. Such widespread economic problems led the U.S. embassy's commercial attaché Thomas Lockett to conclude that the Mexican economy was in bad shape.[116] Officials on both sides of the border were concerned about Mexico's ballooning budget deficit, which grew substantially in 1938.[117] The federal government was so short of cash that it was having difficulty funding the ejidatarios and maintaining its numerous public works projects. Reserves at the Banco de México dropped nearly 45 percent from August 1937 to March 1938, and private banks throughout the country began curtailing loans.[118] Government revenue declined by 14 percent when the oil companies stopped paying taxes after their properties were nationalized in mid-1938. That year, oil exports dropped by 35 percent compared to 1937 levels due to the boycott imposed by the foreign-owned petroleum companies. Throughout 1938 both foreign and domestic capital left the country, and the run on dollars at the Banco de México continued. By August, Mexican trade was declining, factory production was down, and small bankruptcies were increasing. The value of the peso declined 28 percent, which spurred higher inflation and prompted the Banco de México to remove Mexico's currency from the world market. Dollars also were hard to come by in 1938, as tourist income declined by one-third from 1937 levels. Meanwhile, food prices continued to rise; in the month of March the price of beans jumped from 12 to 31 centavos per kilo.[119] The country's increasing economic problems compelled Mexico City, now more than ever, to resolve the issue of compensation in a way that did not further increase its foreign debt or undermine the national economy. The only way to achieve this was to gain economic assistance from Washington in exchange for indemnifying U.S. landowners.

Just as the State Department stepped up pressure during Daniels's three-week absence from Mexico City in June 1938, Cardenista officials took advantage of Welles's absence from Washington during his five-week trip to Europe in September and October 1938 to press their case. In early September, Castillo Nájera initiated private talks with Hull to bring an interim resolution to the agrarian dispute. The Mexican ambassador stated that political circumstances in Mexico prevented Cárdenas from changing his policy via the public exchange of notes that were published in the press, adding that the Mexican president hoped to settle the conflict privately through oral negotiations. During their first of four meetings, Castillo Nájera told Hull that Cárdenas was "very desirous about clearing up the land claims" and planned "to make payments without fail for both the Yaqui Valley lands and all other American-owned rural property seized during the past ten years." According to Castillo Nájera, Cárdenas even agreed "to refrain from any further American land expropriations" and set a time limit in which valuations would be made and the lands paid for.[120] Once again, Mexican officials were telling the Americans what they wanted to hear, and once again, it worked.

Bilateral affairs had become so tense that Daniels pleaded with Roosevelt not to "permit a break in relations between Mexico and our country over the land expropriations." Daniels endorsed Mexico's calls for private talks, arguing that the public exchange of notes got the two countries "nowhere." Seeing that the State Department's forceful policy had severely strained bilateral relations, FDR reversed course and followed the advice of his ambassador. In Daniels's view, the hard-liners did not understand any of the "social implications growing out of the Revolution and the absolute necessity for educating the people and breaking up the big haciendas." To demand, as Welles did in late June, that all the American landowners be compensated in thirty months, the U.S. ambassador argued, was like "trying to extract blood from a turnip."[121] To advance his position with Roosevelt and undermine the State Department's "strong stand," diplomats in Washington complained that Daniels would not allow embassy personnel to send material to the United States that reflected negatively on Mexico.[122]

Hull's turnaround began in mid-September, when, according to Berle, the secretary of state decided to "tackle the job of Mexican relations at the White House."[123] After speaking with FDR, Hull agreed to pursue oral negotiations along the lines laid out by Castillo Nájera, as long as Mexico assured Washington that satisfactory arrangements would be made regarding payment.[124] During their third meeting in late September, Hull expressed his concern about future expropriations of American-owned land. Mexico's ambassador replied that while his "government could not go on record or make any public statement about the matter, it would agree not to make any more seizures . . . [barring] four exceptions."[125] After securing Hull's commitment to stop the exchange of public notes and instead negotiate a private settlement, in their last meeting on September 26, 1938, Castillo Nájera recanted his earlier assurances and told Hull that Mexico could not halt the expropriation of American-owned land.[126]

Both Hull's decision to work at the White House, and his subsequent reversal, stemmed from two factors. First, because over the years Hull had relied heavily on Welles's technical skills and expertise in hemispheric affairs, Hull may have sought White House assistance while Welles was in Europe, especially since he loathed making difficult decisions alone. Second, since inter-American relations were Welles's chief domain, Hull—who was angered by the fact that his subordinate had become FDR's chief foreign affairs adviser—may have seen this as an opportunity to undermine Welles, by changing U.S. policy toward Mexico in his absence. Although it would take Hull a few more years to "ruin Welles" and force his resignation from the State Department, this may have seemed like a good opportunity for him to chip away at the undersecretary, whom he very much disliked.[127]

Roosevelt, for his part, often modified or abandoned ideas that did not work. According to Irwin Gellman, FDR "never followed a consistent set of principles in his conduct of international affairs."[128] Since the State Department's more aggressive approach had failed to get Cárdenas's government to yield publicly to Washington's demands, closed-door talks along the lines suggested by Mexico seemed like a logical alternative. Roosevelt also was probably concerned about losing votes in the midterm elections, which were less than two months away. When bilateral relations reached the breaking point in September, several of the U.S. labor unions (most notably the CIO) and peace lobbies (including the Keep America Out of War Congress and the National Council for the Prevention of War) that comprised an important segment of FDR's New Deal coalition came out publicly against Hull's stern notes to Mexico.[129]

Private oral negotiations between the two governments slowed in October 1938 due to Washington's focus on events in Europe.[130] By late October, Cárdenas was worried that an interim resolution would not be reached prior to his November 20 address celebrating the twenty-ninth anniversary of the revolution. Consequently, he became more conciliatory in his negotiations with U.S. officials. On October 26, for instance, Cárdenas told Daniels that he was willing to make annual payments of $1 million on the agrarian claims, which was double the amount that Mexico had previously offered; he also said that he would "give immediate instructions to the agrarian authorities to cease any further expropriation of American lands while negotiations were in progress."[131] Cárdenas's last-minute overtures paid off. Two months of quiet diplomacy led to a final exchange of notes that laid out the terms of a temporary agrarian

FIGURE 24. Cartoonist Elderman stereotypes the cunning nature of Mexican officials, the feminine innocence of American landowners, and the exasperation of Uncle Sam over the continued expropriation of American-owned land in an attempt to sway U.S. public opinion against Mexico. © 1938, *THE WASHINGTON POST.* REPRINTED WITH PERMISSION.

settlement. Although the diplomatic notes of November 9 and 12, 1938, reiterated each government's initial position, they were much more cordial. By repeating their well-worn arguments, each side avoided the appearance of folding. The State Department wanted to appear firm in its convictions regarding just compensation for expropriated properties as a means to dissuade other countries from following Mexico's lead. Cárdenas, meanwhile, did not want it to appear that the United States had any say in his domestic agrarian reform program.

The notes of November 9 and 12 more closely resembled Mexico's earlier correspondence and proposals than they did those of the State Department. In line with Mexico's earlier suggestion, both governments agreed to establish a bilateral commission to determine the value of all the American-owned land expropriated since 1927. The commission's work was scheduled to be completed by May 31, 1939. On or before that date, the Mexican government would make its first annual reparations payment of $1 million and would continue until all of the agrarian claims were paid in full.[132] The November notes made no mention of future expropriations, and Cárdenas's government continued to seize American-owned estates, much to Washington's chagrin (see figure 24). And although it would appear that after three years Roosevelt's administration got Mexico to commit to a reparations plan, we will see in the next chapter that Mexico City stalled for three more years before signing onto a final agrarian agreement.

EPILOGUE

On November 20, 1938, nine days after the exchange of notes that marked an interim resolution to the agrarian dispute, Cárdenas asked thousands of Mexican landowners to make an enormous sacrifice on behalf of their country. In his public address at the annual parade in Mexico City that celebrates the revolution's anniversary, he called upon Mexican property owners to renounce their compensation claims for their expropriated rural holdings, even though they were guaranteed indemnification by the 1917 Constitution.

> Since the settlement of the international incident that stemmed from the expropriation of American agrarian properties is now known, I think it proper to inform the people that if the agreement has to result in a large expense on the part of the nation, then the outcome of this sacrifice will be the achievement of Mexican independence.
>
> I think it is advisable to ask our brother Mexicans, especially those affected [by expropriation], to act with patriotic fervor and humanitarian feelings, and study their situation, particularly how they maintained and exploited laborers on their lands. . . . And then take into consideration the unfairness of condemning future generations to pay the enormous [domestic] agrarian debt that would weigh down upon the people. Also, in light of the financial capacity of the nation, it must be agreed that many years will elapse before this debt can be paid. Therefore, it would be an example of high morality and true love of the interests of our country if Mexican citizens would disclaim indemnification for their affected lands. . . . If this is done the nation will feel very proud of the true patriotism of its own children. If this message is heeded, it will be the greatest and most deserved homage that has been paid to the martyrs of the Mexican Revolution.[133]

In short, Cárdenas had used the revolution's anniversary to inform Mexican landowners that they would not be indemnified because the federal government did not have the means to pay them. According to the president, Mexico's very independence came from settling the agrarian dispute with the United States. Because the landed elite still wielded a significant amount of power in the countryside, to offset a potential political backlash Cárdenas cleverly addressed his appeal to them in nationalistic terms. Rather than attack Mexico's landed class, which comprised his traditional and most vocal opposition, Cárdenas called on them to liberate Mexico and finish the battle begun by the martyrs of the revolution. Ironically, Mexican landowners would not only redeem those who had sacrificed themselves for their country, but they themselves would become the last heroes of the revolution if they would forgo compensation. Otherwise, they would be seen as unpatriotic, antirevolutionary reactionaries. Due to the establishment of an institutionalized one-party system in the 1930s, and in light of the fact that most Mexicans rallied behind Cárdenas during both the oil crisis and agrarian dispute, Mexican property owners had little option but to forgo indemnification.

This particular Día de la Revolución was the first to occur after the oil nationalization of March 1938. In the eight months between that date and the November twentieth holiday, Cárdenas's popularity reached its zenith. Thus, he probably expected that the nationalistic fervor surrounding the holiday would reduce the likelihood of a political attack by the hacendados. In the late 1930s, the Revolution Day parade through Mexico City's historical district lasted as long as six hours and included as many as fifty thousand peasants, workers, athletes, schoolchildren, government bureaucrats, and soldiers.[134] The parade crossed class lines and marked a novel use of public space for disseminating government decrees and propaganda.[135] Cárdenas, like his predecessors and successors, used the Día de la Revolución, and the social solidarity and patriotism engendered by the parade's spectacle, to shape popular views of the past and legitimate his present and future policies, especially regarding land redistribution, indemnification of American claimants, and the lack of compensation for Mexican rural property owners.[136]

What makes the agrarian dispute interesting is that domestic forces in Mexico shaped Cardenista policies toward Washington, and these same Mexican foreign policies were then used to justify Cárdenas's domestic decisions. By allowing bilateral relations to deteriorate over the agrarian issues, Cárdenas garnered nationwide support in his defiance of Washington. He then quickly and symbolically traded on this political capital to mitigate the backlash that would follow his call for Mexican landowners to forgo compensation. With Welles on vacation, Castillo Nájera approached Hull for a private resolution; there was no need to appeal to Daniels, since the U.S. ambassador already endorsed Mexico's position. Cárdenas's administration simply needed to convince the U.S. secretary of state to compromise. Once Hull was agreeable, Mexico City had the U.S. Embassy, the White House, and the State Department on its side.

THE 1941 GLOBAL SETTLEMENT

*The End of the Agrarian Dispute and the Start
of a New Era in U.S.-Mexican Relations*

The present moment is, from all standpoints, the most favorable for the initiation
of a new era in the history of Mexican and United States international relations.
MEXICAN AMBASSADOR DR. FRANCISCO CASTILLO NÁJERA, FEBRUARY 17,
1941

The early 1940s witnessed the beginning of a new and improved era in U.S.-
Mexican relations. By settling the agrarian, oil, and general claims, the 1941
Global Settlement resolved a number of bilateral controversies that had developed over the preceding six years, as well as others that dated back to 1868. The
agreement also contained generous provisions that both promoted Mexican
economic development along less nationalistic lines and addressed the economic needs of the United States as the country shifted to a wartime economy.
Together, the Global Settlement, World War II, and the economic growth of
each nation after 1945 improved bilateral relations by ending some of the long-
standing conflicts between the two countries, fostering international cooperation against the Axis powers, supplying Mexico with U.S. financial assistance,
making American investments below the Rio Grande more secure, expanding
cross-border trade, and cultivating a broad mutuality of such interests that was
unique in the often-contentious history of bilateral affairs.

The literature that covers the period from 1939 to 1941 plays down the broad
nature of the Global Settlement and focuses overwhelmingly on the conclusion
of the oil crisis. Stressing only one aspect of this important bilateral agreement

distorts the methods of and rationale behind Mexican policymaking. For instance, scholars both have overemphasized the role played by U.S. officials and their security concerns and have credited Mexican diplomats with nothing more than using the war to win a favorable oil deal. But how and exactly when did Mexico start to take advantage of global politics? According to María Paz, Mexican officials did not apply the leverage that they gained from WWII until late 1940 because U.S. hemispheric defense strategy was not fully defined until France fell to Germany that summer.[1] Paz's argument holds true if one looks at the bilateral negotiations that settled the agrarian dispute.

Since the agrarian claims negotiations began in January 1939, Mexico could not yet offer its support as a committed military ally as a point of leverage to extract concessions from its northern neighbor. At this point there was little support within popular or official circles in Mexico for either the war or assisting the Unites States militarily.[2] Even as late as 1941, public opinion polls conducted by Nelson Rockefeller "showed that Mexicans were predominantly anti-American and in many cases supported Germany."[3] As a result, throughout 1939 Mexican officials did not use events in Europe or Asia to bolster their hand in their talks with Washington over the land and oil questions. In fact, Cárdenas's cabinet did not discuss how world affairs would assist them in their relations with the United States until mid-1940. This, coupled with the fact that the traditionally anti-American stance of both the political elite and the general public in Mexico had only been heightened by the land and oil conflicts, explains why the country remained neutral until the spring of 1942 and did not deploy troops until mid-1945. According to Paz, not only was Mexico a "reluctant U.S. ally," but "before Pearl Harbor, Mexico's attitude toward security cooperation remained noncommittal."[4] Cárdenas was astute enough to realize that creating problems over the American agrarian claims in 1939 would enhance his prestige nationwide, whereas aligning with the United States militarily would undermine it. Consequently, Mexican officials did not use the war as a bargaining chip during the agrarian dispute; rather, they played it like a trump card late in the negotiating game.

If Mexico City did not use WWII to strengthen its position against Washington after the November 1938 diplomatic notes, how then did Mexican policymakers gain the upper hand when discussing compensation for American landowners? Rather than immediately play the defense card and accommodate Washington over military issues, Cardenista officials initially and continuously used the agrarian claimants themselves to gain leverage and secure the lucrative Global Settlement.

As agreed to in the November 1938 notes, both governments created the Agrarian Claims Commission to appraise the claims of American landowners who had lost property since 1927 under Mexico's official agrarian reform program. Starting in early 1939, the U.S. and Mexican sections of the commission gathered evidence to evaluate each individual claim. That May, they were supposed to meet and negotiate a fair appraisal for each American landowner. The U.S. section was headed by the former commissioner of the International Boundary Commission, Lawrence Lawson; the Mexican section was led by the former commissioner of the International Water Commission, Gustavo Serrano.[5] The life of the Agrarian Claims Commission was extended twice because landowners needed more time to file and because the U.S. and Mexican sections required additional time to evaluate the claims, in part because Cárdenas's government expropriated additional American-owned properties in 1939 and 1940. In addition, the two commissioners did not start the adjudication process until the spring of 1940, one year after they were first supposed to meet, due to the complexity of the claims and Mexican foot-dragging.[6]

Mexican officials saw little need to reach a quick settlement, knowing full well that the White House remained amiable. In February 1939, Roosevelt told Ambassador Castillo Nájera that despite the differences between the two countries, his "sympathy for President Cárdenas continued invariably."[7] As is often the case in foreign affairs, what is said privately (in this case by FDR) often carries greater weight than what is said publicly, since the latter is sometimes intended only to influence public opinion. A number of U.S. policymakers also recognized this and grew concerned. In early 1939 some State Department officials expected little to change in terms of Mexican diplomacy. Commented one official, "Nothing has transpired since Secretary Hull's [1938] notes, and there is a rumor that the notes represent only the State Department's statements 'for the record,' in view of the protests by the landowners, oil companies, and foreign governments, but that it is privately known that there is nothing for Mexico to worry about."[8]

In early 1939 it was clear to officials in both governments that there were "serious differences of interpretation" regarding the diplomatic notes of November 9 and 12, 1938. Commissioner Lawson argued that if the United States "acceded to the Mexican position on all of the points, [it] would result in excluding a majority of the claims." He estimated nearly 75 percent of the total amount claimed by the landowners involved what Mexican officials considered controversial legal questions.[9] Upset by Mexico's posturing, Undersecretary Welles told Castillo Nájera that the November 1938 agreement was "premised on [their] mutual desire to effect a prompt and fair solution [which] avoided technicalities." In Welles's view, "the clear intent and spirit of [their] conversations was that the claims should be evaluated and settled in a broadminded and non-legalistic manner."[10] U.S. diplomats found themselves in a difficult position because, as one official remarked, the November 1938 notes were not "formal and precise documents." The notes' brevity and lack of specificity allowed the Cardenistas to interpret them narrowly and raise numerous technical points that hampered negotiations and forced Washington to offer Mexico City the type of settlement it wanted.

One of the technical issues raised by Mexico was squatting. Mexican officials won a major diplomatic victory early in the claims negotiations when they convinced U.S. officials to accept a narrow definition of what constituted a legitimate agrarian claim: only land that had been taken by official agrarian authorities. This saved Mexico City an enormous amount of money in reparations for lands occupied by squatters, which could not form the basis of a claim no matter how long they had been occupied. A number of U.S. consulates in Mexico believed that this strict requirement was problematic, especially since squatters could gain legal possession, although not the title, of any vacant land which they occupy continuously for ten years. According to the U.S. consul in Veracruz, "Illegal seizures . . . affected a rather large percentage of American-owned property" in that consular district.[11] In the Yaqui Valley squatters also were common, as seen earlier with Edward Jesson's property. One American in southern Sonora observed, "Groups of peon and Indian families would move onto lands owned by Mexican and American colonist-farmers and erect homes. They would then claim the existence of a settlement or center of population that was entitled to own, use, and cultivate in common a substantial body of communal land."[12] Oftentimes their actions were followed by official decrees that began the government's land redistribution process. However, sometimes the authorities stayed out of the matter. When this happened, the squatters usually remained on the property illegally, and the owner was denied the right to seek any financial compensation.

Washington's concession on squatting proved very beneficial to Mexico. According to Lawson, this decision "accounted for a considerable part of the disparity between the total amount claimed [by the landowners] and the total amount of the appraisals." Lawson's findings should not be too surprising, since many Americans were absentee owners who could do little about the illegal possession of their land, assuming they were even aware of it.[13] The State Department agreed that cases resulting from independent actions by peasants could not be filed as claims but would be "proper subjects of diplomatic protection."[14] Diplomatic protection, though, was usually ineffectual.[15] American landowners were disappointed that Washington yielded on this issue, believing they had little chance of local recourse. James Butler, an American farmer in Oaxaca, expressed the frustration felt by many regarding the occupation of his land by squatters. When U.S. officials told Butler to address state and municipal authorities, he replied, "I do not quite understand what is meant by 'appropriate legal proceedings' and an 'appeal to the local authorities.' The fact that squatters have occupied my land for years, and at the same time the authorities have accepted taxes from me for the same land, would seem to require no further proof that the land is occupied with the acquiescence of the Mexican Government."[16]

Admitting that "the eviction of squatters was always difficult," U.S. officials understood Butler's predicament. According to the U.S. consul, even if Butler had the squatters removed, "they might easily retaliate and petition to expropriate his land."[17] Not only was it hard to get seized lands returned, but, according to Lawson, "a number of Americans who have sustained agrarian losses since 1927 indicated their intention not to file claims . . . due to fear of possible reprisals." In fact, according to the U.S. commissioner, many Americans who lost land after 1927 did not file a claim.[18] Thus, the Mexican government also saved a significant amount of money by not having to compensate American landowners who failed to file a reparations claim.

At what point in the official expropriation process could a property owner file a claim for compensation?[19] This question represents another technicality raised by Mexican diplomats. For Mexican decisionmakers this topic was integral to presidential authority and worthy of drawn-out discussions. The Mexican section of the Agrarian Claims Commission believed a claim could only be filed after the definitive (i.e., presidential) resolution was published in the *Diario Oficial*, the federal government's official periodical, since this was the final act of the expropriation process that officially divested the owner's title. By law, the Mexican president was the nation's highest agrarian authority. If the commission evaluated losses based on a provisional resolution (i.e., the state governor's initial expropriation decree), Mexican officials argued, it would decrease the president's authority. Also, since the amount of land affected sometimes differed between the provisional and definitive resolutions, the Mexican section argued that they should only accept claims based on the latter.[20]

U.S. officials opposed the Mexican position and argued that any action by agrarian authorities that deprived a landowner of property was grounds for a claim.[21] The State Department rightly argued that it often took many years for a provisional resolution to reach the president for signature, and in most cases owners lost control of their lands immediately following the issuance of the provisional decree, if not earlier. U.S. officials worried that using the definitive resolution as the basis for filing would enable the Mexican government to deprive owners of compensation by simply withholding the presidential decree.[22] This was a critical issue, since Mexico continued to expropriate American holdings in 1939 and 1940.[23] For nearly six months Mexican officials debated this issue with their U.S. counterparts. In May 1939, Cárdenas conceded and instructed Commissioner Serrano to consider all provisional expropriations as definitive and constituting a legal claim.[24] Because Cárdenas had already signed most resolutions by this time, the number of outstanding provisional resolutions was low and the total dollar amount involved relatively small; Mexico was therefore willing to compromise.

In determining the value of claims, the Mexican section argued for a very narrow reading of the November 1938 notes: only redistributed land should be compensated, and not the loss of agricultural machinery and personal property, damages to land improvements, or the depreciation of lands not seized.[25] Although Mexican officials agreed that such losses had been sustained, they were unwilling to provide indemnification. U.S. officials saw it necessary to press the point, since fifty-three claims had sustained such damages. According to Lawson, the "seizure of property involved not only the land value, but the improvements placed on the property such as fences, canals, drainage works, pumping plants, storage facilities, buildings, and other items representing expenditures by the claimants."[26] U.S. officials pointed out that under Mexican law, indemnification covered damages that were incurred from expropriation.[27] Although Cárdenas's administration admitted that Washington's position on payment for damages was well grounded in Mexican law, it nevertheless impeded a final settlement by debating this issue with the U.S. section for more than a year before acquiescing.[28]

Mexican officials also argued that indemnification should be based on the property's tax appraisal—which normally was lower than its commercial value. Although never stated openly, Cardenista officials alluded to the fact that most landowners frequently undervalued their property to reduce their tax burden: in other words, since rural property owners had cheated state and federal governments out of much needed revenue, it was only fair that appraisals be based on tax assessments. U.S. officials realized that both the November notes and Mexican law supported this position and quickly conceded this point. Nevertheless, the U.S. section rightly argued that using the land's fiscal value was problematic, since tax forms reflected the value of an entire estate and did not differentiate between different types of land within a single property. Thus, when mostly high-quality lands were expropriated and the undeveloped lands remained with the owner, the tax form that covered the entire property could not accurately reflect the value of the land that was seized. On any given American-owned estate, agrarian authorities often expropriated all the lands that had access to water—making it difficult for property owners to irrigate their remaining holdings. Not only did this leave them "literally high and dry" and force many to sell their "protected" 250 acre *pequeña propiedad* (small property exempt from expropriation); it also shortchanged the U.S. landowners when they sought full compensation for their irrigated lands based on a propertywide tax form. Despite the fact that using tax forms to appraise the claims was detrimental to the American landowners, U.S. officials believed there was little that they could do to rectify these difficulties.[29]

The subject that caused the greatest amount of bilateral contention concerned the fate of American stockholders in "Mexican-owned" companies—many of whom, like Baja California's Colorado River Land Company (CRLC), were colonization or land development firms. As noted in chapter 7, in November 1938 Cárdenas decreed that Mexican landowners and companies would not be indemnified for their expropriated property. Consequently, U.S. nationals holding millions of dollars of stock in Mexican land companies also were prohibited from filing compensation claims. According to the Cardenistas, even if all of a company's stock was owned by U.S. citizens, if the firm was incorporated in Mexico they were barred from indemnification. One can only speculate whether Cárdenas had the foreign stockholders and bilateral negotiations in mind when he announced on Revolution Day that Mexican landowners and companies would not be compensated. If so, he showed a great deal of forethought.

The stockholder issue was critical because these claims represented the largest and most expensive seizures of American-owned land in Mexico, including the hundreds of thousands of acres expropriated from CRLC and United Sugar Companies. In December 1939, Lawson estimated that sixty-five claims totaling 14.5 million acres and worth "approximately $31 million were filed on behalf of American stockholders of Mexican companies."[30] Cárdenas's administration was shrewd in using the stockholders as their main bargaining chip during the latter half of the agrarian dispute, since determining whether they would be compensated would have a significant bearing on the total amount owed by Mexico. The stockholders were the wealthiest and most influential Americans filing claims, and the Cardenistas may have believed that the pressure which they were likely to put on U.S. officials might force Washington to compromise elsewhere to ensure their indemnification. Harry Chandler, for instance, who owned the majority of CRLC's stock, was the publisher of the *Los Angeles Times*. And, if CRLC officials are any measure, the leading stockholders of major "American" companies probably had access to State Department officials and congressional representatives. Also, American stockholders were a vital component of U.S. foreign investment in Mexico, Latin America, and much of the world; for many U.S. policymakers, obtaining compensation for them was critical in order to dissuade other governments from following Cárdenas's lead and thereby protect American investors globally.[31] Because of the importance of stockholders to both countries, Mexican officials used them to gain leverage, slow down negotiations, and force Washington into providing economic incentives to Mexico as part of the final agrarian settlement.

To Mexico's advantage, the November 1938 notes made no mention of the American stockholders' rights. As a result, the Mexican section of the Agrarian Claims Commission argued forcefully against including them in a final agrarian settlement and used the U.S.-Mexican general claims agreement as precedent. According to Cardenista officials, since the stockholder claims were "not specifically referred to in the [November 1938] Agreement, had the two Governments intended to include this class of claims, they would have so stated . . . [and] included an allotment provision similar to the one incorporated in the General Claims Convention of September 8, 1923." Mexican policymakers had a good point: Article I of the General Claims Convention specifically preserved the rights of U.S. partners and stockholders in Mexican corporations and allowed them to file general claims against the Mexican government. Call it poor diplomacy on Washington's part for not including such a provision, but Mexican officials smartly interpreted the November 1938 notes narrowly and used a recent bilateral agreement to argue against compensating the agrarian stockholders.[32]

U.S. officials clearly had their work cut out for them if they hoped to obtain indemnification for the American stockholders, especially since international law was ambiguous on the issue. They staked their claim on two different arguments: first, that Mexican domestic law recognized that when the majority stock of a Mexican company was owned by foreigners, its national status could be altered; second, that Mexico City's position on the stockholders had violated the spirit of the November 1938 notes, which was that all American property owners affected by expropriation were to be compensated.[33]

Realizing the importance that Washington put on the stockholder claims, Mexican diplomats milked it for all it was worth, from the start of negotiations in January 1939, until September 1940 when U.S. officials blinked first. Moreover, when the bilateral agrarian talks faltered over of the stockholder issue, the Cardenistas sometimes blamed Daniels for creating confusion. For example, in a November 1939 meeting with Welles, Castillo Nájera stated that Daniels had told the Mexican Ministry of Foreign Affairs that Washington was more "interested in the claims of the small landholders and not the larger landholders, notably those who had incorporated their properties in Mexico, had no legitimate claim for payment." According to the Mexican ambassador, "Mr. Daniels convinced the Mexican Government that there was no need to find a way out of the [stockholder] difficulty."[34] No evidence has been found verifying that Daniels made any such statements, and Mexican officials may have simply been trying to shift blame for the impasse. This also may have been an attempt by Mexico to increase the discord within the U.S. diplomatic corps, since it was clear to most that the State Department frowned on Daniels's compliant stance toward Cárdenas's government over agrarian matters.

In general, Mexican officials settled their disagreements with their U.S. counterparts quickly when it was to their economic advantage, as seen with squatting and land appraisals based on tax value. On the other hand, they dragged their feet when the discussions pertained to matters that would increase their payments to the United States, including compensation for properties under provisional resolution, for damages incurred, and for the stockholders. And, although Mexican officials yielded on a few of the controversial points, such as provisional resolution and damages, these issues concerned relatively small dollar amounts. However, on the issues that involved the largest claims, namely the American stockholders, the Cardenistas never budged—at least not until Washington made it financially worth their while.

The inability of both sides to agree on these and many other legal questions raised by Mexico could not have worked out better for Cárdenas's administration. In March 1939, Welles instructed Commissioner Lawson not to present any appraisals to Serrano until the controversial questions were first resolved. This halted any bilateral discussion of the individual agrarian claims filed by the American landowners.[35] To make the process even slower and more bureaucratic, Commissioner Serrano was ordered by Cárdenas not to make any decisions without his approval.[36] Some U.S. officials saw early on that reaching a final agrarian settlement with Mexico would be difficult. One member of the U.S. section noted pessimistically that there was "little prospect of any change in the position of the Mexican section on these controversial subjects." He commented, "The Mexican Section does not consider that the purpose of the [1938] agreement is to put an end to all agrarian claims arising since 1927. Rather, its position seems to be to employ every available technicality to prevent the disposition by this Commission of as many such claims as possible."[37]

After nine months of negotiating the technical questions alone, by late 1939 Mexican officials noted the growing consternation within Roosevelt's administration over the fact that no progress was made in appraising the claims, and hence little movement had been made toward a final agrarian settlement. For a developing nation to employ the diplomatic weapons of the weak successfully against a hegemonic power, it cannot prove obstinate on every issue but instead must find some common ground. While Mexican officials held firm during the first year of agrarian claims negotiations, they did demonstrate their solidarity with the United States in the fight against fascism. Since the Western Hemisphere was not under any military threat in 1939, it was unrealistic for Cárdenas to align militarily with the United States at this stage without risking political attack at home. Therefore, in late 1939 and early 1940, Cárdenas granted the U.S. minor security-related concessions that pleased Washington but drew little attention south of the border. After wwii began, Cárdenas told Daniels that Foreign Secretary Hay would give "the heartiest cooperation at the Panama conference toward securing effective continental solidarity."[38]

Cárdenas also assured U.S. officials that his administration would not adopt a pro-German posture like the one held by President Venustiano Carranza between 1916 and 1918. Said Cárdenas, "That was another and distant day. We live in a different period. There should be no fear of German influence or German penetration of Mexico. [Mexico] is in full accord with the policy of the United States whose friendship it prizes and we will be found standing together to prevent any European country's penetration or influence in our policies."[39]

In November 1939, Mexico agreed to allow U.S. aircraft to fly over its airspace in cases of emergency and without prior permission, such as during aerial pursuit of a belligerent submarine or plane. Cárdenas's government also began purchasing limited military supplies from U.S. manufacturers.[40] On one hand, Cárdenas's gestures of solidarity and arms purchases helped to ease the strain in bilateral relations caused by both the agrarian dispute and the oil crisis. On the other hand, they did little to resolve either conflict.

MEXICO'S ECONOMIC AND POLITICAL PROBLEMS AND U.S. ECONOMIC PRESSURE

Just as political and economic constraints had prevented Mexico from presenting an acceptable payment plan to Washington prior to the November 1938 notes, likewise, in 1939 and 1940 Cárdenas's administration carefully avoided a final reparations agreement due to the continued weakness of the Mexican economy and the president's waning political power. In return for the loyalty of Mexico's governors during Saturnino Cedillo's 1938 rebellion, Cárdenas had handed some federal powers over to the states. Not only did this weaken the central government, but it also empowered some of Cárdenas's conservative opponents at the regional level. In fact, despite Cedillo's defeat, the political opposition to Cárdenas continued in 1939, as a coalition of military groups came together and formed the Mexican Constitutional Front (Frente Constitucional Mexicano). Rather than attack the president directly, these conservative generals spoke out against Cárdenas's closest supporters, especially the CTM and its leader, Vicente Lombardo Toledano; they also were critical of Cárdenas's oil policy. To make matters worse for the president, in 1939 and 1940 rumors of a Callista rebellion on the Right and communist uprising on the Left continued to proliferate. During these same years, a conservative movement headed by Juan Andreu Almazán seriously challenged the official selection of Manuel Ávila Camacho as the country's next president. Almazán had ties to local fascist groups, which stirred up fears of a " 'Franco-type' " coup when rumors of his impending rebellion spread.[41] Together, these political developments probably would have made Cárdenas think twice about the fallout that might follow a final agrarian agreement that guaranteed Mexican payment for expropriated American-owned lands.

In addition to these political considerations, economic reality must have weighed heavily on Cárdenas's stance in the negotiations. There simply was not enough money in the federal treasury to immediately compensate American

TABLE 6. Mexico's balance of trade, 1934–1940 (in millions of dollars)

	1934	1935	1936	1937	1938	1939	1940
Exports	178.9	208.3	215.2	247.9	185.4	176.1	177.8
Imports	92.8	112.8	128.9	170.6	109.3	121.4	123.9
Balance	86.1	95.5	86.3	77.3	76.1	54.7	53.9

Source: Hamilton, *The Limits of State Autonomy*, 224.

property owners as the State Department demanded. Table 6 illustrates Mexico's continued downward economic slide after the oil nationalization, showing three years of falling or flat exports beginning in 1938. In January 1939, Mexico exported $12.6 million worth of products, but November's export total of $9.2 million was the lowest of the year, producing the country's first monthly trade deficit in nineteen years.[42] Meanwhile, the outbreak of war in Europe decreased Mexican exports across the Atlantic. Although Mexican trade to Europe had risen during wwi, the British naval blockade during wwii precipitated a dramatic decline in the nation's export of copper, lead, zinc, and silver to the continent. Also, England's preference of importing raw materials from within its empire, which grew stronger during wwii, reduced Mexican exports to the United Kingdom as well.[43]

U.S. silver policy also indirectly contributed to the decrease in Mexican trade. In early 1939, Washington reduced the global price of silver by 10 cents, which destabilized the peso's exchange rate and reduced the value of Mexico's silver exports. Since the peso was closely tied to the price of silver, any reduction in its price weakened the peso's value and made imports more expensive. Unable to boost exports, which usually offsets a lower valued currency, Mexico's exports instead fell dramatically between 1938 and 1940, and inflation grew. Mexican exports to the United States also suffered as a result of the import quota that Washington placed on Mexican oil, which, according to one Cardenista official, "placed Mexico in a situation of marked inferiority with respect to the other oil-producing countries." Mexican officials had reason to complain, since the U.S. quota throttled Mexican oil exports to a trickle compared to Venezuela's. Under the quota, Venezuela sold the United States 71.9 percent of its imported oil, the Netherlands 20.3 percent, Colombia 4 percent, and Mexico just 3.8 percent.[44] Moreover, Mexican oil production dropped significantly in 1938, and from then until 1940, it never exceeded its 1937 prenationalization peak.[45]

As oil exports declined, throughout 1938 and 1939 the price of foodstuffs in Mexico rose dramatically, in part due to the lower production of staples in the Mexican countryside. Aware that they would not be compensated for their land should it be expropriated by the federal government, to reduce their potential losses many Mexican farmers underplanted. Dramatic changes in land tenure and production methods that stemmed from land redistribution also reduced crop yields and increased the price of staples. Although Mexico had long imported basic foodstuffs, the dramatic increase of wheat imports in 1938 and 1939 illustrates the severity of declining food production. In 1935, Mexico imported just 46 tons of wheat, and 95 tons in 1936. This number jumped to 4,932 tons in 1937 and skyrocketed to 89,684 tons in 1938 before declining the following year to 51,086 tons.[46] As the cost of living and food prices increased, the government was forced to increase subsidies on staples, which decreased federal revenue. Meanwhile, agricultural production and real wages declined during Cárdenas's last three years in office.[47]

Federal fiscal policy did little to reverse Mexico's declining economic indicators. In 1939 the Bank of Mexico and the Ministry of Finance issued paper currency with insufficient backing. In fact, the amount of money in circulation increased by 30 percent, from $703 million pesos in 1936 to more than $1 billion pesos by 1940, sparking widespread inflation. Meanwhile, the flight of capital that had begun in 1937 and had accelerated in 1938 continued in 1939 as investors lost confidence in the Mexican economy. Likewise, the decline in silver exports that began in 1938 worsened in 1939 and 1940—so much so that in 1940 silver exports were only one-sixth of their 1937 level. In February 1940, the exchange holdings of the Bank of Mexico reached a record low of $25.3 million. Meanwhile, banks throughout Mexico responded to the economic crisis by reducing loans.[48]

Mexico's economic problems in 1939 made it difficult for Cárdenas's government to pay its first installment on the U.S. agrarian claims. Although the two countries had not reached a final agreement regarding compensation for the American landowners, the November 1938 notes obligated Mexico to pay Washington $1 million annually until there was a final settlement. The first installment was due on June 1, 1939. Just one week before the deadline, representatives of the American Smelting and Refining Company informed U.S. officials that nine of the largest mining companies in Mexico had recently advanced the federal government $1.5 million, in exchange for an agreement whereby the amount loaned could be deducted from future taxes. Another important string attached to the loan required the Mexican government to side with the American mining companies during the 1939 mine workers' strike—which it did. Many U.S. officials, including the U.S. consul general, were convinced that "the loan was tied to the million dollar payment that was due the American government at the end of the month on account of the agricultural claims of American citizens." They also suspected that the loan was used "to pay government salaries, since the [Mexican] government was very hard pressed for money."[49]

Although Washington could do little about the loan advanced by the mining companies, the State Department prevented other large-scale public and private loans from reaching Mexico as a means to put pressure on Cárdenas's government during the oil and agrarian talks. In early 1939, for instance, the State Department blocked a $10 million Export-Import Bank loan to Mexico that Treasury Secretary Eduardo Suárez requested for the construction of a thermoelectric power plant, two sugar mills, and a natural gas pipeline.[50] Unable to gain public loans from Washington, Suárez was forced to look for private credit extensions. Cárdenas's administration had worked out a $20 million loan from National City Bank, Kuhn Loeb, and J. P. Morgan to help finance Mexico's cotton, wheat, sugar, and chickpea production. The loan also was intended to help stabilize the Mexican exchange rate and improve economic conditions south of the border. But in a meeting with representatives of National City Bank, Laurence Duggan, chief of the State Department's Division of American Republics, stressed that with "the present status of the petroleum and land questions . . . it would be greatly preferable if an operation of this character were to follow as a sort of fruit of settlement of the outstanding questions rather than to precede such settlements. That pending a solution of the petroleum and agrarian matters, the Export-Import Bank was not making available its credit facilities to the Mexican Government."[51]

The following day, National City Bank informed Duggan that they would not extend any credit to Mexico City. Mexican officials knew why the loan was canceled. During his meeting in New York, Fernández del Castillo, president of the Central Finance Company (Compañía Central Financiera)—which acted on behalf of the federal government's National Bank of Agricultural Credit and the National Bank of Ejidal Credit—was told by National City Bank officials that they "could not look upon the transaction as an isolated piece of business, and that because the general situation [with Washington] was bad, it would have to be cleared up before the Bank could consider the proposal favorably."[52] The economic pressure this time may have been instigated by the renewed criticism

FIGURE 25. Cartoonist Elderman illustrates through Uncle Sam's actions that the U.S. government had become more assertive in trying to get Mexico to pay for expropriated American-owned property. Although the Mexican figure is portrayed negatively (e.g., as sneaking out of the diner without paying his bill), the cartoon does rightly illustrate Mexico's attempt to circumvent Washington's demands for compensation. © 1938, THE WASHINGTON POST. REPRINTED WITH PERMISSION.

that members of Congress levied in early 1939 against Cárdenas's expropriations, Daniels's ambassadorship, and Roosevelt's overall Mexico policy.[53]

Although the U.S. government neither imposed a trade embargo nor levied other crippling economic sanctions during this period, nor, as Lorenzo Meyer states, "push[ed] Mexico to the breaking point," Washington and the American oil companies did "keep up the pressure" and flex their economic muscles. It is often assumed, especially by dependency scholars, that the economic might of a hegemon allows it to influence the domestic and foreign affairs of weaker states in a manner that suits its own interests. However, U.S.-Mexican relations in the late 1930s show this is not always the case. Cárdenas's government did not acquiesce during either the agrarian or the oil negotiations, even though the American oil companies boycotted sales of Mexican petroleum, cut off industry materials to Mexico, and would not allow Mexico to use their tankers.[54] In addition, even though Washington reduced its silver purchases from Mexico, lowered the world price of silver, placed import quotas on Mexican oil, and blocked public and private loans to its southern neighbor, the Cardenistas would not blink first. In fact, not only did U.S. economic pressure backfire, but Mexico gave the United States a taste of its own medicine. According to Stephen Niblo, Deputy Foreign Minister Beteta "kept a list of U.S. companies that openly opposed Mexican policy so that business could be directed away from them."[55] As the Mexican economy continued to spiral downward, in part because of U.S. policies, Cardenista officials were better able to justify their inability to compensate American property owners on account of the country's economic weakness.

A LUMP-SUM SETTLEMENT

Against the backdrop of Mexico's economic deterioration, the agrarian talks stalled in the fall of 1939 over the stockholder issue. In late November, one year after the formal exchange of notes, Welles met with Castillo Nájera and expressed his frustration. The U.S. undersecretary stated that he was "very greatly dissatisfied with the way in which the work of the Commission had been progressing due to the fact that the Mexican Government had been so utterly unwilling to agree upon the basic principles involved in the work of the two members of the Joint Commission in determining the fair amount of the claims." After noting that within the past year "the two Governments had not agreed upon the valuation of one single claim," Welles gave Castillo Nájera an "aide-mémoire" that invoked the earlier Mexican proposal that both sides work toward a lump-sum settlement of all the agrarian claims—as opposed to evaluating each individual one—to speed up the process and avoid the technicalities that repeatedly hampered negotiations.[56] As was often the case, Castillo Nájera saved face and told Welles that he agreed there should be no discrimination between the different types of claimants and that he supported the idea of a lump-sum agreement.[57] Beteta, on the other hand, recommended to Cárdenas that Mexico neither compensate American stockholders nor accept a "partial global settlement" that was limited solely to the agrarian claims and excluded U.S. financial assistance.[58]

Cárdenas followed Beteta's advice. As late as December 1939 the Mexican president stated that the November 1938 notes pertained only to the indemnification of American landowners, and not stockholders, and that he believed Mexico's position was upheld by international law. Cárdenas was so confident in his position that he suggested submitting the question to an international court of arbitration. Cárdenas's steadfastness stemmed from his anger with the United States for lowering the world price of silver by 10 cents per ounce, even though Washington said it would raise it after the November 1938 notes were exchanged. He also complained that Washington's silver policy destabilized Mexican exchange rates and undermined bilateral trade and the Mexican economy. Cárdenas then instructed his ambassador to tell U.S. officials that if Mexico were to continue payments on the special claims, and undertake payments for the agrarian and general claims, its trade with the United States would need to increase; if it did not, Mexico City would be unable to uphold all of its financial obligations to the various U.S. claimants.[59]

A few days after receiving instructions from Cárdenas, Castillo Nájera met with Welles and tried to capitalize on the idea of a lump-sum settlement, using the American stockholders as bait. Mexico was willing to compromise and compensate the American stockholders, but there were strings attached. According to the ambassador, the "Mexican Government would indemnify American stockholders in Mexican corporations for properties of those corporations which had been expropriated, provided the American Government, by changes in policy in connection with silver purchases and in connection with permitting the importation into the United States of Mexican oil, made it possible for the Mexican Government to find money with which to pay such indemnities."[60] After listening to years of rhetoric concerning the reciprocal nature of the Good Neighbor policy, Mexican officials had turned the tables on Roosevelt's administration. If Washington wanted compensation for the stockholders, then it had to assist Mexico commercially. Cárdenas's government wanted to ease payments on both the agrarian and general claims by increasing Mexican oil and silver exports. Greater exports would increase the production of both products, reduce unemployment, expand trade, and provide the federal government with more revenue.[61]

1940 AND THE SLOW START TO SUBSTANTIVE NEGOTIATIONS

Rather than pursue Mexico's latest proposal, Welles continued, in vain, to press for a lump-sum agreement devoid of both the legal questions raised by Cárdenas's administration and any economic incentives for Mexico City from Washington. In January 1940, he instructed Commissioner Lawson to present his findings to Serrano and appraise the claims "without regard to the technical points, such as the status of the claims of American stockholders, tax assessment valuations, et cetera."[62] Seeing this as a step backward, Cárdenas refused to yield and upped the ante by presenting additional issues that he said required resolution. After the Lawson-Serrano meeting, the Mexican president complained that the material Lawson presented was inadequate, since it did not contain any information regarding the nationality of the claimants, the validity of their claims, or other technical matters that, according to Cárdenas, "had to be discussed fully and informally with the Mexican Commissioner with regard to each specific claim."[63] To justify the disallowance of the stockholder claims, Cárdenas argued that compensation for American stockholders would induce Mexican nationals and corporations to transfer their stock to U.S. citizens and holding companies to obtain indemnification. Cárdenas's intransigence reflected his continued concern that any agreement without corresponding U.S. economic assistance would greatly increase Mexico's foreign debt.[64]

As negotiations continued to make little progress, the stalling tactics employed by Cardenista officials became more apparent. In February 1940, Lawson bemoaned that his Mexican counterparts were disposed "to evade the actual evaluation work," adding, "It is my belief that the present administration in Mexico would welcome an opportunity to delay final action until after the incoming administration assumes office in December [1940]."[65] Assistant Secretary of State Herbert Bursley concurred with Lawson's assessment: "Lawson, de Boal, [Agrarian Claims Commission Executive Officer George] Winters, and myself, in conversations with Mexican officials have seen very pointed indications that the Mexican Government seeks in every possible way to defer the proceedings, probably with the hope of having everything go over until after November 30 (Cárdenas's last day in office). One of the tactics we would anticipate would be the tendency to quibble over every detail of every case."[66]

Meetings between Welles, Castillo Nájera, and Bursley in April and May of 1940 proved fruitless.[67] However, in June, after Castillo Nájera stated that Serrano could now discuss a lump-sum settlement absent of technical points, Hull instructed Lawson to meet with his Mexican counterpart.[68] During the meeting, though, it was clear that Serrano did not have the authority to discuss the claims of American stockholders. Afterwards, Lawson concluded, it was "impossible for the two commissioners to arrive at an acceptable figure for a settlement. . . . However, the two commissioners would serve a very useful purpose by supplying their respective governments with independent appraisals which probably could be adjusted diplomatically particularly if considered in relation to other possible matters."[69] Clearly, Lawson was moving toward Mexico's position and saw the need to broaden the scope of the agrarian settlement.

By June 1940, talks between the two commissioners were again underway. Lawson informed Serrano that the American section had evaluated 347 claims and removed 90 of them as invalid. The remaining 257 claims, which covered nearly 4.8 million acres of land, were appraised by the U.S. section at $23 million. After studying Lawson's proposal, Serrano complained of the meagerness of the data, especially with regard to "the nationality of the claimants, the legitimacy of their title, and their interest in the claim." Serrano also held that many more of the 257 appraised claims should be invalidated. To support his assertion, Serrano raised questions regarding the claims of spouses to estates, exaggerated claims, and the rights of stockholders. Because the Mexican section raised so many questions that needed to be addressed, in July 1940 they requested that the life of the Agrarian Claims Commission again be extended. It was.[70]

Before Serrano submitted his counterproposal, he conferred with Cárdenas.[71] In his subsequent meeting with Lawson, Serrano stated that he had not been instructed to adjudicate the stockholder claims, and therefore Mexico would only pay between $8 and $11 million. A few weeks later, Serrano lowered the offer, stating that due to "Mexico's difficult economic situation . . . Mexico should not be expected to pay more than $5 or possibly $6 million dollars."[72] Mexican officials were not exaggerating their country's economic problems: gross domestic product had barely increased in 1940 over 1939 levels.[73] An internal memorandum written by the Mexican Ministry of Foreign Affairs admitted that the $40 million requested by Washington to liquidate both the agrarian and general claims "did not appear as an exaggerated sum."[74] Nevertheless, at the end of their last meeting Serrano and Lawson agreed on just one thing: "They saw no way in which they could possibly reach an agreement."[75] After examining Mexico's counteroffer, Lawson wrote to Hull:

> I have carefully examined Mexico's statement and find that . . . it does not constitute an appraisal of reasonable value of the expropriated properties. . . . It appears that no real appraisal has been made by the Mexican Section. The principal importance of the Mexican Commissioner's statement seems to be their endeavor to eliminate certain classes of claims,

notably those involving stockholders of Mexican companies, and to raise technical questions in others. . . . It is obvious that [Serrano] is unable to agree upon a lump sum settlement at a sufficient figure to provide reasonable compensation to all claimants, including the stockholders. . . . [The] joint evaluation of individual claims, which originally was intended, was abandoned because of the serious legal questions injected by the Mexican section. . . . Subsequently, and after evading an interpretive agreement clarifying the legal questions raised, the Mexican government suggested a lump sum settlement as a means of avoiding the necessity of discussing these questions and details of individual cases. . . . After a delay of four months, we now find that the Mexican government is bringing up the same legal questions and details of individual cases, which are inconsistent with the idea of a lump sum settlement. . . . [F]urther efforts by the two Commissioners to adjust the wide differences not only are entirely useless, but result in delay which is, of course, entirely acceptable to the Mexican government.[76]

Lawson's analysis was spot on. Cárdenas's administration was not going to pay the amount that he suggested unless the United States increased its silver and oil purchases from Mexico and changed its commercial policy to expand Mexican exports. The flight of approximately $20 million in capital from Mexico, the depletion of foreign assets in Mexico's Exchange Stabilization Fund, and the depletion of gold from Mexico's Metallic Reserve in the summer and fall of 1940 augmented the downward spiral of the economy. Simply put, Mexico was too poor to take on additional debts. To get Washington to reduce the agrarian claims to a figure that was acceptable to Mexico City or provide economic aid so it could afford this increase to its foreign debts, Cárdenas's administration began to play the defense card.[77]

Despite the ambivalence of the Mexican public over the war and their continued skepticism about supporting the United States, following the fall of France in June 1940 Mexican officials made it clear that they would join the United States in a military alliance—which showed Washington that the two nations agreed on the most important global question of the day. In mid-June, Cárdenas held two cabinet meetings to decide Mexico's position on hemispheric solidarity for the upcoming inter-American conference scheduled for July in Havana. With the exception of Mexico's ambassador to the League of Nations, Isidro Fabela, all of the cabinet members present—including Hay, Beteta, Suárez, Interior Minister Ignacio García Téllez, Deputy Minister of Finance Eduardo Villaseñor, and General Jesús Agustín Castro—supported closer military ties with the United States. Villaseñor spoke for most when he stated that an alliance would provide a good opportunity for the two countries to resolve all of their outstanding problems. The cabinet members and Cárdenas agreed to seek as many advantages as possible through military cooperation with their northern neighbor.[78] In June 1940, Téllez announced that Mexico would adopt a pro-Allied foreign policy and cut off oil sales to Italy.[79] Secret talks between U.S. and Mexican army and naval personnel regarding military cooperation were held in Washington, and Cárdenas stated that Mexico would enter into a military alliance with the United States and allow American forces to use Mexican territory and naval bases should the United States enter the war. Due to widespread suspicion concerning the United States and the general apathy regarding the war, it is unlikely the Mexican public would have endorsed military cooperation with the United States. Consequently, in light of Mexico's upcoming presidential election in July, bilateral military talks remained confidential to avoid jeopardizing the campaign of the official party's candidate, Manuel Ávila Camacho.[80]

Although Mexico's decision to side with the allies enabled the country to apply greater leverage in its negotiations with Washington, this stance, at heart, reflected the political disposition of Cárdenas's government and was not a completely Machiavellian move designed purely for domestic economic gain. During the mid-1930s, Mexico was more active in halting the spread of fascism than was the United States. During the Spanish Civil War, Cárdenas supported the Loyalists in Spain with military supplies against the German-backed forces of General Francisco Franco, while the United States would not lift its arms embargo to help the Spanish Republican government. Cárdenas also granted asylum to thousands of Spanish refugees who fled Franco's regime.[81]

Although Cárdenas wanted to stay out of wwii, as it spread across Europe and Asia his government worried about the nation's security, especially since observers on both sides of the border believed that Mexico could be used as a base for an Axis attack against the United States. Cárdenas sought to avoid the fate of weak European countries which, despite declaring their neutrality, were invaded and occupied by more powerful nations. He therefore purchased arms and military aircraft from the United States in order to modernize the nation's ill-prepared and poorly equipped military and increase its security. Mexican Army and Navy officers also sought to professionalize their forces through military arrangements with their northern neighbor. Cárdenas furthermore realized that Mexico's participation in the war would give it a stronger position in the postwar international order.[82] In short, Cárdenas's choice to align with the Allies reflected the ideological slant of his administration, Mexico's military and security needs, and his desire for a larger postwar international role; he would have made the same choice irrespective of the agrarian and oil conflicts. For these and other reasons, the same could be said of the wartime policies of Cárdenas's successor, Ávila Camacho.[83]

WASHINGTON YIELDS AND OFFERS
A COMPREHENSIVE SETTLEMENT

August 1940 saw numerous meetings that made little headway between U.S. and Mexican officials over the agrarian claims. Although both sides spouted familiar rhetoric about their sincerity in wanting to reach a final agreement, the same issues continued to be futilely debated.[84] By September, Welles realized that Mexico would continue to withstand U.S. economic pressure and that it would be impossible to circumvent the technical issues and secure a lump-sum agreement unless Washington first offered Mexico City the "fruits of settlement." As Commissioner Lawson rightly noted, "Negotiating a final settlement without raising any controversial legal questions, particularly that arising in claims of American stockholders of Mexican companies, was the principal reason for a global settlement."[85] Welles gained Roosevelt's approval to discuss all of the pending issues between the two countries, and he, rather than Hull, was in charge of negotiating the all-inclusive agreement.[86] What Welles had in mind was a quid pro quo resolution. In a subsequent meeting with Henry Morgenthau, Welles told the treasury secretary that payment for the expropriated rural properties would provide the basis for an adjustment of other controversies, and that the United States would "cooperate with the Mexican Government in the commercial and financial fields."[87]

In late September 1940, Welles suggested to Mexican Undersecretary of Finance Antonio Espinosa de los Monteros and Castillo Nájera that the two governments should reach a comprehensive "Global Settlement" and resolve all of the outstanding issues between them. Both Mexican officials responded enthusiastically.[88] The negotiations then shifted away from Lawson and Serrano and toward Welles, Duggan, Castillo Nájera, Espinosa, and Treasury Secretary Suárez. The topics discussed included the agrarian and general claims, settlement of the oil crisis, renewed service on Mexico's foreign and railroad debts, the distribution of waters from the Rio Grande and Colorado rivers, peso stabilization, a U.S. loan for Mexican highway construction, and a reciprocal trade agreement. The wide-ranging settlement and assistance package was greatly welcomed in Mexico City, and because of its broad and detailed nature Cárdenas and Roosevelt played a diminished role in setting its specific terms. Moreover, Cárdenas only had two months left in office. Meanwhile, U.S. officials were pleased that discussions now excluded the technical points that plagued earlier agrarian claims negotiations.[89]

In October 1940, Welles suggested to Castillo Nájera and Espinosa that Mexico pay $40 million to liquidate both the agrarian and general claims.[90] A month later Mexican officials made a counteroffer of $25 million to $30 million, using what Bursley described as "the stock Mexican arguments in these matters" to claim that Mexico was financially unable to come up with a greater sum.[91] Welles pointed out that the $40 million should not be difficult to pay, since the Global Settlement would ensure "Mexico would obtain economic benefits that would surely facilitate the fulfillment of the pecuniary obligations which it would contract in accordance with said plan." Shortly thereafter, Castillo Nájera informed Welles that his country would pay the $40 million sum "if, through the functioning of the general plan, there would be brought about an economic situation making it possible for Mexico to fulfill, in a regular and uninterrupted way, any monetary commitments which it accepts."[92]

Shrewd Mexican diplomacy had helped counter the power of the United States. Washington was also more inclined to offer the Global Settlement because the Mexican government had become less radical during Cárdenas's last two years in office and a moderate conservative was poised to succeed him. Additionally, there was a "convergence" of ideas on both sides of the Rio Grande regarding Mexican development that began in Cárdenas's last years in office and accelerated rapidly during the 1940s. Mexico's economic and political elite wanted to industrialize their way out of poverty, while their American counterparts saw renewed economic penetration of Mexico as one way to avoid another depression.[93] For Washington, the Global Settlement was designed primarily to settle the agrarian claims, but it also made Mexico a partner in the Allied war effort, fostered economic development along less radical lines, and made the country more attractive to foreign investment. For Mexico City, the all-inclusive agreement was a face-saving way to settle the agrarian dispute and the oil crisis; it also provided Mexico with much-needed financial assistance and promoted industrialization and commercial expansion.

Since the Global Settlement helped the two nations put their differences behind them, the State Department and Roosevelt were willing to accept Mexico's invitation for Vice President Elect Henry Wallace to attend Ávila Camacho's inauguration. Wallace's appearance in December 1940 marked the first time that a U.S. vice president attended the swearing in of a Mexican president.[94] The invitation and its acceptance indicated both the improved tenor of bilateral relations and Washington's endorsement of the more conservative orientation of Mexico's next administration. As Roosevelt's former secretary of agriculture, Wallace capitalized on his previous position and acted as a goodwill ambassador to Mexico. His visit, along with his humble nature and broken Spanish, had a profound impact on Mexico. Besides attending the inauguration and speaking before the Mexican Congress, Wallace spent a week traveling the countryside, where he visited small villages, agricultural communities, and Cárdenas's home state of Michoacán. During his tour, Wallace also delivered numerous addresses and radio broadcasts that were aired in the United States, Mexico, and other parts of Latin America. At Roosevelt's insistence, he laid a wreath at the tomb of Los Niños Héroes in Mexico City's Chapultepec Park—a monument that honors the boy heroes of the U.S.-Mexican War. Not surprisingly, many Mexicans were greatly moved by the wreath-laying ceremony.[95]

According to Assistant Attorney General Norman Littell, who accompanied the vice president, the Mexicans "hailed Mr. Wallace with cordiality. . . . Not only as the personal friend and representative of the president, and as vice-president elect, but also as a great leader in the agricultural industry on this continent. Mr. Wallace's appointment as ambassador plenipotentiary and extraordinary was an effective move in the interests of solidarity between the two countries."[96] Mexico's new minister of agriculture Marte Gómez appreciated that Wallace understood the need for land redistribution. After his visit, Gómez wrote to the vice president and told him that he was "the first high official of the United States government who has not come to Mexico to make any claims or to hear the complaints of American citizens whose properties have been damaged by any of the measures Mexico had to take in order to transform its economic and political structure, but rather to try to scrutinize the causes of [Mexico's] malaise in order to solve them and help to constitute a new era that will put Mexico on the road to progress and will allow the United States to have an industrious neighbor at the southern border, who can buy from them and sell to them, and who at any moment would be willing to shake hands in a friendly gesture."[97]

Mexico's new president also saw how Wallace's visit would improve economic conditions and bilateral affairs. Ávila Camacho told Wallace that his visit produced "feelings of assurance and stability that were good for Mexican business" and that his "interest in the modest problems of rural life" resulted in "the most cordial comments on the part of the people and had vigorously strengthened the reciprocal confidence between the two countries."[98] Besides conducting a goodwill tour, while in Mexico Wallace discussed the Global Settlement and other pending issues with Cárdenas, Ávila Camacho, Interior Minister Miguel Alemán, and the new Foreign Secretary Ezequiel Padilla. From these meetings, Wallace concluded that Mexico wanted to reach a settlement with the United States because it needed to attract American capital.[99]

A BILATERAL CLAIMS AGREEMENT
OR A U.S. AID PACKAGE?

Many U.S. officials rightly believed that Ávila Camacho viewed his northern neighbor positively and that his government posed less of a threat to U.S. economic interests than did Cárdenas's. Despite the fact that he was a weaker president than Cárdenas, unbeknownst to Washington, Ávila Camacho's administration would continue to employ the same diplomatic tactics used by its predecessor in order to resolve the agrarian dispute in Mexico's favor. In hindsight, this is not too surprising, since he initially kept some members of Cárdenas's cabinet on board. Castillo Nájera remained ambassador to the United States, Suárez continued as finance secretary, former deputy foreign secretary Beteta became deputy secretary of finance, and similarly Eduardo Villaseñor left the Finance Ministry to become the director of the Bank of Mexico. Also, Ignacio García Téllez went from interior secretary to labor secretary, General Heriberto Jara remained minister of the navy, and Antonio Villalobos was appointed president of the official party. Meanwhile, Cardenistas continued to run the Agrarian Department, which was responsible for land redistribution.[100]

Cárdenas himself was appointed defense secretary in 1942. Consequently, not only did he frequently meet with Ávila Camacho, but according to María Paz, the former president had "considerable influence over the terms of defensive collaboration between the two nations" and was frequently a thorn in the side of U.S. military planners.[101] Besides having a role in the new administration, Cárdenas gave Ávila Camacho important advice on the day of his inauguration. In a clear reference to the agrarian and oil conflicts, he told Ávila Camacho that American nationals and the U.S. government must accept Mexican laws and renounce diplomatic protection. Cárdenas further suggested to Ávila Camacho that he work hard to ensure U.S. respect for Mexican sovereignty and that he convey this important nationalistic principle to his successor.[102]

Although Ávila Camacho kept some Cardenistas on his team, this does not mean that he was tightly wedded to them. During the early 1940s, as Ávila Camacho's administration shifted federal policies rightward, many old Callistas also came back, including former presidents Plutarco Elías Calles, Abelardo Rodríguez, and Emilio Portes Gil, while leading leftists, such as the CTM's Vicente Lombardo Toledano, Senator Ernesto Soto Reyes, and cabinet member Francisco Múgica, had their wings clipped. Despite the differences in their domestic programs, accommodation and resistance toward Washington characterized the diplomatic strategy of both the Cárdenas and Ávila Camacho administrations. In fact, the same could be said of the Carranza, Obregón, and Calles presidencies. Hence, it may be safe to conclude that during much of the revolutionary and postrevolutionary eras the policymaking procedures employed by Mexican diplomats saw a good deal of continuity.

With a favorable deal on the table, Ávila Camacho's government deftly played both the poor neighbor and defense cards to strengthen its hand when discussing the final terms of the Global Settlement. As Beteta remarked, "Mexico's cooperation and goodwill should be worth a few million, under the circumstances." The new president agreed with the seasoned deputy secretary.[103] During a year of talks over the exact terms of the agreement, Mexican officials linked the economic benefits of the Global Settlement to Mexico's war effort. In early 1941, Castillo Nájera noted that since his country was prepared to liquidate the agrarian and general claims, honor its foreign debt, and settle the oil problem, the United States should "contribute on its side all the necessary goodwill for establishing international cooperation, capable of improving commercial intercourse between the two republics and of giving to Mexico the opportunity to increase its exports to the extent made necessary, not only by the fact of contracting its [financial] obligations, but also to assume very energetically the responsibilities accruing from the agreements in matters of continental defense."[104]

To prove that this was not empty rhetoric, in April 1941 the Mexican Congress agreed to allow U.S. military planes to use Mexican airfields while en route to Panama. Of even greater importance to the United States was Mexico's decision in July 1941 to prohibit the export of basic and strategic materials to all nonhemispheric countries. The following month Mexico cut economic relations with Germany. Mexico's new commercial policy not only meant that they would no longer trade with the Axis powers, but also that the country's export sector would be tied solely to the Allied war effort and establish monopolistic links to the U.S. economy.[105] As the two countries began to see eye to eye on a number of different issues, it was clear that closer relations would be economically beneficial to Mexico as a result of the windfall that would derive from the war. Hence, it was in Mexico City's interests to be on good terms with Washington—which meant no longer stalling during the agrarian claims negotiations.

Ávila Camacho realized that Mexico should finalize the terms of the Global Settlement as soon as possible. As one observer in Mexico stated in early 1941, "The most valuable time [for Mexico] to make an agreement economically and financially with the States, like settlement of the oil question, land question, and foreign debt was being lost." As the United States got "more mixed up with European affairs, or even as a belligerent into the war," Washington would "not have the time or desire to listen to Mexico's demands."[106] Moreover, the Mexican economy had not yet recovered from its downward spiral.[107] Thus, having secured from Washington the type of settlement they had long sought, Mexican officials no longer employed foot-dragging tactics, and Ávila Camacho's administration made it clear that Mexico would not raise any technical questions when discussing the Global Settlement.[108]

It took another nine months to iron out the details. On November 18, Daniels told Hull that Roosevelt wanted him to sign the agreements—which he did the following day in Washington with Castillo Nájera.[109] Ratifications were exchanged between the two governments on April 3, 1942.[110] The Global Settlement was clearly beneficial to Mexico City. According to Niblo, it was "the most successful settlement in [Mexico's] history of outstanding issues with the United States."[111] Even though Roosevelt's administration provided a great deal of economic aid to Mexico, U.S. officials did not dictate its final terms. Throughout 1941 Mexican officials negotiated hard, causing Bursley to conclude that Washington "had now gone very far in meeting Mexico's requests."[112] It was to the credit of Mexican diplomats that they won such a favorable deal. In addition to resolving the agrarian and general claims, the Global Settlement also stabilized the peso, improved Mexican highways, and produced a new bilateral silver purchase agreement, a reciprocal trade agreement, and a resolution to the oil crisis.[113]

The Global Settlement (known officially as the 1941 Convention between the United States and Mexico) superseded the 1923 General Claims Convention, the 1934 Protocol to the General Claims Convention, and the diplomatic notes exchanged on November 9 and 12, 1938. It provided indemnification for the 257 American landowners who had their property officially expropriated between

August 30, 1927, and October 6, 1940, and that had been ruled upon by Lawson's Agrarian Claims Commission.[114] Under the agreement, Ávila Camacho's administration paid $40 million to liquidate both the agrarian and general claims. Of this amount, $21.5 million was earmarked for the general claims and $18.5 million for the American landowners—even though the market value of their rural holdings was much higher. Mexico paid $3 million when the ratifications were exchanged. The remaining balance on both the general and agrarian claims was paid in annual installments of $2.5 million, beginning in November 1942. Mexico finally liquidated both debts in 1955.[115]

In December 1942, a year after the Global Settlement was signed, the U.S. government established the American Mexican Claims Commission to distribute the monetary compensation that Washington received from Mexico City to the American landowners. This new commission also evaluated ninety-four new claims (known as the Series E Claims) filed by American landowners who either had missed the Agrarian Claims Commission's application deadline of October 6, 1940, or who had lacked the necessary documentation in their initial claims with said commission. Thirty-two of these claims were disallowed, but the sixty-two remaining (which represented an additional 1.5 million acres of expropriated American-owned land) tagged on an extra $3.4 million to Mexico's debt. After combining the work of the two commissions, the Mexican government paid nearly $22 million in compensation to 319 American property owners who lost approximately 6.2 million acres of land between January 1, 1927, and October 6, 1940.[116]

To assist Mexico in making its payments, the Global Settlement stabilized the peso and increased Mexican exports to the United States. After the nationalization of the foreign-owned petroleum industry in March 1938, Mexico witnessed extensive capital flight. Officials on both sides of the border believed that stabilizing Mexico's currency would reverse this trend. Under the Global Settlement, the U.S. Treasury purchased $40 million worth of pesos from the Bank of Mexico. These dollars allowed the Mexican government to repurchase the pesos from the United States at a pegged rate of 4.85 to the dollar, which stabilized the currency. Since Washington did not receive any collateral from Ávila Camacho's administration for this arrangement, one U.S. Treasury official concluded that it was the "most liberal re-purchasing arrangement" the U.S. government had ever given another country.[117]

Both U.S. and Mexican officials believed that improving Mexico's highway system would decrease unemployment in Mexico, stimulate the nation's economy, foster bilateral trade and tourism, and facilitate hemispheric defense. Therefore, the Global Settlement arranged for a $30 million loan from the Export-Import Bank for this end. Of particular emphasis was the completion of the Inter-American Highway from Mexico City to the border of Guatemala, and from Nogales, Arizona, to Guadalajara.[118]

The Global Settlement also included a new silver purchase agreement that would increase and regularize Mexico's silver exports to the United States. Six million ounces of newly mined silver were to be purchased each month directly from the Bank of Mexico by the U.S. Treasury at 35 cents per ounce, totaling $25 million annually. Under this agreement, the United States purchased 17 percent more silver from Mexico than it had during the agreement in place between 1936 and March 1938.[119] Officials on both sides believed that the new silver purchase agreement would expand and stabilize Mexico's silver sales, increase government revenue, and have a positive effect on the overall Mexican economy.[120] They were right.

As for the oil question, Mexico paid $9 million in compensation for the oil properties when they signed the Global Settlement. The agreement then called for the creation of a bilateral commission, modeled on the Agrarian Claims Commission, that would determine the total amount due. By April 1942, the joint commission completed its study, and the two governments agreed that Mexico would pay a total indemnity of $24 million for the nationalized oil properties over a five-year period, an amount that included the initial $9 million installment. For these reasons, diplomats on both sides of the border, and a few scholars since then, considered the oil crisis "officially" over when the Global Settlement was signed in November 1941.[121]

Although it only laid out the general principles of a bilateral trade agreement, the Global Settlement was instrumental in initiating trade talks. Just a few months later, the two nations signed the Bateman-Suárez-Téllez Trade Agreement, which obligated the United States to purchase $100 million worth of Mexican minerals and oil. The commercial agreement also required that the United States assist Mexico with obtaining capital goods for oil and mineral production, as well as manufactured goods and raw materials for industrial development.[122] And in the spring of 1942, the Roosevelt administration offered to assist Mexico in railroad rehabilitation, shipyard construction, and the development of new industries, including oil refineries for high-octane gasoline. During the same month, the White House agreed to purchase additional raw materials from Mexico and advance a $6 million Export-Import Bank loan for the construction of a new steel mill.[123] In July, Deputy Finance Secretary Beteta met with U.S. officials in Washington and convinced them to raise the price of silver from $0.35 to $0.44 per ounce. Then, in December 1942, both countries signed the long-awaited reciprocal trade agreement.[124]

The Global Settlement, which was extremely beneficial to the Mexican economy, came at a good time. Mexico City, in achieving the resolution of the agrarian dispute and the oil crisis, also achieved the stabilization of the peso, development of the country's infrastructure, improvement of access to foreign capital, and an increase in exports to the United States, all of which allowed the Mexican economy to recover fully from the recession that had gripped the country since late 1937. These improvements also hastened the economic boon produced by WWII and helped foster Mexican industrialization. During the war, Mexico channeled raw materials to the United States in return for capital goods and hard currency, stimulating the development of Mexico's textile, chemical, food, and beverage industries. Between 1940 and 1945, the country's industrial sector grew at an annual rate of 10.2 percent, which acted as a springboard for the postwar "Mexican miracle."[125]

Nevertheless, although the Mexican economy grew by 6 percent annually between 1940 and 1978, the benefits of this "miracle" were not equitably distributed among the populace. Worse yet, Mexico continued to be governed by corrupt authoritarian regimes that used force and intimidation against its opponents, especially those who challenged the status quo by calling for a more just economic system and a more democratic political system.

EPILOGUE

Both U.S. and Mexican officials believed the Global Settlement initiated a new and improved era in bilateral relations. In his letter to Roosevelt, Ávila Camacho wrote, "The agreements signed will be of real benefit to the two countries and I am sure that they will mark a point of departure . . . for a fuller understanding between Mexico and the United States." Similarly, Mexican Foreign Minister Ezequiel Padilla proclaimed that "the agreements marked a new milestone in the history of U.S.-Mexican relations."[126] A poll conducted by *Excelsior* found consensus within Mexico City's banking community that the Global Settlement was beneficial to the country's economy. Consequently, Mexico's business sector "warmly congratulated" Ávila Camacho for signing it.[127] The view of the Mexican press was equally favorable. Articles in *Excelsior, El Universal, El Nacional,* and *Novedades* supported the agreement, noting Mexico would benefit economically from both peso stabilization and the revival of the mining industry through the resumption of U.S. silver purchases.[128]

The American press was much more critical. The *New York Journal of Commerce* editorialized that the Global Settlement made "it clearer than ever that the United States would not protect investments in Latin America," a stance that would "discourage such investments." A *New York Times* article complained that "no understanding to halt further expropriations of American agrarian or other properties in Mexico was included." The article derided the agreement, stating that Mexico had "obtained everything it had been insisting upon for the past two months" while the U.S. government had "established the precedent of advancing large sums of money to a foreign government to facilitate that government's making a 'token' payment." "Friendship purchased at a high price," the article concluded, was "scarcely the most secure foundation for international relations."[129] Because Washington provided Mexico with $40 million for currency stabilization and $30 million for highway construction, one American daily charged, U.S. taxpayers would "pay American landowners for their seized land," while Mexican officials could "point with pride to a handsome deal with the U.S."[130] The *New York Herald Tribune* argued that the settlement was unfavorable to the United States: "The United States sets up a stabilization fund of $40,000,000, establishes credits of $30,000,000 not for defense bases but for highways, agrees to negotiate a reciprocal trade agreement, the chief purpose of which would be to relax trade restrictions on American imports of oil from Mexico, and agrees to purchase 6,000,000 ounces of silver monthly from Mexico. Thus, in effect, we shall be making Mexico an outright gift each year of between $15,000,000 and $18,000,000, as against the $2,500,000 she proposes to pay on account of her legitimate debt to us."[131] Even historian David Cronon, whose book offers a sympathetic treatment of Daniels, FDR, and Mexico, concludes, "The agreement showed Washington was now willing to pay a considerable price for a *rapprochement* with Mexico, for it was plain that the United States in effect would be underwriting the Mexican payments."[132]

Roosevelt was not worried about the negative press. After the Global Settlement was signed, FDR stated that he found the accords "eminently satisfactory" and was "glad that they created an immediate and very favorable reaction in Mexico and in many other parts of the New World."[133] Roosevelt, like Ávila Camacho, understood the broader significance of the settlement, especially its role in repairing relations and charting a new and better course for bilateral affairs. In his letter to the Mexican president, FDR wrote that the agreements would "play an important part in the future" by "strengthening friendship and cooperation between Mexico and the United States."[134]

Despite some disagreements over bilateral military relations, starting in April 1941 the two countries signed the first of several defense-related accords. The day after the Japanese bombed Peal Harbor, Mexico broke relations with Japan and quickly granted the United States use of Magdalena and Acapulco bays for military purposes. In January 1942, the two capitals announced the formation of the Joint U.S.-Mexico Defense Commission, which enabled Mexico to receive military aid via the Lend Lease program. That same month, Japanese nationals in Baja California were relocated to Guadalajara and Mexico City because of Washington's fears that the undefended peninsula might become a base for a Japanese attack on the U.S. mainland. Shortly thereafter, three teams of U.S. radar monitors were placed in Baja California to scan the Pacific Ocean for Japanese vessels and aircraft.[135]

After German submarines sunk two Mexican merchant ships in May 1942, killing twelve crew members, Mexico declared a "state of war" against the Axis. In mid-1945 Mexico dispatched the small, American-trained, and mostly symbolic 201st Fighter Squadron to the Philippines. More notably, approximately 250,000 Mexicans and one million Mexican Americans living north of the border were drafted into the U.S. armed forces during the war.[136] Although Mexico did not follow some other Latin American republics in deporting German nationals within its borders to detention centers in the United States, Ávila Camacho's administration did freeze the assets and seize hundreds of properties belonging to Axis nationals and corporations.[137]

More important than its military involvement was Mexico's economic contribution to the Allied war effort. Due to the labor shortages in the United States, in the summer of 1942 Washington and Mexico City initiated the Bracero Program, which brought hundreds of thousands of Mexicans to the United States to work on farms, railroads, and in other industries. Even more Mexican workers entered on their own volition, outside the auspices of the program, and were employed in similar capacities. As Mexican laborers journeyed north, in 1943 U.S. scientists working for the Rockefeller Foundation's Mexican Agricultural Program traveled south to train Mexican agronomists in modern methods of agriculture and plant breeding. Vice President Wallace made good on his earlier trip to Mexico to foster these and other bilateral agricultural projects. And in order to increase Mexican agricultural production to meet wartime

FIGURE 26. April 1943 presidential meeting in Monterrey, Nuevo León. Left to right: Undersecretary of State Welles, Mexican Ambassador Castillo Nájera, Mrs. Ávila Camacho, President Roosevelt, unidentified person, President Ávila Camacho, Mrs. Roosevelt, Foreign Minister Padilla. AGN, ARCHIVO FOTOGRÁFICO, FONDO AVILA CAMACHO, 681/13.

needs in the United States, Washington allotted $4.6 million in farm machinery to help modernize Mexico's rural sector. Likewise, Roosevelt's administration gave the go-ahead for the Export-Import Bank, the Inter-American Development Bank, and private international lenders to help finance the construction of mills, dams, and irrigation works on nationalized Mexican farms, including some ejidos that Cárdenas's government had established on expropriated American-owned estates. In these cases, U.S. "intervention" in the Mexican countryside was for positive ends and helped to spark the country's subsequent Green Revolution.[138]

To mark the improvement in bilateral affairs, on April 20, 1943, Roosevelt traveled to the city of Monterrey, in the northern state of Nuevo León, and met with Ávila Camacho—the first meeting of the two countries' chief executives in thirty-four years. The two leaders got along well, exchanging "strong hugs" and "satisfying smiles." After reviewing a military parade, they drove to the state capital in Monterrey. The route was draped with U.S. and Mexican flags, and bystanders threw confetti and flowers at their convertible motorcade, while shouting "vivas to Mexico, vivas to the United States, vivas to Roosevelt and Ávila Camacho." During his address at a banquet that night, Roosevelt assured Mexico, "The day of exploitation of the resources and the people of one country for the benefit of any group in another country is definitely over."[139] Despite the fact that relations had dramatically improved by 1943, and the agrarian dispute and the oil crisis were over, the White House recognized that they were defining moments for Mexico and its relations with the United States. Consequently, they warranted mentioning. Although Roosevelt's reference to both conflicts was rather starry eyed, he hoped to convince the Mexicans that times had changed and that going forward the United States would pursue a more evenhanded relationship with its southern neighbor.

Roosevelt had much to be proud of, due to the fact that bilateral affairs were now more amicable than they were at most points in the preceding half-century. The peaceful resolution of the agrarian dispute and the oil crisis, Washington's economic aid package to Mexico, and Ávila Camacho's willingness to support the United States in the war signified a commonality of interests that ushered in a new era in U.S.-Mexican relations. None of these developments would have been possible had Roosevelt's administration responded to the expropriation of American-owned land with force or crippling economic and political sanctions designed to unseat Cárdenas. Had Washington applied such heavy-handed policies against Cárdenas's government to thwart Mexican economic nationalism, it is very unlikely that he or his successor would have provided so much assistance to the United States in WWII. As a result, the improvements seen in U.S.-Mexican relations during the last seven decades might not have occurred, and instead bilateral affairs might still be characterized by mutual animosity and distrust.

Conclusion

MOVING AWAY FROM BALKANIZED HISTORY

The presentation of claims by Mexico against the United States and by America against Mexico has bedeviled both countries ever since Poinsett was ambassador to Mexico.

FORMER U.S. AMBASSADOR JOSEPHUS DANIELS, APRIL 29, 1946

The resolution of the agrarian dispute marked a turning point in U.S.-Mexican relations. Ever since the conflict ended in November 1941, there has been little discord between the two nations over the acquisition of land in Mexico by Americans and its expropriation by the Mexican government. This can be attributed to the limitations placed on foreign property ownership by Mexican federal law, as well as the conservatism of most administrations after Cárdenas. With regard to the latter and more notable trend, since 1941 Mexican officials have allowed most remaining landowners to keep their holdings and have generally limited the expropriation of foreign-owned property, as they simultaneously have welcomed investments by transnational corporations south of the border. Consequently, unlike the postrevolutionary era, during the past seven decades the issues of expropriation and compensation have not destabilized bilateral affairs.

Even more significant to the history of U.S.-Mexican relations is the fact that belligerent U.S. policies toward Mexico, such as military intervention and nonrecognition, have been completely curtailed since the 1930s. This has not only helped to level the bilateral playing field to some degree but it has also improved the tenor of U.S.-Mexican affairs, making the relationship between the two countries less antagonistic, as well as more stable and mature. Many of these improvements, especially Washington's evenhanded approach toward its southern neighbor during times of bilateral conflict, find their roots in the Roosevelt administration's handling of the agrarian dispute that began in 1935.

This is not to say that all has been well in U.S.-Mexican relations during the last seventy years. Despite Mexico's economic and demographic growth, the preponderance of wealth and power held by the United States vis-à-vis Mexico still imposes a certain asymmetry on bilateral affairs. And there have been serious disagreements between Washington and Mexico City over a wide range of bilateral issues, including immigration, drug trafficking, economic aid, the Chamizal, border control, water, and the environment. Likewise, Mexico City was often critical of hard-line U.S. policies toward Guatemala, Cuba, Chile, Nicaragua, and El Salvador during the Cold War and distanced itself from Washington by championing nonintervention and self-determination. In addition, political leaders, pundits, and the general public on both sides of the Rio Grande have often pointed an accusatory finger across the border to deflect criticism at home or rally popular support. Nevertheless, despite the asymmetry, the disagreements over bilateral and hemispheric policies, and the negative rhetoric, the long-term impact of the 1941 Global Settlement has been positive, and U.S.-Mexican relations since then have been better than during most preceding historical periods.

By resolving the agrarian dispute, the Global Settlement ended one of the principal bilateral crises of the postrevolutionary era. This conflict was characterized by a number of issues that had repeatedly disrupted relations since the early nineteenth century: the acquisition of Mexican land and natural resources by U.S. nationals and corporations, Washington's protection of U.S. economic interests in Mexico, and the monetary claims filed by Americans against the Mexican government. The agrarian dispute was not the first time that compensation claims were at the center of bilateral affairs. In the mid-1830s, for example, to get Mexico to "compromise on the question of Texas," Washington instructed U.S. Minister Powhatan Ellis "to press the claims of U.S. nationals," knowing full well that Mexico City could not afford to pay the American claimants. A decade later, President James Polk was prepared to justify a U.S. invasion of Mexico because of its failure to pay said claims. In 1876, President Rutherford Hayes agreed to recognize the new Porfirio Díaz government only if it paid more than $4 million to settle the U.S. claims that were filed between 1848 and 1868—a demand to which Díaz agreed. And in 1913, President William Howard Taft made the same threat to Francisco Madero's administration with respect to the post-1868 general claims.[1]

In the late 1930s and early 1940s, it was Mexico City and not Washington who used monetary claims as a diplomatic tool to achieve broader international objectives. Having disavowed military intervention, nonrecognition, trade embargos, or other aggressive tactics to buttress its Mexican policy, Roosevelt's administration could not leverage the agrarian claims to Washington's advantage. Indeed, they became a liability for U.S. diplomats. If the White House wanted compensation for American landowners, stated both the Cárdenas and Ávila Camacho administrations, it first had to provide Mexico City with financial incentives that would offset the costs of indemnification. Some of the plums that Mexico received in exchange for paying the agrarian claims included the resumption of silver purchases, international loans, a peso stabilization program, and a bilateral trade agreement. Hence, to see only U.S. officials as relevant to the Global Settlement, or bilateral affairs more generally, would be a narrow and skewed perspective.

Although Roosevelt never questioned Mexico's right to expropriate private property, and even though his administration had its own reasons for yielding to Mexico during the agrarian dispute, it would be wrong to conclude that the expropriation of American-owned land was without controversy. The main conflict that arose from it concerned proper indemnification for the American landowners. Had the Cárdenas administration met Washington's demands between 1935 and 1940, the conflict over land would never have ended in Mexico's favor. In all likelihood, the two countries would have agreed to a lump-sum agrarian settlement that, like the special claims agreement of 1934, lacked any financial or commercial assistance from Washington to Mexico City. Despite the asymmetrical nature of bilateral affairs, Mexican officials did not succumb to U.S. hegemony.

As I have tried to show here, subalternity can extend beyond the disenfranchised lower classes; a nation's elite can also be understood as subalterns when seeking to advance their interests against more-powerful international actors. Throughout the agrarian dispute, Mexican officials deftly employed the diplomatic weapons of the weak to resolve the compensation question and obtain an agreement with Washington that benefited their country economically, and themselves politically. Years of foot-dragging, obfuscation, noncompliance, and other inventive diplomatic tactics forced Washington to blink first and enabled Mexico City to secure the lucrative Global Settlement. Revealing the manner in which this bilateral conflict was resolved demonstrates that peripheral nations are not at the mercy of hegemonic states, but instead can successfully assert their own national interests. It also shows that great powers are limited in their ability to shape the internal and foreign affairs of weaker countries. This understanding debunks the misperception that in global affairs developing countries are helpless, U.S. influence is all pervasive, and power is exerted in only one direction—from Washington outward.

Mexican diplomacy during the agrarian dispute was shaped by Cárdenas's administration—with Ávila Camacho's government taking the handoff in 1941 —and influenced primarily by structural domestic forces: in particular, the weakness of the Mexican economy and the Cárdenas presidency. During the first half of the conflict, Cárdenas was impelled to take a firm stand because of his political vulnerability at home. From the Calles-Cárdenas imbroglio in 1935 until Saturnino Cedillo's rebellion in 1938, Cárdenas was never in full control of the country. Even in 1939 and 1940, his political strength remained tenuous to some extent because he had ceded some power back to regional officials follow-ing the oil nationalization. For Cárdenas to have backed down to Washington during the agrarian dispute would have exposed an additional weakness to his opponents and invited additional attacks—a situation that would have destabi-lized his government and further reduced his authority. Moreover, had Cár-denas scaled back his land reform program to meet U.S. demands, workers and peasants may have looked for a more radical leader to follow, which would have shrunk his base of support. On the contrary, since anti-Americanism has long been a part of Mexican political culture, Cárdenas gained strength regionally when his government expropriated American-owned land. He similarly in-creased his popularity nationwide when he publicly challenged the State De-partment over indemnifying American landowners while at the same time seizing new American-owned estates.

Like the political stakes, the economic implications were great for Cárdenas and Mexico. In 1936 and 1937, Cárdenas did not pay American property owners because he probably assumed that the government's limited revenue could be better spent on public works projects and land reform programs that reduced unemployment and broadened his political base. And by 1938, the Mexican economy was too weak to dole out tens of millions of dollars in reparations to the United States. After March 1938, Mexican officials also had to proceed carefully since an agrarian resolution would likely set an important precedent for an equally expensive oil settlement. It is fair to conclude that Cárdenas's administration did not settle the agrarian claims in 1939—a deadline stipulated by the November 1938 diplomatic notes—because doing so would have in-creased Mexico's foreign debt without expanding its economic capacity.

To outmaneuver U.S. officials and gain the leverage needed to win the compensation question, Mexican diplomats both accommodated and resisted Washington. To make their policies seem less threatening to FDR's administration, the Cardenistas often compared the 1934–1940 Six-Year Plan to the New Deal and note how the 1934 Special Claims Commission provided a model for resolving the agrarian claims. In addition, they accommodated U.S. policymakers by telling them what they wanted to hear regarding land reform, bilateral trade, and the fight against international fascism. For example, Mexican officials paid lip service to their U.S. counterparts by repeatedly assuring them that they would halt the expropriation of American-owned estates and compensate all U.S. property owners. Since it appeared that Mexican policymakers agreed with Washington regarding the issue of expropriation and compensation, it was difficult for the accommodators within FDR's government, especially Ambassador Daniels, to justify a hard-line policy. Meanwhile, Mexican policymakers were sincere when they stated that they too wanted to increase cross-border commerce and would assist the United States militarily should war erupt. Since positive pronouncements like those noted above made Mexico appear as a U.S. ally, they helped to increase its leverage during the agrarian dispute.

Even as Mexican officials placated Washington, they continued to resist their northern neighbor by continuing to seize American holdings without providing a workable reparations plan. In 1939 and 1940, for instance, Mexican policymakers sidetracked the agrarian claims negotiations with a barrage of technical questions that stalled progress toward a final resolution. Another one of their tactics was to play the "poor neighbor" card. In hard economic times, past Mexican presidents, including Díaz, Obregón, and Calles, had yielded to U.S. demands because of their need for American capital. Cárdenas did not, and instead turned a weakness into a strength. Rather than see his country's economic problems as a liability (as the White House did), Cárdenas used them to gain additional leverage. Throughout the agrarian dispute, Mexican officials repeatedly stated that they could not afford to compensate American landowners unless Washington helped Mexico City generate the money that was needed for indemnification—which they insisted could occur if the United States altered its commercial policies to increase Mexican imports. In short, between 1938 and 1941, Mexican policymakers were savvy enough to avoid a costly confrontation with Washington by playing the role of a good neighbor, while effectively stalling and exploiting the policymaking procedures of Roosevelt's administration, as well as the divisions within the U.S. diplomatic corps.

Mexican diplomacy in the late 1930s and early 1940s appears to have influenced the foreign policies of one of its neighbors. According to Kyle Longley's study of U.S.–Costa Rican relations in the 1940s and 1950s, when President José Figueres nationalized foreign-owned properties, he followed policies that were first established by Cárdenas. While this is true, the similarities did not end there. When comparing Cardenista and Figuerista diplomacy toward the United States, we find that many of the diplomatic strategies used by the Costa Ricans were first employed by Mexican policymakers in the 1930s. For instance, just as the Cardenistas played up the similar agendas of the New Deal and the Plan Sexenal, the Figueristas did the same when they compared the goals of Costa Rica's National Liberation Party with those of U.S. liberal democrats. And in the same way that the Cardenistas pointed out to U.S. officials their mutual understanding of the problems caused by latifundismo, the benefits of bilateral trade, and the threat of fascism, the Figueristas also claimed that they shared with U.S. liberal democrats a common vision for the Western Hemisphere and the world. Similar domestic and international convictions made the Mexicans, and later the Costa Ricans, appear less threatening and more as friends than enemies. In addition, the Figueristas, like the Cardenistas, had a good understanding of the U.S. political establishment that facilitated policymaking, since they each knew "which buttons to push." Thus, just as the Mexicans used Ambassador Daniels to counter their conservative opponents in the State Department, so too did the Costa Ricans employ William Bennett, Nathaniel Davis, and Robert Woodward against Figueres's opponents in Washington. Likewise, just as the Cardenistas had employed Columbia University's Frank Tannenbaum and the CIO's John Lewis to make their case to Roosevelt and Daniels, the Figueristas used influential nonstate actors to "lobby U.S. diplomats at important junctures."[2]

This study upholds Longley's assertion that most Latin American countries "do not employ radical or violent responses to Washington" but instead engage in "more routine and orderly forms of peripheral resistance and accommodation."[3] However, the success of Mexican and Costa Rican diplomats vis-à-vis their U.S. counterparts raises a number of important questions about the foreign policies of their Latin American neighbors. Are the diplomatic weapons of the weak enough to ensure a Latin American victory over Washington? More specifically, between the 1950s and 1980s, why did administrations in Guatemala, Cuba, the Dominican Republic, Chile, and Nicaragua fail in their stand against hard-line U.S. policies and wind up overthrown, forced from power, or internationally isolated? What role did the U.S. economy and global politics play in these bilateral conflicts—many of which also involved the expropriation of American-owned property? Did it matter who occupied the White House? While these substantive questions require lengthy analysis and are beyond the scope of this study, a few comparisons to the agrarian dispute not only will further clarify how Mexico avoided the fate of these countries but also will put the U.S.-Mexican conflict into a broader historical framework and test Longley's general observations regarding Latin American diplomacy.

Although Mexico's foreign policy played a central part in shaping the outcome of the agrarian dispute, the economic, political, and cultural orientation of Roosevelt's administration, along with U.S. policymaking procedures were important in providing Mexican officials with room to maneuver. FDR's arrival in Washington meant that the White House, State Department, and U.S. embassy included policymakers who advocated greater state intervention in both the U.S. and Mexican economies. Likewise, a mutual interest in social justice produced common ideological convictions between the Roosevelt and Cárdenas administrations on how best to relieve the plight of the working classes within their respective countries. Not only did Roosevelt's political rhetoric of defending the "common man" work to Mexico's advantage, but FDR, Daniels, and Assistant Secretary of State Laurence Duggan even endorsed Cárdenas's agrarian reform program. Additionally, because some U.S. officials such as Daniels held romantic and simplistic views of Mexico, at times it was difficult for them to see the hardball nature of Mexican diplomacy. Meanwhile, FDR's management style—especially his bypassing the State Department and giving Daniels direct access to the Oval Office—meant that Mexico's strongest U.S. ally had the president's ear. Similarly, personal and departmental rivalries in Washington (e.g., Hull versus Welles), as well as divisions within the U.S. diplomatic corps regarding policy toward Mexico (e.g., the accommodators versus the hard-liners), worked against a united U.S. front and allowed Mexican diplomats to divide and conquer: first the U.S. Embassy, then the White House, and lastly the State Department. The Cardenistas cleared the State Department hurdles when Secretary of State Hull agreed to Cárdenas's suggestion that both countries stop the inflammatory exchange of public notes in late 1938 and instead use quiet diplomacy to reach an interim agrarian resolution. The second such Mexican victory came in late 1940, when Undersecretary of State Welles accepted Ambassador Castillo Nájera's proposal to make the final agrarian claims settlement part of a broader agreement that addressed a number of economic issues that were important to Mexico City.

Presidents Dwight Eisenhower, Lyndon Johnson, Richard Nixon, Ronald Reagan, and George H. W. Bush were all less accepting of Latin American economic nationalism than was Roosevelt, so it was harder for reformist and revolutionary governments in Guatemala, Cuba, the Dominican Republic, Chile, and Nicaragua to make their statist economic policies seem tolerable to Washington. In fact, when Reagan and Bush were in office, big government was on the wane and free-market principles were popular in U.S. policymaking circles. Thus, with the possible exception of LBJ's Great Society, common ideological principles and economic agendas that previously linked Cardenista and Rooseveltian domestic reforms were rare during the Cold War between Washington and Latin America's leftist reformers. Consequently, during the Cold War few of Latin America's leftist leaders picked up on the economic rhetoric of the U.S. administrations, as the Cardenistas did with Roosevelt's "forgotten man."

In addition to ideological differences, many of the above-mentioned U.S. administrations took a hard line against Latin American economic nationalism for political reasons. During the Cold War, U.S. presidents faced serious political fallout from being labeled "soft on communism." Electoral politics since Eisenhower, for instance, has long driven Washington's aggressive policies toward Fidel Castro's Cuba. So while domestic politics during the Great Depression made FDR hesitant to defend big business overseas, Cold War domestic politics necessitated it because communism and the expropriation of private property were seen as the antithesis of American capitalism. And, despite the fact that elitism, paternalism, and ethnocentrism continued to characterize the U.S. diplomatic establishment after World War II, for leading U.S. officials (e.g., FDR and Daniels), social commentators, and even the general public, Latin American culture was no longer en vogue as it had been during the Good Neighbor era. Consequently, the lack of romanticism on the part of U.S. Cold War policymakers toward the region made it unlikely that they would rationalize the economic nationalism of their southern neighbors.

Besides the character of the Oval Office, larger global forces, such as the Great Depression, also mitigated U.S. policy during the agrarian dispute. Many U.S. officials rightly believed that Cárdenas's agrarian reform program helped the U.S. economy because it increased U.S. exports to Mexico, which aided American industry and reduced unemployment. The Cardenistas' attempt to modernize agricultural production and increase output led Mexico City to import extensive amounts of farm machinery, irrigation and road construction equipment, high-yield seeds, pesticides, and fertilizers from U.S. manufacturers. Also, officials on both sides of the border thought that land redistribution increased the acquisitive capacity of Mexico's rural majority and would lead to a greater demand for American products. In addition, U.S. officials refused to back Cárdenas's opponents—most of whom either represented the far right or far left—out of fear of instigating a Spanish-like civil war below the border that could reduce bilateral trade and spark the migration of refugees to the United States. The weak U.S. economy could ill afford such a scenario. Hence, economic self-interest led many in Washington away from criticizing Cárdenas's overall agrarian reform program.

Roosevelt's administration also accommodated Mexico City for political reasons that were tied to the Depression. Since FDR sought to reduce both job competition among low skilled workers and government assistance to the unemployed, the White House looked favorably on land redistribution in Mexico as a way to keep poor Mexicans at home and reduce the likelihood that they would cross the border for work. Washington similarly championed Cárdenas's repatriation of Mexican agricultural workers from the United States, even though land redistribution was used to induce them to return home. Because most of Roosevelt's New Deal coalition wanted to limit the number of Mexicans in the country, and since land redistribution did just that, he was politically wise to endorse it. Also, the White House saw little political gain in defending the large landowners in Mexico who, like their domestic big business counterparts, were frowned upon by FDR's working-class political base.

During the Cold War, especially in the 1950s, 1960s, and 1980s, the U.S. economy and the nation's political leaders were not as vulnerable as they were in the 1930s. And Washington was not under any great pressure to expand trade with Latin America or expel immigrant labor, as it was during the Depression. Furthermore, Guatemala, Cuba, the Dominican Republic, Chile, and Nicaragua did not import a significant amount of U.S. goods in the post-WWII era. Were any of these countries to fall out of the U.S. commercial orbit (as Cuba did through the U.S. trade embargo), the impact on the American economy would have been negligible. The same could not be said for Mexico. Hence, unlike Depression-era officials, Cold War policymakers in the United States had few economic reasons to seek accommodation with their Latin American adversaries.

The Second World War, like the Depression, worked to Mexico's advantage during the agrarian dispute. wwii and the Cold War similarly influenced Washington's Latin American policy in that U.S. officials sought out hemispheric allies during both conflicts, which increased Latin American leverage. After France fell to Germany in June 1940, for instance, leftist Mexican policymakers, who were also anti-fascist, began to play the defense card to make the final agrarian settlement more lucrative. During the Cold War, it was centrist and rightist governments within the hemisphere that were able to extract concessions from Washington, while leftist governments could not. The nature of the Cold War limited which types of governments could curry favor with the United States. In other words, since wwii was a global war against fascism, it was possible for the United States to align with leftist and Communist governments against their common enemy. However, because the Cold War was fought to contain communism, it was difficult for the United States to align with leftist governments that were perceived, often from their domestic economic policies, to be in the enemy's camp. Consequently, while Mexico and even the Soviet Union were U.S. allies who gained material assistance during wwii, in the Cold War, Washington saw Guatemala, Cuba, the Dominican Republic, Chile, and Nicaragua as adversaries whose governments had to be deposed.

Longley is correct in that weak and middle-power diplomatic tactics based on accommodation and resistance are commonplace among nonindustrialized countries.[4] This tends to be the case because they lack the military, economic, and political tools that are at the disposal of hegemonic states. However, as the brief analysis above indicates, foreign policymaking alone will not enable Latin American officials to triumph over their U.S. counterparts. Besides the art of diplomacy, a variety of international factors and domestic issues that are germane to both countries determine U.S.–Latin American relations. In short, the character of the White House, its policymaking procedures, the state of the U.S. economy, U.S. domestic politics, and global political and military circumstances, along with a host of other issues not addressed here, help to determine whether the diplomatic weapons of the weak will enable Latin American leaders to reach their foreign policy goals when confronting the Colossus of the North. This notion—that international relations are a complex process that takes multiple forces working in tandem to produce a Latin American diplomatic victory —should clarify why certain bilateral conflicts within the hemisphere evolved as they did between the 1930s and the 1990s. It also may give scholars fresh ideas for reinterpreting the past and prove helpful for understanding the future, especially as the United States wages a global war against terrorism and is again looking for regional allies, while at the same time facing a rising tide of leftist economic nationalism within the hemisphere.

THE DOMESTIC SIDE OF THE AGRARIAN DISPUTE

Just as one must examine both U.S. and Mexican diplomacy, as well as the domestic forces that shaped each nation's foreign policy, it is equally important to elucidate the origins of the agrarian dispute that prompted the clash in the first place. While many recent works rightly illustrate the sophistication of Latin America's diplomatic corps, such a focus on the political and economic elite provides little insight into how subaltern actors influence Latin American foreign affairs.[5] To gain a fuller and more balanced understanding of the bilateral conflict over land, I have extended this analysis to include the important roles played by Mexican rural workers, indigenous groups, labor leaders, schoolteachers, regional politicians, federal officials, and diplomats, among others, in sparking and sustaining the crisis. In short, peasant agency (both mestizo and indigenous) contributed to the agrarian dispute, along with the larger social, economic, cultural, and political forces that drove Mexican state building. For example, it is safe to assume that had the agraristas not invaded CRLC's holdings in January 1937, the land tenure system in the Mexicali Valley would have been based on colonization and private property rather than government-financed ejidos. Likewise, had the invasion taken place under a president more conservative than Cárdenas, CRLC's property would likely not have been redistributed.

While some landless peasants in Mexico were inspired by anti-Americanism, including those in Baja California's Mexicali Valley, many coveted American-owned agricultural property because it was generally higher in quality than the nearby public lands and Mexican-owned estates. In fact, American properties in the Mexicali and Yaqui Valleys were among the best-developed agricultural holdings in the country. Whether they sought foreign- or Mexican-owned lands, agraristas petitioned for, squatted upon, or seized private property as a means to improve their quality of life. The physical plight of fieldworkers in Sonora and Baja California, as exemplified by their unemployment, underemployment, low wages, long hours, high rents, and abhorrent working and living conditions, led them to mobilize and demand ejidos rather than the higher wages and better working conditions that most urban and some rural labor unions called for. As with the movements that Ann Craig studied in

Jalisco's Lagos de Moreno, the Mexicali and Yaqui Valley agrarian movements were comprised of "workers turned agraristas."[6]

Although politics mattered some, it appears that most agraristas in Baja California and Sonora were not driven primarily by a burning political philosophy or party allegiances. Rather, bread-and-butter issues precipitated their movement. Most believed that landownership would provide them with disposable income to purchase the modern material items that would facilitate their work in the fields and make life at home easier and more comfortable. Moreover, because many rural workers in northwestern Mexico were migratory laborers, landownership would enable them to stop traveling in search of employment and enroll their children full time in school. Sociocultural issues also instigated agrarista mobilization, alongside these material needs. These included moral outrage that stemmed from years of rejected ejidal petitions by both state and federal governments and, in the case of the Yaqui Indians, the desire to see their culturally rich ancestral homelands returned. For the Yaqui, land restitution was the first critical step toward regaining their cultural and political autonomy. In both the Mexicali and Yaqui Valleys, landless agricultural workers invited the state in to act as a powerful ally that would promote their particular class or ethnic interests. As seen throughout much of the country, Cárdenas's government responded to such calls since it, like the peasantry, sought to improve conditions in the countryside and empower both mestizos and indigenous groups through agrarian reform.

Cárdenas also used agrarian reform to advance a nationalistic state-building project. By expropriating American-owned land, Mexico's government became empowered over foreign economic interests situated in the rural sector. For instance, dividing 412,000 acres of CRLC's property among landless field workers answered the revolutionary call to give land to those who worked it and the nationalistic impulse to allow Mexicans to enjoy the fruits of their country's natural resources. Only 122,300 acres of CRLC's 850,000 acre estate were being farmed before expropriation, and the Cardenistas believed that expanding the amount of land under cultivation through collective ejidos would reduce unemployment, increase cotton yields, stimulate regional economic growth, and foster the development of the nation's textile industry. In addition, the more land that the Mexican government put under plow in the Mexicali Valley, the more water it could claim from the Colorado River and demand from Washington when the two countries negotiated a new water treaty. Land redistribution, therefore, advanced the nation-building goal—as envisioned by the Plan

Pro-Baja California—of pulling the territory out of the U.S. economic orbit and tying it more closely to Mexico's.

Cultural nationalism and social engineering also shaped Cárdenas's rural policies in northern Baja California Norte. Taking so much land away from the Americans and placing it under the control of Mexican farmers and the central government helped to stem the region's Americanization. Likewise, building railroad lines and roads that promoted internal migration to the peninsula fostered its Mexicanization. In light of the large percentage of foreign immigrants living in Baja California, particularly Chinese, local labor leaders and the country's political and intellectual elite justified their Mexicanizing agenda in racialist terms that celebrated the mestizaje myth and denigrated non-Mexican races, especially Asians. Along with Mexicanizing and homogenizing the peninsula, the federal government used its increased presence in the territory to foster the education and social welfare of Mexican residents through the construction of schools and sanitation works. Mexico City also cracked down locally on social vices such as alcoholism and gambling by closing bars and casinos—many of which were operated by Chinese immigrants and frequented by Americans. Together, these paternalistic reforms were designed to lift up Mexican workers by making them healthier, smarter, more modern, and more efficient.

Cárdenas's agrarian policy in Baja California was also based on political expediency. Following the public outcry by the largest peasant and labor organizations in the country on behalf of Mexicali's agraristas after they invaded CRLC's holdings, Cárdenas reversed his initial opposition to the land invasion, then canceled the colonization contract that his government had recently signed with CRLC and redistributed the company's property. Thus, local subaltern actors forced federal officials to recast their economic development program for the Mexicali Valley from colonization and individually owned private property, to a state-run project predicated on expropriation and communal agricultural production. Events in Baja California show how the politics from below radicalized the policies that were implemented from above; they also illustrate that landless campesinos and Cárdenas's government were both leading agents of domestic socioeconomic reform, as well as instigators of the international agrarian dispute.

To an even greater degree than it was in the Mexicali Valley, Cárdenas's decision to redistribute land in the Yaqui Valley was based on domestic politics. Following his split with Calles in mid-1935, Cárdenas aligned with Sonora's conservative Obregonistas to purge the state's political system of the ruling Callistas and thereby thwart any chance that the latter group would rebel against his government. However, because Cárdenas had a more radical agenda for Sonora than did the new ruling Obregonista faction, and since he never had their full political support, the president sought to undermine them. To strengthen his hand throughout the state and pave the way for the election of a Cardenista governor, the president used the CTM and federal teachers to align himself with the Yaqui Valley's well-developed rural labor movement. Then, in October 1937, Cárdenas redistributed millions of acres of land throughout Sonora to broaden his base of support among rural workers and weaken the state's conservative Obregonista faction, led by Governor Román Yocupicio. The governor's loyalty to Mexico City was questionable; he strongly opposed the president's reform program, including land redistribution, and was closely allied with General Saturnino Cedillo—the caudillo from San Luis Potosí who led an armed uprising against the federal government in 1938. Included in the reparto was the restitution of more than one million acres of land to the Yaqui Indians. The Yaqui restitution promoted the administration's new nationwide indigenous policy of local Indian empowerment; it also gained the Yaquis' allegiance should Sonora's conservatives have taken up arms against Cárdenas's government. In short, the president used land reform in Sonora as a political weapon. Caught in the middle of this state and federal conflict were dozens of American and Mexican landowners who lost most of their medium-size farms in the Yaqui River Valley.

Like the agraristas around them, neither the large nor small American property owners in the Mexicali and Yaqui Valleys were passive participants in the struggle over landownership. Rather, to safeguard their holdings from expropriation they sought help from U.S. officials who were located locally, in Mexico City, and in Washington. American landowners even looked to more conservative Mexican politicians for assistance, including former president Abelardo Rodríguez. Also, whether they were individual growers or absentee owners of large colonization companies, the Americans repeatedly blurred their identity by describing themselves to Mexican officials as "locals," "insiders," and "friends" who had invested significant amounts of time and money into their holdings and therefore had the region's best interests at heart. They likewise described the migratory agraristas as "outsiders" and even "foreigners" who did not understand local conditions. By conflating such terms and engaging in identity politics, the American landowners inverted the usual roles played in the foreign-local encounter.[7]

American property owners in the Mexicali and Yaqui Valleys tried in vain to safeguard their holdings, both before and after the official expropriation decrees. In Sonora, the American farmers organized collectively before the reparto and presented Cárdenas with various alternatives to the redistribution of their small estates. Meanwhile, CRLC officials believed that their holdings were secure because they had recently signed a twenty-year colonization agreement with Cárdenas's government. After their property was expropriated, the company's leading stockholders met with U.S. and Mexican officials to get their lands returned. Also, CRLC's representatives in Mexicali assisted a lengthy sit-down strike against the territory's government by the small growers, colonists, and renters. Although Mexicali's counter-agrarian movement proved successful—federal officials returning the properties of Mexican colonists and smallholders—CRLC's stockholders, like the American farmers in Sonora, still lost their lands. This, along with hundreds of additional expropriations of American-owned rural property, produced the bilateral agrarian dispute between the United States and Mexico.

THE INCONSISTENCY AND COMPLEX WHOLENESS OF HISTORY

Although he was the most important figure in the agrarian dispute, Cárdenas was not alone when he challenged the United States; instead, a multiform engagement of elite and subordinate actors confronted American economic interests in rural Mexico and helped to recast U.S.-Mexican relations. These were not nameless masses that acted in a consistent or unified manner; rather, on both sides of the border groups of people and individual actors alike were divided and inconsistent in their positions. As Timothy Henderson points out, during the postrevolutionary era, political solidarity among rural people was "often in short supply."[8] Throughout the 1920s and 1930s, the agraristas in both the Yaqui and Mexicali Valleys, including Sonora's Pascual Ayón, changed political parties and labor unions whenever it suited their needs. Likewise, the Yaqui Indians were considered a "political wild card" because they were willing to join any faction that advocated the return of their ancestral homelands. In addition, many rural workers who initially championed collective agricultural production later wanted their own individual plot of land. Also, many ejidatarios in Baja California abandoned their ejidos and headed to the United States when the U.S. wartime economy offered greater economic opportunities. At the national level, after taking a bold stand against the United States, Presidents Obregón and Calles both yielded to Washington over their constitution's retroactivity. Cárdenas, meanwhile, abruptly canceled his colonization agreement with CRLC and expropriated the company's property; he also slowed land redistribution during his last few years in office and chose a moderate conservative to succeed him as president. Similarly, nationalistic Cardenistas, including Beteta and the CTM's Lombardo Toledano, became increasingly conservative and friendly toward the United States in the early 1940s.

Contradictions existed north of the border as well. Roosevelt's Mexican policy flip-flopped from accommodation, to a firmer line, and back to accommodation. Likewise, Hull and Welles each abandoned their narrow position on expropriation and compensation and agreed to Mexico's demand for a broad economic package to ensure landowner indemnification. And, while Daniels expressed no reservations about the expropriation of American-owned rural property, he thought Cárdenas's nationalization of the foreign-owned oil industry was a mistake. Demonstrating the incongruity of key actors within each country undermines the "formulaic propositions suggested by dependency, world-system, and globalization theories."[9] It also reveals the all-too-human tendency of being practical and changing one's mind as the circumstances warrant. When scholars lump historical figures together into a constant homogenous whole, rather than elucidate both their consistencies and inconsistencies, our understanding of the past becomes skewed.

Besides noting the fluidity of both popular and elite actors, I have tried to show here that the interplay between domestic and foreign affairs is not only constant but also multistranded and multidirectional. At times the relationship between domestic and foreign affairs is obvious, and on other occasions it may not be. An example of the former occurred whenever agraristas demanded and received American-owned property—thereby precipitating and sustaining the bilateral agrarian dispute. A less noticeable example of how foreign affairs shaped domestic policy occurred when Cárdenas spent a year considering U.S. alternatives to the Yaqui Valley redistribution—which delayed Sonora's reparto until late 1937 and probably cost the Cardenista candidate the state's 1936 gubernatorial election.

Recently, scholars have begun to pay greater attention to the link between domestic and foreign policy. While some works that examine this relationship —especially those that focus on U.S.–Latin American cultural relations—ably decenter the foreign-local encounter, many do not then recenter their analysis and explain how, for instance, local "contact zones" influenced the foreign policies of their nation's capital.[10] In this book I have attempted to do just that, by providing a detailed case study of the linkages between peasant actions in the Mexican countryside and important developments nationally and internationally. Furthermore, by integrating broad historical frameworks, including socioeconomic reform, state building, and bilateral affairs, this study has sought to sidestep the balkanization that frequently divides the scholarly literature between domestic and international history, as well as elite and subaltern studies. In short, this investigation has tried to explain what drove human behavior on each side of the border during the U.S.-Mexican agrarian dispute by decentering and then recentering, examining the local, regional, national, and international, covering both the weak and the powerful, and crediting economic, political, social, and cultural forces for precipitating the crisis in Mexico and fostering its peaceful resolution. I have sought to avoid reductionism and instead illustrate "the complex wholeness of social reality" as seen in the four main issues that surrounded the bilateral conflict over land: Mexico City's diplomatic strategy toward the United States, Washington's accommodation of Mexican economic nationalism, Cárdenas's agrarian policies in Sonora and Baja California, and peasant agency in the Mexicali and Yaqui Valleys.[11]

Although some topics may not warrant such a dualistic domestic and international approach, or necessitate the study of both the elite and subaltern, many do and would benefit accordingly. U.S. diplomatic historians, for instance, could pay greater attention to regional developments overseas, and area specialists could tie the local to the international. If neither scholarly community does so, they will continue to speak past one another, to their mutual detriment. Likewise, structuralists could broaden their analysis and also focus on "real people doing real things," just as those who emphasize popular agency could also address larger systemic forces.[12] As it now stands, some scholars tell only half a story, which denies readers insight into life's fullness, its interconnections, its contradictions, and its rich yet gray complexity. Historians should move beyond balkanization, transcend paradigms, incorporate all the central actors that pertain to their studies, and combine the local, regional, national, and international together into one narrative. Although a holistic approach to historical analysis might frustrate attempts at typology, it will likely provide us with a fuller understanding of the past.

NOTES

INTRODUCTION: DOMESTIC AFFAIRS
AND FOREIGN RELATIONS

1. Lawson to Serrano, June 24, 1940, Serrano to Lawson, June 24, 1940, Lawson to
   Welles, August 7, 1940, Lawson Correspondence, vol. 1–3, entry 203, RG 76, NAW;
   Department of State, *American Mexican Claims Commission,* 475–651.

2. Hall, *Oil, Banks, and Politics*, 174, 175.

3. Knight, *U.S.-Mexican Relations, 1910–1940*, 2.

4. *New York Times*, May 24, 1925, and July 9, 1927; Smith, *Talons of the Eagle*, 71.

5. The literature on the oil crisis includes Lorenzo Meyer, *Mexico and the United States in the Oil Controversy;* Jayne, *Oil, War, and Anglo-American Relations;* Jonathan Brown, *Oil and Revolution in Mexico;* Grayson, *The Politics of Mexican Oil;* Koppes, "The Good Neighbor Policy and the Nationalization of Mexican Oil."

6. Just as James Scott's work has revised the discourse on local hegemony, some of his ideas have been applied to the study of U.S. relations with the developing world. See Scott, *Weapons of the Weak* and *Domination and the Arts of Resistance;* Cullather, *Illusions of Influence;* Longley, *The Sparrow and the Hawk;* Buchenau, *In the Shadow of the Giant;* Dwyer, "Diplomatic Weapons of the Weak."

7. Knight, *The Mexican Revolution* and *U.S.-Mexican Relations, 1910–1940;* John Mason Hart, *Revolutionary Mexico* and *Empire and Revolution*. See also their respective chapters in Nugent, ed., *Rural Revolt in Mexico*.

8. RG 76, Office of the Commissioner, U.S. Section, Agrarian Claims Commission, Final Appraisals, Annexes to Final Report, 1940–43, entry 206, NAW; Bowman, Report: Agrarianism in the Mexicali Consular District, March 10, 1938, RG 84, Mexicali, file 852, Confidential Records, NAW; Department of State, *American Mexican Claims Commission*, 629–30.

9. "Many Mexicos" was coined in Simpson, *Many Mexicos*, while Bantjes posits "many Cardenismos" in *As If Jesus Walked on Earth*, xiv.

10. Traditionalist or populist accounts of Cárdenas that portray him favorably include Tannenbaum, *Mexico;* Townsend, *Lázaro Cárdenas;* Weyl and Weyl, *The Reconquest of Mexico;* and Blanco Moheno, *Tata Lázaro*. For revisionist interpretations that are more critical of Cárdenas, see Córdova, *La política de masas del Cardenismo;* Anguiano, *El estado y la política obrera del cardenismo;* Ianni, *El Estado capitalista en la época de Cárdenas;* Hernández Chávez, *La mecánica Cardenista;* Hamilton, *The Limits of State Autonomy;* Basurto, *Cárdenas y el poder sindical;* Friedrich, *The Princes of Naranja;* Gledhill, *Casi Nada;* Becker, "Black and White and Color."

11. Cárdenas's need to stabilize and strengthen his government following his conflict with Calles impelled him to allow a number of conservative, anti-Callista governors to obtain power, such as Maximino Ávila Camacho in Puebla, Gildardo Magaña in Michoacán, Félix Bañuelos in Zacatecas, Miguel Alemán in Veracruz, and Román Yocupicio in Sonora.

12. For postrevisionist and neopopulist accounts of the postrevolutionary era that are more balanced toward Cárdenas, see Knight, "Cardenismo"; Vaughan, *Cultural Politics in Revolution;* Bantjes, *As If Jesus Walked on Earth;* Bliss, *Compromised Positions;* Boyer, *Becoming Campesinos;* Dawson, *Indian and Nation in Revolutionary Mexico;* Olcott, *Revolutionary Women in Postrevolutionary Mexico;* Vaughan and Lewis, eds., *The Eagle and the Virgin*. Fallaw's *Cárdenas Compromised* rejects both the revisionist and neopopulist perspectives on Cardenismo and paints Cárdenas as a somewhat

disengaged president who not only allowed his key collaborators to advance the federal project in Yucatán but also failed to provide full autonomy and adequate legal protection to his regional popular supporters.

13. Indigenismo was an idea that sprung mostly from urban intellectual elites during the postrevolutionary era and which sought to advance the interests of Mexico's various indigenous groups. Indigenistas, the promoters of indigenismo, called for the modernization and material improvement of Indians and were usually more successful in promoting indigenous culture than they were in increasing the political power of indigenous peoples. Mestizaje was an ideology that also gained prominence in Mexico after 1920. One of its leading proponents, José Vasconcelos, in his work *La raza cósmica*, argued that the fusion of various cultures, including European, American, and African, created a new and superior mestizo race whose interests should be promoted. After the revolution ended, influential sociologists such as Manuel Gamio championed mestizaje as a way to unite the country and make it more inclusive, since a majority of Mexicans were of mixed heritage.

14. For structural arguments on revolutions and the peasantry, see Hobsbawm, *Primitive Rebels;* Wolf, *Peasant Wars of the Twentieth Century;* Skocpol, *States and Social Revolutions;* Paige, *Agrarian Revolution.* For postrevisionist accounts of peasants in postrevolutionary Mexico, see Nugent, *Spent Cartridges of Revolution;* Becker, *Setting the Virgin on Fire;* Purnell, *Popular Movements and State Formation in Revolutionary Mexico;* Boyer, *Becoming Campesinos.*

15. Scott, *Weapons of the Weak,* xvi.

16. Ochoa, *Feeding Mexico,* 6.

17. Brown, "Acting for Themselves," 45–71. Although Brown's article covers the role of petroleum workers in the oil takeover, his study is mostly institutional and focuses on the trade unions and the government. When the oil workers speak, it is mostly anecdotal.

18. Nugent, "Rural Revolt in Mexico, Mexican Nationalism and the State, and Forms of U.S. Intervention," 5, 15, italics in original. Throughout this study I use the terms peasant, campesino (rural person engaged in agriculture), field worker, landless rural worker, and rural proletarians, among others, interchangeably. The agrarista rank and file in the Mexicali Valley were comprised of sharecroppers, leaseholders, resident estate workers (*peones acasillados*), day laborers (*jornaleros*), and seasonal migrant workers. The landless wage-earning laborers worked in a variety of positions, such as pickers, packers, and loaders. With the exception of the peones acasillados, similar groups comprised the Yaqui Valley agrarista movement. See Bantjes, *As If Jesus Walked on Earth,* 92–93.

19. Ferry, *Not Ours Alone;* Striffler, *In the Shadows of State and Capital.*

20. For works that blend together Mexico's domestic and international history, see Katz, *The Secret War in Mexico;* Joseph, *Revolution from Without;* Nugent, ed., *Rural Revolt in Mexico and U.S. Intervention;* Niblo, *War, Diplomacy, and Development;* Tenorio-Trillo, *Mexico at the World's Fairs;* Henderson, *The Worm in the Wheat;* Ferry, *Not Ours Alone.*

21. The $2,941,209 awarded to CRLC's stockholders was the largest reparation awarded by the Mexican government to an American landowner. The second and third largest awards went, respectively, to businessman and former U.S. consul William O. Jenkins ($2,270,510) and the stockholders of United Sugar Companies ($2,113,466). While nearly 2 million of the 6.2 million acres expropriated from the Americans was agricultural property, the remaining 4 million acres was pasture, rangelands, and timberlands. RG 76, Office of the Commissioner, U.S. Section, Agrarian Claims, Lawson Correspondence, 1938–43, vol. 1–3, 1942, entry 203, and "Location of Docketed Claims," Final Appraisals, Annexes to Final Report, 1940–43, and April 23, 1940, entry 206, NAW; Department of State, *American Mexican Claims Commission,* 107–11, 475–651.

1. THE ROOTS OF THE AGRARIAN DISPUTE

1. Holden, *Mexico and the Survey of Public Lands;* Jackson, ed., *Liberals, the Church, and Indian Peasants;* John Mason Hart, *Empire and Revolution,* 167–71, 200, 206.

2. Jean Meyer, "Haciendas y ranchos, peones y campesinos en el Porfiriato," 477–509; Fujigake Cruz, "Las rebeliones campesinas en el Porfiriato," 193–97; Markiewicz, *The Mexican Revolution and the Limits of Agrarian Reform,* 15, 185; Thiesenhusen, "Mexican Land Reform, 1934–91," 36; Susan Walsh Sanderson, *Land Reform in Mexico,* 20; John Mason Hart, *Empire and Revolution,* 169–70.

3. Katz, "The Agrarian Policies and Ideas of the Revolutionary Mexican Factions," 21–34.

4. Freeman Smith, *The United States and Revolutionary Nationalism in Mexico,* 72–74; Hall, "Álvaro Obregón and the Agrarian Movement, 1912–1920," 124–39.

5. George Wythe to State Department, March 12, 1926, folder 13/17, U.S. Embassy Collection, 1918–28, Calles and Torreblanca Archives; Hall, "Alvaro Obregón and the Politics of Mexican Land Reform," 213–38; Jean Meyer, "Mexico," 155–94.

6. Although land redistribution increased during President Abelardo Rodríguez's term in office (1932–34), he was largely attempting "to complete the process." See *New York Times,* February 19, 1930, June 24, 1930, December 13, 1930, June 19, 1932, and September 29, 1932; Lorenzo Meyer, *El conflicto social y los gobiernos del maximato,* 211–29; Reyes Osorio, *Estructura agraria y desarrollo agrícola en México.*

7. State Department, "The Economic Effects of the Mexican Agrarian Program," August 10, 1938, RG 84, Mexicali Consulate, General Records, box 7, file 350, NAW. Although land redistribution was relatively limited before Cárdenas entered office, this does not mean that Mexico's postrevolutionary presidents did not carry out other political or socioeconomic reforms. During the 1920s and early 1930s, Mexico's presidents greatly increased federal expenditures on education, the arts, and public works; they also reformed the banking system, advanced the labor movement, and promoted anticlericalism, cooperativism, and corporatism. In addition, they sought to gain some control over the foreign-owned oil industry, and Obregón and Calles, especially, challenged the United States. In other words, we should not view Cár-

denas as reversing the policies of his predecessors. Instead, he built on some of their programs and altered others (such as agrarian reform) with similar goals in mind: economic development, a strong and stable federal government, and a more symmetrical relationship with the United States.

8. The pro-Cárdenas faction of the Liga Nacional met in San Luis Potosí in the spring of 1933 to promote agrarista policies and form the CCM. Tobler, "Peasants and the Shaping of the Revolutionary State," 514–15; Craig, *The First Agraristas,* 112, 249–58.

9. The autonomous Agrarian Department was empowered to carry out the nation's land redistribution program. Its responsibilities were multifold and included dividing large estates, conducting agrarian censuses, collecting ejido petitions, distributing and regulating ejido lands and waters, managing ejidos, marketing ejido products, and maintaining the agrarian register and ejidal statistics. It also ran the National Consulting Body, state-level agrarian delegations, Mixed Agrarian Commissions, private executive committees, ejidal commissariats, and the Office of Attorney for the pueblos. Cárdenas, *Plan Sexenal; Diario Oficial,* January 17, 1934; Escárcega López, "El principio de la reforma agraria," 80–83; Knight, "Mexico, c. 1930–1946," 10.

10. Lyle Brown, "Lázaro Cárdenas," 106; de la Peña, "Rural Mobilizations in Latin America," 316–17.

11. *Diario Oficial,* 20, November 25, 1936, 1–3; Hamilton, *The Limits of State Autonomy,* 162–64.

12. John Mason Hart, *Empire and Revolution,* 171–74, 195–97, 227, 236, 260, 511.

13. American economic penetration was not limited to the agricultural sector. By 1911, U.S. investments in agriculture, mining, oil, and railroads, along with a host of other industries, totaled $1.265 billion, or 38 percent of all foreign investments in Mexico. Those investments increased to $1.325 billion by 1929. See *New York Times,* February 20, 1927, and August 18, 1929.

14. John Mason Hart, *Empire and Revolution,* 180, 233–34, 236.

15. Tinker Salas, *In the Shadow of the Eagles;* Weiner, *Race, Nation, and Market;* Kerig, "Yankee Enclave," 26.

16. Dabdoub, *Historia del Valle del Yaqui,* 139–57; Radding, "Peasant Resistance on the Yaqui Delta, 340–42; Steven Sanderson, *Agrarian Populism and the Mexican State,* 38, 43–46; Hu-DeHart, *Yaqui Resistance and Survival,* 155–200; Spicer, *The Yaquis,* 158.

17. *Los Angeles Times,* April 7, 1909. Chandler Ward was the attorney for CCR and its executives from 1922 onwards. See Chandler Ward, "Background Material on Irrigation Development of the Yaqui Valley, Sonora, and the Sale of the Project to the Mexican Government" (hereafter Ward Report), January 24, 1968, CCR Records, SC UAL; CCR Records, 1918–28, folder 1, Historical Material, 1909–68 (hereafter folder 1), SC UAL; and Richardson to Stockholders, May 20, 1907, CCR Records, folder 3, SC UAL; John Mason Hart, *Empire and Revolution,* 326.

18. Ward Report; Richardson to Stockholders; Yepis to Hull, December 15, 1936, enclosure 2, RG 84, Guaymas, file 350, NAW.

19. Richardson to Stockholders, May 20, 1907, CCR Records, folder 3, SC UAL; Ward Report; John Mason Hart, *Empire and Revolution*, 236.

20. Richardson to Stockholders; Ward Report; Tomás Conant to Obregón, April 30, 1923, file 21, inventory 1037, docket 1, Calles and Torreblanca Archives; *New York Times*, February 20, 1927; Sanderson, *Agrarian Populism and the Mexican State*, 48–49; Vaughan, *Cultural Politics in Revolution*, 164.

21. Richardson to Stockholders, May 20, 1907, CCR Records, folder 3, SC UAL; Ward Report; *New York Times*, February 20, 1927; Murrieta y Graf, *Por el milagro de aferrarse*, 108–9, 111; John Mason Hart, *Empire and Revolution*, 173, 237.

22. *Foreign Relations of the United States* (hereafter FRUS), 1917 (Washington, D.C.: Government Printing Office, 1926), 1:1025–27, 1033–35; FRUS, 1918, 1:668; FRUS, 1919, 1:571–72, 582–83, 614–24, 626–31; Subsecretario de Relaciones Exteriores to Secretario de Gobernación, October 2 and November 14, 1925, and February 8, 1926, DGG 2.382, box 47, AGN.

23. John Mason Hart, *Empire and Revolution*, 326; FRUS, 1917, 1:1033–35; FRUS, 1919, 1:624–25, 631–63.

24. Ward Report, January 24, 1968, CCR Records, folder 1, SC UAL; RG 76, Office of the Commissioner of the U.S. Section, Agrarian Claims, Final Appraisals, Annexes to the Final Report, 1940–43, entry 206, NAW; *New York Times*, February 20, 1927; Bantjes, "Politics, Class and Culture in Postrevolutionary Mexico," 401–2; Vaughan, *Cultural Politics in Revolution*, 68.

25. *New York Times*, February 20, 1927; Ward Report, January 24, 1968, CCR Records, folder 1, SC UAL; RG 76, Office of the Commissioner of the U.S. Section, Agrarian Claims, Final Appraisals, Annexes to the Final Report, 1940–43, entry 206, NAW; Cronon, *Josephus Daniels in Mexico*, 142; Bantjes, *As If Jesus Walked on Earth*, 125; Vaughan, *Cultural Politics in Revolution*, 68; Naylor, Falcon, and Puentes-González, *Policy Reform and Mexican Agriculture*, 2.

26. Sibbet and Richardson were each allowed to keep 5,000 acres of land from the 1927 sale—most of which Cárdenas's government expropriated in 1937. Ward Report, January 24, 1968, CCR Records, folder 1, SC UAL; Ruiz, *The People of Sonora and Yankee Capitalists*, 146–61; Bantjes, "Politics, Class and Culture," 403–4; Bantjes, *As If Jesus Walked on Earth*, 125; Vaughan, *Cultural Politics in Revolution*, 164; Sanderson, *Agrarian Populism and the Mexican State*, 114.

27. U.S. Embassy to State Department, Memo, enclosure 2, December 15, 1936, Yepis to Hull, December 17, 1936, RG 84, Guaymas, file 350, NAW; John Mason Hart, *Empire and Revolution*, 237.

28. U.S. Embassy to State Department, Memo, enclosure 2, December 15, 1936, Yepis to Hull, December 17, 1936, RG 84, Guaymas, file 350, NAW.

29. Mathes, ed., *Baja California*; Piñera Ramírez, *Ocupación y uso del suelo en Baja California*.

30. Consejo Nacional de Población Mexico, *Baja California demográfico*, 17, 39; Peritus, "La población en Baja California."

31. Anguiano Téllez, "La formación social en el Valle de Mexicali a principios de siglo," 27–50; Hendricks, "Guillermo Andrade and Land Development on the Mexican Colorado River Delta"; Kerig, "Yankee Enclave," 21, 36–40.

32. The five leading individual investors in CRLC were Chandler, Otis, Allen, Brant, and Moses Sherman. Chandler became owner and publisher of the *Los Angles Times* and president of CRLC following Otis's death in 1917. These men also owned a 270,000 acre ranch in Los Angeles County, as well as the Los Angeles Steamship Company. See Kerig, "Yankee Enclave," 41, 49, 60, 64–70, 84; Department of National Lands memo to Cárdenas, January 14, 1936, Cárdenas Papers, 705.2/26, AGN; Anguiano Téllez, "La formación social en el Valle de Mexicali," 30.

33. Anguiano Téllez, "La formación social en el Valle de Mexicali," 34; Memo of Areas Leased, 1922–36, no date, Archive of the Colorado River Land Company, General Archives, unnumbered box, SL; Kerig, "Yankee Enclave," 58–88.

34. RG 76, Approved Agrarian Claims Case Files, 1938–47, docket 72, claim 54, box 31, and Agrarian Claims, Final Appraisals, Annexes to Final Report and other Records, 1940–43, entry 206, NAW; Department of State, *American Mexican Claims Commission*, 481–82, 502–11, 559–62, 589–98, 629–30, 637–39, 647–49; Kerig, "Yankee Enclave," 58–88, 152–53, 485; Ward, *Border Oasis*, 36–38.

35. Blaisdell, "Was It Revolution or Filibustering?" 147–64; Macías, ed., *Plutarco Elías Calles*, 210; Werne, "Vice Revenue and the Growth of Government in Baja California Norte," 4–6.

36. Chamberlin, "Mexican Colonization versus American Interests in Lower California," 43–55; Pablo Martínez, *Historia de Baja California*, 461–65; Obregón and Calles Papers, 424-A-9, AGN; Jack Hart, *The Information Empire*, 53; Kerig, "Yankee Enclave,," 152–60, 257.

37. Werne, "Vice Revenue and the Growth of Government in Baja California Norte," 7–9, 13; Kerig, "Yankee Enclave," 170, 185, 233.

38. Macías, ed., *Plutarco Elías Calles*, 250–51; Abelardo Rodríguez, *Autobiografía*, 127–32; Kerig, "Yankee Enclave," 131, 233, 240–41; Knight, "The Political Economy of Revolutionary Mexico," 297.

39. Jiménez to Ortiz Rubio, September 3, 1930, Guerrero to Hernández Cházaro, August 13, 14, 15, 16, 17, 21, 22, 23, 24, 1930, Ortiz Rubio Papers, file 257 (1930), 10089, AGN. For more on Rodríguez's corruption, see Ortiz Rubio Papers, file 257 (1930), 10878, 10933, 10997, 11025, 12119, 14714, 14883, 15203, and Gómez Estrada, *Gobierno y casinos*.

40. Chandler to Governor José Lugo, March 31, 1922, Lugo to Obregón, April 4, April 15, 1922, Obregón and Calles Papers, folder 243-B1-B-4, AGN. The favoritism shown CRLC by Mexican officials was apparent to many, see Varios Mexicanos Conscientes to Calles, October 7, 1925, Obregón and Calles Papers, folder 823-CH-5, AGN; U.S. Consul Horatio Mooers to American Consul General James Stewart, February 13, 1939, RG 76, Approved Agrarian Claim Case Files, AMC docket 72, NAW; Moors to Daniels, August 2, and August 9, 1939, RG 84, Mexicali, file 852, Confidential Records, NAW; Kerig, "Yankee Enclave," 48, 213; Macías, ed., *Plutarco Elías Calles*, 225–26, 236–38.

41. Gómez to Vierhus, September 6, 1934, CRLC, General Archives, box 382; Agustín Loroña memo to Haskell, November 29, 1938, CRLC, General Archives, unnumbered box, General File, SL; Kerig, "Yankee Enclave,," 269, 291–327, 484.

42. Blaisdell, "Henry Lane Wilson and the Overthrow of Madero," 126–35.

43. The greater part of U.S. investments in Mexico were made in mining, smelting, oil, railroads, electric power, banking, and agriculture. Lesser investments were made in telephones, autos, cement, irrigation, and cattle. Still less in volume were printing, press manufacture, salt, and hotels. See *Washington Times*, May 22, 1936.

44. *FRUS*, 1917, 1:949–50, 1061–62; *New York Times*, February 20, 1927.

45. *New York Times*, June 1, 1920; Beelen, "The Harding Administration and Mexico," 177–89; Harrison, *Dollar Diplomat*, 123–24.

46. Summerlin to Pani, May 30, 1921, file 11–9–127, AHSRE; *FRUS*, 1921, 2:473–92, 709.

47. *New York Times*, September 1, 1923, May 20, 1924; Sumner Welles to A. F. Yepis, August 17, 1937, RG 84, Mexico, Guaymas, General Records, file 350, box 12, NAW; Kane, "American Businessmen and Foreign Policy," 293–313.

48. *New York Times*, September 1, 1923, May 24, 1925; Kane, "American Businessmen and Foreign Policy," 309–12.

49. *New York Times*, May 17, June 13, June 17, 1925.

50. *FRUS*, 1925, 2:517–54, for example.

51. Macías, ed., *Plutarco Elías Calles*, 81–82; *FRUS*, 1926, 2:605–30, 688–702. For more on the petroleum conflict in 1926, see file 28–1–105, AHSRE.

52. *FRUS*, 1926, 2:605–30, 688–702.

53. Macías, ed., *Plutarco Elías Calles*, 90, 95–96; *FRUS*, 1925, 2:517–54, *New York Times*, November 17, 1925, January 13, 1927; Buchenau, *In the Shadow of the Giant*, 171–77.

54. Former president Emilio Portes Gil claimed that U.S. naval ships were mobilized for military intervention against Mexico but that Calles's disclosure of the stolen embassy documents led Washington to cancel the incursion. See Portes Gil, *Autobiografía de la revolución mexicana*, 396; Sheffield to Kellogg, February 27, 1926, U.S. Embassy Collection, folder 3/17, Calles and Torreblanca Archives; *Excelsior*, July 3, 1926; *New York Times*, January 31, 1924, June 14, 1925, February 1, 1927; Daniels to Roosevelt, September 28, 1936, Roosevelt Papers, PPF, folder 86, Daniels, FDRL; Horn, "Did the U.S. Plan an Invasion of Mexico in 1927?" 454–71.

55. *New York Times*, February 1, 1927, March 8 and 29, 1928, July 2, 1929, March 24, 1930; Sheffield to Kellogg, February 27, 1926, U.S. Embassy Collection, folder 3/17, Calles and Torreblanca Archives; *Excelsior*, July 3, 1926; Chandler Anderson, "The Mexican Confiscation Policy: Memo on Questions Discussed at Conference," April 19, 1927, Clark Papers, LC; Macías, ed., *Plutarco Elías Calles*, 84; Harrison, *Dollar Diplomat*, 67–81, 119–20.

56. *New York Times*, June 14, 1925, April 29, 1927, July 9, 1927; *FRUS*, 1927, 3:196–209; *FRUS*, 1928, 3:300–8; Macías, ed., *Plutarco Elías Calles*, 89, 104; Bodayla, *Financial Diplomacy*.

57. *New York Times*, December 31, 1927, February 5, 1928; Kellogg to American Consul,

Calexico, March 8, 1929, RG 84, Mexico, Mexicali, decimal file 800–810, vol. 42, NAW; *FRUS*, 1927, 3:196–209; *FRUS*, 1928, 3:300–8.

58. *FRUS*, 1929, 1:653–67; *New York Times*, July 2, 1929.

59. *New York Times*, September 24, 1933.

60. *New York Times*, March 30, May 4, 1929; Morrow also improved U.S.-Mexican relations by resolving the controversies surrounding Mexico's foreign debt and negotiating a cease-fire to the Cristero Rebellion. See *New York Times*, March 24, 1930; Ellis, "Dwight Morrow and the Church-State Controversy in Mexico," 482–505; Ross, "Dwight Morrow and the Mexican Revolution," 506–28.

61. Brief Outline of the History of Claims Negotiations with Mexico, RG 76, American-Mexican Claims Commission, 1942–47, Orders, Decisions and Related Records, entry 227, NAW; Daniels, *Shirt-Sleeve Diplomat*, 115–24; Baker and Flood to Henry Norweb, Chargé d'Affaires of U.S. Embassy, June 3, 1934, and Norweb to Edward Reed, June 4, 1934, Daniels Papers, box 661, LC; Cronon, *Josephus Daniels in Mexico*, 137.

62. Moreno, Memo on Pending Major Problems Between the United States and Mexico, April 24, 1934, Daniels Papers, box 655, LC; Cronon, *Josephus Daniels in Mexico*, 136.

63. Castillo Nájera to Hay, "Reclamaciones por concepto de tierras expropriadas a ciudadanos Norteamericanos . . .," November 14, 1938, Cárdenas Papers, 571.3/1, AGN; *FRUS*, 1935, 4:757–59, 778–79; Cronon, *Josephus Daniels in Mexico*, 138.

64. State Department, memo, March 1936, Daniels Papers, box 653, LC.

2. HOW LOCAL AGENCY SHAPED AGRARIAN REFORM

1. Acosta Montoya, *"Precursores del agrarismo" y "El asalto a las tierras" en el estado de Baja California*, 75.

2. Published interview of Jesús Andrade Romero, Ejido Oaxaca, by Dipp Varela, "Pioneros del movimiento agrario en el Valle de Mexicali," 10.

3. Acosta Montoya, *"Precursores del agrarismo,"* 102–3; Sánchez Ogáz, "Lucha por la nacionalización del Valle de Mexicali," 52; Contreras Mora, "El acuerdo de asaltar la tierra," *Ciguatan*, 22; American Consul Howard Bowman to Secretary of State Cordell Hull, January 29, 1937, RG 84, Mexicali Consulate, file 350, CRLC, NAW.

4. Interviews by author with original agrarista activists Pedro Pérez and Apolinar Pérez, along with initial ejidatarios and descendents of some original agraristas and initial ejidatarios, including Liborio Pérez Fernández, Bonifacio Cabrera Cordova, Manuel Encinos, Pedro Jiménez Figueroa, Marciel López, and Jeremias Guillén (director of the Museo del Asalto a las Tierras, Ejido Michoacán de Ocampo), Ejido Michoacán de Ocampo, Mexicali Valley, Baja California, July 12, 13, 19, and 20, 2001 (hereafter Mexicali Interviews, 2001); U.S. Section, Agrarian Claims Commission, Appraisal of Claim 54, docket 72, RG 76, Approved Agrarian Claims Case File, 1938–1947, NAW.

5. Hobsbawm, "Peasants and Politics," 13; Scott, *Weapons of the Weak*, xvi.

6. See Lázaro Cárdenas, *Obras I*, 293, 301. In 1936 the government began extending the

railroad line southward from the Mexicali Valley to Puerto Peñasco, Sonora. When the port city was reached in May 1940, it linked Baja California to the mainland for the first time. Between then and 1947, the government extended the line from Puerto Peñasco to Benjamin Hill, Sonora—just north of the state capital of Hermosillo. On the construction of the rail line between Mexicali and Puerto Peñasco, see Cárdenas Papers, 545.3/63, AGN; Dirección General de Construcción de Ferrocarriles, *Ferro-carril Sonora–Baja California*, 34–50; Hendricks, "Port Otis," 183–84; Meade, *El distrito norte de Baja California*, 181–82, 192–93.

7. General Ernesto Aguirre Colorado to Cárdenas, November 3, 1935, Cárdenas Papers, 437.1/413, AGN.

8. David Brant, Report from April 12, 1935, trip to Mexicali, Brant Papers, box 68, SL; for quote, see Pizarro Suárez to Vierhus, October 7, 1935, CRLC, file 99, SL; Loroña memo to Haskell, November 29, 1938, General Archives, unnumbered box, CRLC, General File, SL; for the intersecretarial commission, see Presidential Acuerdo no. 435, April 16, 1935, DGG, 2.300(29)518, box 36, AGN.

9. Chandler to Vierhus, February 1, 1936, Cárdenas Papers, 705.2/26, AGN. For a copy of the April 1936 CRLC colonization contract and details regarding it, see RG 84, Mexicali, General Records, file 852, NAW; 852/671.24/3613, Fondo Territorio Norte, AHEBC; *Diario Oficial*, May 7, 1936, 3, and August 14, 1937; CRLC, file 99, folders Colonización, Proyectos y Borradores, Contracto Colonización, and Nuevo Contracto de Colonización, SL; CRLC, General Archives, unnumbered boxes, box U, General File, SL.

10. Chandler to Vierhus, February 1, 1936, Cárdenas Papers, 705.2/26, AGN; Kerig, "Yankee Enclave," 345–46.

11. The colonization commission with a national focus was composed of Secretary of the Agriculture (who identified the lands to be broken up and colonized), the Secretary of Interior (who worked to repatriate Mexican field workers from the U.S.), the National Bank of Agricultural Credit (which provided new colonists with financial support), the National Irrigation Commission (which constructed canals and irrigation works for the new colonies), and the Secretary of Finance (who over saw the project). See *Periódico Oficial*, March 20, and May 10, 1935; Governor of Baja California Gildardo Magaña to Cárdenas, November 8, 1935, Cárdenas Papers, 705.2/26, AGN.

12. A Mexican mestizo is a person of mixed ancestry, most often of indigenous and European descent. Magaña to Cárdenas, October 20, 1935, Cárdenas Papers, 564.1/65; Magaña to Cárdenas, November 16, 1935, Cárdenas Papers, 606.3/2; Parrés to Engineer Antonio Basich (Mexicali Development Agency), July 24, 1935; Gavira to Cárdenas, Report by the Subcommittee on the Colonization of the Northern Territory of Baja California, July 29, 1936, Cárdenas Papers, 437.1/413, AGN; *El Hispano Americano* (Tijuana), November 21, 1935, 1.

13. Secretary of Agriculture, Memo con respecto a la colonización en la Baja California de los terrenos que actualmente está poseyendo la Colorado River Land Co., April 13,

1935, Cárdenas Papers, 705.2/26, Dionisio Mercado, Informes relativos a los problemas y avances del proyecto de colonización del valle de Mexicali, 1935–37, Cárdenas Papers, 534.3/41; AGN.

14. On colonizing Baja California with Mexican repatriates, see Juan Romero to Cárdenas, December 1, 1936, Cárdenas Papers, 503.11/212, AGN; Kerig, "Yankee Enclave," 334.

15. Governor of Baja California, Gabriel Gavira, to Secretary of the Interior, July 21, 1936, Cárdenas Papers, 606.3/2, AGN; *Excelsior,* December 11, 1935.

16. Lázaro Cárdenas, *Obras I,* 280, 358, 431; Cárdenas, "Exposición del presidente de la república sobre la reconstrucción integral de los territorios de Baja California y Quintana Roo, en México," 215; Cárdenas, *El problema de los territorios federales,* 3–4. Baja California Norte was granted statehood in 1952; Baja California Sur achieved statehood in 1974.

17. Lázaro Cárdenas, *Obras I,* 280–81, 284, 292–97, 301, 325; Departamento Autónomo de Prensa y Publicidad, *México en acción;* Bernal, *Breve historia del estado de Baja California,* 79–83.

18. *El Hispano Americano* (Tijuana), May 8 and July 10, 1936, and January 21 and March 19, 1937 all p. 1; *El Mundo,* August 29, 1936, 1; *La Opinión,* June 19, 1936, 3; *El Periódico Oficial,* August 30, 1936, 1. Secretaries of Finance and National Economy, March 27, 1935, Cárdenas Papers, 564.1/26, AGN; Memo on the subject, DGG, 2.382(30)24554, box 70, vol. 1, AGN; Cárdenas, *Obras I,* 293, 301, 358; Lázaro Cárdenas, *El problema de los territorios federales,* 15; Taylor, "La Transformación de Baja California en Estado, 1931–1952," 65–72; Aguilar, *Norte precario,* 244–48.

19. For the hundreds of letters supporting Cárdenas's call for the integration of the territories into the nation, see Cárdenas Papers, 437.1/413, AGN.

20. *La Prensa,* n.d., 2, Cárdenas Papers, 437.1/413. For hundreds of letters from campesinos and peasant leagues in Mexico and the United States to Cárdenas volunteering to colonize CRLC's land, see Cárdenas Papers, 404.1/4227, 437.1/413, 534.3/41, 705.2/26, and especially 503.11/212, AGN.

21. José Valdez Gómez to Cárdenas, July 10, 1936, Cárdenas Papers, 705.2/26; Camilo Alvarado to Cárdenas, March 11, 1936, Cárdenas Papers, 503.11/106; Pedro Gálvez to Cárdenas, July 24, 1937; César Ruiz to Cárdenas, July 30, 1936; Cárdenas Papers, 404.2/81, AGN; Kerig, "Yankee Enclave," 351.

22. Castelo Encinas to Cárdenas, December 14, 1936, Cárdenas Papers, 705.2/26, AGN; Chandler to Cárdenas, January 7, 1937, CRLC, file 99, folder Colonización, SL; Cárdenas to Navarro Cortina, January 20, 1937, Cárdenas Papers, 437.1/413, AGN; Taboada, "Relación de los terrenos enajenados por la Colorado River Land Co., S. A., con fines de colonización," November 23, 1938, 852/651.7/871, AHEBC.

23. Attorney E. J. Guajardo to Miles Bickel, January 10, 1945, CRLC, file 99, folder Colonización; Loroña memo to Haskell, November 29, 1938, General Archives, unnumbered box, CRLC, General File, SL.

24. Cárdenas to Navarro Cortina, January 20, 1937, Cárdenas Papers, 437.1/413; Colonel Rubén García to Cárdenas, January 25, 1937, Cárdenas Papers, 437.1/413; Navarro Cortina to Cárdenas, and attached memo, January 26, 1937, Cárdenas Papers, 534.3/41, AGN.

25. Mexicali Interviews, 2001; Hernández y López, "Campesinos y poder," in Escárcega López, ed., *Historia de la cuestión agraria mexicana,* 491–99.

26. Mexicali Interviews, 2001; Carr, "The Mexican Communist Party and Agrarian Mobilization in the Laguna," 378.

27. Ing. Castro Fernández, November 5, 1941, Tierra y Patria, Mexicali, Baja California, 23/23066, ASRA; Kerig, "Yankee Enclave," 200–1.

28. Andrade was the Secretary General of the Unión de Obreros y Campesinos del Valle de Mexicali. For Andrade's interview, see Dipp Varela, "Pioneros del movimiento agrario en el Valle de Mexicali," 7–8; Gamio, *Mexican Immigration to the United States,* 161–62; Craig, *The First Agraristas,* 178–82.

29. Interview with Pedro Pérez, Mexicali Interviews, 2001; Dipp Varela, "Pioneros del movimiento agrario en el Valle de Mexicali," 8.

30. Photographs from the Museo del Asalto a las Tierras, Ejido Michoacán de Ocampo, Mexicali; Mexicali Interviews, 2001; Cibrián to Villafuerte, August 4, 1936, Alamo Mocho, Mexicali, BCA, 23/7849, ASRA.

31. Mexicali Interviews, 2001; Rentería to Cárdenas, December 7 and 21, 1936, Cárdenas Papers, 705.2/26, AGN; José María Morelos, Algodones, BCA, 23/22748; Tierra y Patria, Mexicali, BCA, 23/23066; Cucapas, Mexicali, BCA, 23/11149, ASRA; interview of Cárdenas Lizarraga by Dipp Varela, in "Pioneros del movimiento agrario en el Valle de Mexicali," 17. Sánchez Ogáz, "La nacionalización de las tierras del Valle de Mexicali y la formación de la organización campesina en Baja California," in Ferrer, ed., *Historia de las ligas de comunidades agrarias,* 46–49.

32. Cardoso, *Mexican Emigration to the United States,* 97–99; Kerig, "Yankee Enclave," 201–2.

33. Kerig, "Yankee Enclave," 200–8; wall display, Museo del Asalto a las Tierras, Ejido Michoacán de Ocampo, Mexicali Valley, Baja California.

34. See interview of Reyes's son, Rosalío Reyes Corona, in Dipp Valera, *Así abrimos la tierra,* 50–55.

35. George Wythe to U.S. Embassy, October 23, 1926, U.S. Embassy Collection, folder 9/17, Calles and Torreblanca Archives; Craig, *The First Agraristas,* 98–99.

36. Martínez to Secretary of Agriculture and Development, January 1927, Alamo Mocho, Mexicali, BCA, 23/7849, ASRA.

37. Palencia, Notice, May 31, 1927, Alamo Mocho, Mexicali, BCA, 23/7849, ASRA; *Periódico Oficial,* June 30, 1927, 13–16; Dipp Valera, *Así abrimos la tierra,* 56–58.

38. Acosta Montoya, *"Precursores del agrarismo,"* 84.

39. Over a sixteen-year period from 1920 to 1936, Baja California Norte had fourteen different governors. Aguirre Bernal, *Compendio histórico-biográfico de Mexicali,* 323,

and "La mexicanización del Valle de Mexicali," in Piñera, ed., *Panorama histórico de Baja California*, 487–96; Hoffman, *Unwanted Mexican Americans in the Great Depression*, 38, 48; Kerig, "Yankee Enclave," 254, 288–91, 304–9; Fitzgerald, "Restructuring through the Depression," 242–65; Cárdenas, "The Great Depression and Industrialization," 222–41.

40. Tapia was Rodríguez's deputy during the latter's term. For the interview of Macrina Lerma Álvarez, see Dueñas Montes, *Territorio Norte de la Baja California*, 62–69; Acosta Montoya, *"Precursores del agrarismo,"* 82.

41. The other agrarista leaders who were arrested included Macario Sánchez, Daniel Bautista, Juan Párez, Benjamin Magaña, Benigno Lama, Miguel Águilar (who died in prison), Florentino Domínguez, Francisco López, Leonardo Prado, and Ignacio Sánchez (the latter two participated in the 1936 agrarian movement and 1937 invasion of CRLC's land). See Acosta Montoya, *"Precursores del agrarismo,"* 45–49; Dueñas, *Territorio Norte de la Baja California*, 67–69; Garduño, *Voces y ecos del Valle de Mexicali*, 35.

42. Pablo Martínez, *Historia de Baja California*, 550–52; Acosta Montoya, *"Precursores del agrarismo,"* 49–52; Duarte Vargas, "La lucha por la tierra en Baja California," 146–47; Camp, *Mexican Political Biographies*, 227–28.

43. Kerig, "Yankee Enclave," 311–312; Dueñas, *Territorio Norte de la Baja California*, 71; Acosta Montoya, *"Precursores del agrarismo,"* 85; interview with Pedro Pérez, Mexicali Interviews, 2001; Ibarra to Olachea, November 9, 1931, Candia to Ministerio Público, September 9, 1932, Rodríguez Papers, file 561.8/12, AGN; León to Rodríguez, June 20, July 17, 1933, González to Olachea, June 16, 1933, Flores to Olachea, July 6, 1933, Rodríguez Papers, file 518.2/15, AGN.

44. Secretary General Juan González to Secretary of the Interior, May 11, 1936, DGG, 2.331.9(30)18333, box 86-A, AGN.

45. Executive Committee Colonia Alamo Mocho, Constituent Accord, August 16, 1936, Alamo Mocho, Mexicali, BCA, 23/7849, ASRA; interview with Pedro Pérez, Mexicali Interviews, 2001; Union of Peasant Day Laborers, Alamo Mocho, Mexicali, BCA, 23/7849, ASRA.

46. Mexicali Interviews, 2001; Acosta Montoya, *"Precursores del agrarismo,"* 73–74; Fallaw, *Cárdenas Compromised*, 16–17, 23–28, 113–14.

47. Fallaw, *Cárdenas Compromised*, 23–28; interview with Pedro Pérez, Mexicali Interviews, 2001.

48. Manuel Godínez to Vázquez, August 17, 1936, Alamo Mocho, Mexicali, BCA, 23/7849, ASRA; Acosta Montoya, *"Precursores del agrarismo,"* 73–74; Fallaw, *Cárdenas Compromised*, 25, 27 Vanderwood, *Juan Soldado*, 162.

49. *La Opinión*, June 8, 1936.

50. Sindicato de Jornaleros Campesinos de Alamo Mocho to Vázquez, July 24, 1936, Gavira to Prado, June 25, 1936, Cibrián to Villafuerte, August 4, 1936, Alamo Mocho, Mexicali, BCA, 23/7849, ASRA.

51. Jesús García to Head of the Agrarian Department, July 8, and September 12, 1936, Alamo Mocho, Mexicali, BCA, 23/7849, ASRA.

52. For ejidal petitions filed by various agrarian communities prior to the 1937 invasion of CRLC's lands, see José María Morelos, Mexicali, BCA, 23/22748, ASRA; Tierra y Patria, today Jalisco, Mexicali, BCA, 23/23066, ASRA; Cucapah Mestizos before Cucapas, Mexicali, BCA, 23/11149, ASRA. The interviewees agreed that the Mexicali government ignored both their petitions for land and their larger socioeconomic interests.

53. The union was affiliated with the CROM. See Declaration of the Bar and Restaurant Employees Union of Mexicali, translation, n.d., General File, CRLC, 1937, SL.

54. See Acting President of Agrarian Community of Alamo Mocho, Ignacio Sánchez to Navaro Cortina, December 21, 1936, Alamo Mocho, Mexicali, BCA, 23/7849, ASRA; Vanderwood, *Juan Soldado*, 162.

55. Rentería's leadership in the CRLC land invasion was twice rewarded. First, in 1937 he was elected Baja California Norte's sole federal deputy to the Mexican Congress. Subsequently, one of the valley's ejidos was named Ejido Rentería in his honor. Agrarista leaders Emigdio Mora and Emeterio Ramírez also were from Michoacán. Interview with Pedro Pérez, Mexicali Interviews, 2001; Rentería to Cárdenas, December 7 and 21, 1936, Cárdenas Papers, 705.2/26, AGN; Sánchez Ogáz, "La nacionalización de las tierras del Valle de Mexicali," 46–49; Contreras, "El acuerdo de asaltar la tierra," 20; Camp, *Mexican Political Biographies*, 791.

56. Sánchez to Vázquez, March 1, 1937, Alamo Mocho, Mexicali, BCA, 23/7849, ASRA; Knight, *The Mexican Revolution*, 1:165–66.

57. Interview with Pedro Pérez, Mexicali Interviews, 2001.

58. Cárdenas Papers, 1939, 404/1 and 705.2/26, AGN.

59. "No hay trabajo para los Nuevos Colonos," in *El Hispano Americano* (Mexicali), January 14, 1937, 1; interview with Pedro Pérez, Mexicali Interviews, 2001.

60. Kerig, "Yankee Enclave," 421; interview with Pedro Pérez, Mexicali Interviews, 2001.

61. Interview with Pedro Pérez, Mexicali Interviews, 2001; Acosta Montoya, "*Precursores del agrarismo*," 105; Interview of Cárdenas Lizarraga by Dipp Varela, in "Pioneros del movimiento agrario en el Valle de Mexicali," 19; Craig, *The First Agraristas*, 8, 99, 183–184.

62. Sánchez Ogáz, "Lucha por la nacionalización del Valle de Mexicali," 56; Rentería to Cárdenas, January 27, 1937, Cárdenas Papers, 404.1/6708, AGN; Craig, *The First Agraristas*, 113–14, 227.

63. Longino González to Cárdenas, January 4, 1937, Cárdenas Papers, 404.1/6708, AGN; wall display at the Museo del Asalto a las Tierras; Contreras, "El acuerdo de asaltar la tierra," 21–22; Dipp Valera, "Pioneros del movimiento agrario en el Valle de Mexicali," 10.

64. Rentería to Cárdenas, January 26, 1937, Cárdenas Papers, 705.2/26, AGN; Sánchez Ogáz, "La nacionalización de las tierras del Valle de Mexicali," 52–56; Celso Aguirre Bernal, "Génesis y destino de la liga de comunidades agrarias y sindicatos campesi-

nos del estado de Baja California," 103–5; Garduño, *Voces y ecos del Valle de Mexicali,* 36–46.

65. Brant's account, January 26 and February 3, 1937, Brant Papers, box 68, SL; Haskell memo, November 29, 1938, file 477, CRLC, SL; wall display in the Museo del Asalto a las Tierras; Mexicali Interviews, 2001; Aguirre Bernal, *Compendio histórico-biográfico de Mexicali,* 326–30.

66. Loroña memo to Haskell, November 29, 1938, General Archives, unnumbered box, CRLC, General File, SL; Rentería to Cárdenas, February 16, 1937, Cárdenas Papers, 705.2/26, AGN.

67. Cárdenas's secretary, Luis Rodríguez to Navarro Cortina and Rodríguez to Rentería, January 28, 1937, Cárdenas Papers, 404.1/6708, AGN; Navarro Cortina to Cárdenas, February 4, 1937, Cárdenas Papers, 705.2/26, AGN.

68. Haskell to Brant, February 3, 1937, Brant Papers, box 68, SL.

69. For Cárdenas's Circular no. 19650 of March 24, 1936, that outlawed land invasions, see Cárdenas Papers, 404.1/2101, AGN; Jonathan Brown, "Acting for Themselves," 61–63, 66; Middlebrook, *The Paradox of Revolution,* 67–70, 83–95; Martínez Ríos, "Las invasiones agrarias en México," 741–83.

70. CGT secretary general Ramírez to Cárdenas, January 28, 1937, secretary of Acción Campesina Morales to Cárdenas, January 29, 1937, Secretary of Confederación de Trabajadores de México, Lombardo Toledano to Cárdenas, February 2, 1937, Presidential Secretary Rodríguez to Morales, February 9, 1937, and Rodríguez to Ramírez, February 9, 1937, all Cárdenas Papers, 705.2/26, AGN; Secretary of the Organización Campesina of the CGT García to Cárdenas and Vázquez, January 28, 1937, Alamo Mocho, Mexicali, BCA, 23/7849, ASRA; Haskell to Brant, February 3, 1937, Brant Papers, box 68, SL; Kerig, "Yankee Enclave," 357–58; Acosta Montoya, *"Precursores del agrarismo,"* 76.

71. Pablo Martínez, *A History of Lower California,* 538; Dipp Valera, "Pioneros del movimiento agrario en Mexicali," 12; Cárdenas to Crespo and Guillén, February 12, 1937, Cárdenas Papers, 705.2/26, AGN; Cárdenas to Navarro Cortina, February 17, 1937, 852/671.6/904, AHEBC; Hamilton, *The Limits of State Autonomy,* 14, 25.

72. Fallaw, *Cárdenas Compromised,* 34.

73. Vanderwood, *Juan Soldado,* 162–63; Ignacio Sánchez to Vázquez, March 1, 1937, Alamo Mocho, Mexicali, BCA, 23/7849, ASRA; Mexicali Interviews, 2001.

74. Wall display, the Museo del Asalto a las Tierras, interview with Pedro Pérez, Mexicali, 2001.

75. Cárdenas to Taboada, March 14, 1937, Taboada to Cárdenas, March 17, 1937, 852/671.6/904, AHEBC; Cárdenas to Cedillo, Cárdenas to Vázquez, March 14, 1937, Vázquez to Cárdenas, March 18, 1937, Cárdenas Papers, 404.1/4227, AGN; González, *Los días del presidente Cárdenas,* 158–163.

76. Cárdenas to Navarro Cortina, February 17, 1937, Cárdenas Papers, 401/21, AGN; Vázquez to Cárdenas, February 24, 1937, Cárdenas Papers, 404.1/4227, AGN; Bowman

to Hull, February 26, 1937, RG 84, Mexicali, file 350, NAW; Loroña to Haskell, November 29, 1938, General Archives, unnumbered box, CRLC, General File, SL; Memo of CRLC Property Expropriated by the Mexican Government, February 10, 1944, file 382, SL; Vera Estañol to CRLC, November 1, 1937, CRLC, file 382, SL; Kerig, "Yankee Enclave," 363–67.

77. A few more American-owned properties were expropriated by Cárdenas's government in the Mexicali Valley before he left office in December 1940. Copia, Department of State Memo, anexo 2, March 31, 1937, Cárdenas Papers, 571.3/1, AGN; Department of State, *American Mexican Claims Commission,* 481–82, 629–30.

78. Bowman, Report: Agrarianism in the Mexicali Consular District, March 10, 1938, RG 84, Mexicali, file 852, Confidential Records, NAW.

79. Interview of Lemus Vargas by Dipp Valera, *Así abrimos la tierra,* 28; Eugenia Anguiano Téllez, *Agricultura y migración en el Valle de Mexicali,* 99.

80. Gonzales, *The Mexican Revolution,* 233; Mexicali Interviews, 2001.

81. Vázquez, *The Agrarian Reform in Lower California,* 7.

82. Buelna of the Federation of Small Farmers to Cárdenas, August 18, 1937, Fernando España to Cárdenas's secretary, Ignacio García Téllez, July 31, 1937, and España and José Roa to Cárdenas, August 18, 1937, Cárdenas Papers, 705.2/26, AGN; Gastélum of the Federation of Small Farmers to Cárdenas, October 2, 1937, Lucerno of the Comité Pro-Justicia to Cárdenas, May 2, 1937, Cárdenas Papers, 404.1/4227, AGN; Ramírez to Cárdenas, Sánchez Tamayo to Cárdenas, Reyes to Cárdenas, and Montoya to Cárdenas, April 20, 1937, Cárdenas Papers, 503.11/106, AGN; Kerig, "Yankee Enclave," 367–70.

83. Interview of Guillermo Canchola Bravo by Dipp Varela, *Así abrimos la tierra,* 9; Boyer, *Becoming Campesinos,* 23.

84. Rancho Dieguinos to Vázquez, March 25, April 15, and May 22, 1937, José María Morelos, Mexicali, BCA, 23/22748, ASRA; Vázquez, *The Agrarian Reform in Lower California,* 7; de Cota to Cárdenas, June 12, 1937, Alamo Mocho, Mexicali, BCA, 23/7849, ASRA. For the hundreds of letters and telegrams sent to Cárdenas by small farmers, colonists, and CRLC tenants regarding the attacks they suffered at the hands of the agraristas and their request for federal protection, as well as for more details on the sit-down strike, see Cárdenas Papers, 404.1/4227, 503.11/106, and 705.2/26, AGN; Craig, *The First Agraristas,* 125.

85. Boyer, *Becoming Campesinos,* 13; Wells and Joseph, *Summer of Discontent, Seasons of Upheaval,* 141–47.

86. In December 1937 España was shot and seriously wounded by a group of agraristas still upset over his participation in the strike. See Brant memo of conversation with Haskell, December 18, 1937, Brant Papers, box 68, SL. Loraño to Chandler, April 22, 1937; España to Chandler, April 24, 1937, and España to Haskell, June 25, 1937, Unnumbered Box, SL; Kerig, "Yankee Enclave," 370–74. For more on the strike, see Cris Celaya to Vierhus, April 28 and April 30, 1937, General Archives, box 131, SL; Pizarro Suárez to Cedillo, May 12, 1937, file 99, folder Colonización, SL; Buelna,

Presidente de Comité Pro-Justicia to Cárdenas, May 2, 1937, and Ramos, Presidente de la Unión de Soldados Veteranos de la Revolución to Cárdenas, May 7, 1937, Cárdenas Papers, 404.1/4227, AGN; Pérez y Ramírez, "La huelga de los sentados," in *La Voz de la Frontera,* January 1977.

87. Cárdenas to Taboada, April 30, 1937; Loroña memo to Haskell, November 29, 1938, General Archives, unnumbered box, box U, General File, CRLC, SL; Cárdenas to Buelna and Lucero, representatives of the colonists, April 27, 1937, Cárdenas Papers, 404.1/4227, AGN.

88. *Diario Oficial,* March 16, 1937; Bowman to Hull, May 14, 1937, and Bowman to Aram and Wretman, May 29, 1937, RG 84, Mexicali, file 350, NAW; Vázquez, *The Agrarian Reform in Lower California,* 7–9; Sánchez Ramírez, *Crónica agrícola del Valle de Mexicali,* 121–25.

89. Cárdenas to Taboada, August 12, 1938; Taboada to Cárdenas, August 22, 1938, Cárdenas Papers, 404.1/4227, AGN.

90. Mexicali Consul, Horatio Mooers to Hull, September 12, 1938, RG 84, Mexicali, file 350, NAW; Loroña memo to Haskell, November 29, 1938, General Archives, unnumbered box, General File, CRLC, SL; Bowman to Hull, April 2, 1937, with attachment, March 27, 1937, RG 84, Mexicali, file 350, NAW. For CRLC's official objections filed with the Agrarian Department, see Vierhus to Mixed Agrarian Commission, March 13, 1937, Alamo Mocho, Mexicali, BCA, 23/7849; Tierra y Patria, Mexicali, BCA, 23/23066; Cucapah, Mexicali, BCA, 23/11149; Lázaro Cárdenas, Mexicali, BCA, 23/10851, ASRA; Vierhus to Mixed Agrarian Commission, April 6, 1937, José María Morelos, Mexicali, BCA, 23/7849, ASRA; Bowman to Hull, March 9, 1937, RG 84, Mexicali, file 350, NAW.

91. Vierhus to Secretary of Agriculture, April 3, 1937, General Archives, unnumbered box, box U, CRLC, SL.

92. Haskell to Chandler, April 12, 1937, box 3A, Harry Chandler, SL.

93. Colorado River Land Company to Hull, April 15, 1937, General File, CRLC; Haskell to Pike Brant, April 26, 1937, box 3A, Harry Chandler, SL.

94. State Department, "Requesting Investigation of the Legal Aspects of the Expropriation of Lands of the Colorado River Land Company," n.d., Cárdenas Papers, 705.2/26, AGN.

95. Haskell to Pike, April 26, 1937; Haskell to Chandler, April 28, 1937, box 3A, Harry Chandler, SL.

96. Chandler to Rodríguez, April 22 and May 8, 1937, General Archives, unnumbered box, SL; Kerig, "Yankee Enclave," 125 n. 74, 169, 210–11; Medina Robles, "The Colorado River and the All-American Canal" 119.

97. Rodríguez to Chandler, April 26, 1937, General Archives, unnumbered box, SL.

98. Vierhus, memo, n.d., General Archives, unnumbered box, box U, General File, CRLC, SL.

99. Rodríguez and Vierhus messages regarding Cárdenas's reply, May 1, 1937, unsigned [Vierhus] narrative of events between 1935 and 1938, n.d.; Chandler to Cárdenas, December 13, 1938, General Archives, unnumbered box, SL.

100. Translation of Agrarian Code, file 382, Memos to ADH, SL; Bowman to Hull, March 26, 1937, RG 84, Mexicali, file 350, NAW.

101. Vera Estañol to Vierhus, November 1, 1937, Vierhus to Haskell and Vierhus to Risheberger, November 7, 1937, General Archives, General File, unnumbered box, box U, CRLC, SL.

102. Vierhus to Castillo Nájera, November 2, 1937, Castillo Nájera to Vierhus, November 4, 1937, Castillo Nájera to Haskell, November 30, 1937, Risheberger telegram to Haskell, January 23, 1938, Loroña memo to Haskell, November 29, 1938, Vierhus memo summarizing developments to then, n.d., General Archives, unnumbered box, box U, General File, CRLC, SL; Bowman to Hull, November 13 and December 16, 1937, RG 84, Mexicali, file 350, NAW.

103. Vázquez, *The Agrarian Reform in Lower California*, 7.

104. Haskell to Risheberger, November 18, 1938, file 382, Mexican Claims, General File, SL.

105. Daniels to Hull, March 9, 1938, RG 84, Mexicali, file 852, Confidential Records; U.S. Vice Consul Myers to Anderson, October 6, 1941, RG 84, Mexicali, file 350, NAW.

106. Daniels to Hull, March 9, 1938; Mooers to Hull, September 22, 1938, RG 84, Mexicali, file 852, Confidential Records, NAW. Chandler blamed Daniels for many of CRLC's postinvasion difficulties and said that had the U.S. ambassador been "a real he man," rather than "that old foo-foo Daniels," CRLC would not have had the problems it did. See Chandler to Haskell, March 14, 1938, and December 17, 1938, box 3A, File Harry Chandler, SL.

107. Parrés to Pizarro Suárez, June 2, 1937, 852/671.24/3613, box 377, AHEBC; Taboada, certificate, n.d., and report appraising CRLC's land and the ejidos established from it, 852/671.24/3613, box 377, AHEBC; Chandler to American Consul, Baja California, February 25, 1939, RG 84, Mexicali, file 350, NAW; Langston Secretary, American Mexican Claims Commission to Chandler, June 22, 1943, U.S. Section, Agrarian Claims Commission, Appraisal of Claim 54, docket 72, RG 76, Approved Agrarian Claims Case File, 1938–47, NAW; Department of State, *American Mexican Claims Commission*, 108, 481–82.

3. ECONOMIC, SOCIAL, AND CULTURAL FORCES

1. Representative of the Campesinos of Michoacán in Mexicali, Jesús Juárez Coria to Cárdenas, March 22, 1937, Secretary General of the Confederation of Unions and Worker Syndicates of the Northern Territory of Baja California, Higuera to Cárdenas, June 5, 1937, Cárdenas Papers, 437.1/413, AGN; President of the League of Agrarian Communities of the Northern Territory of Baja California, Santos Lara to Cárdenas, June 6, 1937, Cárdenas Papers, 503.11/212; for numerous letters and telegrams to Cárdenas applauding the redistribution of land in the Mexicali Valley, see Cárdenas Papers, 404.1/4227, AGN.

2. For a copy of the photograph of the ceremony, see Pérez y Ramírez, "Un gran proyecto de colonización," *La Voz de la Frontera*, January 1977, 2.

3. Hernández Chávez, *La mecánica cardenista*, 176–78; Kerig, "Yankee Enclave," 359–60.

4. Lázaro Cárdenas, *Obras I*, 240–41; Boyer, *Becoming Campesinos*, 188–222; Knight, "Populism and Neo-Populism in Latin America," 223–48.

5. Lázaro Cárdenas, *Obras I*, 241, 280, 286, 312; on his campaign tour, see 226–89; Escobar Toledo, "La ruptura cardenista," 19–27, and "El cardenismo más allá del reparto," 427–55; Escárcega López, "El principio de la reforma agraria," 76–79.

6. Hamilton, *The Limits of State Autonomy*, 238.

7. According to Cárdenas's son, Cuauhtémoc Cárdenas, the primary goal of his father's presidency was to implement the Plan Sexenal and uphold the 1917 Constitution. In addition, his father's "radical" socioeconomic policies did not stem from the president's personal background or upbringing but were informed by his participation in the revolution and his nationwide campaign tour in 1934. Interview with author, March 1, 1996, Mexico City.

8. Lázaro Cárdenas, *Obras I*, 311–12; Departamento Agrario, Estadística de firma del presidente de la Republica, December 1934–December 1935, Cárdenas Papers, 565.4/80, AGN.

9. Fallaw, *Cárdenas Compromised*, 133.

10. Larroa Torres, "Cárdenas y la doble vía del desarrollo agrario," 283–86.

11. Cárdenas's speech of October 6, 1936, to the new ejidatarios in the Laguna is cited in Hamilton, *The Limits of State Autonomy*, 165. Agricultural production in Mexico was modernized through agricultural credit and federal support of irrigation, sanitation, potable water, electric plants, sugar mills, forest reserves, livestock breeding, rural schools, technical institutions, scientific agricultural stations, producers' associations, rural cooperative societies, commodity price regulating committees, and agricultural fairs. Cárdenas's speech to State Legislature of Guerrero, February 20, 1940, Daniels Papers, box 653, LC; Hewitt de Alcantara, *Modernizing Mexican Agriculture*; Cotter, "The Origins of the Green Revolution in Mexico," 224–47.

12. *New York Herald Tribune*, March 6, 1938.

13. Ochoa, *Feeding Mexico*, 39–70.

14. Susan Walsh Sanderson, *Land Reform in Mexico*, 56–57; Knight, "The Political Economy of Revolutionary Mexico," 306; Gutelman, *Capitalismo y reforma agraria en México*, 101–11; Craig, *The First Agraristas*, 127. For commercial reasons, Mexican officials sought to increase yields of cotton, henequen, sugarcane, coffee, wheat, alfalfa, rice, barley, potatoes, chickpeas, corn, tomatoes, limes, pineapple, melon, bananas, maguey, vanilla, and grapes. See American Vice Consul Kent Leavitt, Report: Mexico—Economic and Financial, May 2, 1936, RG 59, 812.51/2152, NAW; Secretary of Agriculture, Report on the Work Carried out by the Secretary of Agriculture in agreement with the Six Year Plan 1934–39, November 1939, Cárdenas Papers, 704.1/13, AGN.

15. "La independencia económica en México en materia agraria se conseguirá" and Cárdenas to Cliserio Villafuerte, February 1936 and November 6, 1936, all in Cár-

denas Papers, 565.4/80, AGN; General Adrián Castrejón and Engineer Gumaro García de la Cadena, Report, July 1936, Cárdenas Papers, 404/1, AGN; Susan Walsh Sanderson, *Land Reform in Mexico*, 109–15. Following the establishment of the Banco Nacional de Crédito Ejidal in 1935, 289 million pesos were lent to nearly 250,000 ejidatarios during Cárdenas's presidency. See Knight, "The Political Economy of Revolutionary Mexico," 305; Ochoa, *Feeding Mexico*, 41–42.

16. De la Peña, "Rural Mobilizations in Latin America since *c.* 1920," 320–21.

17. Haskill to American Embassy, March 11, 1938, RG 84, Torreón, Coahuila, Consulate, file 350 and 852, NAW; Hernández Chávez, *La mecánica cardenista*, 176; Escárcega López, "El principio de la reforma agraria," 223–27.

18. Fallaw, *Cárdenas Compromised*, 81–84; Bantjes, *As If Jesus Walked on Earth*, 123–49; Restrepo and Eckstein, *La agricultura colectiva de la Laguna*, 38–54; Hernández Chávez, *La mecánica cardenista*, 176–78.

19. Escárcega López, "El principio de la reforma agraria," 85–120; Knight, "Mexico *c.* 1930–1946," 20; Gonzales, *The Mexican Revolution*, 236–39; Meyer, Sherman, and Deeds, *The Course of Mexican History*, 527–30.

20. Knight, "The Political Economy of Revolutionary Mexico," 306; Cárdenas established the Banco Nacional de Comercio Exterior to promote agricultural exports. See Hamilton, *The Limits of State Autonomy*, 199.

21. Guillermo Rodríguez, Study in conjunction with the Office of Economic Agricultural Geography, Secretary of Agriculture, July 18, 1938, Cárdenas Papers, 437.1/556, AGN; Craig, *The First Agraristas*, 123–24.

22. Fallaw, "Cárdenas and the Caste War That Wasn't," 569; Craig, *The First Agraristas*, 124.

23. Lázaro Cárdenas, *Obras I*, 325–26; Knight, "Mexico *c.* 1930–46," 7.

24. Federal Territories Commission for Development, "Cincuenta pensamientos," November 11, 1936, Cárdenas Papers, 437.1/413, AGN; Ward, *Border Oasis*, 4.

25. Lázaro Cárdenas, *Obras I*, 348, 350; Newcomer, *Reconciling Modernity*, 8. Moreno, *Yankee Don't Go Home!* 229; Gonzales, *The Mexican Revolution*, 237–38.

26. Lázaro Cárdenas, *Obras I*, 293, 301; Meyer, Sherman, and Deeds, *The Course of Mexican History*, 529.

27. Federal Territories Development Commission, "Cincuenta pensamientos."

28. Bortz, "The Genesis of the Mexican Labor Relations System," 53–57; Haber, *Industry and Underdevelopment*, 180–86.

29. Lázaro Cárdenas, *Obras I*, 293.

30. Cárdenas to Taboada, August 17, 1937, Cárdenas Papers, 404.1/4227, AGN; Moors to Hull, September 12, 1938, RG 84, Mexicali, file 350, NAW; Lázaro Cárdenas, *Obras I*, 362; Gabino Vázquez, *The Agrarian Reform in Lower California*, 10.

31. Lázaro Cárdenas, *Obras I*, 312; *Sol de Mayo*, May 1939, 7.

32. Henson, "United States Business Interests in the Structure of State-Society Relations in Mexico," 483.

33. Acres planted in cotton and bales produced decreased in the Mexicali Valley in the late 1930s but recovered fully by 1941 and reached record levels in the early 1940s. After wwii, cotton acreage and yields decreased some, but still outpaced pre-expropriation levels. See Kerig, "Yankee Enclave," 481.

34. Gabino Vázquez, *The Agrarian Reform in Lower California*, 12; Medina Robles, "The Colorado River and the All-American Canal," 116; Arizona state legislator Hugo Farmer is cited in Ward, *Border Oasis*, 23.

35. Cárdenas's government undertook an extensive road-building program. In 1930, there were only 1,426 kilometers of roads in Mexico, but by 1940 there were 9,929 kilometers. See Haber, *Industry and Underdevelopment*, 176; Waters, "Remapping Identities," 226, 228, 239.

36. In 1930, Baja California Norte held only 0.3 percent of the national population. By 1960, 1.5 percent of Mexico's population lived in the state. See Ward, *Border Oasis*, 15, 36–38; Lorey, ed., *United States–Mexico Border Statistics*, 7, 9, 431, 432.

37. José Ángel Cisneros, memos, July 8 and 22, 1935, and Ing. Lorenzo Hernández to Jaime Torres Bodet, Sintesis cronológica de problema de las aguas de los ríos internacionales entre los Estado Unidos y México, October 2, 1937, file III-358–13, ahsre; Kerig, "Yankee Enclave," 349; Ward, *Border Oasis*, 17, 24.

38. Cárdenas to Navarro Cortina, January 20, 1937, Cárdenas Papers, 437.1/413, agn; Ward, *Border Oasis*, 25.

39. Secretaría de Relaciones Exteriores, *El Tratado de Aguas Internacionales, Celebrado entre México y los Estados Unidos el 3 de Febrero de 1944;* Ward, *Border Oasis*, 31–37.

40. More-modern and efficient agricultural production can be seen in the fact that output increased from 51,313 bales in 1950 to 84,226 bales in 1960, despite the fact that the amount of acres planted to cotton in Baja California decreased from 309,000 acres to 285,000 over the same period. See Ward, *Border Oasis*, 36–38; Lorey, *United States–Mexico Border Statistics*, 119, 120, 124, 125, 253, 325, 404, 405.

41. Mexicali Interviews, 2001; Ward, *Border Oasis*, 36–38; Lorey, *United States–Mexico Border Statistics*, 67, 74, 90.

42. Gabino Vázquez, *The Agrarian Reform in Lower California*, 11.

43. Lázaro Cárdenas, *Obras I*, 275–77, 308, 311–12, 334; Haber, *Industry and Underdevelopment*, 172.

44. Cotter, *Troubled Harvest*, 90–101.

45. Tannenbaum, "How Cárdenas Governs in Mexico," clipping from unknown newspaper, General File, crlc, 1937, sl.

46. Lázaro Cárdenas, *Obras I*, 256, 283, 297, 311–12, 328, and 366; Lerner, *La educación socialista;* Vaughan, *Cultural Politics in Revolution*, 67–71, 169, 175–84; Bliss, *Compromised Positions*, 186–212; Vanderwood, *Juan Soldado*, 159.

47. Lázaro Cárdenas, *Obras I*, 256, 283, 297, 311–12, 328, and 366; Benjamin, *La Revolución*, 110–14; Lorey, "Postrevolutionary Contexts for Independence Day," 233–45; Fallaw, *Cárdenas Compromised*, 41–42, 90–96; Boyer, *Becoming Campesinos*, 205–11.

48. Guerrero to Ortiz Rubio, August 1930, Jiménez to Ortiz Rubio, September 3, 1930, file 257 (1930): 10089, Ortiz Rubio Papers, AGN. For a sense of the overwhelming number of bars, cantinas, casinos, horse tracks, opium users, and prostitutes in border towns such as Tijuana and Mexicali in the 1920s, see Gómez Estrada, *Realidad y ensueños,* 43–80, and *Gobierno y casinos,* 12–26; Schantz, "All Night at the Owl," 91, 96; Schantz, "From the Mexicali Rose to the Tijuana Brass," 481; Vanderwood, *Juan Soldado,* 159–63.

49. According to Fallaw, the Federal Labor Code of 1931 prohibited cantinas from operating near places of employment. See Fallaw, *Cárdenas Compromised,* 92. Cárdenas, *Obras I,* 293, 311–12; *Sol de Mayo,* 3, 33; Schantz, "All Night at the Owl," 125–26; Schantz, "From the Mexicali Rose to the Tijuana Brass," 485–86; Vanderwood, *Juan Soldado,* 159–62.

50. Gabino Vázquez, *The Agrarian Reform in Lower California,* 12.

51. *Sol de Mayo,* May 1939, 3, 33; Gabino Vázquez, *The Agrarian Reform in Lower California,* 11–12.

52. Secretary of Agriculture, Report on the Work Carried out by the Secretary of Agriculture in Agreement with the Six-Year Plan 1934–39, November 1939, Cárdenas Papers, 704.1/13, AGN; Lorey, *United States–Mexico Border Statistics,* 89, 90.

53. Knight, "Racism, Revolution, and 'Indigenismo,'" 95, 102 n. 1; John Mason Hart, *Empire and Revolution,* 238, 253.

54. Hewitt de Alcántara, *Anthropological Perspectives on Rural Mexico,* 10–13, 27–29.

55. Stern, "From Mestizophilia to Biotypology," 190–92.

56. Knight, "Racism, Revolution, and 'Indigenismo,'" 84–86, 98; Stern, "From Mestizophilia to Biotypology," 190–91.

57. Gilberto Loyo, "Los problemas de la población en México," *Eugenesia* 7, no. 78, quoted in Stern, "From Mestizophilia to Biotypology," 194–95.

58. Based on national averages that exclude Baja California Norte, in 1930 there was approximately one Chinese resident in Mexico for every one thousand Mexicans. In northern Baja California there were approximately sixty Chinese residents for every one thousand Mexicans. These ratios grew further apart when thousands of Chinese were deported from Sonora and entered Baja California Norte in the early 1930s. See Cardiel Marín, "La migración china en el Norte de Baja California, 203, 211, 234.

59. Abelardo Rodríguez, *Autobiografía,* 127–30; Gabino Vázquez, *The Agrarian Reform in Lower California,* 4.

60. Cárdenas is quoted in Henson, "United States Business Interests in Mexico," 64–65; Gabino Vázquez, *The Agrarian Reform in Lower California,* 3–4.

61. Knight, "Populism and Neo-Populism in Latin America," 230.

62. For a copy of the April 1936 CRLC colonization agreement, see RG 84, Mexicali Consulate, General Records, file 852, NAW; for a sample of the individual colonization contract, see 852/671.24/3613, AHEBC; *Diario Oficial,* March 16, 1937; Bowman to Hull, May 14, 1937, and Bowman to Aram and Wretman, May 29, 1937, RG 84, Mexicali, file 350, NAW.

63. For the extensive amount of material on anti-Chinese sentiment outside of Baja California Norte, see Comité Directivo del Anti-Chinismo Nacional to Calles, April 16, 1924, February 4, 1925, October 31, 1925, and August 9, 1927, Obregón and Calles Papers, folders 104-CH-1, legs.1, 2, and 3, AGN; Werne, "Vice Revenue and the Growth of Government in Baja California Norte," 11–12; José María Dávila, quoted in José Ángel Espinoza, *El problema chino en México* (Mexico City: Porrúa, 1931), 16–17, cited in Rénique, "Race, Region, and Nation," 223; Kerig, "Yankee Enclave," 157–60.

64. Knight, "Racism, Revolution, and 'Indigenismo,'" 96; Rénique, "Race, Region, and Nation," 214, 223, 228.

65. *New York Times*, August 31, 1931, September 3, 1931, August 6, 1932, March 1, 1933, and August 7, 1933; Rénique, "Race, Region, and Nation," 220. For complaints by the Chinese legation about the treatment of Chinese nationals, see DGG, file 2.367(30)6, box 5, AGN.

66. Cardiel Marín, "La migración china," 241–49; Rénique, "Race, Region, and Nation," 230; Knight, "Racism, Revolution, and 'Indigenismo,'" 96–97.

67. *New York Times*, March 1, 1933.

68. Secretary General of the Workers Union of Agua Caliente, Juan González, to Rodríguez, March 30, 1934, Olachea to Secretary of the Interior, June 22, 1934, Department of Labor Official Haro to Secretary of the Interior, May 29, 1934, DGG, file 2.331.8 (30) 33, box 53A, AGN.

69. Secretary General of the Union of Employees and Workers of Various 'Progressive' Offices, Carrillo to Rodríguez, April 7, 1934, Secretary General of the Dockworkers Union, Davíd Miranda to Rodríguez, April 11, 1934, Secretary General of the Felipe Carrillo Puerto Union, Guillermo Alva to Rodríguez, April 23, 1934, Rodríguez Papers, file 519/1, AGN; Secretary General of the Agua Caliente Workers Union, Juan González, to Rodríguez, March 30, 1934, Agustín Haro to Secretary of the Interior, May 29, 1934, DGG, file 2.331.8 (30) 33, box 53A, AGN; translation of declaration of the Bar and Restaurant Employees Union of Mexicali, n.d., General File, CRLC, 1937, SL.

70. Interview with Pedro Pérez, Mexicali Interviews, 2001.

71. Translation of declaration of the Bar and Restaurant Employees Union of Mexicali, n.d., General File, CRLC, 1937, SL.

72. Rénique, "Race, Region, and Nation," 216; Pedro Pérez, Mexicali Interviews, 2001.

73. Cardiel Marín, "La migración china," 222, 225, 247.

74. Knight, "Racism, Revolution, and 'Indigenismo,'" 96–97.

75. Bowman to Hull, April 2, 8, and 23, 1937, RG 84, Mexicali, file 350, NAW; Ishibáyama, Asociación Japonesa to Cárdenas, April 3, 1937, and Foreign Minister Eduardo Hay to president's secretary, September 23, 1937, Cárdenas Papers, 404.1/4227, AGN; Otokichi Nakamura to Cárdenas, April 6, 1937, Cárdenas Papers, 705.2/26, AGN.

76. Knight, "Racism, Revolution, and 'Indigenismo,'" 96–97.

77. Camposortega Cruz, "Análisis demográfico de las corrientes migratorias a México," 36.

78. Niblo, *Mexico in the 1940s*, 119.

79. Cardiel Marín, "La migración china," 213–14.

80. Between 1937 and 1944, 5,353 ejidatarios and over 1,500 colonists benefited from the division of CRLC's lands. See Anguiano Téllez, *Agricultura y migración en el Valle de Mexicali*, 99–100; Mexicali Interviews, 2001.

81. Loroña to Haskell, December 14, 1943, General File, CRLC, SL; John Ketcham, American Consul at Mexicali, Memo: Sale of Colorado River Land Company to Mexican Government Interests, May 23, 1945, RG 84, Mexicali, file 852, NAW; and Kerig, "Yankee Enclave," 393–96.

82. Guillermo Caballero Sosa, radio bulletin, May 12, 1945, 852/671.24/3613, AHEBC.

83. Kerig, "Yankee Enclave," 1–2.

4. DOMESTIC POLITICS AND EXPROPRIATION

1. *New York Times*, May 4, 1929; Guadarrama, Martínez, and Martínez, "Las alianzas políticas," 38–47.

2. José Lamas to Colonel Manuel Medina Chávez, October 14, 1935, Manuel Duarte to Ramos, October 16, 1935, municipal president to Lindorfe García, October 22, 1935, Ramos to Ures municipal president, October 30, 1935, Ramos to Ramón Armenta, December 6, 1935, 231.14"35"/1 a 111, AAGES; Bantjes, "Politics, Class and Culture," 105–8, 113; Moncada, *La sucesión política en Sonora*, 45–50.

3. The Cristiada was a three-year conservative counterrevolutionary uprising in parts of rural Mexico during the mid- to late 1920s that stemmed in large measure from the federal government's anticlerical policies and land reform programs. Bantjes, *As If Jesus Walked on Earth*, 43–52.

4. De la Peña, "Rural Mobilizations in Latin America Since c. 1920," 320.

5. Portes Gil, *Quince años de política mexicana*, 495–511; Medin, *El minimato presidencial*, 148–61; Hernández Chávez, *La mecánica cardenista*, 45, 91; Hamilton, *The Limits of State Autonomy*, 124–28; Sanderson, *Agrarian Populism and the Mexican State*, 99–101.

6. Daniels to Hull, June 18, 1935, Roosevelt Papers, PPF, 86, Daniels, FDRL; Bantjes, *As If Jesus Walked on Earth*, 64; Hernández Chávez, *La mecánica Cardenista*, 54–60.

7. Some of the Callista threats may have come from individual actors denouncing their adversaries as Callistas in order to sideline them and advance their own position. For these and other examples of the Callista threat toward Cárdenas's government, see Cárdenas Papers, 559/23, AGN.

8. Cárdenas's removal of the Sonoran governor was not unique. After expelling Calles from Mexico, Cárdenas deposed five other Callista state governors in December 1935, charging each with sedition. See Ramón Miranda to Gutiérrez, April 15, 1936, 231.14"35"/1 a 111, AAGES; Bantjes, *As If Jesus Walked on Earth*, 52–55; Bantjes, "Politics, Class and Culture," 172–78, 575; Vaughan, *Cultural Politics in Revolution*, 63; Sanderson, *Agrarian Populism and the Mexican State*, 101–2.

9. Secretaría de Acción Agraria Arturo Flores López to Sonoran secretary of the interior, July 16, 1936, Francisco Salazar, Substitute Governor to federal secretary of the interior, September 14, 1936, Ramón Medina Guzmán, jefe de gobernacíon, to secretary of the Sindicato de Campesinos de Quechehueca, September 26, 1936, DGG, 2.382(22)19646, AGN.

10. The fact that Gutiérrez owned a large ranch in the Yaqui Valley may have reinforced the image of his running the territory like a hacendado. See Vaughan, *Cultural Politics in Revolution*, 150.

11. 233.6"38"/1 and 414.6"39"/2, AAGES; Moncada, *La sucesión polítca en Sonora*, 51–62; Bantjes, "Politics, Class and Culture," 179, 189, 217–18; Sanderson, *Agrarian Populism and the Mexican State*, 110–12.

12. Bantjes, *As If Jesus Walked on Earth*, 62. Against Cárdenas's wishes and in return for vast sums of money, General Otero Pablos helped to unseat Yucatecan governor Fernando López Cárdenas in 1936 and replace him with Florencio Palomo Valencia. The latter official was considered a "radical agrarista" who headed the Agrarian Department's Yucatecan delegation and had the support of Francisco Múgica. For more on Otero Pablos's questionable activities in Yucatán, see Fallaw, *Cárdenas Compromised*, 43, 70, 73–76.

13. Cedillo attended Yocupicio's inauguration on January 4, 1937, in Hermosillo. Yocupicio also had close ties to a number of pseudofascist organizations, such as Acción Mexicanista, the successor of the outlawed Gold Shirts, and the Unión de Veteranos de la Revolución. See Moncada, *La sucesión política en Sonora*, 51–62; Bantjes, "Politics, Class, and Culture," 179, 189, 217–18; Sanderson, *Agrarian Populism and the Mexican State*, 110–12; Yepis to Hull, October 13, 1936, RG 84, Guaymas, file 350, box 3, NAW; Yepis to Hull, January 9, 1937, RG 84, Guaymas, General Records, file 350, box 12, NAW.

14. Bantjes, *As If Jesus Walked on Earth*, 69–73; Sanderson, *Agrarian Populism and the Mexican State*, 111.

15. Yepis to Hull, December 12, 1936, RG 84, Guaymas, General Records, file 350, box 3; Yepis to Hull, January 26, 1937, RG 84, Guaymas, General Records, box 12, NAW.

16. Yocupicio also opposed Cárdenas's pro-labor policy and endorsed reopening the churches in Sonora. Yepis to Hull, September 14, 1937, RG 84, Guaymas, General Records, file 350, box 12, NAW; *Excelsior*, September 13, 1937.

17. Yepis to Hull, June 15, 1938, RG 84, Guaymas, General Records, file 350, NAW. Although a federation, the CTS was similar to a company union and was commonly referred to as a "*sindicato blanco*" (white union) or "*sindicato de paja*" (straw union). See Bantjes, "Politics, Class, and Culture," 351, 356–57, 392–94, and Sanderson, *Agrarian Populism and the Mexican State*, 112–13.

18. Jonathan Brown, "Acting for Themselves," 45–71.

19. Vaughan, *Cultural Politics in Revolution*, 21, 174; Dabdoub, *Historia de el Valle del Yaqui*, 346–47.

20. Interview of Vicente Padilla, in Murrieta and Graf, *Por el milagro de aferrarse,* 112; *Excelsior,* June 24, July 9, September 6, and September 13, 1937; Cárdenas Papers, 534.1/8, AGN, and 411.12"37"/2, AAGES; for the hundreds of complaints filed against Yocupicio by a cross-section of Sonorans, see DGG, 2.384 (22) 23760, box 23, and 2.331.8 (22) 30108, box 38-A, AGN; Sanderson, *Agrarian Populism and the Mexican State,* 112–13.

21. Sanderson, *Agrarian Populism and the Mexican State,* 112.

22. Yepis to Hull, February 16, 1937, RG 84, Guaymas, General Records, file 350, box 12, NAW.

23. U.S. Vice Consul Charles Gidney to U.S. Embassy, February 12, 1937, RG 84, Guaymas, General Records, circular file 350, NAW; *Heraldo del Yaqui,* November 4, 1937.

24. Ayón to Agrarian Department, April 17, 1936, El Yaqui, Cajeme, Sonora, 23/4670, ASRA; Murrieta and Graf, *Por el milagro,* 63; Vaughan, *Cultural Politics in Revolution,* 173.

25. Sanderson, *Agrarian Populism and the Mexican State,* 62–63, 68–69, 80–94; Bantjes, "Politics, Class and Culture," 413.

26. Bantjes, *As If Jesus Walked on Earth,* 91–93; interview of Marcelina Saldívar Cabrales, in Murrieta y Graf, *Por el milagro de aferrarse,* 84–85; Vaughan, *Cultural Politics in Revolution,* 164–65.

27. Within a few years Padilla was the general secretary of the Sindicato Central del Valle. See interview of Vicente Padilla Hernández, in Murrieta and Graf, *Por el milagro de aferrarse,* 108–9, 111.

28. Interview of Padilla and Aurora Ayala de Ayón, in Murrieta and Graf, *Por el milagro de aferrarse,* 65, 111.

29. Interviews of Alfonso Encinas García and Ayala de Ayón, in Murrieta and Graf, *Por el milagro de aferrarse,* 13, 56. Peloso, *Peasants on Plantations,* 6.

30. Boyer, *Becoming Campesinos,* 10–12.

31. Interviews of García and Ayala de Ayón, in Murrieta and Graf, *Por el milagro de aferrarse,* 13, 56; Vaughan, *Cultural Politics in Revolution,* 165–66.

32. Yepis to Hull, December 15, 1936, enclosure 2, RG 84, Guaymas, file 350, NAW; Lawson to Hull, August 29, 1939, July 1, 1940, RG 76, Lawson Correspondence, vol. 1–3, entry 203, NAW.

33. Some settlements in the Yaqui Valley, such as Ayón's, did not require assistance from teachers. A commonality of interests between elite and subordinate actors in both the agricultural and industrial sectors can be seen in Joseph, *Revolution from Without;* Jonathan Brown, "Acting for Themselves," 45–71; Ochoa, *Feeding Mexico;* and Olcott, *Revolutionary Women in Postrevolutionary Mexico.*

34. Bantjes, *As If Jesus Walked on Earth,* 107; Vaughan, *Cultural Politics in Revolution,* 167–69; Henderson, *The Worm in the Wheat,* 223.

35. Knight, "Land and Society in Revolutionary Mexico," 97.

36. Bantjes, "Politics, Class, and Culture," 310, 412–13.

37. W. E. Richardson to Yepis, October 12, 1936, RG 84, Guaymas, General Records, file 350, box 3, NAW.

38. Interviews of Viviano Alatorre Valenzuela and Francisco Schwarsbeck Ramírez, in Murrieta and Graf, *Por el milagro de aferrarse,* 78, 223; Richardson to Yepis, October 12, 1936, RG 84, Guaymas, General Records, file 350, box 3, NAW; Yepis to Hull, February 16, 1937, RG 84, Guaymas, General Records, file 350, box 12, NAW.

39. Ayón to Rafael Castro, Oficial Mayor of the Department of Indian Affairs, July 2, 1936, Ayón to secretary of the interior, August 8 and 10, October 9, 1936, Subsecretary of the Interior Agustín Arroyo to Secretary of Agriculture Saturnino Cedillo, September 22, 1936, Arroyo to Secretary of Foreign Affairs Eduardo Hay, September 22, 1936, DGG, 2.365(22)19355, AGN; interviews of García and Ayala de Ayón, in Murrieta and Graf, *Por el milagro de aferrarse,* 10, 60, 63, 66, 68.

40. Interview of Ayala de Ayón, in Murrieta and Graf, *Por el milagro de aferrarse,* 56–59. For the 1923 purchase and distribution of CCR's land, see Obregón and Calles Papers, 818-T-133, AGN. For a summary of the history of pueblo El Yaqui's ejidal petitions, see Jefe de Procuradores Graciano Sánchez to procuradores del pueblos, December 7, 1935, Ayón to Agrarian Department, April 17, 1936, El Yaqui, Cajeme, Sonora, 23/4670, ASRA; see also Cárdenas Papers, 404.1/928, AGN.

41. See interviews of Ayala de Ayón and Padilla, in Murrieta and Graf, *Por el milagro de aferrarse,* 58–61, 110–11.

42. Ayón to Ortiz Rubio, June 30, 1931, Ortiz Rubio Papers, file 3746-T, AGN; Jefe de Procuradores Graciano Sánchez to procuradores del pueblos, December 7, 1935, Ayón to Agrarian Department, April 17, 1936, El Yaqui, Cajeme, Sonora, 23/4670, ASRA; interview of Ayala de Ayón, in Murrieta and Graf, *Por el milagro de aferrarse,* 58–59, 61.

43. Interviews of Ayala de Ayón and Padilla, in Murrieta and Graf, *Por el milagro de aferrarse,* 59–61, 110–11; Vaughan, *Cultural Politics in Revolution,* 172. Bantjes, "Politics, Class and Culture," 293.

44. The Union of Workers and Peasants represented 201 families and 669 people in pueblo El Yaqui. See Secretary General of the Union de Obreros y Campesinos Manuel Romero to municipal president of Ciudad Obregón, May 21, 1932, 411.12"32"/25, AAGES.

45. Censo General de la Union de Obreros y Campesinos del Pueblo Yaqui, March 20, 1934, Secretary General of the Union Ramón Martínez to Rodolfo Calles, March 20, 1934, Rodolfo Calles to the secretaries of the union, April 18, 1934, 411.12"32"/25, AAGES; Vaughan, *Cultural Politics in Revolution,* 179.

46. For agrarista petitions requesting ejidal land in the Yaqui Valley during the early 1930s, see president of the Comité Particular Ejecutivo Agrario to president of the Local Agrarian Commission, March 14, 1933, 411.12"32"/25, AAGES. Bantjes, "Politics, Class and Culture," 313; Lorenzana Durán, "Política agraria y movimientos campesinos en los Valles del Yaqui y Mayo," 41–59; Guadarrama, Martínez, and Martínez, "La integración institucional," 142.

47. Bantjes, "Politics, Class and Culture," 312, 323; Boyer, *Becoming Campesino*, 14, 24, 28–30; Vaughan, *Cultural Politics in Revolution*, 172.

48. *Diario Oficial*, January 10, 1936; Yepis to Hull, December 15, 1936, Enclosure 2, RG 84, Guaymas, file 350, NAW.

49. Yepis to Hull, November 11, 1936, enclosure no. 7, RG 84, Guaymas, file 350, NAW; Secretary General of the Union de Obreros y Campesinos Jesús Andrade Romero to Cárdenas, November 8, 1935, El Yaqui, Cajeme, Sonora, 23/4670, ASRA.

50. Ayón to Cedillo, May 4, 1936, El Yaqui, Cajeme, Sonora, 23/4670, ASRA; Ayón to Cárdenas, November 20, 1937, Cárdenas Papers, 404.1/928, AGN.

51. Otero, *Farewell to the Peasantry?* 128.

52. El Yaqui, Cajeme, Sonora, 23/4670, ASRA; and Cárdenas Papers, 404.1/928, AGN; interview of Ayala de Ayón, in Murrieta and Graf, *Por el milagro de aferrarse*, 62. As Dawson notes, "The postrevolutionary period was replete with examples of communities that cooperated with officials in return for help in pursuing land and other claims." See Dawson, *Indian and Nation in Revolutionary Mexico*, 114.

53. Despite the shift in educational emphasis, Cárdenas still viewed religious fanaticism as one of the leading causes of ignorance among the rural population. See Lázaro Cárdenas, *Obras I*, 283, 297–98, 334; Vaughan, *Cultural Politics in Revolution*, 67–68, 178; Boyer, *Becoming Campesinos*, 206.

54. Interview of Ayala de Ayón, in Murrieta and Graf, *Por el milagro de aferrarse*, 64–65; Vaughan, *Cultural Politics in Revolution*, 173–74. For more on Sonora's defensas sociales in 1935 and 1936, see 231.14"35"/1 al 111, AAGES. It appears that most landowners did not use white guards, and those who did tended to be Mexican rather than U.S. nationals. Also, from Murrieta and Graf's interviews, it appears that a few landowners were very progressive and even supported the workers' right to unionize. In addition, following the reparto some landowners helped the new ejidatarios, loaning them farming tools, machinery, and money, while instructing them in modern farming techniques. See interviews of Encinas and Padilla, in Murrieta and Graf, *Por el milagro de aferrarse*, 11, 13, 113, 115.

55. Fallaw, "Cárdenas and the Caste War That Wasn't," 570–73; Craig, *The First Agraristas*, 130–31.

56. See memo, January 7, 1937, III-2354–2, AHSRE; Yepis to Hull, November 5, 1937, RG 84, Guaymas, General Records, file 350, box 12, NAW.

57. Stocker to Yepis, December 12, 1937, RG 84, Guaymas, file 350, box 13, NAW; Bantjes, "Politics, Class and Culture," 428.

58. Cárdenas's papers are filled with hundreds of requests for arms. See Cárdenas Papers, 551.1/24 and 404/1, AGN. Cárdenas claims to have armed around two hundred thousand campesinos nationwide, sixty thousand of whom received military training. See Cornelius, "Nation Building, Participation, and Distribution," 458.

59. Carr, "The Mexican Communist Party and Agrarian Mobilization in the Laguna," 395–99; Bantjes, "Politics, Class and Culture," 348–49; Bantjes, *As If Jesus Walked on Earth*, 100–1, 214, 222.

60. *Excelsior,* February 25, 1937, 1; Bantjes, "Politics, Class and Culture," 287–90; Sanderson, *Agrarian Populism and the Mexican State,* 111.

61. Yepis to Hull, March 31, 1937, RG 84, Guaymas, General Records, file 350, box 12, NAW.

62. Lázaro Cárdenas, *Obras I,* 269. On the benefits of worker and campesino unity and mobilization, see also 281 and 286.

63. Bantjes, *As If Jesus Walked on Earth,* 100–1, 214, 222; interview of Padilla, in Murrieta and Graf, *Por el milagro de aferrarse,* 113.

64. Bantjes, "Politics, Class and Culture," 317–19; Vaughan, *Cultural Politics in Revolution,* 69–70; interview of Padilla, in Murrieta and Graf, *Por el milagro de aferrarse,* 113. For more on the conflict between Lombardo Toledano and Yocupicio, see the multiple pieces of correspondence in DGG, 2.384 (22) 23760, AGN; on demonstrations in Sonora, see 231.5"35"/69–119, and 231.5"38"/1–18, AAGES.

65. Lombardo Toledano to Cárdenas, May 18, 1937, Cárdenas Papers, 404.1/202, AGN; Yepis to Hull, July 31, 1937, RG 84, Guaymas, General Records, file 350, box 12, NAW; interviews of Ayala de Ayón and Padilla, in Murrieta and Graf, *Por el milagro de aferrarse,* 65, 112.

66. Interview of Padilla, in Murrieta and Graf, *Por el milagro de aferrarse,* 114, Vaughan, *Cultural Politics in Revolution,* 175.

67. *Excelsior,* October 29, 1937; *Diario Oficial,* October 30, 1937, 9–10; Ayón and Ibarra to Cárdenas, November 20, 1937, Cárdenas Papers, 404.1/928, AGN; Alfonso Meza Gómez, Representative of the Mixed Agrarian Commission for Sonora, October 18, 1937, Cosme Verdura Mier to president of the Mixed Agrarian Commission, November 2, 1937, Chief of the Agrarian Department, Office of Statistics, November 1 and 10, 1937, El Yaqui, Cajeme, Sonora, 23/4670, ASRA; Lázaro Cárdenas, *Obras I,* 375–76; RG 76, Office of the U.S.-Section, Agrarian Claims, Final Appraisals, Annexes to Final Report, 1940–43, entry 206, NAW.

68. Sheridan, "The Yoemem (Yaquis)," 36; Hernández Silva, *Insurgencia y autonomía,* 35–50; Dabdoub, *Historia del Valle del Yaqui,* 14.

69. Griffin-Pierce, *Native Peoples of the Southwest,* 214.

70. Tomás Conant to Obregón, April 30, 1923, file 21, inventory 1037, docket 1, Calles and Torreblanca Archives; FRUS, 1917, 1:1025–27, 1033–35, Spicer, *The Yaquis,* 261; Vaughan, *Cultural Politics in Revolution,* 144.

71. The eight original Yaqui pueblos were Cocorit, Bácum, Torim, Vícam, Potam, Rahum, Huirivis, and Belem. Spicer, *The Yaquis,* 262; Vaughan, *Cultural Politics in Revolution,* 147; John Mason Hart, *Empire and Revolution,* 57.

72. George Wythe to U.S. Embassy, October 23, 1926, U.S. Embassy Collection, folder 9/17, Calles and Torreblanca Archives; *New York Times,* February 7 and 10, 1927; March 28, 1927; Hu-DeHart, "Peasant Rebellion in the Northwest," 167–68; Radding, "Peasant Resistance on the Yaqui Delta," 349; Otero, *Farewell to the Peasantry?* 126–28.

73. Buitimea to Rodolfo Calles, July 20, August 15, 1932, Rodolfo Calles to Ortiz Rubio, September 7, 1932, Jecari to Rodríguez, January 26, April 6, 1933, Ybarra to Rodrí-

guez, September 20, 1934, Rodríguez Papers, 106/2, AGN; Padilla to Rodríguez, March 17, 1933, Rodríguez Papers, 534.1/87, AGN; Conant to Rodríguez, January 15, 1934, Rodríguez Papers, 534.1/260, AGN.

74. Cited in Spicer, *The Yaquis*, 263.

75. Lázaro Cárdenas, *Obras I*, 427–28.

76. Untitled newspaper clipping in Cárdenas Papers, 533.11/1, AGN.

77. Lázaro Cárdenas, *Obras I*, 375–76.

78. Ibid., 296.

79. Ibid., 255–56, 260, 276. For the extreme poverty of the Yaquis, see Moisés, Holden Kelly, and Curry Holden, *A Yaqui Life*, 129–49. Dawson repeatedly shows that many indigenous groups "wanted schools, lands, roads, health programs, and all the implements of modernity, from plows to gasoline lamps and radios." See Dawson, *Indian and Nation in Revolutionary Mexico*, 86, 102, 109–13.

80. Cárdenas is quoted in Dawson, *Indian and Nation in Revolutionary Mexico*, 73, 85; Lázaro Cárdenas, *Obras I*, 256, 260.

81. Lázaro Cárdenas, *Obras I*, 277; Stern, "From Mestizophilia to Biotypology," 191.

82. Dawson, *Indian and Nation in Revolutionary Mexico*, 81, 85, 96–98, 104, 122; Lewis, "The Nation, Education, and the 'Indian Problem' in Mexico," 189–90.

83. Dawson, *Indian and Nation in Revolutionary Mexico*, 81, 85, 104; Lewis, "The Nation, Education, and the 'Indian Problem' in Mexico," 189–90.

84. Vaughan, *Cultural Politics in Revolution*, 151; McGuire, *Politics and Ethnicity on the Río Yaqui*, 68–78. Turner, "The Yaqui Deer Dance at Pascua Pueblo, Arizona," 82–95.

85. González, *Los días del presidente Cárdenas*, 157–63; Vaughan, *Cultural Politics in Revolution*, 150; Sheridan, "The Yoemem (Yaquis)," 35, 53.

86. Yepis to Hull, February 22, 1938, RG 84, Guaymas, General Records, file 350, NAW.

87. Sheridan, "The Yoemem (Yaquis)," 40; Griffin-Pierce, *Native Peoples of the Southwest*, 212.

88. Griffin-Pierce, *Native Peoples of the Southwest*, 213, 217.

89. Lázaro Cárdenas, *Obras I*, 375–76; Spicer, *The Yaquis*, 263; McGuire, *Politics and Ethnicity on the Río Yaqui*, 20–39; *Excelsior*, February 26, 1938.

90. Construction on Angostura Dam began in 1937 and was completed in 1941. *La Gaceta* (Guaymas), February 19, 1938; *El Heraldo de Yaqui* (Ciudad Obregón), February 20, 1938; *Washington Star*, February 20, 1938; *El Universal*, February 20, 1938. For multiple pieces of correspondence on the Yaqui development project from 1938 through 1940, see Cárdenas Papers, 533.11/1, microfilm reel 20, AGN; Lázaro Cárdenas, *Obras I*, 427; Sheridan, "The Yoemem (Yaquis)," 35; Spicer, *The Yaquis*, 263; Dawson, *Indian and Nation in Revolutionary Mexico*, 55.

91. Yepis to U.S. embassy, June 25, 1938, RG 84, Guaymas, file 350-J, NAW.

92. Yepis to Hull, June 26, 1938, RG 84, Guaymas, file 350-J, NAW.

93. Yepis to Hull, June 26, 1938, RG 84, Guaymas, file 350-J, NAW; Bantjes, "Politics, Class and Culture," 393, 460–61.

94. Spicer, *The Yaquis*, 265.

95. Dawson, *Indian and Nation in Revolutionary Mexico,* 55–56; Cassigoli Salamón, "Educación e indigenismo en México," 605–13; Lewis, "The Nation, Education, and the 'Indian Problem' in Mexico," 190.

96. Becker, *Setting the Virgin On Fire,* 162.

97. Spicer, *The Yaquis,* 274.

98. Colonel José Dosal Guzmán to Cárdenas, June 30, 1937, the eight Yaqui governors Mariano Flores, Ignacio Molina, Miguel Buitimea, Marcos Ramírez, Félix Miranda, Juan Aldama, Juan Huiqui, and Juan María Molina to Cárdenas, March 25, 1938, Henríquez Guzmán to Cárdenas, March 25, 1938, Cárdenas Papers, 533.11/1, AGN.

99. Lázaro Cárdenas, *Obras I,* 425–28.

100. Sanderson, *Agrarian Populism and the Mexican State,* 234; Vaughan, *Cultural Politics in Revolution,* 175; Sheridan, "The Yoremem (Mayos)," 41. Although some Mayo Indians received ejidos from the October 1937 reparto, most continued to work as wage laborers on private commercial farms. In December 1939, a small group of Mayo Indians rebelled following rumors that the federal government was going to close local churches and persecute priests. During this brief and unsuccessful Mayo uprising, the Yaqui Indians pledged their support to Cárdenas's administration. See Luis Matuz, general of the Yaqui Tribe, to Cárdenas, January 6, 1940, Presidentes Comisariado Ejidales Ramón Rochin and Juan Alcala to Cárdenas, January 6, 1940, Macías to Cárdenas, January 17, 1940, Cárdenas to Vázquez, November 22, 1940, Cárdenas Papers, 559.3/25, AGN; Sheridan, "The Yoremem (Mayos)," 41. For more on the Mayo's religiosity, see Vanderwood, *The Power of God against the Guns of Government.*

5. THE SONORAN REPARTO

1. Edward Jesson, Affidavit of Claim, and Thomas Everall, Affidavit of Claim, June 1, 1939, RG 76, Records of the U.S. and Mexican Claims Commission, Approved Agrarian Claims, Jesson, claim 91, docket 11, box 5, NAW.

2. Jesson to Yepis, March 29, 1936, Yepis to Hull, April 27, 1936, RG 84, Guaymas, file 350, box 3, NAW; Yepis to U.S. Ambassador to Mexico Josephus Daniels, April 24, 1936, RG 59, 412.11 J494/4, NAW.

3. Yepis to Hull, February 22, 1938, RG 84, Guaymas, General Records, file 350, NAW; Yepis to Hull, February 24, 1938, RG 84, Guaymas, file 350-J, NAW. For more on Jesson's problems, see Palo Parado, Guaymas, Sonora, 23/22270, ASRA, and 411.12"36"/10, AAGES.

4. Jesson to Hull, April 9, 1938, RG 76, Approved Agrarian Claims, Jesson, claim 91, docket 11, box 5, NAW; Jesson to Yepis, March 2, 1938, Yepis to Hull, May 3, 1938, Jesson to U.S. Consul, June 5, 1938, RG 84, Guaymas, file 350, box 23, NAW.

5. Municipal President at Empalme Sonora Miguel Sesma to Jesson, April 28, 1938, Thomas Everall, Affidavit, December 30, 1938, RG 76, Approved Agrarian Claims, Jesson, claim 91, docket 11, NAW.

6. Yepis to Hull, June 6, 1938, RG 84, Guaymas, file 350, box 23, NAW; Sesma to Comisario de Policía, February 22, 1938, Yepis to Hull, March 8, 1938, RG 84, Guaymas, file 350-J, NAW.

7. Jesson complained that the agraristas, besides threatening his life and invading his property, had also stolen his crops, timber, tools, and farming equipment, making it impossible for him to collect rent from his legal tenants or to find new ones. See Jesson to Yepis, March 11, 1938, and May 2, 1938, RG 84, Guaymas, file 350-J, NAW.

8. Yepis to Governor Yocupicio, March 8, 1938, Acting Governor Enrique Fuentes Frías to Yepis, March 25, 1938, Yepis to Hull, March 28, 1938, RG 84, Guaymas, file 350-J, NAW.

9. Welles to Daniels, April 19, 1938, RG 59, 812.5200 Jesson, Edward R./9, NAW; Welles to Daniels, June 14, 1938, de Boal to Foreign Minister Eduardo Hay, June 17, 1938, Daniels to Hay, June 29, 1938, RG 59, 812.5200 Jesson, Edward R./25, NAW; Yepis to Hull, February 24, 1938, RG 84, Guaymas, file 350-J, NAW.

10. U.S. Vice Consul, Charles Gidney to U.S. embassy, February 12, 1937, RG 84, Guaymas, General Records, file 350, NAW.

11. Lázaro Cárdenas, *Obras I*, 422–28.

12. Tanis, Division of Mexican Affairs, State Department, to Assistant Secretary of State Moore, December 30, 1936, Roosevelt Papers, PSF, Diplomatic Correspondence, Mexico, 1936–37, box 43, FDRL.

13. Yepis to Hull, March 19, April 27, June 10, September 21, October 5 and 10, 1936, December 18, 1936, enclosure 3, RG 84, Guaymas, file 350, NAW.

14. Yepis to Hull, September 21, October 5 and 10, 1936, RG 84, Guaymas, file 350, NAW.

15. Yepis to Hull, December 29, 1936, enclosure 3, RG 84, Guaymas, file 350, NAW; Bantjes, *As If Jesus Walked on Earth*, 133.

16. Congressman Anthony Dimond to Hull, May 1 and 11, 1936, RG 59, 412.11 J494/1, and /6, NAW; Senator Hiram Johnson to Hull, May 12, 1936, RG 59, 412.11 J494/7, NAW; Hull to Johnson, May 16, 1936, RG 59, 412.11 J494/15, NAW; Hull to Congressman Richard Welch, May 12, 1936, RG 59, 412.11 J494/10, NAW; Congresswomen Florence Kahn to Hull, May 21, 1936, RG 59, 412.11 J 494/13, NAW; Hull to Kahn, May 27, 1936, RG 59, 412.11 J 494/15, NAW.

17. Yepis to Hull, October 10, 1936, Hull to Yepis, October 14, 1936, RG 84, Guaymas, file 350, NAW.

18. For the October 22, 1936 landowner meeting, see Vice Consul Charles Gidney to Hull, October 26, 1936, RG 84, Guaymas, General Records, file 350, box 3, NAW. Out of Stocker's 4,844 acre estate, 4,589 acres would be expropriated by Cárdenas's government in late 1937. For more on Stocker's losses and compensation claim, see RG 76, Commissioner of the U.S. Section, Agrarian Claims, Final Appraisals, 1940–43, entry 206, NAW.

19. Vice Consul Charles Gidney to Hull, October 26, 1936, RG 84, Guaymas, General Records, file 350, box 3, NAW.

20. The landowners also suggested that Mexico City settle the extensive, idle, and now federally owned property of the former Richardson Construction Company and give each agrarian 25 acres from it. Yepis to Hull, November 12 and 27, 1936, January 7, 1937, Pierre L. de Boal, chargé d' affaires ad interim, January 7, 1937, Yepis memo, n.d., RG 84, Guaymas, General Records, file 350, box 12, NAW.

21. Yepis memo, January 13, 1937, Gidney to U.S. Embassy, February 12, 1937, Yepis to Hull, February 16, 1937, RG 84, Guaymas, General Records, file 350, box 12, NAW; *Heraldo de Yaqui,* February 13, 1937.

22. Yepis to Hull, February 16, 1937, RG 84, Guaymas, General Records, file 350, box 12, NAW.

23. Ibid.

24. Most American landowners, oil companies, and U.S. business interests attacked Cárdenas as a communist. However, leading U.S. officials, including FDR, Daniels, Hull, and Welles believed otherwise. See Daniels to George Creel, March 23, 1936, Daniels Papers, box 647, LC.

25. The proposed compensation lands were expected to be irrigated in 1941 following the completion of the Angostura Dam on the Yaqui River. See *FRUS,* 1937, 5:614–15. For more on the Angostura Dam, see RG 84, Guaymas, General Records, 1937, file 350-T, box 12, 1938, file 350, NAW.

26. Presidente del Comité Ejecutivo Agrario, Jesús M. Villa and residents of Palo Parado to Gutiérrez, February 11, 1936, 411.12"36"/10, AAGES; *Boletín Oficial,* April 8, 1936, 2; Yocupicio, Provisional Resolution, September 26, 1937, Jesús Medina Mayorga, Sonoran Delegate of Agrarian Department to Secretary General of Agrarian Department, December 21, 1937, Luis Alcerreca to Cuerpo Consultivo Agrario, June 26, 1944, Palo Parado, Guaymas, Sonora, 23/22270, ASRA.

27. Stocker to Yepis, March 31, 1938, Welles to Yepis, April 21, 1938, Yepis to Stocker, April 28, 1938, RG 84, Guaymas, General Records, file 350, NAW; Yepis to Hull, June 13, 1938, RG 84, Guaymas, file 350-J, NAW.

28. James Ryan to Stocker, October 28, 1937, Yepis to Hull, November 5, 1937, Daniels to Hull, November 9, 1937, RG 84, Guaymas, General Records, file 350, NAW.

29. Cárdenas to Castillo Nájera, October 29, 1937, III-2353–1, AHSRE.

30. Cárdenas to Castillo Nájera, December 6, 1937, Castillo Nájera to Welles, December 17, 1937, III-2353–1, AHSRE.

31. Welles to Castillo Nájera, November 4, 1937, III-2353–1, AHSRE.

32. *La Gaceta,* February 19, 1938; *Excelsior* and *El Heraldo de Yaqui,* February 20, 1938; Yepis to Hull, February 23 and April 22, 1938, Daniels to Yepis, March 25, 1938, RG 84, Guaymas, General Records, file 350, NAW; Stocker to Yepis, May 2, 1938, Yepis to Hull, May 3, 1938, RG 84, Guaymas, General Records, file 350-J, NAW.

33. Boyle, Basic Report on Agrarianism in the Agua Prieta Consular District, March 9, 1938, RG 84, Nogales Consulate, Confidential Records, box 1, NAW. Although there is no evidence of American landowners taking up arms, they did complain about the

irregularities in the application of the agrarian laws, such as the amount of land they were allowed to retain as small property, additional invasions by agraristas, the illegal occupation of nonagricultural property, including houses, and the illegality of expropriating land under a colonization contract. See the multiple correspondence in RG 84, Guaymas, General Records, file 350, NAW; *El Diario,* November 14, 1938.

34. The $30,368 that Jesson's family received as compensation was based on his claim of $162,486. See RG 76, Office of the Commissioner of the U.S. Section, Agrarian Claims Commission, Final Appraisals, Annexes to Final Report 1940–43, entry 206, NAW; Yepis to Hull, June 30, 1938, RG 84, Guaymas, General Records, file 350, NAW; Department of State, *American Mexican Claims Commission,* 105–6.

35. Yepis to Hull, March 8, 1938, RG 84, Guaymas, file 350, box 26, NAW; See Bantjes, *As If Jesus Walked on Earth,* 134.

36. Saldívar is cited in Vaughan, *Cultural Politics in Revolution,* 184.

37. *Heraldo de Yaqui,* October 23 and 24, 1937, November 3, 1937; *El Boletín Oficial,* March 19, 23, 26, and 30, 1938, and April 2, 1938; *Diario Oficial,* July 12, 13, and 14, 1938; Stephen Worster, U.S. vice consul, to Hull, August 1, 1938, RG 84, Guaymas, General Records, file 350, NAW; Steven Sanderson, *Agrarian Populism and the Mexican State,* 233; Griffin-Pierce, *Native Peoples of the Southwest,* 215.

38. Vaughan, *Cultural Politics in Revolution,* 186; Steven Sanderson, *Agrarian Populism and the Mexican State,* 145–47; Ramírez, *Hipótesis sobre la historia económica y demográfica de Sonora en la era contemporánea del capital,* 45–46; Otero, *Farewell to the Peasantry,* 128.

39. McCullough, "Coping with Drought," 4–6.

40. Cardenista and agrarista candidates—whether self-proclaimed or legitimate—failed to win their elections in a number of states between 1937 and 1940. Moncada, *La sucesión política en Sonora,* 63–74; Bantjes, *As If Jesus Walked on Earth,* 148–49, 225.

41. Yepis to Hull, April 30, May 31, and June 20, 1938, RG 84, Guaymas, General Records, file 350, NAW; Lombardo Toledano to Cárdenas, February 18, 1939, DGG, 2.384 (22) 23760, AGN. The final result of the statewide PRM primaries was close. Macías received 35,530 votes, Otero Pablos 33,449, and Bórquez 1,413. In the Yaqui Valley, Otero Pablos tallied 2,705 votes, Macías 1,385 and Bórquez 714. For more on the election results, including widespread fraud, see Bantjes, *As If Jesus Walked on Earth,* 197–202. Otero Pablos did well in regions like the Yaqui Valley because the federal government's "Open-Door Plan" increased voter participation by "automatically registering all members of federally recognized unions and ejidos." For more on the Open-Door Plan and how it failed in Yucatán, see Fallaw, *Cárdenas Compromised,* 97, 107.

42. Steven Sanderson, *Agrarian Populism in Sonora,* 123; Bantjes, *As If Jesus Walked on Earth,* 199.

43. Sherman, *The Mexican Right,* 80–83, 107–14; Fallaw, *Cárdenas Compromised,* 156–57.

44. Yepis to Hull, May 31, 1938, RG 84, Guaymas, General Records, file 350, NAW;

Vaughan, *Cultural Politics in Revolution*, 71; Bantjes, *As If Jesus Walked on Earth*, 192–98.

45. Lombardo Toledano to Secretary of the Interior Ignacio García Téllez, July 20, 1938, DGG, 2.382(22)19646, AGN; Vaughan, *Cultural Politics in Revolution*, 70–71. Bantjes argues that part of Yocupicio's success stemmed from "his immense local popularity," which he gained "not so much [from] his opposition to the policies of the federal government as [to] the opposition of the federal government to him." See Bantjes, *Politics, Class and Culture*, 556–57.

46. Yepis to Hull, October 18, 1938, RG 84, Guaymas, General Records, file 350, NAW; Bantjes, *As If Jesus Walked on Earth*, 200; Boyer, *Becoming Campesinos*, 23; Vaughan, *Cultural Politics in Revolution*, 71; de la Peña, "Rural Mobilization in Latin America since c. 1920," 321; interview of Alfonso Encinas García, in Murrieta and Graf, *Por el milagro de aferrarse*, 12–13.

47. Bantjes, "Politics, Class and Culture," 452–59, 611; Otero, *Farewell to the Peasantry*, 125–48; Boyer, *Becoming Campesinos*, 225, 227, 230.

48. De la Peña, "Rural Mobilization in Latin America since c. 1920," 293, 308.

49. Both quotes cited in Vaughan, *Cultural Politics in Revolution*, 182–183.

50. Knight, "Populism and Neo-Populism in Latin America," 232; Saldívar is cited in Vaughan, *Cultural Politics in Revolution*, 186.

51. Dawson, *Indian and Nation in Revolutionary Mexico*, 117; Vaughan, *Cultural Politics in Revolution*, 158.

6. THE END OF U.S. INTERVENTION IN MEXICO

1. Department of State, *American Mexican Claims Commission*, 47–50, 71–74; summary of reappraisal of claims, June 14, 1941, RG 76, Office of the Commissioner of the U.S. Section, Agrarian Claims Commission, Lawson Correspondence, 1938–43 (hereafter Lawson Correspondence), vols. 1–3, 1942, entry 203, NAW.

2. Commissioner Lawson's Report, annex 2, and Lawson to Hull, June 10, 1940, RG 76, Lawson Correspondence, vols. 1–3, entry 203, NAW.

3. Lawson to Daniels, March 2, 1939, RG 76, Office of the Commissioner, U.S. Section, Agrarian Claims Commission, Correspondence of the Commissioner with the Executive Officer of the United States, Administrative Decisions to Memo Report (hereafter Commissioner's Correspondence with the Executive Officer), entry 204, NAW.

4. Lawson to Welles, March 7, 1939, RG 76, Lawson Correspondence, vols 1–3, entry 203, NAW.

5. Lawson to Bursley, July 17, 1941, RG 76, Lawson Correspondence, vol 1–3, entry 203, NAW.

6. John Mason Hart, *Empire and Revolution*, 2, 372, 373, 382. Niblo shows that in 1946 Americans still owned land along the border and Pacific coast, thereby throwing doubt on Hart's claims. See Niblo, *Mexico in the 1940s*, 135–37.

7. Assistant Secretary of State Robert Walton Moore to Hull, n.d., RG 84, Mexicali, Confidential Records, 1936–39, file 852, NAW.

8. John Mason Hart, *Empire and Revolution,* 407, 541.

9. State Department, *American Mexican Claims Commission,* 71–74, 475–651; Message from the President of the United States to the Senate of the United States, 77th Congress, 1st Session, December 9, 1941, entitled "Mexico—Adjustment and Settlement of Certain Outstanding Claims"; Lawson to Bursley, July 17, 1941, RG 76, Lawson Correspondence, entry 203, vols. 1–3, NAW; *Diario Oficial,* May 30, 1942; Castillo Nájera to Hull, November 19, 1942, RG 59, 412.11(41) Agreements/122, NAW.

10. Lorenzo Meyer, *Mexico and the United States in the Oil Controversy,* 223.

11. For more on the general and agrarian claims settlements, see Department of State, *American Mexican Claims Commission,* 7–74.

12. One reason the American Mexican Claims Commission was established in late 1942 was to enable the ninety-four American landowners who had missed the Agrarian Claims Commission's October 6, 1940, filing deadline to file a compensation claim for their expropriated property. See Department of State, *American Mexican Claims Commission,* 3–8.

13. Niblo, *War, Diplomacy, and Development,* 39. See also John Mason Hart, *Empire and Revolution,* and Henderson, *The Worm in the Wheat.*

14. Josephus Daniels, diary entry, November 14, 1938, Daniels Papers, LC.

15. State Department, memo for the President, March 26, 1937, Roosevelt Papers, PSF, Departmental File, State, box 70, FDRL.

16. Knight, *U.S.-Mexican Relations,* 2.

17. Paz, *Strategy, Security, and Spies,* 10–12.

18. Pike argues that due to the apparent failure of industrial capitalism, during the Depression a strong Jeffersonian influence ran through the Democratic Party and fostered a noninterventionist U.S. foreign policy. See Pike, *FDR's Good Neighbor Policy,* 177–90.

19. Freidel, *Franklin D. Roosevelt,* 85. In his 1933 inaugural address FDR stated "We must recognize the overabundance of population in our industrial centers and, by engaging on a national scale in a redistribution, endeavor to provide a better use of the land for those best fitted for the land." For a copy of the speech, see Hunt, ed., *The Essential Franklin Delano Roosevelt,* 30–35.

20. *Harper's Magazine,* February 1937, vol. 174, 235.

21. Roosevelt to Allred, April 11, 1938, Roosevelt Papers, PSF, Confidential File, State Department, box 8, FDRL.

22. Before entering politics, Daniels was editor of the *Raleigh News and Observer,* one of the most distinguished newspapers in the South. Daniels to Roosevelt, December 1, 1934, Roosevelt Papers, PSF, 43, Mexico 1933–35, FDRL.

23. Duggan, *The Americas,* 130.

24. Tugwell to Roosevelt, August 26, 1937, Roosevelt Papers, PPF, 564, FDRL.

25. Park, *Latin American Underdevelopment*, 142–45, 151–53; Britton, *Revolution and Ideology*, 17, 141–42, 147; Delpar, *The Enormous Vogue of Things Mexican*, ix, 195, 202–3.

26. Roosevelt to Tugwell, August 29, 1937, Roosevelt Papers, PPF, 564, Tugwell, Rexford, FDRL; Pike, *FDR's Good Neighbor Policy*, 179–90; Delpar, *The Enormous Vogue of Things Mexican*, x, 41–46, 198; Hurlburt, *The Mexican Muralists in the United States*, 4–11.

27. Delpar, *The Enormous Vogue of Things Mexican*, 10, 193; Park, *Latin American Underdevelopment*, 140–42; Britton, *Revolution and Ideology*, 171–72.

28. Britton, *Revolution and Ideology*, 140, 172.

29. Daniels to Roosevelt, April 11, 1938, Roosevelt Papers, PSF, Diplomatic Correspondence, Mexico, 1938, box 44, FDRL; Daniels memorandum, April 19, 1938, Daniels Papers, box 656, LC. On one occasion FDR advised Undersecretary of State Edward Stettinius that it was necessary to treat the Argentineans "like children." For Roosevelt's suggestion to Stettinius, see Schoultz, *Beneath the United States*, 320.

30. Roosevelt speech, April 14, 1938, Berle Papers, Diary, box 210, FDRL.

31. Renda, *Taking Haiti*, 89–130; Schoultz, *Beneath the United States*, xv–xvi; Kenworthy, *America/Américas*, 32; Cottam, *Images and Interventions*, 19.

32. López, "Un órgano eficaz para intervenir la economía," 39–52; Espinosa de los Monteros, "La controversia monetaria actual," 131–54.

33. Cárdenas, "Discurso ante el congreso de la unión," 11–15.

34. Daniels memo of conversation with Cárdenas, July 10, 1935, Daniels Papers, box 647, LC.

35. Although both FDR and Cárdenas sought to improve socioeconomic conditions in the countryside, because the United States and Mexico had very different problems with their rural economies, the two administrations usually pursued distinct agricultural policies. Since the mid- to late nineteenth century, the main problem in American agriculture was overproduction and its associated depressed commodity prices. For Mexico the central problem was land concentration, underproduction, and its associated inflated commodity prices. See Olson, ed. *Historical Dictionary of the Great Depression*, 8–12, 162–66, 500–2, 525–27; Ciment, ed., *Encyclopedia of the Great Depression and the New Deal*, 60 and 235; Simonian, *Defending the Land of the Jaguar*, 219.

36. Freidel, *Franklin D. Roosevelt*, 84; O'Brien, *The Revolutionary Mission*, 6, 285–86, 310–11; Finegold and Skocpol, *State and Party in America's New Deal*, 3–30.

37. Collier is cited in Delpar, *The Enormous Vogue of Things Mexican*, 121–24; Ciment, ed., *Encyclopedia of the Great Depression and the New Deal*, 192, 344. Dawson questions the extent to which Gamio was an indigenista. See Dawson, *Indian and Nation in Revolutionary Mexico*, 147–51.

38. Collier is cited in Delpar, *The Enormous Vogue of Things Mexican*, 121–24.

39. According to Cárdenas's son Cuauhtémoc Cárdenas, his father did have a great deal of respect for Roosevelt. Interview with author, March 1, 1996, Mexico City.

40. Duggan speech on Good Neighbor policy, April 2, 1938, Daniels Papers, box 662, LC; Tasca, *The Reciprocal Trade Policy of the United States,* 29–44, 100–21; Gellman, *Good Neighbor Diplomacy,* 24, 40, 47–49, 57–58; Gardner, *Economic Aspects of New Deal Diplomacy,* 52.

41. O'Brien, *The Century of U.S. Capitalism in Latin America,* 97.

42. Hull, "The Path to Recovery," address, April 23, 1934 (Washington: Government Printing Office, 1934); Hull, "International Trade and Domestic Prosperity," address, November 1, 1934 (Washington: Government Printing Office, 1934).

43. Memo of conversation, Tannenbaum and Duggan, December 13, 1937, RG 59, 812.52/2529, NAW; Enrique Cárdenas, "The Great Depression and Industrialization," 226; Sugiyama, "Reluctant Neighbors," 43–44.

44. *El Universal,* June 30, 1939; U.S. Embassy dispatch, July 7, 1939, RG 59, 812.51/2375, NAW; Cotter, *Troubled Harvest,* 94–95; Sugiyama, "Reluctant Neighbors," 83.

45. State Department study, "Economic Effects of the Mexican Agrarian Program," August 10, 1938, RG 84, Mexicali Consulate, General Records, 1938, file 350, box 7, NAW; Cotter, *Troubled Harvest,* 86–105, 129.

46. Cárdenas's quote on foreign investment is cited by Ambassador Castillo Nájera in an address he delivered at the Academy of World Economics, May 21, 1936, file III-327–13, AHSRE; *Washington Times,* May 22, 1936; *Excelsior,* April 16, 1935.

47. Gamio is cited in Niblo, *Mexico in the 1940s,* 34.

48. De Boal to Daniels, December 18, 1936, Daniels Papers, box 649, LC.

49. Halperin, "Mexico Bursts the Old Bonds," *New York Times Magazine,* February 28, 1937.

50. Ibid.; Britton, *Revolution and Ideology,* 161.

51. Haber, *Industry and Underdevelopment,* 189.

52. Welles to Castillo Nájera, November 4, 1937, Castillo Nájera to Welles, December 17, 1937, Cárdenas Papers, 571.3/1, anexo 3 and 5, AGN.

53. State Department, "Economic Effects of the Mexican Agrarian Program," August 10, 1938, RG 84, Mexicali, General Records, 350, NAW.

54. *Nogales Herald,* December 16, 1937; Steward, *Trade and Hemisphere,* 202.

55. Daniels strongly advocated lower tariffs and increased U.S.-Mexican trade. See Daniels speech, November 8, 1940, Welles Papers, box 59, folder 6, FDRL.

56. Castillo Nájera, Report on the American agrarian claims, November 14, 1938, Cárdenas Papers, 571.3/1, AGN.

57. Memo of the National Foreign Trade Council to Hull, August 11, 1938, file III-2353–1 (IV), AHSRE.

58. Alanís Enciso, "Las políticas migratorias de Estados Unidos y los trabajadores mexicanos," 441.

59. Senate Joint Resolution 242, 76th Congress, 3rd Session, April 8, 1940; Enciso, "Las políticas migratorias de Estados Unidos y los trabajadores mexicanos," 436–40, 443.

60. Balderrama and Rodriguez, *Decade of Betrayal,* 121, 216.

61. Roosevelt Papers, POF, 4245g, FDRL; Hoffman, *Unwanted Mexican Americans in the Great Depression,* 18–24; Garcia, "Chicana/o and Latina/o Workers in a Changing Discipline," 89.

62. Garcia, "Chicana/o and Latina/o Workers in a Changing Discipline," 89.

63. Balderrama and Rodriguez, *Decade of Betrayal,* 2, 121; Carreras de Velasco, *Los Mexicanos que devolvió la crisis,* 7–9.

64. Alanís Enciso, "Las políticas migratorias de Estados Unidos y los trabajadores mexicanos," 441; Senate Joint Resolution 242, 76th Congress, 3rd Session, April 8, 1940.

65. Cárdenas's papers are filled with numerous telegrams from Mexican nationals and consulate officials in the United States complaining about racism and the terrible living and working conditions for Mexicans immigrants. See Cárdenas Papers, 575.1/50, AGN.

66. Until 1945 most demographers expected the populations in colonial and postcolonial societies to decline. Cárdenas may have subscribed to this belief since he intensified the drive toward repatriation and sent the repatriados to underpopulated regions of the country. See Cárdenas, *Plan Sexenal;* Cárdenas's form letter regarding repatriation to each Mexican state governor, April 12, 1939, Cárdenas Papers, 503.11/3, AGN; on colonization, see Cárdenas Papers, 549.5/87, AGN; Balderrama and Rodriguez, *Decade of Betrayal,* 144; Nodín Valdés, "Mexican Revolutionary Nationalism and Repatriation during the Great Depression," 1–24.

67. Jesús M. González, "Un estudio sobre la situación económica actual de los trabajadores mexicanos en los Estados Unidos: Sobre el problema de la repatriación y colonización . . ." (hereafter González, "Estudio"), January 18, 1936, Cárdenas Papers, 503.11/3, AGN; Cotter, *Troubled Harvest,* 87, 101

68. González, "Estudio."

69. As early as December 1934, Baja California Governor Agustín Olachea suggested to Cárdenas that the government should settle Mexican repatriates in the Mexicali Valley on the property owned by the Colorado River Land Company. See Olachea to Cárdenas, December 26, 1934, Cárdenas Papers, 564.1/65, AGN.

70. González, "Estudio." Secretaría de Comunicaciones to Cárdenas, n.d., Cárdenas Papers, 503.11/3–1, AGN; Beteta to Leñero to Cárdenas, April 24, 1939, file III-240–8, AHSRE; *Los Angeles Times,* July 20, 1939; *New York Times,* July 26, 1939; Balderrama and Rodriguez, *Decade of Betrayal,* 147–50.

71. Examples of letters and telegrams describing the difficulties faced by Mexicans in the United States and their requests for assistance can be found in the Cárdenas Papers, see 503.11/3, 503.11/212, and 437.1/413, AGN.

72. Lázaro Cárdenas, *Cárdenas Habla,* 182–83.

73. Although Colonia 18 de Marzo seemingly got off to a good start, by 1940—like most other colonies filled with repatriates—it fell on hard times, since federal funding was reduced, infrastructure remained undeveloped, and economic opportunities were

limited. Eduardo Chávez, memo, April 24, 1939, Beteta to Cárdenas, April 27, May 5, August 11, 1939, Cárdenas Papers, 503.11/3–1, AGN. For more on Colonia 18 de Marzo, see Cárdenas Papers, 503.11/3–1; Balderrama and Rodriguez, *Decade of Betrayal*, 158–84.

74. Ladd and Hadley, *Transformations of the American Party System*, 84–86; Balderrama and Rodriguez, *Decade of Betrayal*, 52–61.

75. State Department memo, December 29, 1937, Welles Papers, box 178, folder 10, FDRL. The Yaqui Indians threatened to take up arms should their ancestral homelands not be returned to them. See Yepis to U.S. Embassy, June 25, 1938, RG 84, Guaymas, file 350-J, NAW.

76. Tannenbaum, *Whither Latin America*, chaps. 4, 5, and 7.

77. Daniels to Roosevelt, August 21, 1936, cited in Kilpatrick, *Roosevelt and Daniels*, 165.

78. Tannenbaum to Daniels, July 6, 1938, Roosevelt Papers, PPF, Diplomatic Correspondence, Mexico, box 44, FDRL; Tannenbaum, *Mexico*, 180, 142–43.

79. While in exile, Rodríguez stated that the Mexican Gold Shirts had eight hundred thousand members. This figure appears greatly exaggerated, since most estimates claimed that the organization had only one thousand members. See *New York Times*, July 24, August 15, 1938; *Herald Post*, January 4, 1937.

80. Ankerson, *Agrarian Warlord*, 167, 178; Lorenzo Meyer, *Mexico and the United States in the Oil Controversy*, 175.

81. Some contemporary estimates put Sinarquista membership as high as 1 million, although this figure was excessive. More recently, Jean Meyer claims that there were approximately 310,000 Sinarquistas nationwide in 1940—still a sizeable number. For more on the Sinarquistas, see Jean Meyer, *El Sinarquismo, el Cardenismo y la Iglesia*, 64. The far-right religious groups did not pose a significant threat because of Cárdenas's agreement with the church hierarchy to relax most Callista-era regulations against it in return for its support—which he received after the oil nationalization. Moreover, since the end of the Cristiada, church leaders in Mexico (reflecting papal wishes) were against another violent confrontation with the state. Knight, "The Rise and Fall of Cardenismo," 292; Michaels, "Fascism and Sinarquismo," 234–50.

82. Ankerson, *Agrarian Warlord*, 165–67. Founded in 1939, the PAN would become the most powerful opposition party in Mexico. See Mabry, *Mexico's Acción Nacional*, 8–22.

83. Sherman, *The Mexican Right*, 71–83.

84. Cárdenas's main defense against an insurrection was to keep Mexico's generals in line by rewarding loyal ones and retiring suspect ones. Matesanz, *Las raíces de exilio*, 7–12; Lorenzo Meyer, *Mexico and the United States in the Oil Controversy*, 192.

85. Daniels to Roosevelt, September 30, 1936, Roosevelt Papers, PSF, box 44, Mexico, Daniels, FDRL.

86. Rosenman, ed., *The Public Papers and Addresses of Franklin D. Roosevelt*, 255–56.

87. *New York Enquirer*, August 14, 1938. During this period dozens of American dailies ran jingoistic articles that exaggerated German penetration of Mexico. See Friedman, "There Goes the Neighborhood," 571.

88. Hull cited in Sugiyama, "Reluctant Neighbors," 93.

89. Daniels to Hull, August 7, 1938, Roosevelt Papers, PSF, Diplomatic Correspondence, Mexico, Daniels, box 44, FDRL.

90. *Evening Globe,* May 24, 1938.

91. Sugiyama, "Reluctant Neighbors," 92.

92. Memo, Communist Activities in the American Republics, Berle Papers, Latin American Republics, General, box 60, FDRL.

93. Ibid.; Letter and newspaper clipping from White to Cárdenas, July 13, 1937, Cárdenas Papers, 571.1/6, AGN; Hernández Chávez, *La mecánica cardenista,* 154–64.

94. Confidential Report, June 4, 1938, Daniels Papers, box 662, LC. Although the legitimacy of Toledano's "confidential" letter is questionable, it was probably widely read, since copies were found in two separate depositories.

95. *The Nation,* April 16, 1938.

96. O'Brien, *The Century of U.S. Capitalism in Latin America,* 97.

97. Under the special claims agreement, the Mexican government acknowledged that it was liable for the damages caused by all Mexicans during the revolution, including federal, state, and local governments, the national military, and local police forces, as well as revolutionaries, rebels, bandits, and mobs. FRUS, 1918, 1:792–816; *New York Times,* March 29, 1928, June 19, 1932; State Department, *American Mexican Claims Commission,* 29–32, 71–74.

98. FRUS, 1927, 3:228–29; FRUS, 1928, 3:337–39; FRUS, 1929, 3:434–40; FRUS, 1930, 3:495–508; FRUS, 1932, 5:732–56; State Department, *American Mexican Claims Commission,* 72–74; Estrada to Téllez, April 16 and 21, 1931, Téllez to Estrada, April 18, 1931, file 14–15–30, AHSRE.

99. Daniels to Roosevelt, May 2, 1933, Roosevelt Papers, PPF 86, Daniels, FDRL; Daniels to Roosevelt, August 14, 1933, Roosevelt Papers, PSF, Diplomatic Correspondence, Mexico, box 43, FDRL; FRUS, 1933, 5:800–1; Edgar Witt, "Statement Regarding the Work of the Special Claims Commission," June 8, 1938, Roosevelt Papers, POF, 146d, Mexican Special Claims Commission, box 3, FDRL; Cronon, *Josephus Daniels in Mexico,* 76–81.

100. Secretary of Foreign Affairs José Manuel Puig Casauranc to Secretary of the Interior, May 29, 1934, DGG, 2.300(29)444, box 32, AGN; Brief Outline of the History of Claims Negotiations with Mexico, RG 76, U.S.-Mexican Claims Commission, Orders, Decisions, and Related Records, 1943–47, entry 227, NAW; State Department, *American Mexican Claims Commission,* 72; Witt, "Statement Regarding Work of Special Claims Commission," June 8, 1938, Roosevelt Papers, POF, 146d, Mexican Special Claims, box 3, FDRL; Secretaría de Hacienda to Cárdenas, August 29, 1938, Cárdenas Papers, 576/5, AGN; FRUS, 1932, 5:739–56; *Washington Herald,* July 21, 1934; Abelardo Rodríguez, *Autobiografía,* 147.

101. FRUS, 1938, 5:663.

102. Roosevelt Press Conference, April 1, 1938, in *Complete Presidential Press Conferences of Franklin D. Roosevelt,* 266–67.

103. Daniels to Hull, April 30, 1938, Welles Papers, FDRL.

104. Téllez to Obregón, September 10, 1923, file 8–9–24, AHSRE; State Department, *American Mexican Claims Commission,* 22, 71–72; Brief Outline of the History of Claims Negotiations with Mexico, RG 76, U.S.-Mexican Claims Commission, Orders, Decisions, and Related Records, 1943–47, Entry 227, NAW; Edgar Witt, "Statement Regarding the Work of the Special Claims Commission" June 8, 1938, Roosevelt Papers, POF, 146d, Mexican Special Claims Commission, Box 3, FDRL; *New York Times,* March 29, 1928, June 19, 1932.

105. Brief Outline of the History of Claims Negotiations with Mexico, RG 76, American-Mexican Claims Commission, 1942–47, Orders, Decisions and Related Records, Entry 227, NAW; Daniels, *Shirt-Sleeve Diplomat,* 115–124; *FRUS,* 1938, 5:763–64.

106. Baker and Flood to Henry Norweb, chargé d'affaires of U.S. Embassy, June 3, 1935; Norweb to Edward Reed, June 4, 1935, Daniels Papers, box 661, LC; Cronon, *Josephus Daniels in Mexico,* 137.

107. Roorda, *The Dictator Next Door,* 236–37.

108. Press release/conference, March 30, 1938, Moore Papers, group 55, Monroe Doctrine, box 10, FDRL, emphasis mine.

109. Berle, diary entry, July 9, 1938, Berle Papers, Diary, box 210, FDRL.

110. *The Evening Star,* October 30, 1938.

7. DIPLOMATIC WEAPONS OF THE WEAK

1. Lorenzo Meyer, *Mexico and the United States in the Oil Controversy,* 154.

2. Ibid., 198–200.

3. Memo for the president, March 26, 1937, Roosevelt Papers, PSF, Departmental File, State, box 70, FDRL; Daniels, diary entry, November 14, 1938, Daniels Papers, LC.

4. This term is borrowed from Scott, *Weapons of the Weak.*

5. Hobsbawm, "Peasants and Politics," 13; Longley, *The Sparrow and the Hawk,* x.

6. Scott, *Weapons of the Weak,* xv–xvii.

7. Gambone, *Eisenhower, Somoza, and the Cold War in Nicaragua;* Ewell, *Venezuela and the United States;* Longley, *The Sparrow and the Hawk;* Roorda, *The Dictator Next Door;* Buchenau, *In the Shadow of the Giant;* Paz, *Strategy, Security, and Spies;* Friedman, "Retiring the Puppets, Bringing Latin America Back In," 626–27.

8. Schuler, *Mexico between Hitler and Roosevelt,* 1–2.

9. Daniels memo, April 21, 1938, Daniels Papers, box 656, LC. For more on the paradoxical nature of U.S. involvement in Nicaragua, see Michel Gobat, *Confronting the American Dream,* 203–66. For more on how the Good Neighbor policy's nonin-terventionism emboldened Latin American leaders, including Rafael Trujillo, see Roorda, *The Dictator Next Door,* 27–62, 90–99.

10. Roosevelt, Pan-American Day speech, April 14, 1938, Berle Papers, Diary, January–June 1938, box 210, FDRL.

11. For the complete text of FDR's speech, see Hunt, ed., *The Essential Franklin Delano Roosevelt,* 46–48.

12. Duggan speech on the Good Neighbor policy, April 2, 1938, Daniels Papers, box 662, LC.

13. Longley, *The Sparrow and the Hawk,* 170. For more on the lack of unity in U.S. policy toward the Dominican Republic, Costa Rica, Mexico, Argentina, Cuba, and Brazil, see Roorda, *The Dictator Next Door;* Schuler, *Mexico between Hitler and Roosevelt,* Randall Woods, *The Roosevelt Foreign-Policy Establishment and the "Good Neighbor";* Gellman, *Roosevelt and Batista;* McCann, *The Brazilian-American Alliance.*

14. Daniels to Roosevelt, June 4, 1938, Roosevelt Papers, PSF, Diplomatic Correspondence, Daniels, box 44, FDRL.

15. Daniels to Lawrence Duggan, January 29, 1938, Daniels Papers, box 662, LC.

16. Daniels to Roosevelt, April 11, 1938, Roosevelt Papers, PSF, Diplomatic Correspondence, Mexico, 1938, box 44, FDRL; Daniels memo, April 19, 1938, Daniels Papers, box 656, LC.

17. Daniels memo, April 21, 1938, Daniels Papers, box 656, LC.

18. To help cement the Good Neighbor policy, FDR attended the 1936 Pan-American conference in Argentina. See Gellman, *Good Neighbor Diplomacy,* 22–26, 61–65.

19. Daniels to Roosevelt, June 4, 1938, Roosevelt Papers, PSF, Diplomatic Correspondence, Daniels, box 44, FDRL.

20. *New York Times,* July 4, 1937.

21. Conversation between Hull and Morgenthau, July 13, 1938, Morgenthau Diary, reel 36, book 134, FDRL; Niblo, *War, Diplomacy, and Development,* 35.

22. Kilpatrick, ed., *Roosevelt and Daniels,* vii.

23. Littell to Franklin Roosevelt Jr., December 16, 1940, Roosevelt Papers, PSF, Diplomatic Correspondence, Mexico, box 44, FDRL; Gellman, *Secret Affairs,* 152, 164–65.

24. Gellman, *Secret Affairs,* 15; Freidel, *Franklin D. Roosevelt,* 121, 124.

25. Pike, FDR's Good Neighbor Policy, xxv; Cronon, *Josephus Daniels in Mexico,* 4–5; Gellman, *Secret Affairs,* 12–19, 152.

26. Acheson is quoted in Gellman, *Secret Affairs,* 164.

27. Jim (last name unknown) to Wallace, January 5, 1941, Wallace Papers, reel, 22, LC.

28. Francisco Castillo Nájera to Foreign Secretary Eduardo Hay, March 11, 1938, 30–3–10 (1), AHSRE.

29. Castillo Nájera to Hay, March 11, 1938, 30–3–10 (1), AHSRE; Cobbs, "Why They Think Like Gringos," 315; Pike, FDR's Good Neighbor Policy, 137.

30. Longley, *The Sparrow and the Hawk,* 163.

31. Martínez de Alba, Memo de relaciones exteriores, July 25, 1934, Cárdenas Papers, 570/8, AGN.

32. Beteta to Cárdenas, January 4, 1940, Cárdenas Papers, 571.1/1, AGN; Halperin, "Mexico Shifts Her Foreign Policy," 207–21.

33. Martínez de Alba, Memo de relaciones exteriores, July 25, 1934, Cárdenas Papers, 570/8, AGN; Weintraub, *Financial Decision-Making in Mexico,* 18; Gilderhus, *The Second Century,* 54–55.

34. Martínez de Alba, Memo de relaciones exteriores, July 25, 1934, Cárdenas Papers, 570/8, AGN.

35. Castillo Nájera described Hay as "both stupid and superficial." Welles conversation with Castillo Nájera, December 12, 1935, Welles Papers, box 178, folder 9, FDRL; Schuler, *Mexico between Hitler and Roosevelt*, 9–32.

36. Schuler, *Mexico between Hitler and Roosevelt*, 4–5.

37. FDR, Daniels, and Duggan were the accommodators, Hull, Welles, and Moore were the hard-liners, and Berle and Morgenthau vacillated between the two groups. Commenting years later on the issue of land reform in Latin America, Berle wrote, "In U.S. official thinking it is accepted that [agrarian] reform must be encouraged and indeed must take place." See Berle, *Latin America*, 51.

38. *FRUS*, 1936, 4:776; State Department memo, "Brief Chronology of Recent Important Developments in the Department's Efforts to Work Out a Policy Providing for the Relief of American Citizens Affected by the Mexican Agrarian Laws," March 27, 1936 (hereafter March 1936 State Department memo), Daniels Papers, box 653, LC.

39. On the agrarista invasions in Sinaloa, see DGG, 2.367(21)15358, box 3, AGN; on Tamaulipas, see DGG, 2.367(24)17125, box 3, AGN.

40. Moore and Armstrong memo, October 4, 1938, Moore Papers, Mexico, Expropriation of Land and Oil, FDRL.

41. *Time*, January 19, 1937. For examples of agrarista invasions and the reaction of U.S. congressmen, see Castillo Nájera, Informe de los reclamaciones Norteamericanos, November 14, 1938, Cárdenas Papers, 571.3/1, AGN.

42. Haber, *Industry and Underdevelopment*, 174–76; Sugiyama, "Reluctant Neighbors," 59.

43. Cárdenas later offered to set aside $2 million pesos for paying American landowners. *FRUS*, 1936, 5:715–19; Memo of conversation between Daniels and Cárdenas, October 7, 1937, Daniels Papers, box 662, LC.

44. *FRUS*, 1936, 5:714.

45. Ibid., 715–19.

46. Castillo Nájera, Informe de los reclamaciones Norteamericanos, November 14, 1938, Cárdenas Papers, 571.3/1, AGN.

47. Moore memo, January 16, 1937, Roosevelt Papers, PSF, Diplomatic Correspondence, Mexico, 1936–37, box 43, FDRL.

48. Roosevelt memo for Assistant Secretary Moore, January 16, 1937, Roosevelt Papers, PSF, Diplomatic Correspondence, Mexico, 1936–37, box 43, FDRL.

49. Memo for the president, March 26, 1937, Roosevelt Papers, PSF, Departmental File, State, box 70, FDRL.

50. Berle, diary entry, December 17, 1937, Berle Papers, box 210, FDRL.

51. Cronon, *Josephus Daniels in Mexico*, 147.

52. George Wythe, Chief, Latin American Section, Department of Commerce, memo, September 16, 1937, Roosevelt Papers, POF, Commerce Department, box 3, FDRL.

53. Cotter, *Troubled Harvest*, 125, 132–33; Ochoa, *Feeding Mexico*, 45–48; Hertford,

Sources of Change in Mexican Agricultural Production, 38; Brown, "Acting for Themselves," 61–64; Schuler, *Mexico between Hitler and Roosevelt*, 73–77.

54. In 1938, loans dropped to $406,536 million pesos, while in 1939, they were $387,494 million and in 1940 they were $352,641 million. Hewitt de Alcántara, *La modernización de la agricultura Mexicana*, 68.

55. Sugiyama, "Reluctant Neighbors," 60–65; Lorenzo Meyer, *Mexico and the United States in the Oil Controversy*, 166; Schuler, *Mexico between Hitler and Roosevelt*, 73–74.

56. State Department, Memo on Important Matters Affecting the Relations between the United States and Mexico, September 15, 1937, RG 59, 711.12/1354 1/2, NAW.

57. *Excelsior*, October 14, 1937; Lorenzo Meyer, *Mexico and the United States in the Oil Controversy*, 156. Cardenista officials frequently offered agrarian bonds as compensation, which they preferred in lieu of cash because the latter would quickly drain the country's limited supply of foreign exchange. Between 1931 and 1934, the Mexican government reimbursed a small percentage of foreign and domestic landowners for the loss of their holdings with federal bonds. However, because Mexico defaulted on them in 1934, the State Department rejected all subsequent offers to compensate American landowners with agrarian bonds. See Daniels to Roosevelt, September 28, 1936, Roosevelt Papers, PPF, 86, Daniels, FDRL.

58. *FRUS*, 1938, 5:663.

59. *FRUS*, 1937, 5:614–15; Daniels to Hull, September 8, 1937, RG 59, 812.52/2237, NAW.

60. Lazaro Cárdenas, *Obras I*, 376. By August 1938, Mexico's debt to both foreign and domestic landowners was estimated in the Mexican press to be approximately $1.5 billion pesos. See State Department, "Economic Effects of the Mexican Agrarian Reform Program," August 10, 1938, RG 84, Mexicali Consulate, General Records, file 350, box 7, NAW. In mid-December Cárdenas asked Tannenbaum to tell the State Department that he wanted to remain on friendly terms with the United States. After emphasizing the similarities between Mexico's Six-Year Plan and FDR's New Deal, Cárdenas stated that he could not stop land redistribution, since he considered it his mission, nor could he pay $194 million in agrarian compensation to the Americans. See Memo of conversation between Tannenbaum and Duggan, December 13, 1937, RG 59, 812.52/2529, NAW.

61. On separate occasions Cárdenas, Beteta, and Suárez offered the American oil companies compensation in the form of cash, oil, bonds, or a combination of the three. Mexican officials even proposed that the companies return to Mexico and operate their installations under a government contract. See Lorenzo Meyer, *Mexico and the United States in the Oil Controversy*, 193–94, 198.

62. Meeting between Morgenthau, Castillo Nájera, Suárez, Feis, Taylor, Lochhead, and White, December 14, 1937, Morgenthau Diary, diary 101, reel 26, FDRL.

63. Berle, diary entry, December 10, 1937, Berle Papers, box 210, FDRL.

64. Ibid.; Berle and Jacobs, eds., *Navigating the Rapids*, 151; Lorenzo Meyer, *Mexico and the United States in the Oil Controversy*, 165.

65. Cedillo also disagreed with the poor treatment of foreign capital in Mexico, the

Cárdenas administration's support of radical labor groups, the federal attacks on the church, and the nationalization of the foreign-owned petroleum industry. Walter Jones to Roosevelt, November 23, 1936, Roosevelt Papers, PSF, Departmental File, State, box 69, FDRL; *El Universal,* June 19, 1938.

66. *New York Times,* August 17, 1937.

67. Ankerson, *Agrarian Warlord,* 165–81.

68. Ibid., 182, 186.

69. *El Universal,* June 19, 1938; Falcón, *Revolución y caciquismo,* 264–70.

70. *New York Times,* August 1, 1938; Lorenzo Meyer, *Mexico and the United States in the Oil Controversy,* 175; González, *Los días del presidente Cárdenas,* 195–98.

71. Daniels to Roosevelt, September 28, 1936, Roosevelt Papers, PPF 86, Daniels, FDRL; Tannenbaum to Daniels, July 6, 1938, Roosevelt Papers, PPF, Diplomatic Correspondence, Mexico, box 44, FDRL.

72. Hale, "Frank Tannenbaum and the Mexican Revolution," 215–46, John Mason Hart, *Empire and Revolution,* 544.

73. De Boal to Yepis, March 16, 1938, RG 84, Guaymas, General Records, file 350, NAW.

74. Mexico offered American property owners in the Yaqui Valley 1.5 hectares of non-irrigated land on the north bank of the Yaqui River for each expropriated hectare. The compensation lands also would be exempt from expropriation. See Meeting between Welles and Castillo Nájera, February 28, 1938, RG 59, 711.12/1362, NAW, and Cárdenas Papers, 571.1/6, AGN.

75. Hull to Daniels, September 8, 1937, RG 59: 812.52/2237, NAW.

76. Franklin D. Roosevelt, Roosevelt Press Conference, April 1, 1938, *The Complete Presidential Press Conferences of Franklin D. Roosevelt,* 11:266–67.

77. Meeting between Roosevelt and Castillo Nájera, April 5, 1938, Berle Papers, State Department 1938–45, Roosevelt, box 66, FDRL; Memo of conversation with Roosevelt, April 5, 1938, 30–3–10, AHSRE. After discussing the agrarian claims, FDR proceeded to discuss the oil claims with the Mexican ambassador and made little distinction between the issues involved in the two separate disputes.

78. Leff, *The Limits of Symbolic Reform,* 8, 292; Gordon, *New Deals,* 280–87.

79. *New York Times,* August 27 and 28, 1938; Keep America Out of War Congress to Roosevelt, September 25, 1938, 30–3–10 (I), AHSRE; Cárdenas Papers, 571.3/1–2, AGN; Pike, *FDR's Good Neighbor Policy,* xxiii, 11–38, 165–67; Lorenzo Meyer, *Mexico and the United States in the Oil Controversy,* 215.

80. Castillo Nájera to Welles, May 26, 1938, Cárdenas Papers, 571.3/1 anexo 8, AGN.

81. Daniels to Roosevelt, Roosevelt Papers, PSF, Diplomatic Correspondence, Mexico, Daniels, box 44, FDRL; Castillo Nájera, Informe de los reclamaciones Norteamericanos, November 14, 1938, Cárdenas Papers, 571.3/1, AGN.

82. Berle, diary entry, March 23, 1938, Berle Papers, box 210, FDRL; Berle believed that if the United States did not take a hard line over the compensation issue, Washington would look timid. See Berle and Jacobs, eds., *Navigating the Rapids,* 169.

83. Meeting between Hull and Castillo Nájera, April 2, 1938, RG 59, 711.12/1367, NAW; Schuler, *Mexico between Hitler and Roosevelt*, 93, 121.

84. Hull to Daniels, April 12, 1938, Daniels Papers, box 662, LC.

85. Daniels to Duggan, April 11, 1938, Daniels Papers, box 662, LC; *New York Times*, June 19, 1938.

86. Daniels was in the United States for three weeks in June celebrating his fiftieth wedding anniversary. See *New York Times*, July 10, 1938.

87. Welles to Castillo Nájera, June 29, 1938, Roosevelt Papers, PSF, Confidential File, State Department, box 8, FDRL. Cárdenas's administration never returned the list of American landowners to U.S. officials. Daniels to Welles, July 1, 1938, Welles Papers, box 45, folder 3, FDRL.

88. Castillo Nájera, Informe de los reclamaciones Norteamericanos, November 14, 1938, Cárdenas Papers, 571.3/1, AGN; Welles to Castillo Nájera, June 29, 1938, Roosevelt Papers, PSF, Confidential File, State Department, box 8, FDRL.

89. Memo of conversation, Welles and Castillo Nájera, June 29, 1937, Welles Papers, box 178, folder 12, FDRL.

90. Castillo Nájera to Welles, July 1, 1938, Cárdenas Papers, 571.3/1 anexo 11, AGN, and Welles Papers, box 179, folder 2, FDRL.

91. Daniels to Welles, July 7, 1938, Daniels Papers, box 662, LC.

92. *New York Times*, July 13, 1938.

93. Cronon, *Josephus Daniels in Mexico*, 217; Conversation between Hull and Morgenthau, July 13, 1938, Morgenthau Diaries, reel 36, book 134, FDRL.

94. Castillo Nájera to Cárdenas, July 16, 1938, III-2353–1, AHSRE; Lorenzo Meyer, *Mexico and the United States in the Oil Controversy*, 185–91.

95. Hull to Castillo Nájera, July 21, 1938, III-2352–17 (Parte 1) AHSRE; Conversation between Hull and Castillo Nájera, August 22, 1938, RG 76, State Department, Correspondence of Commissioner Lawson, 1938–43, box 1, entry 203, NAW.

96. Lorenzo Meyer, *Mexico and the United States in the Oil Controversy*, 191.

97. *Washington Post*, July 25, 1938; *New York Times*, July 23 and 25, 1938.

98. Hull published his note because he did not trust Daniels. After the oil seizure in March 1938, Hull wrote a strongly worded note to Mexico and had Daniels deliver it to the Mexican Ministry of Foreign Affairs. Since Daniels thought that Hull's note would break diplomatic relations, he told Foreign Secretary Hay to consider it "not delivered." To circumvent Daniels and force Mexico to reply to his notes regarding the agrarian dispute, Hull had his statements published in the press. See Lorenzo Meyer, *México y los Estados Unidos en el conflicto petrolero*, 384.

99. Memo of the Foreign Secretary regarding Hull's July 21 note, III-2352–17(Parte 1), AHSRE; Castillo Nájera to Cárdenas, July 22, 1938, III-2353–1, AHSRE.

100. Hay to Daniels, August 3, 1938, III-2352–17 (Parte 1), AHSRE.

101. Ibid.

102. *New York Times*, August 4, 1938.

103. Daniels to Hull, August 7, 1938, Roosevelt Papers, PSF, Diplomatic Correspondence, Mexico, Daniels, box 44, FDRL. *Excelsior* suggested that Mexicans should be indemnified before foreigners. See *Excelsior,* August 4, 1938.

104. For the multiple pieces of correspondence in support of Cárdenas, see Cárdenas Papers, 571.3/1–2, AGN.

105. Daniels to Hull, August 7, 1938, Roosevelt Papers, PSF, Diplomatic Correspondence, Mexico, Daniels, box 44, FDRL.

106. Castillo Nájera, Informe de los reclamaciones Norteamericanos, November 14, 1938, Cárdenas Papers, 571.3/1, AGN; Conversation between Hull and Castillo Nájera, August 22, 1938, RG 76, Agrarian Claims, Correspondence of Commissioner Lawson, 1938–43, box 1, entry 203, NAW.

107. Hull to Castillo Nájera, August 22, 1938, III-2353–1 (Parte 2), AHSRE; *New York Times,* August 26, 1938; Conversation between Hull and Castillo Nájera, August 22, 1938, RG 76, Agrarian Claims, Correspondence of Commissioner Lawson, 1938–43, box 1, entry 203, NAW.

108. Articles cited in *New York Times,* August 27 and 28, 1938; *Excelsior,* August 26, 1938.

109. Newspaper clipping in Cárdenas Papers, 571.3/1–1, AGN; *Washington Herald,* August 27, 1938.

110. *The Evening Star,* August 28, 1938.

111. Daniels to Bowers, September 6, 1938, Daniels Papers, box 662, LC; Articles are cited in *San Antonio Express,* August 29, 1938.

112. Niblo, *War, Diplomacy, and Development,* 41.

113. Hay to Daniels, September 1, 1938, III-2353–1 (Parte 2), AHSRE. Cárdenas's second note also received widespread support from the Mexican press, including newspapers that were often critical of his administration, such as *Excelsior.*

114. *New York Times,* September 5, 1938; *New York Herald Tribune,* September 5, 1938; *Washington Herald,* September 6, 1938; *Kansas City Star,* September 7, 1938; Cárdenas Papers, 571.3/1–2, AGN.

115. Conversation between Hull and Castillo Nájera, September 6, 1938, Hull Papers, Reel 31, Mexico, 1933–44, LC; Daniels to Hull, September 3, 1938, Roosevelt Papers, PSF, Diplomatic Correspondence, Mexico, Daniels, box 44, FDRL; *Washington Herald,* September 6, 1938.

116. Lockett estimated that by the end of 1938, the Mexican deficit would reach $153 million pesos. See Lockett to Daniels, October 19, 1938, RG 59, 812.51/2336, NAW.

117. George Wythe, chief, Latin American Section, Department of Commerce, memo, September 16, 1937, Roosevelt Papers, POF, Commerce Department, box 3, FDRL.

118. The extensive nature of Cárdenas's land reform program drained the government's revenues. According to a State Department memo, "Cárdenas realized that the mere transfer of land to the Indians was not enough but that it must be accompanied by instruction in many branches of agricultural science, by the furnishing of implements and seeds, by the establishing of agricultural credit agencies, and by the creation of cooperatives for purchasing and marketing the production. In short, to

make the agrarian program a success the government must invest vast sums of capital, which it has been doing in large amounts." See State Department memo, December 29, 1937, Welles Papers, box 178, folder 10, FDRL. During his first three years in office, Cárdenas deposited $100 million pesos into the Ejidal Bank. See State Department, "Economic Effects of the Mexican Agrarian Program," August 10, 1938, RG 84, Mexicali, General Records, file 350, box 7, NAW; Niblo, *War, Diplomacy, and Development,* 44.

119. *New York Times,* August 21, 1938; Sugiyama, "Reluctant Neighbors," 83–84; Lorenzo Meyer, *Mexico and the United States in the Oil Controversy,* 16, 203–05; Ochoa, *Feeding Mexico,* 49–50; Schuler, *Mexico between Hitler and Roosevelt,* 87–89; Niblo, *War, Diplomacy, and Development,* 41–42.

120. Castillo Nájera, Informe de los reclamaciones Norteamericanos, November 14, 1938, Cárdenas Papers, 571.3/1, AGN; Memo of meeting between Hull and Castillo Nájera, September 6, 1938, Hull Papers, reel 31, Mexico, 1934–44, LC; Hull, *The Memoirs of Cordell Hull,* 1:610.

121. Daniels to Roosevelt, September 15, 1938, Roosevelt Papers, PSF, Diplomatic Correspondence, Mexico, Daniels, box 44, FDRL.

122. Berle memo, September 19, 1938, Berle Papers, Diary, box 210, FDRL.

123. Ibid.

124. Memo of meeting between Hull and Castillo Nájera, September 10, 1938, Hull Papers, reel 31, Mexico, 1933–44, LC; Castillo Nájera, Informe de los reclamaciones Norteamericanos, November 14, 1938, Cárdenas Papers, 571.3/1, AGN.

125. Memo of meeting between Hull and Castillo Nájera, September 20, 1938, Hull Papers, reel 31, Mexico, 1933–44, LC; Castillo Nájera, Informe de los reclamaciones Norteamericanos, November 14, 1938, Cárdenas Papers, 571.3/1, AGN.

126. Memo of meeting between Hull and Castillo Nájera, September 26, 1938, Hull Papers, reel 31, Mexico, 1933–44, LC; Castillo Nájera, Informe de los reclamaciones Norteamericanos, November 14, 1938, Cárdenas Papers, 571.3/1, AGN.

127. Due to Hull's pressure, Welles resigned from the State Department in 1943. See Gellman, *Secret Affairs,* 302–31.

128. Freidel, *Franklin D. Roosevelt,* 120; Gellman, *Secret Affairs,* 16.

129. *New York Times,* August 27 and 28, 1938; Davidson to Cherrington, December 8, 1938, Roosevelt Papers, POF, 146, Mexico, box 2, FDRL; Keep America Out of War Congress to Roosevelt, September 25, 1938, 30–3–10 (I), AHSRE; Cárdenas Papers, 571.3/1–2, AGN.

130. Castillo Nájera, Informe de los reclamaciones Norteamericanos. On Daniels's role regarding payment, see Daniels to Roosevelt, October 29, 1938, Roosevelt Papers, PSF, Diplomatic Correspondence, Mexico, Daniels, box 44, FDRL.

131. *FRUS,* 1938, 5:712–13.

132. Hull to Castillo Nájera, November 9, 1938, Hay to Daniels, November 12 1938, III-2353–1 (Parte 2), AHSRE.

133. For a complete text of the address, see Lázaro Cárdenas, *Cárdenas Habla,* 182–86.

134. Benjamin, *La Revolución*, 112, 115.

135. Lorey, "Postrevolutionary Contexts for Independence Day," 245.

136. Benjamin, *La Revolución*, 99–100.

8. THE 1941 GLOBAL SETTLEMENT

1. Paz, *Strategy, Security, and Spies,* 14, 236.

2. Ibid., 103–22.

3. Moreno, *Yankee Don't Go Home,* 10.

4. Paz, *Strategy, Security, and Spies,* 6.

5. Memo from Lawson to Bursley, May 14, 1941, RG 76, Lawson Correspondence, vol. 1–3, entry 203, NAW.

6. Hackworth to Welles, February 8, 1939, RG 76, Lawson Correspondence, vol. 1–3, entry 203; Winters, Memo for the American Commissioner, November 23, 1940, RG 76, Lawson Correspondence, entry 203, NAW.

7. Memo of conversation, Castillo Nájera and Roosevelt, February 4, 1939, III–2353–1; Cárdenas to Castillo Nájera, February 9, 1939, III–2353–1, AHSRE; Lázaro Cárdenas, *Obras I,* 407.

8. Confidential memo on Mexico, Matton to Bursley to Welles, January 26, 1939, RG 59, 711.12/1402, NAW.

9. Lawson to Welles, March 7, 1939, and Lawson to Hull, October 2, 1939, RG 76, Lawson Correspondence, vol. 1–3, entry 203, NAW.

10. Welles to Castillo Nájera, April 4, 1939, 39–10–2 (I), AHSRE.

11. Burt to Daniels, RG 84, Veracruz Consulate, file 350, box 49, NAW.

12. Chandler Ward, "Background Material on Irrigation Development of the Yaqui Valley, Sonora, and the Sale of the Project to the Mexican Government," January 24, 1968, RCCR, MS113, folder 1: Historical Material, 1909–68, SC UAL.

13. Lawson to Daniels, May 28, 1946, RG 76, Office of the Commissioner, U.S. Section, Agrarian Claims, Correspondence of the Commissioner, A-1 to A-6, entry 204, NAW.

14. Lawson to Daniels, March 2, 1939, RG 76, Office of the Commissioner U.S. Section, Agrarian Claims, Correspondence of the Commissioner with the Executive Officer of the United States, Administrative Decisions to Memo Report (hereafter Commissioner's Correspondence with the Executive Officer), entry 204, NAW.

15. Winters to Burlsey, November 7, 1938, RG 76, Commissioner's Correspondence with the Executive Officer, entry 204, NAW.

16. Butler to Hackworth, February 21, 1939, RG 84, Veracruz, General Records, fle 350, box 50, NAW; John Mason Hart, *Empire and Revolution,* 373–92.

17. Cochran to Hull, January 2, 1940, RG 84, Veracruz, General Records, file 350, box 65, NAW.

18. Lawson to Welles, March 7, 1939, Lawson to Bursley, July 17, 1941, RG 76, Lawson Correspondence, vol. 1–3, entry 203, NAW.

19. An agrarian claim was defined broadly to incorporate the variety of circumstances

under which land was affected by Mexico's agrarian reform laws. Claims were based on the restitution of lands, woodlands, and waters; on the granting of ejidos; on the nullification of titles to lands, waters, and the natural resources of the country; on the application of the Idle Lands Law; and on expropriation for colonization purposes. See Memo of C. M. Bishop, December 29, 1938, RG 76, Lawson Correspondence, vol. 1–3, entry 203, NAW.

20. Shaner, "Memo Regarding Divergence's in the Views of Representatives of the American Section and the Mexican Section of the Agrarian Claims Commission Regarding the Interpretation of the Agreement of November 9–12, 1938" (hereafter Shaner memo), March 1939, RG 76, Lawson Correspondence, vol. 1–3, entry 203, NAW.

21. Welles to Lawson, February 18, 1939, and Shaner memo, March 1939, RG 76, Lawson Correspondence, vol. 1–3, entry 203, NAW.

22. Welles to Lawson, February 18, 1939, and Shaner memo, March 1939, RG 76, Lawson Correspondence, vol. 1–3, entry 203, NAW.

23. *FRUS*, 1938, 5:712–13.

24. Memo for Cárdenas from Castillo Nájera, May 19, 1939, 39–10–2 (I), AHSRE; Roberto Córdova to Castillo Nájera, August 22, 1939, Cárdenas Papers, 571.3/1, AGN.

25. Hull to Castillo Nájera, November 9, 1938, Hay to Daniels, November 12, 1938, III-2353–1 (Parte 2), AHSRE; Shaner memo, March 1939, RG 76, Lawson Correspondence, vol. 1–3, entry 203, NAW; memo for Cárdenas from Castillo Nájera, May 19, 1939, 39–10–2(I), AHSRE.

26. Lawson to Hull, August 29, 1939, July 1, 1940, RG 76, Lawson Correspondence, vol. 1–3, entry 203, NAW.

27. According to Mexican law, compensation was based on: (1) the fiscal value of the property, (2) improvements made subsequent to the declaration of value, (3) objects whose value was not included in the declaration of value (such as personal property) (4) interest at 5 percent from the date on which the owner was deprived of possession until payment or the determination of the amount of indemnity was made. See Memo of C. M. Bishop, December 29, 1938, RG 76, Lawson Correspondence, vol. 1–3, entry 203, NAW.

28. Córdova to Castillo Nájera, August 22, 1939, Cárdenas Papers, 571.3/1, AGN.

29. Moore to Hull, RG 84, Mexicali, Confidential Records, 1936–39, file 852, NAW; John Mason Hart, *Empire and Revolution*, 388–89.

30. State Department memo, May 20, 1941, Bishop memo, December 29, 1938, RG 76, Lawson Correspondence, vol. 1–3, entry 203, NAW; Memo, Córdova to Castillo Nájera, August 22, 1939, Cárdenas Papers, 571.3/1, AGN.

31. State Department, Memo for the President, March 26, 1937, Roosevelt Papers, PSF, Departmental File, State, box 70, FDRL.

32. Shaner memo, March 1939, RG 76, Lawson Correspondence, vol. 1–3, entry 203, NAW.

33. Bishop memo, December 29, 1938, RG 76, Lawson Correspondence, vol. 1–3, entry 203, NAW.

34. *FRUS*, 1939, 5:660–61. I found no evidence after the November 1938 notes to support Castillo Nájera's claim.

35. Welles to Lawson, March 20, 1939, RG 76, Lawson Correspondence, vol. 1–3, entry 203, NAW.

36. Lawson to Welles, March 7, 1939, RG 76, Lawson Correspondence, vol. 1–3, entry 203, NAW.

37. Shaner memo, March 1939, RG 76, Lawson Correspondence, vol. 1–3, entry 203, NAW.

38. Daniels to Hull, September 23, 1939, Daniels Papers, box 664, LC.

39. Ibid.

40. Memo of conversation, Daniels and Cárdenas, November 3, 1939, RG 59, 711.12/1441; American Consul General William Blocker to Hull, November 4, 1939, RG 59, 711.12/1440, NAW; Castillo Nájera to Cárdenas, November 2 and 13, 1939, Cárdenas Papers, 705.2/232, AGN.

41. According to Daniels, large investors hoped to see either U.S. military intervention or a fascist coup to bring down Cárdenas's government. See Lorenzo Meyer, *Mexico and the United States in the Oil Controversy,* 176–80.

42. Banco de México, Oficina de Estudios Económicos, "Comercio exterior de México," Cárdenas Papers, 704.1/13, AGN.

43. Telegram from Mexico City attached to memo of conversation between Welles and Castillo Nájera, December 18, 1939, Welles Papers, box 179, folder 3, FDRL; John Mason Hart, *Empire and Revolution,* 396.

44. Telegram attached to memo of conversation between Welles and Castillo Nájera, December 18, 1939, Welles Papers, box 179, folder 3, FDRL.

45. Aguilar Camín and Meyer, *In the Shadow of the Mexican Revolution,* 137.

46. Hewitt de Alcántara, *La modernización de la agricultura mexicana,* 105.

47. Cotter, "The Origins of the Green Revolution in Mexico," 224–47. From 1938 to 1939, the per kilogram cost of beans rose from $3 pesos to $9.9 pesos, while corn rose from $9 to $25.5 pesos, lard from $9.24 to $16.47 pesos, and meat from $9 to $23.7 pesos. See Sugiyama, "Reluctant Neighbors," 117.

48. Sugiyama, "Reluctant Neighbors," 117–20; Hernández Chávez, *La mecánica cardenista,* 191; Lorenzo Meyer, *Mexico and the United States in the Oil Controversy,* 205; Ochoa, *Feeding Mexico,* 64; Niblo, *War, Diplomacy, and Development,* 48.

49. Stewart, Political Report, May 25, 1939, RG 59, 812.00/30744, NAW; American Consul General William Blocker to Hull, May 25, 1939, RG 59, 812.51/2387, NAW; Winters memo, May 18, 1939, RG 59, 812.51/2368, NAW.

50. Memo of conversation, Duggan, Bursley, and Lancaster of National City Bank, June 23, 1939, RG 59, 812.51/2378, NAW.

51. Ibid.

52. Conversation between Duggan and Lancaster, June 26, 1939, RG 59, 812.51/2380, NAW; Sugiyama, "Reluctant Neighbors," 119.

53. Lorenzo Meyer, *Mexico and the United States in the Oil Controversy,* 214; Niblo, *War, Diplomacy, and Development,* 52.

54. Lorenzo Meyer, *Mexico and the United States in the Oil Controversy,* 200–13.

55. Niblo, *War, Diplomacy, and Development,* 52.

56. FRUS, 1939, 5:660–61; Castillo Nájera to Cárdenas, November 21 and 24, 1939, 39–10–2 (II), AHSRE.

57. Ibid.

58. It appears that Beteta coined the term "global settlement." See Beteta to Cárdenas, November 22, 1939, 39–10–2 (II), AHSRE.

59. Cárdenas also argued that the U.S. quota on Mexican oil was undermining the Mexican economy. See Cárdenas to Castillo Nájera, December 14, 1939, 39–10–2 (II), AHSRE.

60. Memo of conversation, Welles and Castillo Nájera, December 18, 1939, Welles Papers, box 179, folder 3, FDRL.

61. Castillo Nájera to Cárdenas, December 30, 1939, 39–10–2 (II), AHSRE.

62. Cárdenas to Castillo Nájera, January 31, 1940, memo of conversation, Castillo Nájera and Welles, February 5, 1940, 39–10–2 (II), AHSRE; Welles to Lawson, January 9, 1940, RG 59, 812.52 Agrarian Commission/113a, NAW; Lawson to Hull, February 20, 1940, RG 59, 812.52 Agrarian Commission/125, NAW.

63. Duggan to Welles, February 5, 1940, RG 59, 812.52 Agrarian Commission/119, NAW; Cárdenas to Castillo Nájera, January 31, 1940, 39–10–2 (III), AHSRE.

64. Cárdenas to Castillo Nájera, February 17, 1940, 39–10–2 (III), AHSRE.

65. Lawson to Hull, February 13 and 20, 1940, RG 76, Lawson Correspondence, vol. 1–3, entry 203, NAW.

66. Bursley to Duggan, February 23, 1940, RG 76, Lawson Correspondence, vol. 1–3, entry 203, NAW.

67. State Department memo to Castillo Nájera, April 9, 1940, 39–10–2 (III), AHSRE; Memo of conversation between Castillo Nájera and Bursley, May 6, 1940, 39–10–2 (IV), AHSRE.

68. Hull to Lawson, June 8, 1940, RG 59, 812.52 Agrarian Claims Commission/150, Telegram, NAW.

69. FRUS, 1940, 5:963.

70. Lawson to Serrano, June 24, 1940, Serrano to Lawson, June 24, 1940, Lawson to Welles, August 7, 1940, RG 76, Lawson Correspondence, vol. 1–3, entry 203, NAW.

71. Telegram, Winters to Lawson, July 24, 1940, RG 76, Lawson Correspondence, vol. 1–3, entry 203, NAW.

72. Minutes of meeting between Serrano, Lawson, Winters, Sánchez Gómez, and Bursley, August 12, 1940, RG 76, Lawson Correspondence, vol. 1–3, entry 203, NAW.

73. In 1939, Mexico's GDP stood at $46.1 million pesos, in 1940 it inched up to only $46.7 million. However, in 1941 Mexico's GDP shot up to $51.2 million pesos and increased again in 1942 to $54.1 million. See Aguilar Camín and Meyer, *In the Shadow of the Mexican Revolution,* 172.

74. Memo, "Sobre problemas internacionales pendientes de solución entre México y Estados Unidos," February 7, 1941, Ávila Camacho Papers, 577/3, AGN.

75. Minutes of meeting between Serrano, Lawson, Winters, Sánchez Gómez, and Bursley, August 12, 1940, RG 76, Lawson Correspondence, entry 203, NAW.

76. Lawson to Bursley, July 16, 1940, Lawson to Hull, August 9, 1940, RG 76, Lawson Correspondence, vol. 1–3, entry 203, NAW.

77. Division of American Republics memo, September 17, 1940, RG 59, 412.11 (41) Agreement/9, NAW.

78. Minutes of cabinet meeting, June 19 and 21, 1940, Cárdenas Papers, 550/46–8, AGN; Cárdenas to Romeo, June 19, 1940, 39–10–5, AHSRE; Paz, *Strategy, Security, and Spies*, 103.

79. *New York Times,* June 12, 1940.

80. Memo of conversation, Welles and Castillo Nájera, June 4, 1940, Welles Papers, box 179, folder 4, FDRL; Schuler, *Mexico between Hitler and Roosevelt*, 164–67; Niblo, *War, Diplomacy, and Development*, 83–84.

81. Lázaro Cárdenas, *Obras I,* 354–55, 370. For Cárdenas's role in combating international fascism vis-à-vis Spain, see Powell, *Mexico and the Spanish Civil War*, 24–68.

82. Lázaro Cárdenas, *Obras I,* 390, 398–99, 440. Schuler, *Mexico between Hitler and Roosevelt,* 153, 161, 164; Niblo, *War, Diplomacy, and Development,* 76; Paz, *Strategy, Security, and Spies,* 53; Schwab, "The Role of the Mexican Expeditionary Air Force in World War II," 1129, 1138.

83. Niblo, *War, Diplomacy, and Development,* 84.

84. *FRUS,* 1940, 5:965–76; memo of conversation between Suárez, Welles, and Castillo Nájera, August 16, 1940, Cárdenas Papers, 571.3/1, AGN.

85. Telegram, Lawson to Hull, June 9, 1940, RG 76, Lawson Correspondence, vol. 1–3, entry 203, NAW.

86. Castillo Nájera to Cárdenas, September 21, 1940, and memo of the same date, Cárdenas Papers, 571.3/1, AGN.

87. Minutes of conversation, October 6, 1941, Morgenthau Diaries, reel 124, book 448, FDRL.

88. Duggan to Welles, September 26, 1940, and memo of conversation between Welles, Duggan, Castillo Nájera, and Espinosa, September 30, 1940, RG 59, 412.11(41) Agreements/10 and /12, NAW.

89. State Department, Plan for Settling the Mexican Claims and Petroleum Expropriation through an Agreement between the Mexican and United States Government, n.d., RG 59, 412.11(41) Agreements/13, NAW; Division of American Republics memo, September 17, 1940, RG 59, 412.11(41) Agreements/9, NAW; Plan para el arreglo de los problemas importantes que están pendientes entre los Estados Unidos y México, October 7, 1940, 39–10–3, AHSRE.

90. Memo of conversation, Welles, Bursley, Castillo Nájera, and Espinosa, October 7,

1940, Welles Papers, box 179, folder 4, FDRL; Plan para el arreglo de los problemas importantes que están pendientes entre los Estados Unidos y México, October 7, 1940, 39–10–3, AHSRE.

91. Memo of conversation, Welles, Castillo Nájera, Córdova, Hackworth, and Bursley, November 11, 1940, RG 59, 412.11(41) Agreement/19, NAW.

92. Memo from Castillo Nájera to Welles, November 16, 1940, RG 59, 412.11(41) Agreements/21, NAW.

93. Niblo, *War, Diplomacy, and Development*, 16.

94. Schuler, *Mexico between Hitler and Roosevelt*, 192.

95. Daniels to Hull, December 3, 1940, Roosevelt Papers, Diplomatic Correspondence, Mexico, box 44, FDRL; Schuler, *Mexico between Hitler and Roosevelt*, 192–97.

96. Littell to Franklin Roosevelt Jr., December 16, 1940, Roosevelt Papers, PSF, Diplomatic Correspondence, Mexico, box 44, FDRL; Governor Félix Ireta to Ávila Camacho, December 26, 1940, Ávila Camacho Papers, 577/2, AGN.

97. Gómez to Wallace, February 21, 1941, Wallace Papers as Vice President, Gómez, Marte, box 29, FDRL.

98. Ávila Camacho to Wallace, January 3, 1941, Wallace to Hull, December 16, 1941, Wallace Papers, reel 22, LC.

99. Wallace to Hull, December 16, 1940, Wallace Papers, reel 22, LC, and Roosevelt Papers, POF 146, Mexico, box 1, FDRL; Welles to Roosevelt, January 10, 1941, Roosevelt Papers, POF 4104, Wallace, Henry, FDRL.

100. Medina, *Del cardenismo al ávilacamachismo*, 18–22; Camp, *Mexican Political Biographies, 1935–1981*; Niblo, *Mexico in the 1940s*, 90–91.

101. Paz, *Strategy, Security, and Spies*, 107–22, 139, 215.

102. Lázaro Cárdenas, *Obras I*, 441–42.

103. Betty Kirk, interview with Beteta, June 3, 1941, Daniels Papers, box 654, LC.

104. To get the highest possible price for Mexican silver, when negotiating the Global Settlement's new silver purchase agreement, Mexican officials told Washington that any amount fixed above 45 cents per ounce would "be applied to the construction and conditioning of naval bases, air-fields and, in general, to material works intended to perfect the defensive system of the territory." See Memo of Castillo Nájera, February 17, 1941, Daniels Papers, box 663, FDRL.

105. Lorenzo Meyer, *Mexico and the United States in the Oil Controversy*, 219; Niblo, *War, Diplomacy, and Development*, 75, 91, 101; Paz, *Strategy, Security, and Spies*, 75–88.

106. Copy of letter from A to Morgenthau, January 21, 1941, Morgenthau Diaries, reel 97, book 349, FDRL.

107. Between March 1941 and April 1942, the foreign exchange held by the Bank of Mexico dropped from $67 million to $46 million, while overdrafts rose from $15 million pesos at the end of the Cárdenas term to $60 million pesos by May 1941. See Sugiyama, "Reluctant Neighbors," 157.

108. *FRUS*, 1941, 5:376.

109. This was Daniels's last trip to Washington as U.S. ambassador. According to Castillo Nájera, Daniels was the U.S. official who was most responsible for securing FDR and Hull's acceptance of the Global Settlement. See Castillo Nájera to Ávila Camacho, November 22, 1941, L-E-2134, AHSRE; Cronon, *Josephus Daniels in Mexico*, 267–68.

110. For a copy of the Global Settlement, see Padilla to Secretary of the Interior, November 22, 1941, DGG, 2.364(29)24, box 2, AGN. Lawson estimated that the total appraisals made by the U.S. section equaled 26 percent of the original amount claimed by the American landowners. See Lawson to Daniels, May 28, 1946, RG 76, Office of the Commissioner, U.S. Section, Agrarian Claims, Correspondence of the Commissioner, A-1 to A-6, entry 204, NAW.

111. Niblo, *War, Diplomacy, and Development*, 84.

112. Bursley noted, "The financial arrangements must be very attractive to the Mexican Government." See Bursley to Welles, October 4, 1941, RG 59, 412.11(41) Agreement/67, NAW; Memo of conversation, Córdova, English, and Bursley, October 6, 1941, RG 59, 412.11(41) Agreements/69, NAW.

113. James Langston to Charles Reed, June 20, 1945, RG 76, Approved Agrarian Claims Case Files, AMC docket 72, claim 54, box 30, NAW; Hull to Representative Thomas Rolph, May 26, 1943, RG 59, 412.11(41), Commission/3, NAW.

114. U.S. Consul George Shaw to All U.S. Consular Officers in Mexico, February 3, 1942, RG 84, Mexicali, General Records, file 350, NAW; Department of State, *American Mexican Claims Commission*, 47–50.

115. In addition to the 257 agrarian claims, the Global Settlement also settled thousands of U.S. and Mexican general claims that arose between 1868 and 1927. The U.S. never made any payments to Mexican nationals on account of the general claims; instead, the indemnity was computed into the $40 million which Mexico paid the United States. See Message from the President of the United States to the Senate of the United States, 77th Congress, 1st Session, December 9, 1941, "Mexico—Adjustment and Settlement of Certain Outstanding Claims"; Lawson to Bursley, July 17, 1941, RG 76, Lawson Correspondence, entry 203, vol. 1–3, NAW; *Diario Oficial*, May 30, 1942; Castillo Nájera to Hull, November 19, 1942, RG 59, 412.11(41) Agreements/122, NAW.

116. The agrarian claims before the American Mexican Claims Commission covered the period from January 1, 1927, to October 6, 1940. Agrarian claims filed after October 6, 1940, were reserved for a future diplomatic agreement. As with the initial Agrarian Claims Commission, most of the land expropriations that were submitted to the American Mexican Claims Commission occurred during Cárdenas's presidency. American claimants had until December 1, 1943, to file a claim before this new commission, which also was charged with reviewing the findings of both the General and Agrarian Claims Commissions and evaluating petitions filed by claimants who disagreed with the awards that were granted by the earlier commissions. For more on the work of the American Mexican Claims Commission, see Department of State, *American Mexican Claims Commission*, 3–50, 71–74, 77–207, 475–651; Hull to

Roosevelt, May 11, 1942, RG 59, 412.11(41), Agreement/102, NAW; Senator Tom Connally to Roosevelt, November 30, 1942, Roosevelt Papers, POF, 146d, Mexican Special Claims Commission, box 3, FDRL.

117. Press Release, Treasury Department, November 19, 1941, Daniels Papers, box 656, LC; Cochran, Treasury Department, Inter-office communication, August 25, 1941, Morgenthau Diaries, reel 121, book 435, and October 3, 1941, reel 124, book 447, FDRL.

118. Division of American Republics memo, September 17, 1940, RG 59, 412.11(41) Agreement/9, NAW; Press Release, Federal Loan Agency, November 19, 1941, Daniels Papers, box 656, LC.

119. Treasury Department, Inter-office Communication, October 3, 1941, Morgenthau Diaries, reel 124, book 447, FDRL; Press Release, Treasury Department, November 19, 1941, Daniels Papers, box 656, LC; Cronon, *Josephus Daniels in Mexico*, 268.

120. Division of American Republics memo, September 17, 1940, RG 59, 412.11 (41) Agreement/9, NAW.

121. *New York Times*, November 29, 1941; *Diario Oficial*, March 12, 1942, vol. 131, no. 10, 2–4; Niblo, *War, Diplomacy, and Development*, 106; John Mason Hart, *Empire and Revolution*, 396.

122. Bernstein, *The Mexican Mining Industry, 1890–1950*, 226–27. Mineral exports to the U.S. helped to fuel a wartime boom in Mexico, see Sugiyama, "Reluctant Neighbors," 225.

123. Hull to Roosevelt, July 24, 1942, Roosevelt Papers, PPF 146, FDRL; Joint statement issued by Welles and Padilla, April 1942, III-617–6 AHSRE; Sugiyama, "Reluctant Neighbors," 168.

124. Beteta to Suárez, July 17, 1942, Beteta to Castillo Nájera, July 28, 1942, Beteta to Suárez, August 1942, 39–10–29, AHSRE; Bernstein, *The Mexican Mining Industry*, 226.

125. Aguilar Camín and Meyer, *In the Shadow of the Mexican Revolution*, 161–68.

126. *FRUS*, 1941, 5:397–98.

127. Press Summary, November 23, 1941, Daniels Papers, box 656, LC.

128. *Excelsior* and *El Universal*, November 24, 1941; *El Nacional* and *Novedades*, November 27, 1941.

129. *New York Journal of Commerce*, November 21, 1941; *New York Times*, November 20, 1941.

130. *News-Democrat*, November 21, 1941.

131. *New York Herald Tribune*, November 24, 1941.

132. Cronon, *Josephus Daniels in Mexico*, 269.

133. Roosevelt to Supreme Court Justice Frank Murphy, November 26, 1941, Roosevelt Papers, PPF, 1662, Frank Murphy, FDRL.

134. Roosevelt to Ávila Camacho, November 28, 1941, Roosevelt Papers, PPF, 7075, Ávila Camacho, FDRL.

135. Memo of conversation, Castillo Nájera and Welles, December 17, 1941, Welles Papers, box 179, folder 5; letter to Welles, September 5, 1942, Welles Papers, box 81, folder 7,

FDRL; Paz, *Strategy, Security, and Spies,* 66–72, 82; Niblo, *War, Diplomacy, and Development,* 77, 96, 101; Niblo, *Mexico in the 1940s,* 119.

136. *New York Times,* April 21, 1943; Langley, *Mexico and the United States,* 25–26; Paz, *Strategy, Security, and Spies,* 135–45 and 221–22; Niblo, *Mexico in the 1940s,* 115, 141; Niblo, *War, Diplomacy, and Development,* 97–98.

137. Mexico did restrict the movement of 550 German sailors within the country. See Friedman, *Nazis and Good Neighbors,* 150, 188; Niblo, *Mexico in the 1940s,* 117–18; Moreno, *Yankee Don't Go Home,* 53–58; Paz, *Strategy, Security, and Spies,* 123–34.

138. Roosevelt Press Conference, October 20, 1942, *The Complete Presidential Press Conferences of Franklin D. Roosevelt,* 20:155–56; Gardner Jackson to Roosevelt, October 1, 1942, RG 59, 811.505/895, NAW; Cotter, *Troubled Harvest,* 11; John Mason Hart, *Empire and Revolution,* 418–19; Niblo, *War, Diplomacy, and Development,* 94–95, 100–1, 114; Niblo, *Mexico in the 1940s,* 31; Acuña, *Occupied America,* 254–63.

139. *New York Times* and *New York World-Telegram,* April 21, 1943; Casasola, *Historia gráfica de la revolución Mexicana* 7:2496–99.

CONCLUSION: MOVING AWAY FROM
BALKANIZED HISTORY

1. Vázquez and Meyer, *The United States and Mexico,* 36–38, 41–43, 80–83, 104–5.

2. Longley, *The Sparrow and the Hawk,* 162–67.

3. Ibid., x.

4. Ibid., 169–70. Mexico's geography makes it a unique middle power.

5. Ewell, *Venezuela and the United States;* Longley, *The Sparrow and the Hawk;* Buchenau, *In the Shadow of the Giant;* Schuler, *Mexico between Hitler and Roosevelt;* Roorda, *The Dictator Next Door.*

6. Craig, *The First Agraristas,* 8–11, 234–39.

7. Joseph, "Close Encounters," 16.

8. Henderson, *The Worm in the Wheat,* 2. Craig also sees few ideological purists in Lagos's agrarista movement. Instead, the Jalisco peasant leaders were "pragmatic eclectics" who "used various organizational alliances and ideological perspectives" to reach their goal of land redistribution. See Craig, *The First Agraristas,* 238. Boyer also notes the lack of a dominant political ideology in rural Michoacán and the contradictory positions held by the region's peasants. See Boyer, *Becoming Campesinos,* 10–12.

9. Striffler, *In the Shadows of State and Capital,* 9–10.

10. Buchenau, *In the Shadow of the Giant,* xi; Joseph, "Close Encounters," 21.

11. Coronil, "Foreword," xii.

12. Mintz, "The Rural Proletariat and the Problem of Rural Proletarian Consciousness," 299.

BIBLIOGRAPHY

ARCHIVAL SOURCES

Mexico City

Archivo General de la Nación (AGN)
    Ramo Presidentes,
        Fondo Álvaro Obregón y Plutarco Elías Calles (Obregón and Calles Papers)
        Fondo Pascual Ortiz Rubio (Ortiz Rubio Papers)
        Fondo Emilio Portes Gil (Portes Gil Papers)
        Fondo Abelardo L. Rodríguez (Rodríguez Papers)
        Fondo Lázaro Cárdenas del Río (Cárdenas Papers)
        Fondo Manuel Ávila Camacho (Ávila Camacho Papers)
      Ramo Gobernación, Dirección General de Gobierno (DGG)
      Centro de Información Gráfica, Archivo Fotográfico
Archivo Histórico de la Secretaría de Relaciones Exteriores (AHSRE)
Fideicomiso Archivos Plutarco Elías Calles y Fernando Torreblanca (Calles and
   Torreblanca Archive)
    Archivo Álvaro Obregón
    Archivo Plutarco Elías Calles
    Colección Documental de la Emajada de los Estados Unidos en México
Archivo Central del Registro Agrario Nacional
    Archivo de la Secretaría de la Reform Agraria (ASRA)
Instituto Nacional de Antropología e Historia
    Archivos Institucionales de los Estados: Serie Sonora
    Hemerografía y Publicaciones Periódicas: Serie Periódicos de la Ciudad de
      México; Serie Periódicos de los Estados
Hermoteca, Universidad Nacional Autónoma de México

Mexicali, Baja California Norte

Archivo Histórico del Estado de Baja California (AHEBC)
   Fondo Territorio Norte
Museo del Asalto a las Tierras, Ejido Michoacán de Ocampo

Hermosillo, Sonora

Archivo del Gobierno del Estado de Sonora (AGES)
   Archivo Administrativo del Gobierno del Estado de Sonora (AAGES)

Washington D.C., Suitland and College Park, Maryland

National Archives (NAW)
   Record Group 59 (RG 59): General Records of the Department of State
   Record Group 76 (RG 76): Records of Boundary and Claims Commissions and
     Arbitrations
   Record Group 84 (RG 84): Records of the Foreign Service Posts of the Depart-
     ment of State
Library of Congress (LC)
   Papers of Edward Tracy Clark
   Papers of Josephus Daniels
   Papers of Herbert Fies
   Papers of Cordell Hull
   Papers of Henry Wallace

Hyde Park, New York

Franklin Delano Roosevelt Library (FDRL)
   Papers of Adolf Berle
   Papers of Robert Walton Moore
   Papers of Henry Morgenthau Jr.
   Diary of Henry Morgenthau Jr.
   Papers of Franklin D. Roosevelt
     President's Official File (POF)
     President's Personal File (PPF)
     President's Secretary's File (PSF)
   Papers of Henry Wallace
   Papers of Sumner Welles

New York, New York

Butler Library, Columbia University
   Papers of Frank Tannenbaum

Tucson, Arizona

Special Collections, University of Arizona Library (sc ual)
  Records of the Compañia Constructora Richardson, S.A. (ccr Records)
Arizona Historical Society
  Photographic Collection

Corona del Mar, California

Sherman Library (sl)
  Archive of the Colorado River Land Company (crlc)

INTERVIEWS

Cuauhtémoc Cárdenas, March 2, 1996, Mexico City
Ejidatarios Pedro Pérez, Apolinar Pérez, Liborio Pérez Fernández, Bonifacio Cabrera
  Cordova, Manuel Encinos, Pedro Jiménez Figueroa, and Marciel López, Ejido
  Michoacán de Ocampo, Mexicali, July 12, 13, 19, and 20, 2001 (Mexicali Interviews)
Director Jeremias Guillén, Museo del Asalto a las Tierras, Mexicali, July 19, 2001

NEWSPAPERS AND PERIODICALS

Boletín Oficial (government organ of Sonora)
Brooklyn Daily Eagle
Diario Oficial (federal government organ of Mexico)
Evening Globe (Boston)
The Evening Star (Washington, D.C.)
Excelsior (Mexico City)
La Gaceta (Guaymas)
Harper's Magazine
Heraldo de Yaqui (Ciudad Obregón)
Herald Post
El Hispano Americano (Mexicali)
El Hispano Americano (Tijuana)
Kansas City Star
Los Angeles Times
El Mundo (Mexicali)
El Nacional (Mexico City)
The Nation
Newark Evening News
New York Enquirer
New York Herald Tribune
New York Journal of Commerce
New York Times

New York Times Magazine

New York World-Telegram

News-Democrat (Goshen, Ind.)

Nogales Herald (Nogales, Ariz.)

Novedades

La Opinión (Los Angeles)

Periódico Oficial (government organ of Baja California)

San Antonio Express

Sol de Mayo: Revista Anual de Literatura y Variedades (Mexicali)

Time (Geneva, N.Y.)

El Universal (Mexico City)

La Voz de la Frontera (Mexicali)

Washington Herald

Washington Post

Washington Star

Washington Times

PUBLISHED PRIMARY SOURCES, BOOKS, ARTICLES,
AND DISSERTATIONS

Aboites Aguilar, Luis. *Norte precario: Poblamiento y colonización en México, 1760–1940.* Mexico City: El Colegio de México, 1995.

Acosta Montoya, David. *"Precursores del agrarismo" y "El asalto a las tierras" en el estado de Baja California.* Baja California, Mexico: Instituto de Investigaciones Históricas, 1985.

Acuña, Rodolpho. *Occupied America: A History of the Chicanos.* New York: Harper and Row, 1988.

Aguilar Camín, Héctor. *La frontera nómada: Sonora y la Revolución Mexicana.* Mexico City: Siglo Veintiuno, 1977.

Aguilar Camín, Héctor, and Lorenzo Meyer. *In the Shadow of the Mexican Revolution: Contemporary Mexican History, 1910–1989.* Austin: University of Texas Press, 1993.

Aguilar Zéleny, Alejandro, ed. *Tres procesos de lucha por la sobrevivencia de la tribu Yaqui: Testimonios.* Hermosillo: Universidad de Sonora, 1994.

Aguirre Bernal, Celso. *Compendio histórico-biográfico de Mexicali, 1539–1966,* and *Suplemento, 1966–1968.* 2 vols. Mexicali, Baja California: n.p., 1968.

——. "La mexicanización del Valle de Mexicali." In *Panorama histórico de Baja California,* ed. David Piñera. Tijuana: Centro de Investigaciones Históricas, UNAM/UABC, 1983.

——. *Breve historia del estado de Baja California.* Mexico City: Ediciones Quinto Sol, 1987.

——. "Génesis y destino de la liga de comunidades agrarias y sindicatos campesinos del estado de Baja California." In *Historia de las ligas de comunidades agrarias y sindicatos campesinos,* vol. 4, ed. Edén Ferrer. Mexico City: Centro de Estudios Históricos del Agrarismo en México, 1988.

Alanís Enciso, Fernando Saúl. "Las políticas migratorias de Estados Unidos y los trabajadores mexicanos, 1840–1940." In *Encuentro en la frontera: Mexicanos y norte americanos en un espacio común,* ed. Manuel Ceballos Ramírez. Mexico City: El Colegio de México, 2001.

Alvarez, Robert. *Familia: Migration and Adaptation in Baja and Alta California, 1800–1975.* Berkeley: University of California Press, 1987.

Alvear Acevedo, Carlos. *Lázaro Cárdenas: El hombre y el mito.* Mexico City: Editorial Jus. 1961.

American Mexican Claims Commission. *Report to the Secretary of State.* Washington, D.C.: Government Printing Office, 1948.

Anguiano, Arturo. *El estado y la política obrera del Cardenismo.* Mexico City: Ediciones Era, 1975.

Anguiano Téllez, María Eugenia. "La formación en el Valle de Mexicali a principios de siglo." In *Historia y Cultura,* vol. 6. Tijuana: El Colegio de la Frontera Norte, 1992.

——. *Agricultura y migración en el Valle de Mexicali.* Tijuana: El Colegio de la Frontera Norte, 1995.

Ankerson, Dudley. *Agrarian Warlord: Saturnino Cedillo and the Mexican Revolution in San Luis Potosí.* DeKalb: Northern Illinois University Press, 1984.

Appelbaum, Nancy, Anne Macpherson, and Karin Rosemblatt, eds. *Race and Nation in Modern Latin America.* Chapel Hill: University of North Carolina Press, 2003.

Ashby, Joe. *Organized Labor and the Mexican Revolution under Lázaro Cárdenas.* Chapel Hill: University of North Carolina Press, 1967.

Atkins, G. Pope. *Latin America and the Caribbean in the International Political System.* 4th ed. Boulder, Colo.: Westview Press, 1999.

Balderrama, Francisco, and Raymond Rodriguez. *Decade of Betrayal: Mexican Repatriation during the 1930s.* Albuquerque: University of New Mexico Press, 1995.

Ballesteros, Juan, Sergio Reyes Osorio, Rodolfo Stavenhagen, and Salomón Eckstein. *Estructura agraria y desarrollo agrícola en México: Estudio sobre las relaciones entre la tenencia y uso de la tierra y el desarrollo agrícola de México.* Mexico City: Fondo de Cultura Económica, Centro de Investigaciones Agrarias, 1974.

Bantjes, Adrian. "Politics, Class and Culture in Post-Revolutionary Mexico: Cardenismo and Sonora, 1929–1940." PhD diss., University of Texas, Austin, 1991.

——. *As If Jesus Walked on Earth: Cardenismo, Sonora, and the Mexican Revolution.* Wilmington, Del.: Scholarly Resources Inc., 1998.

Bartra, Armando. *Los herederos de Zapata: Movimientos campesinos postrevolucionarios en México, 1920–1980.* Mexico City: Ediciones Era, 1985.

Bartra, Roger. "Peasants and Political Power in Mexico: A Theoretical Approach." *Latin American Perspectives* 2, no. 2 (1975): 125–45.

Basurto, Jorge. *Del ávilacamachismo al alemanismo, 1940–1952.* Mexico City: El Colegio de México, 1981.

——. *Cárdenas y el poder sindical.* Mexico City: Ediciones Era, 1983.

Bayly, C. A. "Rallying around the Subaltern." *Journal of Peasant Studies* 16, no. 1 (1988): 110–20.

Becker, Marjorie. "Black and White and Color: 'Cardenismo' and the Search for a Campesino Ideology." *Comparative Studies in Society and History* 29, no. 3 (1987): 453–66.

——. "Cardenistas, Campesinos, and the Weapons of the Weak: The Limits of Everyday Resistance in Michoacán, 1930–1940." *Journal of Peasant Studies* 16 (1989): 233–50.

——. *Setting the Virgin On Fire: Lázaro Cárdenas, Michoacán Peasants, and the Redemption of the Mexican Revolution.* Berkeley: University of California Press, 1995.

Beelen, George. "The Harding Administration and Mexico: Diplomacy by Economic Persuasion." *The Americas* 41 (1984): 177–89.

Benítez, Fernando. *Lázaro Cárdenas y la revolución mexicana: El cardenismo.* 3 vols. Mexico City: Fondo de Cultura Económica, 1978.

Benjamin, Thomas. "The Leviathan on the Zócalo: Recent Historiography of the Postrevolutionary Mexican State." *Latin American Research Review* 20, no. 3 (1985): 195–217.

——. *La Revolución: Mexico's Great Revolution as Memory, Myth, and History.* Austin: University of Texas Press, 2000.

Berle, Adolf. *Latin America: Diplomacy and Reality.* New York: Harper & Row, 1962.

Berle, Beatrice Bishop, and Travis Beal Jacobs, eds. *Navigating the Rapids, 1918–1971: From the Papers of Adolf A. Berle.* New York: Harcourt Brace Jovanovich, Inc., 1973.

Bernstein, Marvin. *The Mexican Mining Industry, 1890–1950: A Study of the Interaction of Politics, Economics, and Technology.* Albany: State University of New York, 1965.

Beteta, Ramón. "Economic Aspects of the Six Year Plan." In *The Economic and Social Program of Mexico,* ed. Ramón Beteta. Mexico City: DAPP, 1935.

Black, George. *The Good Neighbor: How the United States Wrote the History of Central America and the Caribbean.* New York: Pantheon, 1988.

Blaisdell, Lowell. "Was It Revolution or Filibustering? The Mystery of the Flores Magón Revolt in Baja California." *Pacific Historical Review,* 23 (1954): 147–64.

——. "Henry Lane Wilson and the Overthrow of Mexico." *Southwestern Social Science Quarterly* 43 (1962): 126–35.

——. "Harry Chandler and Mexican Border Intrigue, 1914–1917." *Pacific Historical Review* 35 (1966): 385–93.

Blanco Moheno, Roberto. *Tata Lázaro: Vida, obra y muerte de Cárdenas, Múgica y Carrillo Puerto.* Mexico City: Editorial Diana, 1972.

Blasier, Cole. *The Hovering Giant: U.S. Responses to Revolutionary Change in Latin America, 1910–1985.* Pittsburgh: University of Pittsburgh Press, 1985.

Bliss, Katherine Elaine. *Compromised Positions: Prostitution, Public Health, and Gender*

Politics in Revolutionary Mexico City. University Park: Penn State University Press, 2001.

Bodayla, Stephen. *Financial Diplomacy: The United States and Mexico, 1919–1933.* New York: Garland Publishing, Inc., 1987.

Bortz, Jeffrey. "The Genesis of the Mexican Labor Relations System: Federal Labor Policy and the Textile Industry 1925–1940." *The Americas* 52, no. 1 (1995): 43–69.

Bosques, Gilberto. *The National Revolutionary Party of Mexico and the Six Year Plan.* Mexico City: Bureau of Foreign Information, 1937.

Boyer, Christopher. *Becoming Campesinos: Politics, Identity, and Agrarian Struggle in Postrevolutionary Michoacán, 1920–1935.* Stanford: Stanford University Press, 2003.

Brass, Tom. "Latin American Peasants—New Paradigms for Old?" *Journal of Peasant Studies* 29, no. 3 (2002): 1–40.

Britton, John. *Revolution and Ideology: Images of the Mexican Revolution in the United States.* Lexington: University Press of Kentucky, 1995.

Brown, Jonathan. *Oil and Revolution in Mexico.* Berkeley: University of California Press, 1994.

——. "Acting for Themselves: Workers and the Mexican Oil Nationalization." In *Workers' Control in Latin America, 1930–1979,* ed. Jonathan Brown. Chapel Hill: University of North Carolina Press, 1997.

Brown, Lyle. "Mexican Church-State Relations, 1933–1940." *A Journal of Church and State* 7 (1964): 202–22.

——. "Cárdenas: Creating a Campesino Power Base for Presidential Policy." In *Essays on the Mexican Revolution: Revisionist Views of the Leaders,* ed. George Wolfskill and Douglas Richmond. Austin: University of Texas Press, 1979.

Buchenau, Jürgen. *In the Shadow of the Giant: The Making of Mexico's Central America Policy, 1876–1930.* Tuscaloosa: University of Alabama Press, 1998.

Caballero, Manuel. *Latin America and the Comintern, 1919–1943.* Cambridge: Cambridge University Press, 1986.

Camou Healy, Ernesto. "Yaquis y Mayos: Cultivadores de las valles." In *Historia general de Sonora: Historia contemporánea de Sonora, 1929–1984,* ed. Sergio Calderón Valdés. Hermosillo: El Colegio de Sonora, 1988.

Camp, Roderic Ai. *Mexican Political Biographies, 1935–1993.* Austin: University of Texas Press, 1995.

Campbell, Hugh. *La derecha radical en México, 1929–1949.* Mexico City: Sepsetentas, 1976.

Camposortega Cruz, Sergio. "Análisis demográfico de las corrientes migratorias a México desde finales de siglo XIX." In Ota Mishima, *Destino México.*

Cárdenas, Enrique. "The Great Depression and Industrialization: The Case of Mexico." In *Latin America in the 1930s: The Role of the Periphery in World Crisis,* ed. Rosemary Thorp. New York: Macmillan, 1984.

——. *La hacienda pública y la política económica, 1929–1958.* Mexico City: Fondo de Cultura Económica, 1994.

Cárdenas, Lázaro. *Plan Sexenal.* Mexico City: Comisión Nacional Editorial, 1933.

——. *El problema de los territorios federales, un llamamiento al patriotismo y al sentido de responsabilidad del pueblo mexicano.* Mexico City: Talleres Gráficos de la Nación, 1936.

——. *Cárdenas Habla.* Mexico City: La Impresora, 1940.

——. "Discurso ante el congreso de la unión, el 30 de noviembre de 1934." In *Los Presidentes de México ante la nación: Informes, manifiestos y documentos de 1821 a 1966,* vol. 4, ed. Luis González. Mexico City: Legislatura de la Camera de Diputados, 1966.

——. *Obras I—Apuntes, 1913–1940.* Mexico City: Universidad Nacional Autónoma de México, 1972.

——. "Exposición del presidente de la república sobre la reconstrucción integral de los territorios de Baja California y Quintana Roo, en México, D.F." In Lázaro Cárdenas, *Palabras y documentos públicos de Lázaro Cárdenas: Informes de gobierno y mensajes presidenciales de año nuevo, 1928–1940,* 2 vols. Mexico City: Siglo Veintiuno, 1978.

Cardiel Marín, Rosario. "La migración china en el norte de Baja California, 1877–1949." In Ota Mishima, *Destino México.*

Carr, Barry. "The Mexican Communist Party and Agrarian Mobilization in the Laguna, 1920–1940: A Worker-Peasant Alliance?" *Hispanic American Historical Review* 67, no. 3 (1987): 371–404.

——. *Marxism and Communism in Twentieth-Century Mexico.* Lincoln: University of Nebraska Press, 1992.

Carreras de Velasco, Mercedes. *Los mexicanos que devolvió la crisis.* Mexico City: Secretaría de Relaciones Exteriores, 1974.

Casasola, Gustavo. *Historia gráfica de la Revolución Mexicana, 1900–1970,* vols. 1–10. Mexico City: Editorial Trillas, 1973.

Cassigoli Salamón, Rossana. "Educación e indigenismo en México: La géstión cardenista." In Escárcega López and Escobar Toledo, *El cardenismo.*

Chamberlin, Eugene Keith. "Mexican Colonization versus American Interests in Lower California." *Pacific Historical Review* 20 (1951): 43–55.

Chassen de López, Francie. *Lombardo Toledano y el movimiento obrero mexicano, 1917–1940.* Mexico City: Editorial Extemporaneos, 1977.

Ciment, James, ed. *Encyclopedia of the Great Depression and the New Deal,* vols. 1–2. Armonk, N.Y.: M. E. Sharpe, Inc., 2001.

Clark, Marjorie Ruth. *Organized Labor in Mexico.* New York: Russell & Russell, 1973.

Cline, Howard. *The United States and Mexico.* Rev. ed. New York: Atheneum, 1969.

Coatsworth, John. "Comment on 'The United States and the Mexican Peasantry.'" In *Rural Revolt in Mexico and U.S. Intervention,* ed. Daniel Nugent. La Jolla: Center for U.S.-Mexican Studies, 1988.

Cobbs, Elizabeth. "Why They Think Like Gringos." *Diplomatic History* 21, no. 2 (1997): 307–16.

Consejo Nacional de Población, Mexico. *Baja California demográfico.* Mexico City: Talleres Gráficos de la Nación, 1985.

Contreras, Ariel. *México 1940: Industrialización y crisis política*. Mexico City: Siglo Veintiuno, 1977.

Contreras Mora, Francisco. "El acuerdo de asaltar la tierra." *Ciguatan* 7 (1987): 22–44.

Córdova, Arnaldo. *La política de masas del cardenismo*. Mexico City: Ediciones Era, 1975.

Cornejo Murrieta, Gerardo, ed. *Historia general de Sonora*. Vol. 5 of *Historia contemporánea de Sonora, 1929–1984*. Hermosillo: Gobierno del Estado de Sonora, 1985.

Cornelius, Wayne. "Nation Building, Participation, and Distribution: The Politics of Social Reform under Cárdenas." In *Crisis, Choice, and Change: Historical Studies of Political Development*, eds. Gabriel Almond, Scott Flanagan, and Robert Mundt. Boston: Little, Brown, 1973.

Coronil, Fernando. "Foreword." In *Close Encounters of Empire: Writing the Cultural History of U.S.-Latin American Relations*, eds. Gilbert Joseph, Catherine LeGrand, and Ricardo Salvatore. Durham: Duke University Press, 1998.

Cothran, Dan. "Budgetary Secrecy and Policy Strategy: Mexico under Cárdenas." *Mexican Studies* 2, no. 1 (1986): 35–58.

Cottam, Martha. *Images and Intervention: U.S. Policies in Latin America*. Pittsburgh: University of Pittsburgh Press, 1994.

Cotter, Joseph. "The Origins of the Green Revolution in Mexico." In *Latin America in the 1940s: War and Postwar Transitions*, ed. David Rock. Berkeley: University of California Press, 1994.

——. *Troubled Harvest: Agronomy and Revolution in Mexico, 1880–2002*. Westport, Conn.: Praeger, 2003.

Craig, Ann. *The First Agraristas: An Oral History of a Mexican Agrarian Reform Movement*. Berkeley: University of California Press, 1983.

Cronon, Edmund. *Josephus Daniels in Mexico*. Madison: University of Wisconsin Press, 1960.

Cuevas Cancino, Francisco. *Roosevelt y la buena vecindad*. Mexico City: Fondo de Cultura Económica, 1954.

Cullather, Nick. *Illusions of Influence: The Political Economy of United States–Philippine Relations, 1942–1960*. Stanford: Stanford University Press, 1994.

Cumberland, Charles. "The Sonora Chinese and the Mexican Revolution." *Hispanic American Historical Review* 40 (1960): 191–211.

Dabdoub, Claudio. *Historia del Valle del Yaqui*. Mexico City: Editorial Porrúa, 1964.

Dallek, Robert. *Franklin D. Roosevelt and American Foreign Policy, 1932–1945*. New York: Oxford University Press, 1979.

Daniels, Josephus. *Shirt-Sleeve Diplomat*. Chapel Hill: University of North Carolina Press, 1947.

Davids, Jules. *American Political and Economic Penetration of Mexico, 1877–1920*. New York: Arno Press, 1976.

Davis, Harold, and C. Wilson. *Latin American Foreign Policies: An Analysis*. Baltimore: Johns Hopkins University Press, 1975.

Davis, Kenneth. *FDR: Into the Storm, 1937–1940*. New York: Random House, 1993.

Dawson, Alexander. *Indian and Nation in Revolutionary Mexico*. Tucson: University of Arizona Press, 2004.

De la Peña, Guillermo. "Rural Mobilizations in Latin America Since *c*. 1920." In *Latin America: Politics and Society Since 1930*, ed. Leslie Bethell. Cambridge: Cambridge University Press, 1998.

Delpar, Helen. *The Enormous Vogue of Things Mexican: Cultural Relations between the United States and Mexico, 1920–1935*. Tuscaloosa: University of Alabama Press, 1992.

Departamento Autónomo de Prensa y Publicidád, *México en acción*. Mexico City: D.A.A.P., 1938.

Department of State. *Report of the Delegation of the United States of America to the Inter-America Conference for the Maintenance of Peace: Buenos Aires, December 1– 23, 1936*. Conference Series 33. Washington, D.C.: Government Printing Office, 1937.

———. *American Mexican Claims Commission*. Publication 2859, Arbitration Series 9. Washington, D.C.: Government Printing Office, 1948.

Dipp Varela, Alfredo. "Pioneros del movimiento agrario en el Valle de Mexicali." *Ciguatan* 16 (1989): 1–81.

———. *Así abrimos la tierra: Compilación testimonial de los primeros colonizadores del Valle de Mexicali*. Mexicali: Instituto de Investigaciones Históricas del Estado de Baja California, 1991.

Dirección General de Construcción de Ferrocarriles. *Ferrocarril Sonora–Baja California*. Mexico City: Secretaría de Comunicaciones y Obras Públicas, 1948.

Duarte Vargas, Marcelino. "La lucha por la tierra en Baja California." In *Historia de las ligas de comunidades agrarias y sindicatos campesinos*, vol. 4, ed. Edén Ferrer. Mexico City: Centro de Estudios Históricos del Agrarismo en México, 1988.

Dueñas Montes, Francisco. *Territorio Norte de la Baja California: Temas históricos, 1932–1953*. Mexicali: Instituto de Investigaciones Históricas de Baja California, 1984.

Duggan, Laurence. *The Americas: The Search for Hemispheric Security*. New York: Henry Holt and Company, 1949.

Duncan, Robert. "The Chinese and the Economic Development of Northern Baja California, 1889–1929." *Hispanic American Historical Review* 74 (1994): 615–47.

Durán, Marco Antonio. *El agrarismo mexicano*. 2nd ed. Mexico City: Siglo Veintiuno, 1972.

Dwyer, John J. "The End of U.S. Intervention in Mexico: Franklin Roosevelt and the Expropriation of American-Owned Agricultural Property." *Presidential Studies Quarterly* 28, no. 3 (1998): 496–510.

———. "Diplomatic Weapons of the Weak: Mexican Policymaking during the U.S.-Mexican Agrarian Dispute, 1934–1941." *Diplomatic History* 26, no. 3 (2002): 375–95.

Eckstein, Salomón. *El ejido colectivo en México*. Mexico City: Fondo de Cultura Económica, 1966.

Ellis, L. Ethan. "Dwight Morrow and the Church-State Controversy in Mexico." *Hispanic American Historical Review* 38, no. 4 (1958): 482–505.

Escárcega López, Everado. "El principio de la reforma." In Escárcega López and Escobar Toledo, *El cardenismo.*

Escárcega López, Everado, and Saúl Escobar Toledo. *El cardenismo: Un parteaguas en el proceso agrario nacional, 1934–1940.* Vol. 5 of *Historia de la cuestión agraria mexicana.* Mexico City: Siglo Veintiuno, 1990.

Escobar Toledo, Saúl. "El cardenismo más allá del reparto: Acciones y resultados." In Escárcega López and Escobar Toledo, *El cardenismo.*

——. "La ruptura cardenista." In Escárcega López and Escobar Toledo, *El cardenismo.*

Espinosa de los Monteros, Antonio. "La controversia monetaria actual." *El Trimestre Económico* 1, no. 2 (1934).

Ewell, Judith. *Venezuela and the United States: From Monroe's Hemisphere to Petroleum's Empire.* Athens: University of Georgia Press, 1996.

Fabela, Isidro. *Buena y mala vecindad.* Mexico City: Editorial América Nueva, 1958.

Fabila, Alfonso. *Las tribus Yaquis de Sonora: Su cultura y anhelada autodeterminación.* Mexico City: Departamento de Asuntos Indígenas, 1940.

Falcón, Romana. "El surgimiento de agrarismo cardenista: Una revisión de las tesis populistas." *Historia Mexicana* 27, no. 3 (1978): 333–86.

——. *Revolución y caciquismo: San Luis Potosí, 1910–1938.* Mexico City: Colegiode México, 1984.

Fallaw, Ben. "Cárdenas and the Caste War That Wasn't: State Power and Indigenismo in Post-Revolutionary Yucatán." *The Americas* 53, no. 4 (1997): 551–77.

——. *Cárdenas Compromised: The Failure of Reform in Postrevolutionary Yucatán.* Durham: Duke University Press, 2001.

Feller, H. Abraham. *The Mexican Claims Commissions, 1923–1934: A Study in the Law and Procedure of International Tribunals.* New York: Macmillan, 1935.

Ferrer, Edén. *Historia de las ligas de comunidades agrarias y sindicatos campesinos,* vol. 4. Mexico City: Centro de Estudios Históricos del Agrarismo en México, 1988.

Ferry, Elizabeth. *Not Ours Alone: Patrimony, Value, and Collectivity in Contemporary Mexico.* New York: Columbia University Press, 2005.

Finegold, Kenneth, and Theda Skocpol. *State and Party in America's New Deal.* Madison: University of Wisconsin Press, 1995.

Fitzgerald, E. V. K. "Restructuring through the Depression: The State and Capital Accumulation in Mexico, 1925–1940." In *Latin America in the 1930s: The Role of the Periphery in World Crisis,* ed. Rosemary Thorp. New York: Macmillan, 1984.

Foreign Relations of the United States. Washington, D.C.: Government Printing Office, 1917–1941.

Foweraker, Joe, and Ann Craig, eds. *Popular Movements and Political Change in Mexico.* Boulder, Colo.: Lynne Rienner Publishers, Inc., 1990.

Frank, Waldo. "Cárdenas of Mexico." *Foreign Affairs* 18 (1939): 91–102.

Freeman Smith, Robert. *The United States and Revolutionary Nationalism in Mexico, 1916–1932.* Chicago: University of Chicago Press, 1972.

Freidel, Frank. *Franklin D. Roosevelt: A Rendezvous with Destiny*. Boston: Little, Brown and Company, 1990.

Friedman, Max Paul. *Nazis and Good Neighbors: The United States Campaign against the Germans of Latin America in World War II*. Cambridge: Cambridge University Press, 2003.

——. "There Goes the Neighborhood: Blacklisting Germans in Latin America and the Evanescence of the Good Neighbor Policy." *Diplomatic History* 27 (2003): 569–97.

Friedrich, Paul. *Agrarian Revolt in a Mexican Village*. Englewood Cliffs, N.J.: Prentice-Hall, Inc., 1970.

Fugigake Cruz. "Las rebelliones campesinas en el Porfiriato." In *Historia de la cuestión agraria mexicana: La tierra y el poder 1800–1910*, ed. Enrique Semo. Mexico City: Siglo Veintiuno, 1988.

Gambone, Michael. *Eisenhower, Somoza, and the Cold War in Nicaragua*. Westport, Conn.: Praeger, 1997.

Gamio, Manuel. *Mexican Immigration to the United States*. 1927. Reprint, New York: Dover Press, 1971.

Garcia, Matt. "Chicana/o and Latina/o Workers in a Changing Discipline." *Humbolt Journal of Social Relations* 22, no. 1 (1996): 83–95.

Garcia-Gonzalez, Camille. *Mexican Workers and American Dreams: Immigration, Repatriation, and California Farm Labor, 1900–1939*. New Brunswick, N.J.: Rutgers University Press, 1994.

Gardner, Lloyd. *Economic Aspects of New Deal Diplomacy*. Madison: University of Wisconsin Press, 1964.

Garduño, Everardo. *Voces y ecos del Valle de Mexicali: Introducción a la historia agraria del Valle de Mexicali*. Mexicali: Universidad Autónoma de Baja California, 1991.

Garibaldi, Lorenzo. *Memoria de la gestión gubernamental del C. Gral. Román Yocupicio en el estado de Sonora, 1937, 1938, 1939: Aspectos principales de su labor social y constructiva*. Hermosillo: J. C. Gálvez, 1939.

Gellman, Irwin. *Roosevelt and Batista: Good Neighbor Diplomacy in Cuba, 1933–1945*. Albuquerque: University of New Mexico Press, 1973.

——. *Good Neighbor Diplomacy: United States Policies in Latin America, 1933–1945*. Baltimore: Johns Hopkins University Press, 1979.

——. *Secret Affairs: Franklin Roosevelt, Cordell Hull, and Sumner Welles*. Baltimore: Johns Hopkins University Press, 1995.

Gilderhus, Mark. *The Second Century: U.S.–Latin American Relations since 1889*. Wilmington, Del.: Scholarly Resources, 2000.

Gilly, Adolfo. *El cardenismo, una utopía mexicana*. Mexico City: Lleón y Cal Editores, 1994.

Gledhill, John. *Casi Nada: A Study of Agrarian Reform in the Homeland of Cardenismo*. Albany: Institute for Mesoamerican Studies, University at Albany, State University of New York, 1991.

Gobat, Michel. *Confronting the American Dream: Nicaragua under U.S. Imperial Rule.* Durham: Duke University Press, 2005.

Gómez Estrada, José Alfredo. *Realidad y ensueños: Historia parcial de Baja California a través de las leyendas.* Mexicali: Universidad Autónoma de Baja California, 1992.

——. *Gobierno y casinos: El origen de la riqueza de Abelardo L. Rodríguez.* Mexicali: Universidad Autónoma de Baja California, 2002.

Gonzales, Michael. *The Mexican Revolution, 1910–1940.* Albuquerque: University of New Mexico Press, 2002.

González, Luis. *Los días del presidente Cárdenas.* Mexico City: El Colegio de México, 1981.

González Feliz, Maricela. *El proceso de aculturación de la población de origen chino en la ciudad de Mexicali.* Mexicali: Universidad Autónoma de Baja California, 1990.

González Ibarra, Juan de Dios. *Interpretaciones del Cardenismo.* Mexico City: Universidad Autónoma Metropolitana, 1988.

González Navarro, Moisés. *La Confederación Nacional Campesina: Un grupo de presión en la reforma agraria mexicana.* Mexico City: Universidad Nacional Autónoma de México, 1977.

Gordillo, Gustavo. *Campesinos al asalto del cielo: Una reforma agraria con autonomía.* Mexico City: Siglo Veintiuno, 1988.

Gordon, Colin. *New Deals: Business, Labor, and Politics in America, 1920–1935.* New York: Cambridge University Press, 1994.

Gould, Jeffrey. *To Lead As Equals: Rural Protest and Political Consciousness in Chinandega, Nicaragua, 1912–1979.* Chapel Hill: University of North Carolina Press, 1990.

Grayson, George. *The Politics of Mexican Oil.* Pittsburgh: University of Pittsburgh Press, 1980.

Green, David. *The Containment of Latin America: A History of the Myths and Realities of the Good Neighbor Policy.* Chicago: Quadrangle Books, 1971.

Griffin-Pierce, Trudy. *Native Peoples of the Southwest.* Albuquerque: University of New Mexico Press, 2000.

Grijalva Larrañaga, Edna Aide. "La Colorado River Land Company." In *Panorama histórico de la Baja California,* ed. David Piñera Ramírez. Tijuana: Centro de Investigaciones Históricas UABC, 1983.

Guardarrama, Rocío, Cristina Martínez, and Lourdes Martínez. "Las alianzas políticas." In Cornejo Murrieta, *Historia general de Sonora.*

Guardino, Peter. *Peasants, Politics, and the Formation of Mexico's National State.* Stanford: Stanford University Press, 1996.

Guerrant, Edward. *Roosevelt's Good Neighbor Policy.* Albuquerque: University of New Mexico Press, 1950.

Guha, Ranajit. *Subaltern Studies: Writing on South Asian History and Society.* Oxford: Oxford University Press, 1992.

Gutelman, Michel. *Capitalismo y reforma agraria en México.* Mexico City: Ediciones Era, 1974.

Gutiérrez, Natividad. *Nationalist Myth and Ethnic Identities: Indigenous Intellectuals and the Mexican State.* Lincoln: University of Nebraska Press, 1999.

Haber, Stephen. *Industry and Underdevelopment: The Industrialization of Mexico, 1890–1940.* Stanford: Stanford University Press, 1989.

Haddox, John. *Vasconcelos of Mexico: Philosopher and Prophet.* Austin: University of Texas Press, 1967.

Hall, Linda. "Álvaro Obregón and the Agrarian Movement, 1912–1920." In *Caudillo and Peasant in the Mexican Revolution,* ed. David Brading. Cambridge: Cambridge University Press, 1980.

——. "Álvaro Obregón and the Politics of Mexican Land Reform, 1920–1924." *Hispanic American Review* 60 (1980): 213–38.

——. *Oil, Banks and Politics: The U.S. and Postrevolutionary Mexico, 1917–1924.* Austin: University of Texas Press, 1995.

Halperin, Maurice. "Mexico Shifts Her Foreign Policy." *Foreign Affairs* 19, no. 1 (1940): 207–21.

Hamilton, Nora. *The Limits of State Autonomy: Post-Revolutionary Mexico.* Princeton: Princeton University Press, 1982.

Hansen, Alvin. "Hemispheric Solidarity." *Foreign Affairs* 19 (1940): 12–21.

Harrison, Benjamin. *Dollar Diplomat: Chandler Anderson and American Diplomacy in Mexico and Nicaragua, 1913–1928.* Pullman: Washington State University Press, 1988.

Hart, Jack. *The Information Empire: The Rise of the "Los Angeles Times" and the Times Mirror Corporation.* Washington, D.C.: University Press of America, 1981.

Hart, John Mason. *Revolutionary Mexico: The Coming and Process of the Mexican Revolution.* Berkeley: University of California Press, 1987.

——. *Empire and Revolution: The Americans in Mexico Since the Civil War.* Berkeley: University of California Press, 2002.

Hay, Eduardo. *Discursos.* Mexico City: Talleres Gráficos de la Nación, 1940.

Henderson, Timothy. *The Worm in the Wheat: Rosalie Evans and the Agrarian Struggle in the Puebla-Tlaxcala Valley of Mexico, 1906–1927.* Durham: Duke University Press, 1998.

Hendricks, William. "Guillermo Andrade and Land Development on the Mexican Colorado River Delta, 1874–1905." PhD diss., University of Southern California, 1967.

——. "Port Otis." In *San Diego Corral of the Westerners,* Brand Book no. 2. San Diego: San Diego Corral of the Westerners, 1971.

Henson, James. "United States Business Interests in the Structure of State-Society Relations in Mexico, 1920–1935." PhD diss., University of Texas, 1996.

Hermida Ruiz, Ángel J. *Cárdenas: Comandante del Pacífico.* Mexico City: Ediciones El Caballito, 1982.

Hernández, Luis, and Pilar López. "Campesinos y poder: 1934–1940." In Escárcega López and Escobar Toledo, *El cardenismo.*

Hernández Chávez, Alicia. *La mecánica cardenista*. Mexico City: El Colegio de México, 1979.

Hernández Silva, Héctor Cuauhtémoc. *Insurgencia y autonomía: Historia de los pueblos Yaquis, 1821–1910*. Mexico City: Centro de Investigaciones y Estudios Superiores en Antropología Social, 1996.

Hertford, Reed. *Sources of Change in Mexican Agricultural Production, 1945–1965*. Washington, D.C.: Department of Agricultural, Economic Research Service, 1971.

Hewitt de Alcántara, Cynthia. *Modernizing Mexican Agriculture: Socioeconomic Implications of Technological Change*. Geneva: United Nations Research Institute for Social Development, 1976.

——. "Land Reform, Livelihood, and Power in Rural Mexico." In *Environment, Society, and Rural Change in Latin America: The Past, Present, and Future in the Countryside*, ed. David Preston. New York: John Wiley & Sons, 1980.

——. *Anthropological Perspectives on Rural Mexico*. London: Routledge & Kegan Paul, 1984.

Hobsbawm, Eric. *Primitive Rebels: Studies in Archaic Forms of Social Movement in the 19th and 20th Centuries*. New York: W. W. Norton & Company, 1959.

——. "Peasants and Politics." *Journal of Peasant Studies* 1, no. 1 (1973): 3–22.

Hoffman, Abraham. *Unwanted Mexicans in the Great Depression: Repatriation Pressures, 1929–1939*. Tucson: University of Arizona Press, 1974.

Hogan, Michael, and Thomas Paterson, eds. *Explaining the History of American Foreign Relations*. New York: Cambridge University Press, 1991.

Holden, Robert. *Mexico and the Survey of Public Lands: The Management of Modernization, 1876–1911*. DeKalb: Northern Illinois University Press, 1994.

Horn, James. "Did the U.S. Plan an Invasion of Mexico in 1927?" *Journal of Inter-American Studies and World Affairs* 15, no. 4 (1973): 454–71.

Horner, Richard. "Agrarian Movements and Their Historical Conditions," *Journal of Peasant Studies* 8, no 1 (1979): 1–16.

Hu-DeHart, Evelyn. "Racism and Anti-Chinese Persecution in Sonora, Mexico, 1876–1932." *Amerasia* 9, no. 2 (1982): 1–28.

——. *Yaqui Resistance and Survival: The Struggle for Land and Autonomy, 1921–1910*. Madison: University of Wisconsin Press, 1984.

——. "The Chinese of Baja California, 1910–1934." *Proceedings of the Pacific Coast Branch American Historical Association* 12 (1985/86): 9–30.

——. "Peasant Rebellion in the Northwest: The Yaqui Indians of Sonora, 1740–1976." In *Riot, Rebellion, and Revolution: Rural Social Conflict in Mexico*, ed. Friedrich Katz. Princeton: Princeton University Press, 1988.

Huizer, Gerrit. *The Revolutionary Potential of Peasants in Latin America*. Lexington, Mass.: D. C. Heath and Company, 1972.

Hull, Cordell. "International Trade and Domestic Prosperity." Washington, D.C.: Government Printing Office, 1934.

——. "The Path to Recovery." Washington, D.C.: Government Printing Office, 1934.

——. *The Memoirs of Cordell Hull.* 2 vols. New York: The Macmillan Company, 1948.

Hundley, Norris. *Dividing the Waters: A Century Controversy between the United States and Mexico.* Berkeley: University of California Press, 1966.

Hunt, Gabriel Hunt. *The Essential Franklin Delano Roosevelt.* New York: Gramercy Books, 1995.

Hurlburt, Laurance. *The Mexican Muralists in the United States.* Albuquerque: University of New Mexico Press, 1989.

Ianni, Octavio. *El Estado capitalista en la época de Cárdenas.* Mexico City: Ediciones Era, 1977.

Ibarra Mendivil, Jorge Luis. *Propiedad agraria y sistema político en México.* Hermosillo: El Colegio de Sonora, 1989.

Irigoyen, Ulises. *Carretera transpeninsular de la Baja California.* Mexico City: Editorial América, 1943.

Jackson, Robert, ed. *Liberals, the Church, and Indian Peasants: Corporate Lands and the Challenge of Reform in Nineteenth-Century Spanish America.* Albuquerque: University of New Mexico Press, 1997.

Jacobson, Nils. *Mirages of Transition: The Peruvian Altiplano, 1780–1930.* Berkeley: University of California Press, 1993.

Jayne, Catherine. *Oil, War, and Anglo-American Relations: American and British Reactions to Mexico's Expropriation of Foreign Oil Properties, 1937–1941.* Westport, Conn.: Greenwood Press, 2001.

Johnston, Bruce, Cassio Luiselli, Celso Cartas Contreras, and Roger Norton. *U.S.-Mexico Relations: Agrarian and Rural Development.* Stanford: Stanford University Press, 1987.

Joseph, Gilbert. *Revolution from Without: Yucatán, Mexico, and the United States, 1880–1924.* 2nd ed. Durham: Duke University Press, 1988.

——. "On the Trail of Latin American Bandits: A Reexamination of Peasant Resistance." *Latin American Research Review* 25, no. 3 (1990): 7–53.

——. "Close Encounters: Towards a New Cultural History of U.S.-Latin American Relations." In *Close Encounters of Empire: Writing the Cultural History of U.S.-Latin American Relations,* eds. Gilbert Joseph, Catherine LeGrand, and Ricardo Salvatore. Durham: Duke University Press, 1998.

Joseph, Gilbert, and Daniel Nugent, eds. *Everyday Forms of State Formation: Revolution and the Negotiation of Rule in Modern Mexico.* Durham: Duke University Press, 1994.

Kane, N. Stephen. "American Businessmen and Foreign Policy: The Recognition of Mexico, 1920–1923." *Political Science Quarterly* 90, no. 3 (1975): 293–313.

Katz, Friedrich. *The Secret War in Mexico: Europe, the United States, and the Mexican Revolution.* Chicago: University of Chicago Press, 1981.

——. "The Agrarian Policies and Ideas of the Revolutionary Mexican Factions Led by Emiliano Zapata, Pancho Villa, and Venustiano Carranza." In *Reforming Mexico's*

Agrarian Reform, ed. Laura Randall. Armonk, N.Y.: M. E. Sharpe, Columbia University Seminar Series, 1996.

Kenworthy, Eldon. *America/Américas: Myth and the Making of U.S. Policy toward Latin America.* University Park: Penn State University Press, 1994.

Kerig, Dorothy Pierson. "Yankee Enclave: The Colorado River Land Company and Mexican Agrarian Reform in Baja California, 1902–1944." PhD diss., University of California, Irvine, 1988.

Kilpatrick, Carroll, ed. *Roosevelt and Daniels: A Friendship in Politics.* Chapel Hill: University of North Carolina Press, 1952.

Kirk, Betty. *Covering the Mexican Front: The Battle of Europe versus America.* Norman: University of Oklahoma Press, 1942.

Knight, Alan. "The Mexican Revolution: Bourgeois? Nationalist? Or Just a 'Great Rebellion'?" *Bulletin of Latin American Research* 4, no. 2 (1985): 1–37.

——. "The Political Economy of Revolutionary Mexico, 1900–1940." In *Latin America, Economic Imperialism and the State: The Political Economy of the External Connection from Independence to the Present,* eds. Christopher Abel and Colin Lewis. London: The Athlone Press, 1985.

——. *The Mexican Revolution.* Cambridge: Cambridge University Press, 1986.

——. *U.S.-Mexican Relations, 1910–1940: An Interpretation.* La Jolla: Center for U.S.-Mexican Studies, 1988.

——. "Mexico, 1930–1946." In *The Cambridge History of Latin America,* vol 7, *Latin America since 1930,* ed. Leslie Bethell. Cambridge: Cambridge University Press, 1990.

——. "Racism, Revolution, and 'Indigenismo': Mexico, 1910–1940." In *The Idea of Race in Latin America,* ed. Richard Graham. Austin: University of Texas Press, 1990.

——. "Land and Society in Revolutionary Mexico: The Destruction of the Great Haciendas." *Mexican Studies/Estudios Mexicanos* 7, no. 1 (1991): 73–107.

——. "The Rise and Fall of Cardenismo, c. 1930–c. 1946." In *Mexico Since Independence,* ed. Leslie Bethell. Cambridge: Cambridge University Press, 1991.

——. "Cardenismo: Juggernaut or Jalopy?" *Journal of Latin American Studies* 26, no. 1 (1994): 73–107.

——. "Populism and Neo-populism in Latin America, Especially Mexico." *Journal of Latin American Studies* 30, no. 2 (1998): 223–48.

——. "Subalterns, Signifiers, and Statistics: Perspectives on Mexican Historiography." *Latin American Research Review* 37, no. 2 (2002): 136–58.

Koppes. "The Good Neighbor Policy and the Nationalization of Mexican Oil: A Reinterpretation." *Journal of American History* 69, no. 1 (1982): 62–81.

Krauze, Enrique. *General misionero: Lázaro Cárdenas.* Mexico City: Fondo de Cultura Económica, 1987.

Krenn, Michael. *U.S. Policy towards Economic Nationalism in Latin America, 1917–1929.* Wilmington, Del.: Scholarly Resources Inc., 1990.

Ladd, Everett Carl, and Charles Hadley. *Transformations of the American Party System:*

Political Coalitions from the New Deal to the 1970s. New York: W. W. Norton & Company, 1975.

Landsberger, Henry. "The Role of Peasant Movements and Revolts in Development." In *Latin American Peasant Movements,* ed. Henry Landsberger. Ithaca: Cornell University Press, 1969.

Langley, Lester. *Mexico and the United States: The Fragile Relationship.* Boston: Twayne Publishers, 1991.

Larroa Torres, Rosa Maria. "Cárdenas y la doble vía del desarrollo agrario." In *Perspectivas sobre el cardenismo: Ensayos sobre economía, trabajo, política y cultura en los años treinta,* eds. Marcos Tonatiuh Águila M. and Alberto Enríquez Perea. Mexico City: Universidad Autónoma Metropolitana, 1996.

Leff, Mark. *The Limits of Symbolic Reform: The New Deal and Taxation, 1933–1939.* Cambridge: Cambridge University Press, 1984.

León, Samuel, and Ignacio Marván. *La clase obrera en la historia de México: En el Cardenismo, 1934–1940.* Mexico City: Siglo Veintiuno, 1985.

Lerner, Victoria. *La educación socialista.* Mexico City: El Colegio de México, 1979.

Leuchtenberg, William. *Franklin Roosevelt and the New Deal, 1932–1940.* New York: Harper and Row, 1963.

Lewis, Stephen. "The Nation, Education, and the 'Indian Problem' in Mexico, 1920–1940." In *The Eagle and the Virgin: Nation and Cultural Revolution in Mexico, 1920–1940,* eds. Mary Kay Vaughan and Stephen Lewis. Durham: Duke University Press, 2006.

Libecap, Gary. "Government Policies on Property Rights to Land: U.S. Implications for Agricultural Development in Mexico." *Agricultural History* 60 (1986): 32–49.

Longley, Kyle. *The Sparrow and the Hawk: Costa Rica and the United States during the Rise of José Figueres.* Tuscaloosa: University of Alabama Press, 1997.

López, Robert. "Un órgano eficaz para intervenir la economía." *El Trimestre Económico* 1, no. 1 (1934): 39–52.

Lorenzana Durán, Gustavo. *Política agraria y movimientos campesinos en los Valles del Yaqui y Mayo, 1915–1934.* Mexico City: Instituto de Investigaciones Históricas, Universidad de Sonora, 1991.

Lorey, David, ed. *United States–Mexico Border Statistics Since 1900.* Los Angeles: UCLA Latin American Center Publications, 1990.

——. *The U.S.-Mexico Border in the Twentieth Century.* Wilmington, Del.: Scholarly Resources, Inc., 1999.

——. "Postrevolutionary Contexts for Independence Day: The 'Problem' of Order and the Invention of Revolution Day, 1920s–1940s." In *Viva Mexico! Viva la Independencia!* ed. William Beezley and David Lorey. Wilmington, Del.: Scholarly Resources, Inc., 2001.

Mabry, Donald. *Mexico's Acción Nacional: A Catholic Alternative to Revolution.* Syracuse, N.Y.: Syracuse University Press, 1973.

Macías, Carlos, ed. *Plutarco Elías Calles: Pensamiento político y social. Antología (1913–1936)*. Mexico City: Fondo de Cultura Económica, 1994.

——. *Correspondencia personal, 1919–1945,* vols. 1–2. Mexico City: Fondo de Cultura Económica, 1996.

Mallon, Florencia. *Peasant and Nation: The Making of Postcolonial Mexico and Peru.* Berkeley: University of California Press, 1995.

María Carreno, Alberto. *La diplomacia extraordinaria entre México y los Estado Unidos.* Mexico City: Editorial Jus, 1951.

Markiewicz, Dana. *The Mexican Revolution and the Limits of Agrarian Reform, 1915–1946.* Boulder, Colo.: Lynne Rienner Publishers, 1993.

Marks, Frederick. *Wind Over Sand: The Diplomacy of Franklin Roosevelt.* Athens: University of Georgia Press, 1988.

Martínez, Pablo. *A History of Lower California.* Mexico City: Editorial Baja California, 1960.

Martínez Ríos, Jorge. "Las invasiones agrarias en México: O la crisis del modelo de incorporación-participación marginal." *Revista Mexicana de Sociologia* 3, no. 4 (1972): 741–83.

Matesanz, José Antonio. *Las raíces de exilio: México ante la Guerra Civil española, 1936–1939.* Mexico City: El Colegio de México, 1999.

Mathes, Miguel, ed. *Baja California.* 2 vols. Mexico City: Instituto de Investigaciones Dr. José María Luis Mora, 1988.

McCann, Frank. *The Brazilian-American Alliance, 1937–1945.* Princeton, N.J.: Princeton University Press, 1973.

McConnell, Burt. *Mexico at the Bar of Public Opinion: A Survey of Editorial Opinion in Newspapers of the Western Hemisphere.* New York: Mail and Express Publishing Company, 1939.

McGuire, Thomas. *Politics and Ethnicity on the Río Yaqui: Potam Revisited.* Tucson: University of Arizona Press, 1986.

Meade, Adalberto Walther. *El distrito norte de Baja California.* Mexicali: Universidad Autónoma de Baja California, 1986.

——. *Origen de Mexicali.* Mexicali: Universidad Autónoma de Baja California, 1991.

——. *El Valle de Mexicali.* Mexicali: Universidad Autónoma de Baja California, 1996.

Medin, Tzvi. *Ideología y praxis política de Lázaro Cárdenas.* Mexico City: Ediciones Era, 1981.

Medina, Luis. *Del cardenismo al ávilacamachismo.* Mexico City: El Colegio de México, 1978.

Medina Robles, Fernando. "The Colorado River and the All-American Canal: The Historical and Cultural Perspective of Water in the U.S. Southwest." In *The U.S.-Mexican Border Environment: Lining the All-American Canal,* ed. Vicente Sánchez Munguía. San Diego: San Diego State University Press, 2006.

Mertz, Paul. *New Deal Policy and Southern Rural Poverty.* Baton Rouge: Louisiana State University Press, 1978.

Meyer, Jean. "Haciendas y ranchos, peones y campesinos en el Porfiriato: algunas falacias estadísticas." *Historia Mexicana* 35, no 3 (1986): 477–509.

——. "Mexico: Revolution and Reconstruction in the 1920s." In *Cambridge History of Latin America*. Vol. 5, *1870–1930*, ed. Leslie Bethell. Cambridge: Cambridge University Press, 1986.

——. *El Sinarquismo, el Cardenismo y la Iglesia (1937–1947)*. Mexico City: Tiempo Dememoria Tusquets Editores, 2003.

Meyer, Jean, Enrique Krauze, and Cayetano Reyes. *Estado y sociedad con Calles*. Mexico City: El Colegio de México, 1977.

Meyer, Lorenzo. "Los límites de la política cardenista: La presión externa." *Revista de la Universidad Autónoma de México* 25 (1971): 1–8.

——. *México y los Estados Unidos en el conflicto petrolero, 1917–1942*. Mexico City: El Colegio de México, 1972.

——. *Los grupos de presión extranjeros en el México revolucionario, 1910–1940*. Mexico City: Secretaría de las Relaciónes Exteriores, 1973.

——. *Mexico and the United States in the Oil Controversy, 1917–1942*. Austin: University of Texas Press, 1977.

——. *El conflicto social y los gobiernos del maximato*. Mexico City: El Colegio de México, 1978.

Meyer, Michael, William Sherman, and Susan Deeds. *The Course of Mexican History*. 8th ed. New York: Oxford University Press, 2007.

Michaels, Albert. "Fascism and Sinarquismo: Popular Nationalism against the Mexican Revolution." *A Journal of Church and State* (1966): 234–250.

——. "The Crisis of Cardenismo." *Journal of Latin American Studies* 2, no. 1 (1970): 51–79.

——. "Mexico and the U.S.: The Historical Structure of their Conflict." *Journal of International Affairs* 43, no. 2 (1990): 251–71.

Middlebrook, Kevin. *The Paradox of Revolution: Labor, the State, and Authoritarianism in Mexico*. Baltimore: Johns Hopkins University Press, 1995.

Mignolo, Walter. *Local Histories/Global Designs*. Princeton: Princeton University Press, 2000.

Mintz, Sydney. "The Rural Proletariat and the Problem of Rural Proletarian Consciousness." *Journal of Peasant Studies* 1, no. 3 (1974): 291–325.

Moisés, Rosalio, Jane Holden Kelly, and William Curry Holden. *A Yaqui Life: The Personal Chronicle of a Yaqui Indian*. Lincoln: University of Nebraska Press, 1971.

Moncada, Carlos. *La sucesión política en Sonora, 1917–1985*. Mexico City: Editorial Latino Americana, 1988.

Moore, Barrington. *Injustice: The Social Bases of Obedience and Revolt*. White Plains, N.Y.: M. E. Sharpe, 1978.

Moreno, Julio. *Yankee Don't Go Home! Mexican Nationalism, American Business Culture, and the Shaping of Modern Mexico, 1920–1950*. Chapel Hill: University of North Carolina Press, 2003.

Morett Alatorre, Luis. *La lucha por la tierra en los Valles del Yaqui y Mayo: Historia oral del sur de Sonora*. Mexico City: Universidad Autónoma Chapingo, 1989.

Muñoz, Hilda. *Lázaro Cárdenas: Síntesis ideológica de su campaña presidencial*. Mexico City: Fondo de Cultura Económica, 1976.

Murrieta, Mayo, and María Eugenia Graf. *Por el milagro de aferrarse: Tierra y vecindad en el Valle del Yaqui*. Mexico City: El Colegio de Sonora, 1991.

Naylor, Rosamond, Walter Falcon, and Arturo Puente-González. *Policy Reform and Mexican Agriculture: Views from the Yaqui Valley*. Mexico City: International Maize and Wheat Improvement Center, 2001.

Newcomer, Daniel. *Reconciling Modernity: Urban State Formation in 1940s León, Mexico*. Lincoln: University of Nebraska Press, 2004.

Niblo, Stephen. *War, Diplomacy, and Development: The United States and Mexico, 1938–1954*. Wilmington, Del.: Scholarly Resources Inc., 1995.

——. *Mexico in the 1940s: Modernity, Politics, and Corruption*. Wilmington, Del.: Scholarly Resources Inc., 1999.

Nugent, Daniel. "Rural Revolt in Mexico, Mexican Nationalism and the State, and Forms of U.S. Intervention." In *Rural Revolt in Mexico and U.S. Intervention*, ed. Daniel Nugent. La Jolla: Center for U.S.-Mexican Studies, University of California, San Diego, 1988.

——. *Spent Cartridges of Revolution: An Anthropological History of Namiquipa, Chihuahua*. Chicago: University of Chicago Press, 1993.

O'Brien, Thomas. *The Revolutionary Mission: American Enterprise in Latin America, 1900–1945*. Cambridge: Cambridge University Press, 1996.

——. *The Century of U.S. Capitalism in Latin America*. Albuquerque: University of New Mexico Press, 1999.

Ochoa, Enrique. *Feeding Mexico: The Political Use of Food Since 1910*. Wilmington, Del.: Scholarly Resources, 2000.

Ojeda, Mario. *Alcances y límites de la política exterior de México*. Mexico City: El Colegio de México, 1976.

Olavarría, María Eugenia. *Yaquis pueblos indígenas de México*. Mexico City: Instituto Nacional Indigenista Secretaría de Desarrollo Social, 1995.

Olcott, Jocelyn. *Revolutionary Women in Postrevolutionary Mexico*. Durham: Duke University Press, 2005.

Olson, James Stuart, ed. *Historical Dictionary of the Great Depression, 1929–1941*. Westport, Conn.: Greenwood Press, 2001.

O'Malley, Ilene V. *The Myth of the Revolution: Hero Cult and the Institutionalization of the Mexican State, 1920–1940*. New York: Greenwood Press, 1986.

Ota Mishima, María Elena, ed. *Destino México: Un estudio de los migraciones asiáticas a México, siglos XIX y XX*. Mexico City: El Colegio de México, 1997.

Otero, Gerardo. *Farewell to the Peasantry? Political Class Formation in Rural Mexico*. Boulder, Colo.: Westview Press, 1999.

Paige, Jeffrey. *Agrarian Revolution: Social Movements and Export Agriculture in the Underdeveloped World.* New York: Free Press, 1975.

Palacios, Guillermo. *La pluma y el arado: Los intelectuales pedagogos y la construcción sociocultural del "problema campesino" en México, 1932–1934.* Mexico City: El Colegio de México, 1999.

Palomares Peña, Noé. *Propietarios norteamericanos y reforma agraria en Chihuahua, 1917–1942.* Ciudad Juárez: Universidad Autónoma de Ciudad Juárez, 1991.

Pani, Alberto. *Apuntes autobiográficos.* Mexico City: Editorial Stylo, 1945.

Park, James William. *Latin American Underdevelopment: A History of Perspectives in the United States, 1870–1965.* Baton Rouge: Louisiana State University Press, 1995.

Partido Revolucionario Institucional. *Historia documental de la confederación nacional campesina.*Vol. 1, *1938–1942.* Mexico City: Instituto de Capacitación Política, 1981.

Paz, María Emilia. *Strategy, Security, and Spies: Mexico and the U.S. as Allies in World War II.* University Park: Pennsylvania State University Press, 1997.

Peloso, Vincent. *Peasants on Plantations: Subaltern Strategies of Labor and Resistance in the Pisco Valley, Peru.* Durham: Duke University Press, 1999.

Pérez Tejada, José. "General Abelardo L. Rodríguez." In *Pasajes históricos de la revolución en el Distrito Norte de Baja California.* Tijuana: Instituto de Investigaciones Históricas del Estado de Baja California, 1956.

Petras, James and Henry Veltmeyer. "Are Latin American Peasant Movements Still a Force for Change? Some New Paradigms Revisited," *Journal of Peasant Studies* 28, no. 2 (2001): 83–118.

Pike, Frederick. *FDR's Good Neighbor Policy: Sixty Years of Generally Gentle Chaos.* Austin: University of Texas Press, 1995.

Piñera Ramírez, David, ed. *Panorama histórico de Baja California.* Tijuana: Centro de Investigaciones Históricas, Universidad Autónoma de Baja California, 1983.

——. "Tierras deshabitadas y concesionarios extranjeros." In *Panorama histórico de Baja California,* ed. David Piñera Ramírez. Tijuana: Universidad Autónoma de Baja California, 1983.

——. *Ocupación y uso del suelo en Baja California: De los grupos aborígenes a la urbanización dependiente.* Mexico City: Universidad Nacional Autónoma de México, 1991.

Pletcher, David. "The Development of Railroads in Sonora." *Inter-American Economic Affairs* 1 (1948): 3–45.

Portes Gil, Emilio. *Quince años de política mexicana.* Mexico City: Ediciones Botas, 1941.

——. *Autobiografía de la revolución mexicana.* Mexico City: Instituto Mexicano de Cultura, 1964.

Powell, T. G. *Mexico and the Spanish Civil War.* Albuquerque: University of New Mexico Press, 1981.

Purnell, Jennie. *Popular Movements and State Formation in Revolutionary Mexico: The 'Agraristas' and 'Cristeros' of Michoacán.* Durham: Duke University Press, 1999.

Raat, W. Dirk. *Mexico and the United States: Ambivalent Vistas.* 2nd ed. Athens: University of Georgia Press, 2005.

Radding, Cynthia. "Las estructuras formativas del capitalismo en Sonora, 1900–1930." In *De los Borbones a la Revolución: Ocho estudios regionales,* ed. Mario Cerutti. Monterrey: Universidad Autónoma de Nuevo León, 1986.

——. "Peasant Resistance on the Yaqui Delta: An Historical Inquiry in the Meaning of Ethnicity." *Journal of the Southwest* 31, no. 2 (1989): 330–61.

Ramírez, José Carlos. *Hipótesis sobre la historia económica y demográfica de Sonora en la era contemporánea del capital, 1930–1990.* Mexico City: El Colegio de Sonora, 1991.

Randall, Laura, ed. *Reforming Mexico's Agrarian Reform.* Armonk, N.Y.: M. E. Sharpe, 1996.

Recio, Gabriela. "Drugs and Alcohol: U.S. Prohibition and the Origins of the Drug Trade in Mexico, 1910–1930." *Journal of Latin American Studies* 34, no. 1 (2002): 21–42.

Renda, Mary. *Taking Haiti: Military Occupation and the Culture of U.S. Imperialism, 1915–1940.* Chapel Hill: University of North Carolina Press, 2001.

Rénique, Gerardo. "Race, Religion, and Nation: Sonora's Anti-Chinese Racism and Mexico's Postrevolutionary Nationalism, 1920s–1930s." In Appelbaum, Macpherson, and Rosemblatt, *Race and National in Modern Latin America.*

Restrepo, Iván, and Salomón Eckstein. *La agricultura colectiva de la Laguna.* Mexico City: Siglo Veintiuno, 1975.

Reyes Osorio, Sergio, et al. *Estructura agraria y desarrollo agrícola en México.* Mexico City: Fondo de Cultura Económica, 1974.

Ríos Manzano, Santa Victoria. *Francisco Múgica: Su pensamiento agrario y su tesis ideológicas.* Mexico City: Centro de Estudios Históricos del Agrarismo en Mexico, 1982.

Riquelme Inda, Julio. "Vías de comunicación de la Baja California." *Boletín de la Sociedad de Geográfica y Estadística* 45 (1936): 115–60.

——. "El problema del agua en el región mexicana del Colorado, Baja California." *Boletín de la Sociedad de Geográfica y Estadística* 60 (1945): 509–23.

Rodríguez, Abelardo. *Autobiografía.* Mexico City: Novaro Editores, 1962.

——. *Memoria administrativa del gobierno del Distrito Norte de la Baja California, 1924–1927.* Mexico City: Universidad Autónoma de Baja California, reprint 1993.

Rodríguez, Ileana, ed. *The Latin American Subaltern Studies Reader.* Durham: Duke University Press, 2001.

Roorda, Eric. *The Dictator Next Door: The Good Neighbor Policy and the Trujillo Regime in the Dominican Republic, 1930–1945.* Durham: Duke University Press, 1998.

Roosevelt, Franklin D. *Looking Forward.* New York: The John Day Company, 1933.

——. *Complete Presidential Press Conferences of Franklin D. Roosevelt,* vol. 2. New York: Da Capo Press, Inc., 1972.

Rosenman, Samuel, ed. *The Public Papers and Addresses of Franklin D. Roosevelt,* vol. 7. New York: Harper, Random House, and Macmillan, 1941.

Ross, Stanley. "Dwight Morrow and the Mexican Revolution." *Hispanic American Historical Review* 38, no. 4 (1958): 506–28.

Rubin, Jeffrey. *Decentering the Regime: Ethnicity, Radicalism, and Democracy in Juchitán, Mexico.* Durham: Duke University Press, 1997.

Ruiz, J. Hermida. *Cárdenas: Comandante del Pacífico*. México: Ediciones El Caballito, 1982.

Ruiz, Ramón Eduardo. *The Great Rebellion: Mexico, 1905–1924*. New York: W. W. Norton & Company, 1980.

———. *The People of Sonora and Yankee Capitalists*. Tucson: University of Arizona Press, 1988.

Salamini, Heather Fowler. *Agrarian Radicalism in Veracruz, 1920–1938*. Lincoln: University of Nebraska Press, 1978.

Salazar Ramírez, Alfonso. *Historia del estado de Baja California*. Mexico City: Ediciones Económicas, 1980.

Sánchez Ogáz, Yolanda. "Lucha por la nacionalización del Valle de Mexicali." *Ciguatan* 7 (1987): 45–58.

———. "La nacionalización de las tierras del Valle de Mexicali y la formación de la organización campesina en Baja California." In *Historia de las ligas de comunidades agrarias y sindicatos campesinos*, vol. 4, ed. Edén Ferrer. Mexico City: Centro de Estudios Históricos del Agrarismo en México, 1988.

Sánchez Ramírez, Óscar. *Crónica agrícola del Valle de Mexicali*. Mexicali: Universidad Autónoma de Baja California, 1990.

Sanderson, Susan Walsh. *Land Reform in Mexico: 1910–1980*. Orlando: Academic Press, 1984.

Sanderson, Steven. *Agrarian Populism and the Mexican State: The Struggle for Land in Sonora*. Berkeley: University of California Press, 1981.

———. *The Transformation of Mexican Agriculture: International Structure and the Politics of Rural Change*. Princeton: Princeton University Press, 1986.

Schantz, Eric. "All Night at the Owl: The Social and Political Relations of Mexicali's Red Light District, 1909–1925." In *On the Border: Society and Culture between the United States and Mexico*, ed. Andrew Wood. Lanham, Md.: Scholarly Resources, 2001.

———. "From the Mexicali Rose to the Tijuana Brass: Vice Tours of the United States–Mexico Border, 1910–1965." PhD diss., University of California, Los Angeles, 2001.

Schmitt, Karl. *Mexico and the United States, 1921–1973: Conflict and Coexistence*. New York: John Wiley & Sons, Inc., 1974.

Schoultz, Lars. *Beneath the United States: A History of U.S. Policy toward Latin America*. Cambridge: Harvard University Press, 1998.

Schuler, Friedrich. *Mexico between Hitler and Roosevelt: Mexican Foreign Relations in the Age of Lázaro Cárdenas, 1934–1940*. Albuquerque: University of New Mexico Press, 1998.

Schwab, Stephen. "The Role of the Mexican Expeditionary Force in World War II: Late, Limited, but Symbolically Significant." *Journal of Military History* 66, no. 4 (2002): 1115–40.

Scott, James. *Weapons of the Weak: Everyday Forms of Peasant Resistance*. New Haven: Yale University Press, 1985.

——. *Domination and the Arts of Resistance: Hidden Transcripts.* New Haven: Yale University Press, 1990.

Scroggs, W. O. "Mexican Anxieties." *Foreign Affairs* 18 (1940): 266–79.

Secretaría de Gobernación y Gobierno del Estado de Sonora. *Los municipios de Sonora.* Mexico City: Talleres Gráficos de la Nación, 1988.

Secretaría de la Economía Nacional, Dirección General de Estadística. *Quinto Censo de Población, 1930, Estados Unidos Mexicanos, Resumen General.* Mexico City: D.A.A.P., 1934.

——. *Sexto Censo de Población, 1940, Estados Unidos Mexicanos, Resumen General.* Mexico City: D.A.A.P., 1943.

Secretaría de las Relaciones Exteriores. *El Tratado de Aguas Internacionales, Celebrado entre México y los Estados Unidos el 3 de Febrero de 1944.* Mexico City: Talleres Gráficos de la Cía Editora y Librería, 1947.

Sheridan, Thomas E. "The Yoemem (Yaquis): An Enduring People." In Sheridan and Parezo, *Paths of Life.*

——. "The Yoremem (Mayos)." In Sheridan and Parezo, *Paths of Life.*

Sheridan, Thomas E. and Nancy J. Parezo, eds. *Paths of Life: American Indians in the Southwest and Northern Mexico.* Tucson: University of Arizona Press, 1996.

Sherman, John. *The Mexican Right: The End of Revolutionary Reform, 1929–1940.* Westport, Conn.: Praeger, 1997.

Silva Herzog, Jesús. *Lázaro Cárdenas: Su pensamiento económico, social y político.* Mexico City: Editorial Nuestro Tiempo, 1975.

Simonian, Lane. *Defending the Land of the Jaguar: A History of Conservation in Mexico.* Austin: University of Texas Press, 1995.

Simpson, Eyler. *The Ejido: Mexico's Way Out.* Chapel Hill: University of North Carolina Press, 1937.

Simpson, Lesley Byrd. *Many Mexicos.* 4th ed., rev. Berkeley: University of California Press, 1971.

Skocpol, Theda. *States and Social Revolutions.* Cambridge: Cambridge University Press, 1979.

Sloan, John. "United States Policy Responses to the Mexican Revolution: A Partial Application of the Bureaucratic Politics Model." *Journal of Latin American Studies* 10 (1978): 283–308.

Smith, Peter. *Talons of the Eagle: Dynamics of U.S.–Latin American Relations.* New York: Oxford University Press, 1996.

Smith, Peter, and Rosario Green. "Introduction." In *Foreign Policy in U.S.-Mexican Relations,* eds. Peter Smith and Rosario Green. La Jolla: Center for U.S.-Mexican Studies, 1989.

Spicer, Edward. *The Yaquis: A Cultural History.* Tucson: University of Arizona Press, 1980.

Stern, Alexandra Minna. "From Mestizophilia to Biotypology: Racialization and Science in Mexico, 1920–1960." In Appelbaum, Macpherson, and Rosemblatt, *Race and Nation in Modern Latin America.*

Stern, Steve, ed., *Resistance, Rebellion, and Consciousness in the Andean Peasant World.* Madison: University of Wisconsin Press, 1987.

Steward, Dick. *Trade and Hemisphere: The Good Neighbor Policy and Reciprocal Trade.* Columbia: University of Missouri Press, 1975.

Stowe, Noel, ed. "Pioneering Land Development in the Californias: An Interview with David Otto Brant." Parts 1–3. *California Historical Society Quarterly* 47 (1968): 15–39, 141–55, 237–50.

Striffler, Steve. *In the Shadows of State and Capital: The United Fruit Company, Popular Struggle, and Agrarian Restructuring in Ecuador, 1900–1995.* Durham: Duke University Press, 2002.

Sugiyama, Shigeru. "Reluctant Neighbors: U.S.-Mexican Relations and the Failure of Cardenista Reforms, 1934–1948." PhD diss., University of California, Santa Barbara, 1996.

Tannenbaum, Frank. *Whither Latin America? An Introduction to Its Economic and Social Problems.* New York: Thomas Crowell, Co., 1934.

——. *Mexico: The Struggle for Peace and Bread.* New York: Knopf, 1950.

Tasca, Henry. *The Reciprocal Trade Policy of the United States: A Study in Trade Philosophy.* New York: Russell & Russell, 1967.

Taylor Hansen, Lawrence Douglas. "La transformación de Baja California en estado, 1931–1952." *Estudios Fronterizos* 1 (2000): 47–87.

Tenorio-Trillo, Mauricio. *Mexico at the World's Fairs: Crafting a Modern Nation.* Berkeley: University of California Press, 1996.

Thayer Painter, Muriel. *With Good Heart: Yaqui Beliefs and Ceremonies in Pascua Village.* Tucson: University of Arizona Press, 1986.

Thiesenhusen, William. "Mexican Land Reform, 1934–91: Success or Failure." In *Reforming Mexico's Agrarian Reform*, ed. Laura Randall. Armonk, N.Y.: M. E. Sharpe, 1996.

Tinker Salas, Miguel. *In the Shadow of the Eagles: Sonora and the Transformation of the Border during the Porfiriato.* Berkeley: University of California Press, 1997.

Tobler, Hans. "Peasants and the Shaping of the Revolutionary State, 1910–1940." In *Riot, Rebellion, and Revolution*, ed. Friedrich Katz. Princeton: Princeton University Press, 1986.

Torres Bodet, Jaime. *Memorias.* 5 vols. Mexico City: Editorial Porrúa, 1969–1974.

Torres Ramírez, Blanca. *México en la segunda guerra mundial.* Mexico City: El Colegio de México, 1979.

Townsend, William Cameron. *Lázaro Cárdenas: Mexican Democrat.* Ann Arbor: George Wahr, 1952.

Tutino, John. *From Insurrection to Revolution in Mexico: Social Bases of Agrarian Violence, 1750–1940.* Princeton: Princeton University Press, 1986.

Valenzuela, José. "La evolución agrícola en el Valle de Mexicali." In *Memoria del primer Congreso de Historia Regional.* Mexicali: Dirección General de Acción Cívica y Cultural, 1958.

Van Young, Eric. "To See Someone Not Seeing: Historical Studies of Peasants and Politics in Mexico." *Mexican Studies/Estudios Mexicanos* 6, no. 1 (1990): 133–59.

——. "Introduction: Are Regions Good to Think?" In *Mexico's Regions: Comparative History and Development,* ed. Eric Van Young. La Jolla: Center for U.S.-Mexican Studies, 1992.

Vanderwood, Paul. *Disorder and Progress: Bandits, Police, and Mexican Development.* Lincoln: University of Nebraska Press, 1981.

——. "Building Blocks but Not Yet a Building: Regional History and the Mexican Revolution." *Mexican Studies/Estudios Mexicanos* 3, no. 2 (1987): 421–31.

——. *The Power of God against the Guns of Government: Religious Upheaval in Mexico at the Turn of the Nineteenth Century.* Stanford, Calif.: Stanford University Press, 1998.

——. *Juan Soldado: Rapist, Murderer, Martyr, Saint.* Durham: Duke University Press, 2004.

Vargas-Lobsinger, María. *La Comarca Lagunera: De la Revolución a la expropiación de las haciendas, 1910–1940.* Mexico City: Universidad Nacional Autónoma de México, 1999.

Vaughan, Mary Kay. *Cultural Politics in Revolution: Teachers, Peasants, and Schools in Mexico, 1930–1940.* Tucson: University of Arizona Press, 1997.

Vázquez, Gabino. *The Agrarian Reform in Lower California.* Mexico City: D.A.P.P., 1938.

Vázquez, Josefina Zoraida, and Lorenzo Meyer. *The United States and Mexico.* Chicago: University of Chicago Press, 1985.

Velasco Toro, José. *Política y legislación agraria en México.* Xalapa: Universidad Veracruzana, 1993.

Walker, J. Samuel. *Henry Wallace and American Foreign Policy.* Westport, Conn.: Greenwood Press, 1976.

Ward, Evan. *Border Oasis: Water and the Political Ecology of the Colorado River Delta, 1940–1975.* Tucson: University of Arizona Press, 2003.

Waters, Wendy. "Remapping Identities: Road Construction and Nation Building in Postrevolutionary Mexico." In *The Eagle and the Virgin: Nation and Cultural Revolution in Mexico, 1920–1940,* eds. Mary Kay Vaughan and Stephen Lewis. Durham: Duke University Press, 2006.

Weiner, Richard. *Race, Nation, and Market: Economic Culture in Porfirian Mexico.* Tucson: University of Arizona Press, 2004.

Weintraub, Sidney. *Financial Decision-Making in Mexico: To Bet a Nation.* Pittsburgh: University of Pittsburgh Press, 2000.

Welles, Sumner. *Seven Major Decisions.* London: Hamish Hamilton, 1951.

Wells, Allen and Gilbert Joseph. *Summer of Discontent, Seasons of Upheaval: Elite Politics and Rural Insurgency in Yucatán, 1876–1915.* Stanford: Stanford University Press, 1996.

Werne, Joseph. "Esteban Cantú y la soberanía mexicana en Baja California." *Historia Mexicana* 30 (1980): 1–32.

———. "Vice Revenue and the Growth of Government in Baja California, 1910–1920." Paper presented at the XI Reunión de Historiadores Mexicanos, Estadounidenses y Canadienses, Monterrey, Mexico, October 2003.

Weyl, Nathaniel, and Sylvia Weyl. *The Reconquest of Mexico: The Years of Lázaro Cárdenas.* London: Oxford University Press, 1939.

White, Graham, and John Maze. *Henry Wallace: His Search for a New World Order.* Chapel Hill: University of North Carolina Press, 1995.

Widenor, William. *Henry Cabot Lodge and the Search for an American Foreign Policy.* Berkeley: University of California Press, 1980.

Winn, Peter. *Weavers of Revolution: The Yarur Workers and Chile's Road to Socialism.* New York: Oxford University Press, 1986.

Wolf, Eric. *Peasant Wars of the Twentieth Century.* New York: Harper and Row, 1969.

Woods, Bryce. *The Making of the Good Neighbor Policy.* New York: Columbia University Press, 1961.

Woods, Randall Bennett. *The Roosevelt Foreign Policy Establishment and the "Good Neighbor": The United States and Argentina, 1941–1945.* Lawrence: University of Kansas Press, 1979.

Zorrilla, Luis. *Historia de las relaciones entre México y los Estados Unidos de América, 1800–1958.* Mexico City: Editorial Porrúa, 1966.

Campeche, 150

Campesinos. *See* peasantry

Cantú Jiménez, Esteban, 32–33, 98

Cárdenas, Cuauhtémoc, 303 n. 7, 321 n. 39

Cárdenas, Lázaro (domestic issues), 42, 60, 127; agrarian policies of, *see* Agrarian policies of Cárdenas; as governor, 79; Ávila Camacho and, 256; Baja California's counter agrarian movement and, 69–73, 75–76; Callista threat against, 8, 105–6, 242, 308 n. 7, 308 n. 8; centrism of, 81, 83, 188; commerce and, 83, 225, 243, 303 n. 14, 304 n. 20; conservatism of, 84; consumerism and, 81, 83, 132, 174–75; deficit spending by, 49, 206–10, 225, 244, 332 n. 116, 332–33 n. 118; demographics and, 94, 99, 323 n. 66; economic policies of, 80–85, 89–91, 94, 206, 209–10, 244; education program of, 68, 79–81, 89–93, 123, 131, 279, 312 n. 53; inconsistency of, 66–67, 72, 77–78, 133, 143, 279, 281–82; Indian policy of, 131–37, 171–72, 280; industrial policies of, 80–84, 175, 254; interventionist state and, 48–49, 79–81, 89–92, 122, 131–32, 135–37, 152–53, 169–75; land redistribution by, 29, 79–83, 89–91, 94–95, 103, 112–13, 123, 128, 132, 137, 141, 150, 213–14; literature on, 7–8, 140, 286 n. 10, 286 n. 12; Mexican landowners compensated by, 208–11, 229–31, 238, 249; military and, 105–6, 324 n. 84; opponents and Baja California, 70, 82–83, 91; opponents and Sonora, 105, 108, 137, 140, 145; opponents of, 8, 183–87, 206, 209, 212–14, 230, 242, 308 n. 8, 324 n. 79, 324 n. 81; paternalism of, 66, 79, 90–92, 94, 279; peasants and workers armed by, 65, 72, 124, 186, 312 n. 58; political expediency of, 13, 48, 62–67, 77–79, 103–13, 122–

25, 132, 133, 137, 140–43, 147, 150, 206, 229–30, 279, 286 n. 11; political orientation of, 79, 104, 107, 112, 145, 188, 252–54, 288 n. 7, 303 n. 7; political power of, 8, 67, 78–79, 82–83, 103–7, 112–13, 124, 135, 140–42, 145, 150, 152, 186, 203–6, 221–22, 230, 242, 270; presidential campaign of, 21, 46, 51, 59, 79, 91, 131, 179, 303 n. 7; public works projects of, 48–49, 86–87, 173, 206, 209, 224, 225, 270, 305 n. 35; Ramos deposed by, 105–7, 140; social reforms of, 89–92, 94, 131–32, 206, 279; social vices attacked by, 79, 90–92, 131, 279, 306 n. 49; Sonora and, 109–12, 116, 120, 122, 126, 128, 132, 135–37, 140–42, 152; state-building project of, 8–9, 277–78; states visited by, 64, 113, 131, 133, 137, 141; textile industry and, 84–85, 278; Yocupicio and, 110–12, 135, 140, 145, 148, 150, 152, 309 n. 16, 319 n. 45

Cárdenas, Lázaro (international issues): American landowners compensated by, 76, 219–28, 237, 256, 267–70, 273, 328 n. 43; diplomatic tactics of, 5, 13; divisions within cabinet of, 219–20, 251–52; economic constraints and, 197, 202–3, 206–10, 225, 242–51, 254, 270, 271, 336 n. 47, 337 n. 59, 337 n. 73; expropriation of American land, *see* Expropriation of American land; fascism and, 241, 252; foreign debt and, 225, 249, 251, 253, 257, 270; Mexican press and, 221, 222–23, 225, 332 n. 113; as minister of war, 256; New Deal and, 169–72; opponents of, 141–42, 145, 199, 212, 245, 317 n. 24, 336 n. 41; political constraints against, 147, 197, 206, 242, 270; public opinion and, 206, 221–25, 230, 233, 251–52; railroads and, 46; repatriation and, 46, 48, 179–81, 323 n.

Mexican Nationalist League of Baja California, 96

Mexican policy toward United States, 5–6, 203–4, 232–33, 265, 268, 269–72; accommodation, 38, 142–46, 224, 227, 237, 240–41, 248, 257–58, 339 n. 104; domestic forces and, 37, 142–45, 197, 202; manipulation of U.S. actors, 142, 146–47, 169, 201–2, 329 n. 60; resistance, 37–40, 148, 189–91, 195–97, 219–28, 230, 234–42, 246, 247, 253, 257

Mexico: communists in, 182, 187–88, 222, 242; economic downturn in, 207–10, 225, 242–48, 251, 270, 336 n. 47, 337 n. 59, 337 n. 73, 339 n. 104; fascists in, 182–187, 242; National Chamber of Commerce of, 209; national congress of, 214, 221, 223, 255, 257

Michoacán, 58, 62, 70, 79, 81, 115, 213, 255, 286 n. 11, 298 n. 55

Middle and weak power diplomacy, 195–97, 241, 246–47, 269–70, 272–73, 276, 342 n. 4

Mining industry, 260, 262, 341 n. 122

Ministry of Foreign Affairs, 202–3

Mixed Agrarian Commissions, 22, 289 n. 9; Baja California and, 61, 67–68, 70, 72–73; Sonora and, 113, 124, 140

Modernization, 174–76, 179–81, 274–75, 287 n. 13; Baja California and, 89–92, 94, 303 n. 11; Sonora and, 115–16, 120

Monroe Doctrine, 202

Monterrey, 264

Moore, Robert Walton, 205, 208, 217

Morelos, 19, 81, 141

Morelos Dam, 88

Morgenthau, Henry, 202, 211, 219, 328 n. 37; Roosevelt and, 204

Morones, Luis, 56

Morrow, Dwight, 41, 293 n. 60

Múgica, Francisco, 58, 77, 219, 257, 309 n. 12

Muñoz, José Eliseo, 35

Mussolini, Benito, 184

National Bank of Agricultural Credit, 20, 28, 34, 39, 69, 135, 245, 294 n. 11

National Bank of Ejidal Credit, 170, 209, 245, 304 n. 15, 329 n. 54, 333 n. 118; Baja California and, 67, 72, 85; Sonora and, 149, 151

National City Bank, 245

National Club for the Homeland, 50

National Irrigation Commission, 134–35, 294 n. 11

Navarro Cortina, Rafael, 44, 50, 62–63, 87, 91; agrarista crackdown and, 65–66; removal from office, 67

Nayarit, 114, 174

Neilan, Marshall, 31

New Deal: Mexican immigrants and, 178; Mexico's Indian policies vs., 171–72; political coalition of, 177–78, 181–82, 216, 227, 275; rural programs of, 165, 170–72, 320 n. 19, 321 n. 35; Six Year Plan vs., 169–73, 220, 271, 272, 329 n. 60; U.S. foreign policy and, 197–98

Nicaragua, 40, 197, 268, 272–76

Nixon, Richard, 274–76

Nuevo León, 141, 264

Oaxaca, 106, 141, 236

Obregón, Álvaro, 25, 103, 108, 288 n. 7; agrarian policies of, 20, 22, 34, 38, 113–14, 118–19, 121; assassination of, 104, 118–19; United States and, 2–3, 34–39, 74, 257, 271, 282

Obregonistas, 42, 103–6, 118–19, 212, 279

Oil crisis, 3–5, 141, 150, 153; literature on, 9, 162–64, 232–33; after November

Vasconcelos, José, 93, 287 n. 13

Vázquez, Gabino, 179–180; Mexicali Valley and, 61, 67–72, 75, 77, 79, 89, 92, 95; Yaqui Valley and, 112, 127, 141, 144–45

Velázquez, Felipa, 58–59

Velázquez, Fidel, 126

Venezuela, 192

Veracruz, 106, 235, 286 n. 11

Vierhus, Albert, 72–73, 75–76

Villa, Francisco "Pancho," 2, 19, 65

Villalobos, Antonio, 84, 256

Villaseñor, Eduardo, 251–52, 256

Wallace, Henry, 166–67, 202; Mexico visited by, 174, 255–56, 263

Welles, Sumner, 43, 202, 207, 210, 231, 235, 264, 282, 328 n. 37; compensation and, 217–26, 241, 247–49, 253–54, 274; Hull and, 200, 201, 218, 227, 253, 333 n. 127; Roosevelt and, 200, 204, 227, 253; U.S. accommodation and, 166, 175–76

Weyl, Nathaniel, 167

Weyl, Sylvia, 167

White, Harry, 175

Wilson, Henry Lane, 35

Wilson, Woodrow, 36, 199, 200

Winters, George, 249

Works Progress Administration, 172, 178

World War I, 33, 55, 167, 186, 243

World War II, 5, 14, 164, 192, 232–33, 241, 243, 275–76; Ávila Camacho and, 251–53, 258, 261–65; Baja California and, 87–89

Xenophobia, 7, 60, 62, 100

Yaqui Indians: agrarian reform and, 129, 131–36; autonomy of, 128–29, 131–36, 154, 313 n. 71; Calles and, 129; Cárdenas and, 113, 130–37, 154, 315 n. 100; Carranza and, 129; Commission for Yaqui

Agricultural Development, 135; culture and identity of, 128–29, 132–36, 154, 278; Díaz and, 23, 128, 138; federal development program for, 131–37, 154; goals of, 9, 129–34, 278, 281, 314 n. 79; Gutiérrez and, 107; living conditions of, 129–30, 133, 136, 314 n. 79; loss of homelands by, 23–24, 117, 128, 131, 136, 138; Mexican Revolution and, 128–29; modernization of, 132–35, 314 n. 79; number of, 23–24, 128–29; Obregón and, 129–30; political orientation of, 132, 135, 154; resistance and squatting by, 25–27, 129–31, 135, 154; repression of, 23–24, 128–31; restitution of homelands of, 113, 128–40, 146–49, 154, 211, 278, 280, 324 n. 75; rituals and beliefs of, 9, 128–29, 132–36, 154; Yaqui Regional Commission on Irrigation, 134–35

Yaqui River, 12, 29, 128–29, 133–38, 142, 149

Yaqui Valley, 10, 40, 108, 318 n. 41; agrarian reform in, 6, 12, 149; American expropriated land in, see Expropriation of American land; American presence in, 23–29, 110, 114–18, 129, 138, 141, 148, 206–8; Calles's policies toward, 26; Cárdenas and peasantry in, 113, 120–23, 145; Cárdenas's visit to, 113, 137; Colonia Esperanza, 139; colonization in, 24–26, 29, 120, 235; compensation for Americans in, 146–48, 207–8, 215–17, 222, 226, 330 n. 74; defensas rurales, 124; Ejido El Yaqui, 128, 152; economic development in, 24, 28, 114, 129, 149; irrigation and modernization of, 24–25, 28, 149; living and working conditions in, 28, 107, 114–19, 122, 153–54, 277; Mexicali Valley vs., 6–7, 11–13, 70–71, 89, 112–16, 119–22, 134, 140, 145, 154,

John J. Dwyer is an assistant professor in the Department of History at Duquesne University in Pittsburgh, Pennsylvania.

Library of Congress Cataloging-in-Publication Data
Dwyer, John Joseph, 1965–
The agrarian dispute : the expropriation of American-owned rural land in postrevolutionary Mexico / John J. Dwyer.
p. cm. — (American encounters/global interactions)
Includes bibliographical references and index.
ISBN 978-0-8223-4295-3 (cloth : alk. paper)
ISBN 978-0-8223-4309-7 (pbk. : alk. paper)
1. Land reform—Mexico. 2. Land tenure—Mexico. 3. Mexico—Boundaries—United States. 4. United States—Boundaries—Mexico. 5. Mexico—Relations—United States. 6. United States—Relations—Mexico. I. Title.
HD1333.M6D99 2008
333.1'4097209041—dc22   2008013524